Uncle John's
BATHROOM READER
PLUNGES INTO
NEW YORK

The Bathroom Readers' Institute
Ashland, Oregon, and San Diego, California

OUR "REGULAR" READERS RAVE

"Before the BRI came along, I had a small library of just books. After BRI, I now have a great library filled with incredible books."
—**Green S.**

"I just happened to see one of these sitting on the back of a friend's toilet one time 8 years ago. Instead of reading the shampoo bottle, I picked this up. I have been hooked every since."
—**Angela D.**

"*Uncle John's Bathroom Readers* are the entire reason I started collecting rubber ducks. I have over seventy."
—**Sara C.**

"My hubby was on a couple of game shows, and I know we can thank his love of the *Bathroom Reader* books for the winnings."
—**Donna E.**

"I have them all, and cherish every one! My 20th anniversary edition sadly fell into the (clean) toilet. I managed to dry it out sufficiently enough to continue reading."
—**Butch H.**

"My friend in school was reading *Bathroom Readers*, so then I bought a couple, and now my mom says I'm just threatening her with my intelligence."
—**Chase O.**

"Your *Bathroom Reader* is like a high-powered flush—it sucks you in. I drink more liquids so I can make more pit stops. Thanks for all the fun!"
—**Kara D.**

UNCLE JOHN'S BATHROOM PLUNGES INTO NEW YORK

For information, write...
The Bathroom Readers' Institute
P.O. Box 1117, Ashland, OR 97520
www.bathroomreader.com
e-mail: mail@bathroomreader.com

ISBN 13: 978-1-60710-235-9 / ISBN 10: 1-60710-235-8

Library of Congress Cataloging-in-Publication Data

Uncle John's bathroom reader plunges into New York.
  p. cm.
 ISBN 978-1-60710-235-9 (pbk.)
 1. New York (N.Y.)—Miscellanea. 2. New York (N.Y.)—Anecdotes.
3. New York (N.Y.)—Humor. 4. Curiosities and wonders—New York
(State)—New York. I. Bathroom Readers' Institute (Ashland, Or.)
 F128.36.U53 2011
 974.7—dc22
                           2011004399

Printed in the United States of America

11 12 13 14 15   5 4 3 2 1

THANK YOU!

The Bathroom Readers' Institute thanks the following people whose hard work, advice, and assistance made this book possible.

Gordon Javna

JoAnn Padgett

Melinda Allman

Lorraine Bodger

Sue Steiner

Derek Fairbridge

Amy Miller

Jay Newman

Michael Brunsfeld

J. Carroll

Jeff Altemus

Carl Lavo

Stephanie Spadaccini

Thom Little

Brian Boone

Jenness Crawford

Leslie Elman

Ryan Murphy

Terri Schlichenmeyer

Dan Mansfield

Bonnie Vandewater

John Hogan

Beth Fhaner

Amy Ly

Monica Maestas

Annie Lam

Ginger Winters

Mana Monzavi

Jennifer Frederick

Kim Griswell

Sydney Stanley

David Cully

Karen M. and David C.

R. R. Donnelley

Nuray Celebi

Bobby James

Sam and Gideon

Sophie and JJ

CONTENTS

Because the BRI understands your reading needs, we've divided the contents by length as well as subject.

Short—a quick read

Medium—2 to 3 pages

Long—for those extended visits, when something a little more involved is required.

*   *   *

NEW YORK CITY FACTS

• In the early 1890s, 100 European starlings were released in Central Park, the first in North America. Today 200 million starlings live throughout the United States.

• The 4,269-foot Verrazano–Narrows Bridge is so long that its towers have to be a few inches off of parallel to accommodate for the curvature of the Earth.

START SPREADING THE NEWS!

WELCOME TO THE CONCRETE JUNGLE
Around Grandma and Grandpa Uncle John's house, the
story of the first time little Uncle John visited New York
is legendary: He gazed up at the dizzying array of buildings in Midtown, breathed in the fragrant mixture of hot dogs and exhaust,
took a bite of his cherry Italian ice, and announced, "It's good to be
home." Then, right there on the sidewalk, he broke into the chorus
of "New York, New York." (There was dancing, too.)

Years later, when it came time to choose the next book in our
regional series, Uncle John handed each of us a bagel with lox and
then told us that our next project would focus on everyone's
favorite town: New York City.

So we dug deep into our tank of knowledge, looking for
nuggets of all things New York: history, pop culture, science,
obscure facts, and some really strange stuff. Have you heard the
story behind the guy who plays guitar in Times Square, wearing
only a cowboy hat, boots, and his underwear? Did you ever witness
Manhattanhenge? Do you know that there are people in history
who have actually "sold" the Brooklyn Bridge? We didn't, either.
We even added some cool stories, fun facts, and bounce-in-yourseat trivia about the state—after all, New Yorkers occasionally
explore outside the boroughs. Here's what awaits you on the pages
of this book:

• New York's greatest hoaxes—from the 140-year-old hot dog at
Coney Island to discoveries of life on the moon.

• A guy who gives free math tours of Manhattan.

• The day they "turned off" Niagara Falls.

• A park built on top of a Manhattan wastewater treatment plant.

• The New York City murder case that inspired Edgar Allan Poe
to create one of his most famous characters.

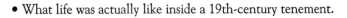
- What life was actually like inside a 19th-century tenement.

- The history of Bellevue Hospital, John Jacob Astor, and the Apollo Theater.

- Rules at the New York Public Library. (Examples: You must wear clothes, and the librarians don't babysit.)

- The answer (finally!) to the burning question: "Can a penny dropped from the top of the Empire State Building really kill you?"

ONE LAST THING

Before we go, we want to give a big New York shout-out and an extra round of jazz hands to Lorrie, Derek, Sue, JoAnn, Bonnie, and Dan who deserve a knish, a hot dog with everything, and an supersized egg cream for all their hard work.

And now, let's take a trip over the river and through the woods, across the bridge, under the city, around the harbor, and down the yellow brick road of weird and interesting stories about the best city and state in the world. We ♥ you, New York!

And as always...

Go with the flow!

—Uncle John and the BRI Staff

TALKING ABOUT NYC

How would you describe New York City?

"New York is the biggest collection of villages in the world."
—**Alistair Cooke**

"I moved to New York City for my health. I'm paranoid, and it was the only place where my fears were justified."
—**Anita Weiss**

"Cut off as I am, it is inevitable that I should sometimes feel like a shadow walking in a shadowy world. When this happens I ask to be taken to New York City. Always I return home weary, but I have the comforting certainty that mankind is real and I myself am not a dream."
—**Helen Keller**

"New York attracts the most people in the world in the arts and professions. It also attracts them in other fields. Even the bums are talented."
—**Edmund Love**

"In New York it's not whether you win or lose—it's how you lay the blame."
—**Fran Lebowitz**

"When it's three o'clock in New York, it's still 1938 in London."
—**Bette Midler**

"The city is not a concrete jungle, it is a human zoo."
—**Desmond Morris**

"One belongs to New York instantly, one belongs to it as much in five minutes as in five years."
—**Thomas Wolfe**

"One day, there were four innocent people shot. That's the best shooting done in this town. Hard to find four innocent people in New York."
—**Will Rogers**

"This is New York, and there's no law against being annoying."
—**William Kuntsler**

"I miss New York. I still love how people talk to you on the street—just assault you and tell you what they think of your jacket."
—**Madonna**

YOU KNOW YOU'RE A NEW YORKER WHEN...

- You're living in a 350-square-foot studio apartment that costs $2,000 a month, and you think it's a fantastic deal.

- Your navigational directions are east, west, uptown, and downtown.

- You've never been to the Empire State Building, the Statue of Liberty, or Times Square on New Year's Eve, but you have seen Ground Zero at midnight, and you've walked the Highline.

- You say "the city" but mean "Manhattan."

- You sprint to catch the subway even when you're not in a hurry.

- You consider yourself multilingual if you can curse in more than one language.

- All the clothes in your closet are black.

- Your front door has at least three locks (and possibly a snow shovel propped under the knob for extra protection).

- You'd climb three flights of subway stairs with crutches to avoid the subway elevator.

- You think of Central Park as "nature" and the Staten Island Ferry as a "romantic boat ride."

- Westchester is considered "upstate."

- You're able to concentrate on your morning paper while standing in a crowded subway with a mariachi band playing in the middle of the car.

- You live in a building with 100 apartments, but know only three of your neighbors.

- You know someone who knows someone who knows the mayor.

Shipping magnate Cornelius Vanderbuilt's first business venture was...

ALMOST FAMOUS

*New York has so many world-famous attractions that many
lesser-known ones get overshadowed...like these.*

NEW YORK HALL OF SCIENCE
Location: Queens
Located in Flushing Meadows–Corona Park, the Hall of
Science opened in 1964 for the World's Fair. (*More about that on
page 277.*) When the fair ended and the other exhibits closed, the
Hall of Science stayed open. Today, it's the only hands-on science
center in New York City and has more than 450 exhibits—you
can peer into powerful microscopes and watch microbes move, figure out how much of your body weight is actually water, and play
minigolf to learn that spaceships and golf balls are powered by the
same forces.

PELHAM BAY PARK

Location: The Bronx
At more than 2,700 acres, Pelham Bay Park is three times larger
than Central Park and offers a much wilder experience. There's a
wildlife sanctuary full of egrets, racoons, blackbirds, and a salt
marsh; Orchard Beach, the only public beach in the Bronx; and
Split Rock, where 17th-century activist and reformer Anne
Hutchinson supposedly hid before she was killed by a group of
Native Americans fighting a war with the Dutch settlers.

ROOSEVELT ISLAND SKYTRAM

Location: Manhattan
Instead of driving or taking a bus or the F train to visit Roosevelt
Island, you can fly...sort of. The skytram takes about three minutes
(and $2.25) to cross the East River from 59th Street/Second
Avenue to Roosevelt Island, and from 250 feet above ground, the
views are spectacular. The tram made an appearance in the 2002
movie *Spider-Man:* The Green Goblin throws Mary Jane over the
Queensboro bridge at the same time that he drops a tram full of
children, trying to force Spider-Man to choose between the
woman he loves and the kids. (Spidey, of course, saves them all.)

HOLE IN ONE

In more than 100 years of bagel making, New Yorkers have acquired such a passion for the doughy bread that it has become an internationally known icon of the city. But the bagel isn't a native New Yorker.

BAGEL TALES
There's a lot of debate over how bagels came to be. One story says a 17th-century Austrian baker wanted to make a gift for King John III Sobieski of Poland, who saved Austria from a Turkish invasion. The king was a famous horseman, so the baker shaped the dough like a stirrup. (The Austrian word for "stirrup" is *bügel*.)

Another story goes like this: Around 1610, the first bagel, called a *beygl* in Yiddish, came out of a Jewish oven in Krakow, Poland. Historians say the doughnut-shaped rolls were designed to be gifts for Jewish women with infants—the hole in the bread represented the gift of life and the crusty roll was a useful teething ring. Also, unlike other breads, bagels could be boiled before the Jewish Sabbath, left until after the religious observance 24 hours later (Jewish law forbade cooking on the Sabbath), and then quickly baked to perfection. People loved them.

In the late 19th century, bagels invaded the U.S. by way of Jewish immigrants from Eastern Europe. Vendors typically sold them as street food, but by 1907, one group of prominent New York bagel makers had founded the International Bagel Bakers Union to protect their recipes. Not just anyone could join; only the sons of former members were eligible. The union's leader, Moishe Soprano, was tough and no-nonsense—he secured contracts with nearly all the bakeries in the New York City area, ensuring bagel-making consistency for decades. A union contract also gave the consumers piece of mind—Soprano and his bakers kneaded their dough by hand, unlike "lower-end" bagel makers outside the union who, rumor had it, often kneaded the dough with their feet.

BAGELS FOR ALL

After World War I, Canadian bagel-maker Meyer Mickey Thompson tried to create an automated bagel maker. He failed because his invention was too expensive, but his son Daniel succeeded, creating the Thompson Bagel Machine, and started churning them out in the 1960s in a six-car garage in New Haven, Connecticut. Thompson Bagel Machines could produce about 400 bagels an hour at minimal cost. Bagel bakers Harry Lender and Florence Sender took it from there, using the machines to mass-produce frozen bagels and selling them to supermarkets everywhere.

In 1988, Americans ate an average of one bagel a month. But an upsurge in bagel sales soon chewed up the competition: Five years later, it was a bagel every two weeks and growing.

BAGEL BITS

• In North America, there are two types of bagel: The New York version and the Montreal. The New York contains salt and malt, and is boiled in water and then baked so that it's puffy with a moist crust. The Montreal is smaller, due to a larger hole, and has no salt; it's boiled in honey-sweetened water and then baked in a wood-fired oven, making it crunchy and sweet. To New York's chagrin, the first bagel in space was the Montreal version. Canadian-born astronaut Gregory Chamitoff lifted off in the 2008 Space Shuttle *Discovery* with a shipment of 18 sesame-seeded bagels from his cousin's bakery in Montreal...and delivered them to the International Space Station.

• In the spring of 2009, New York State tax collectors shut down the H&H bagel factory in Manhattan (popularized on the TV show *Seinfeld*) for failing to pay $100,000 in back taxes. For three hours, customers stood forlorn outside the closed bagel emporium until owner Helmer Toro came up with a $25,000 tax bill installment that allowed H&H to reopen.

* * *

BITE ME
In 1996...
• 9,655 New Yorkers were bitten by dogs.
• 184 were bitten by rats.
• 1,102 were bitten by people.

The name Schenectady is from a Mohawk word meaning "the other side of the pine lands."

SO YOU THINK YOU KNOW NEW YORK CITY

*A few strange facts and stories that even a
seasoned New Yorker might not know.*

• There are more than 2,000 bridges in New York City. Two of
them are *retractile*, meaning they can slide open or even be pulled
ashore to let ships through.

• The life-size bronze elephant that stands in the United Nations
Sculpture Garden on 46th Street was given to the U.N. in 1998
by the governments of Kenya, Namibia, and Nepal. But the
anatomically correct animal sports a two-foot long…um…
appendage. Today, plants strategically hide the controversial body
part, but sadly, the garden is closed. You can still glimpse his front
quarters from the street, though.

• Why are water towers and tanks so common on the rooftops of
New York buildings? Because a water code from the 19th century
specifies that all New York City buildings over six stories must
have individual water storage enough to douse a fire above the
sixth floor. Aqueducts and water pressure can take care of the first
six floors; the amount of extra water and the size of the tank are
commensurate with the number of extra floors.

• You can't fly directly to California from LaGuardia Airport. A
Perimeter Rule set by the Port Authority limits the number of
miles an airplane can fly nonstop out of LaGuardia. Maximum:
1,500. After Flushing airport closed in 1984, most of its traffic was
diverted to LaGuardia, so the Port Authority instituted the
Perimeter Rule to avoid overcrowding. Two exceptions: 1) There
is no cap on Saturday, and 2) the rule doesn't apply to flights to
Denver (just over 1,700 miles) and some parts of the Caribbean—
because nonstops from LaGuardia to those places were allowed
before the rule was made.

• The next total solar eclipse visible from New York will happen
on May 1, 2079.

In 1918 cartoonist Robert Ripley introduced his "Believe It or Not" feature in the *New York Globe*.

THE SWINGINGEST BOROUGH

New Orleans is often cited as the birthplace of jazz, and Chicago, Harlem, and Kansas City are recognized as critical launching pads for the music. But the borough of Queens is where the coolest cats chose to crash when they were beat, ya dig?

WHAT A WONDERFUL NEIGHBORHOOD
In 1943, after more than two decades of traveling and performing, jazz great Louis "Satchmo" Armstrong and his wife, Lucille, settled down for the first time and bought a house at 34-56 107th Street in Corona, Queens. It remained his home until his death in 1971, and after Lucille passed away in 1983, the two-story house became the Louis Armstrong House Museum. To this day, the interiors are preserved as the Armstrongs left them, and the den features an extensive archive of Satchmo's personal reel-to-reel recordings. And although Armstrong mostly maintained a level of modesty appropriate for a man who grew up in the New Orleans Home for Colored Waifs, he did allow himself certain household indulgences, including a kitchen with all its appliances built-in (including the blender) and gold faucets in the bathroom.

Why did Satchmo settle in Queens? The cultural diversity and domestic possibilities that Queens offered are best summed up by Armstrong himself: "I am here with the black people, with the Puerto Rican people, the Italian people, the Hebrew cats, and there's food in the Frigidaire. What else could I want?" And he wasn't the only jazz great to call Queens home.

THE SAINTS OF ST. ALBANS
Many notable musicians made their homes in the Queens neighborhood of St. Albans, particularly in the enclave of Addisleigh Park. A list of the notable residents reads like a poster for a jazz festival:

• **Fats Waller (173-19 Sayres Avenue):** This master "tickler" (jazz slang for "piano player") and writer of such classics as "Ain't Misbehavin'" and "Honeysuckle Rose" came to the neighborhood in 1938. Many jazz historians name him as the first African American to call Addisleigh Park home. His house boasted a Steinway grand piano and a built-in Hammond organ.

• **Count Basie (174-27 Adelaide Road):** A native of Red Bank, New Jersey, Basie and his wife, Catherine, lived in Addisleigh Park from 1946 to 1971. The couple was popular among neighborhood youths for generously granting access to their backyard pool.

• **Ella Fitzgerald (179-07 Murdock Avenue):** The "First Lady of Song" never had a stable home as a child. Her parents separated when she was young, her mother died when she was a teenager, her stepfather abused her—and there were stopovers at reform school, a period of homelessness, and a short stint working lookout at a New York bordello. But as a teenager, she won an amateur talent show at Harlem's storied Apollo Theater, and a star was born. She moved into the house in Queens with her husband, bassist Ray Brown, in 1949. The couple divorced in 1953, but Fitzgerald stayed put until 1956.

• **Milt Hinton (173-05 113th Avenue):** A resident of Queens for 50 years until his death in 2000, Hinton was a bassist and sideman for a staggering number of artists (as a studio musician, he appeared on 1,174 recordings), including Cab Calloway, Benny Goodman, Ben Webster, and neighbors Louis Armstrong and Count Basie.

• **Cootie Williams (175-19 Linden Boulevard):** From 1947 to 1953, this star trumpet player of the Duke Ellington Band lived in a three-story Tudor-style house that featured a prominent fairy-tale-style turret. Another notable musician lived there in the 1960s: Godfather of Soul James Brown.

ROYAL FLUSHING

The Flushing Cemetery in Flushing, Queens, is the final resting place for two prominent jazz trumpeters: "King of Jazz" Louis Armstrong (1901–71) and "Crown Prince of Bop" Dizzy Gillespie (1917–93).

* * *

"There's two kinds of music: good and bad. I play the good kind."

—Louis Armstrong

MANHATTANHENGE

*Want to see a perfect sunset? Twice a year,
you can get your wish right in Manhattan.*

L ET THE SUN SHINE
Most of the time, the tall buildings in Manhattan block the
sunset. But twice a year, above 14th Street, the sun aligns
with the streets' east–west grid pattern and sets perfectly between
the buildings. It lasts only about 15 minutes, but it's so striking that
people stop on the streets to watch. As solar rays light up the tow-
ering buildings, a glowing orange light filters along the streets.

The reflection off the buildings also scatters the sunshine, send-
ing bright light along the north–south avenues as well. Because the
phenomenon resembles sunsets seen at Great Britain's mysterious
Stonehenge ruins, Neil deGrasse Tyson, an astrophysicist at the
American Museum of Natural History in Manhattan, calls it
"Manhattanhenge."

PERFECTION...ALMOST

Stonehenge was built by the ancient Celtic Druids to mark the
exact moment of the spring and fall equinoxes, when the sun rises
and sets due east and due west of true north. But Manhattan's
street grid was established in 1811 for efficiency, not science, so it's
slightly off center—it's turned 28.9 degrees from true east and west
to be exact. As a result, the city's "equinoxes" occur on different
days each year

Usually the dates are in late May and mid-July. But if you miss
the exact dates, not to worry. The day before or after Manhattanhenge also creates a celestial glow—it's not quite as magnificent,
but still pretty good.

According to deGrasse Tyson, who calculates the dates each
year for the museum's planetarium, the best way to see Manhattanhenge is this: "Position yourself as far east in Manhattan as
possible. But ensure that when you look west across the avenues
you can still see New Jersey. Clear cross streets include 14th, 23rd,
34th, 42nd, 57th, and several streets adjacent to them. The
Empire State Building and the Chrysler Building render 34th
Street and 42nd Streets especially striking vistas."

PUNKED

*Even gritty New Yorkers are gullible. Take a trip
through some of the silliest hoaxes ever perpetrated
on a city (supposedly) full of skeptics.*

THE GREAT MOON HOAX
Perpetrator: The *New York Sun* newspaper
Story: The paper printed its first issue in 1833, and by
1835, it was looking for a circulation boost. So to drum up interest,
editors announced the upcoming publication of six articles covering renowned British astronomer Sir John Herschel's fantastic new
discoveries of life on the moon: forests and seas, cranes and peli-
cans, herds of bison and goats, flocks of blue unicorns, sapphire
temples with 70-foot pillars—even a race of bat-like humanoid
creatures. According to the *Sun*, the articles would be reprinted
from the *Edinburgh Journal of Science*.

The day the first article appeared, *Sun* sales were 15,000; by the
sixth day, they were over 19,000, the highest of any New York
paper of the time. Other newspapers, racing to catch up, claimed
to have acquired the "original" *Edinburgh Journal* articles, but they
actually just reprinted the *Sun's* stories.

Exposed! There were no original *Edinburgh Journal* articles...it was
a hoax. In fact, that paper had gone out of business several years
earlier. And Herschel, perhaps the most eminent astronomer of his
time, was totally ignorant of the hoax (and amused by it until he
got sick of answering questions about moon men). The articles
were reportedly written by *Sun* reporter Richard Adams Locke.
The *Sun* never formally admitted the deception, but it did publish
a column speculating that a hoax was "possible." Regardless, the
paper got what it wanted: Circulation remained high.

THE 140-YEAR-OLD HOT DOG HOAX
Perpetrator: The Coney Island History Project
Story: In 2009 and 2010, the Astroland amusement park at Coney
Island was being demolished to make room for new games and
rides. On Wednesday, February 24, 2010, the old kitchen building
of the block-long Feltman's restaurant on Surf Avenue was sched-

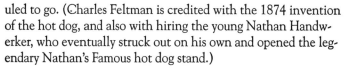

uled to go. (Charles Feltman is credited with the 1874 invention of the hot dog, and also with hiring the young Nathan Handwerker, who eventually struck out on his own and opened the legendary Nathan's Famous hot dog stand.)

According to CNN (which got the story from a local TV station), in the middle of the demolition, an amateur archaeologist unearthed an ice-encrusted object that he claimed was an original Feltman's hot dog…140 years old. Officials of the Coney Island History Project swore that the dog, the bun, and an original receipt from Feltman's had been preserved by the ice, and they immediately put the thawing relic on display. CNN, Grub Street (a New York food blog), and thousands of Tweeters bought it.

Exposed! On February 26, a spokeswoman for the History Project admitted that it was all a publicity stunt in the "grand tradition of Coney Island ballyhoo." The point? To get people out to Coney Island to see the Project's exhibit about Feltman's. It was a success—hundreds of people hurried out to Coney Island to see the show.

THE CENTRAL PARK INTERNATIONAL AIRPORT HOAX

Perpetrator: The Manhattan Airport Foundation (MAF)

Story: On July 21, 2009, a group calling itself the Manhattan Airport Foundation (MAF) ran an Internet posting with an unusual idea: to bulldoze Central Park and turn it into an airport. The MAF called for "the immediate development of a viable and centrally located international air transportation hub in New York City." Where? Central Park. Strawberry Fields would be replanted inside the new terminal, Tavern on the Green restaurant could move to the Food Court, and the Central Park Zoo would be relocated. *The Huffington Post* ran the story on its front page.

Exposed! Who is the Manhattan Airport Foundation? No one knows. The group has a Web site and claimed to have offices on the 58th floor of the Woolworth Building (which has only 57 floors). According to MAF's Web site, a petition to destroy the park in favor of the airport got 19,000 signatures.

For more hoaxes, turn to page 134.

THERE GOES THE NEIGHBORHOOD: THE BRONX

The Bronx is the only borough of New York City that isn't an island.
It's also the only place where you'll find these neighborhoods.

• **The Bronx** was named for the nearby Bronx River, which, in turn, was named for Jonas Bronck, an immigrant from Sweden who settled in the area in the 17th century.

• The town of **Spuyten Duyvil**, a wooded neighborhood near the Hudson and Harlem rivers, also gets its name from a body of water: the Spuyten Duyvil Creek. Depending on how you pronounce them, the words mean "devil's whirlpool" or "spite the devil" in Dutch. (It's unclear why the Dutch had such a low opinion of the creek.)

• New Yorkers can thank Jordan L. Mott, who opened an iron-works in the Bronx in the mid-1800s, for the neighborhood of **Mott Haven**. When the previous owner of the land—Gouverneur Morris II, who'd called the area Morristown—was asked if he minded Mott changing the neighborhood's name, he quipped, "I don't care...while he is about it, he might as well change the Harlem River to the Jordan."

• **Tremont** got its name from a 19th-century mailman who combined three (tre) neighborhoods in the West-Central Bronx: Fairmount, Mount Hope, and Mount Eden.

• Between 1968 and 1970, the City of New York built a housing project of 15,372 units on 300 acres of filled marshland in the northeastern Bronx. It was one of the largest housing projects in the country and had room for about 60,000 people. Today, it's called **Co-op City**, and if it weren't part of the Bronx, it would be the tenth-largest city in the state of New York.

The first retail Christmas tree lot in the U.S. opened in 1851 in NYC.

THE MATH MAN

Do you suffer from arithmophobia…the fear of math? (Yeah, we do, too.) Mathematician Glen Whitney has a remedy for that: a hands-on math museum, where he plans to make numbers fun for everyone.

EVERYDAY MATH

Glen Whitney of Long Island loves math, and he wants everyone else to love it too…or at least understand it. In his view, schools typically get math "wrong" by promoting that there's only one right answer, when the true essence—and the fun part—of math is actually exploration and discovery. According to Whitney, many people don't know that "Mathematics Underlies Simply Everything" in the arts, sciences, and life in general. So on his Web site, he encourages people to "let mathematics be your MUSE!"

Whitney was fascinated when he took his two kids on a trip to a small museum of mathematics, the Goudreau Museum, in Herricks. But he was dismayed to hear in 2006 that the museum was closing, so Whitney quit his job at a hedge fund in 2008 and began a crusade to open his own math museum. He is now the president of Math Factory, a group he created to spark interest in math, and executive director of the Museum of Mathematics, which exhibits around New York and is looking for a permanent home.

Contrary to popular belief, Whitney says, math isn't just about numbers and calculations. It also has fun and practical uses. A card player can learn how to shuffle a deck to increase the probability of winning the next hand, and a musician can benefit from knowing how drums of different sizes and shapes will produce different pitches. Artists may experiment with a *harmonograph*, a pendulum with a pen attached, which makes spiral patterns that change depending on how it's swung.

MATH TOURS

To get his message out to the public, Whitney leads free, appointment-only math tours of Manhattan. Groups meet at Lincoln Center outside the Alice Tully Hall theater and first learn how straight lines fit together to create the curved surface of the theater's grandstand. From there, Whitney follows the most efficient route (jaywalking) across 66th Street to Lincoln Center Plaza. Stopping by a clock near Columbus Avenue, he explains that all clocks work by math, using ellipses and theories by the ancient Greek mathematician Pythagoras. Stopping at a fire hydrant, Whitney demonstrates how pentagonal lug nuts make it impossible for random mischief-makers to break open a hydrant with a simple wrench (city workers use special tools).

The tour then moves on to Times Square, where, under the debt clock, Whitney discusses each household's share of the U.S. national debt. Then he dashes gamblers' dreams by exposing the unlikelihood of winning the lottery—it is, says Whitney, "a tax on the mathematically illiterate." The tour typically ends an hour or so later with information useful to any New Yorker: Whitney calculates that, when possible, walking across blocks diagonally along the hypotenuse of a triangle (instead of traveling straight up and over), saves two blocks for every nine traveled.

MATH MIDWAY

The tours are just one way that Whitney gets the word out about math; another way is the traveling Math Midway, a carnival of sorts where every game has a mathematical punchline. It's the first of several exhibits Whitney has planned for his museum. Some favorites:

• Guests can ride a square-wheeled tricycle. How? By wheeling it over a wavy surface. The edges of the square wheels fit perfectly into the trough of each wave to smooth out what would otherwise be a bumpy ride.

• As an introduction to graph theory, visitors navigate a giant maze without making any left turns.

• Putting calculus into action, the Roller Graphicoaster has a wire track that people curve into shapes and then race a metal ball down to see which configuration allows it to travel fastest.

• A funhouse mirror adjusts from concave to convex with the pull of a rope, so visitors can see how their reflections look different as the mirror changes.

MATH MUSEUM

Eventually, Whitney plans to open his nonprofit math museum in a 15,000–20,000-square-foot space. It will be the first museum of its kind in the country. He explains, "You won't need to be a math whiz or a math lover to enjoy our museum. We'll highlight the connections between math and a huge range of topics: art, biology, music, finance, sports, games, physics, juggling, photography, design, and so on."

When he talks about math, Glen Whitney's enthusiasm for a subject that usually gets a bad rap seems to rub off on those around him. With some hands-on problem-solving and exploration, even the greatest cases of arithmophobia can be eased. Go figure.

*　　*　　*

NEW YORK'S STATE SYMBOLS

- Fruit: apple

- Animal: beaver

- Insect: ladybug

- Shell: bay scallop

- Reptile: snapping turtle

- Saltwater fish: striped bass

- Fossil: Eurypterus remipes (a distant relative of the horseshoe crab)

- Freshwater fish: brook trout

- Bird: bluebird

- Tree: sugar maple

- Bush: lilac

- Gem: garnet

- Beverage: milk

NY'S FINEST (PARKS)

A quick tour through some of New York State's crown jewels.

LETCHWORTH STATE PARK. Located 60 miles southeast of Buffalo in Livingston County, this 14,350-acre park is home to "The Grand Canyon of the East," Letchworth Gorge. It's a 22-mile section of the Genesee River that contains three deep, stunning gorges, the middle of which, the Great Bend Gorge, plunges to 550 feet. The river forms three sizeable waterfalls within the park, and dozens more flow into it from the cliffs above—several of which are more than 500 feet tall themselves. The park was named after William Pryor Letchworth, a Buffalo businessman and philanthropist who donated the land to the state as a public park in 1906.

RIVERBANK STATE PARK. The amazing thing about this park is its location: on top of a building in Manhattan. And not just any building; it's on the roof of a working wastewater treatment plant, covered with tons of trucked-in soil. Situated along the Hudson River, the 28-acre park features a grassy area for picnics, several trees, an Olympic-size swimming pool, a skating rink (roller skating in the summer and ice-skating in the winter), an 800-seat theater, tennis and basketball courts, a restaurant, and a pedestrian esplanade that allows walkers views of Manhattan and the New Jersey Palisades across the river.

GOOSEPOND MOUNTAIN STATE PARK. Near the village of Chester in New York State's Lower Hudson Valley is this park for people who like a rustic experience: It's almost completely undeveloped. There are no toilets, no running water—it's even hard to find a parking space. Most of the park is pure woods and wetlands, and there are many miles of trails, which include wooden walkways over the wetlands, offering especially good viewing of a wide variety of waterfowl. Goosepond also has some interesting history: A rocky outcrop in the park hides a small rock shelter that, according to legend, was used as a hideout by the notorious Claudius Smith, leader of a group of Loyalist guerrillas known as the "Cowboys," who terrorized the region during the Revolutionary War.

JONES BEACH STATE PARK. This park takes up almost all of Jones Beach Island, one of the long, narrow barrier islands off Long Island. Its most popular feature: more than six miles of sandy beach along the Atlantic Ocean. Jones Beach is the most-visited beach on the East Coast—with some 6 million people passing through every year—so don't go there for a quiet getaway. The park also has two huge old bathhouses, built in 1920s art deco style, a 231-foot water tower, and a two-mile-long stretch of boardwalk. All of the buildings were designed by the park's chief founder, Robert Moses.

ADIRONDACK PARK. The largest state-protected park in the contiguous United States, Adirondack Park covers an astounding 9,375 square miles—an area roughly the size of Vermont. It's home to the Adirondack Mountains, more than 3,000 lakes (including Lake Placid, the site of two Winter Olympics), more than 2,000 miles of hiking trails, thousands of miles of rivers and streams, and a huge variety of mammals, including black bears, moose, coyotes, lynx, otters, beavers, and porcupines.

• Adirondack Park is larger than Yellowstone and Yosemite National Parks…combined.

• It's considered a unique example of publicly and privately owned parkland. About 46 percent of the park—2.7 million acres—is a state-owned forest preserve. That land is protected by the New York State constitution as "forever wild." The rest of the park is privately owned, although most of it is forest and sparsely developed farmland.

• There are 103 towns and villages within the park's boundaries, and about 137,000 people live there year-round.

• The Adirondack Mountains have 46 peaks more than 4,000 feet high, including Mt. Marcy, the state's highest, at 5,344 feet.

• There are no official entrances to Adirondack Park, and there is no entrance fee. Just drive, bike, walk—or canoe—right in.

Manhattan is the birthplace of Elizabeth Ann Seton, the first American-born saint.

THIS GUY'S IN–SAAAA–NE!

Electronics is a dirty business…just ask ex-con "Crazy" Eddie Antar, who went from high to low in a New York minute.

EDDIE TAKES OVER

In the 1970s and '80s, just about everybody in New York knew Crazy Eddie—or at least knew his TV commercials. His electronics stores were expanding throughout New York and into the surrounding states. And the commercials for those stores were legendary: They proclaimed that the prices at Crazy Eddie's stores were "Insaaaane!" and spoofed everything from Superman to football. Crazy Eddie made millions after taking his family company public. Wall Street brokers and investors praised him as a retailing revolutionary and a business genius. But by the 1990s, all the Crazy Eddie stores were shut down, and Eddie was in prison. What happened?

ALL IN THE FAMILY

The Crazy Eddie saga began in 1969, when Eddie Antar, his cousin Ronnie, and his father Sam, founded a company called ERS Electronics (for Eddie, Ronnie, and Sam) and opened an electronics store called Sights and Sounds on Kings Highway in Brooklyn. The Antars were a close-knit family, and Sam Antar hoped that the store would expand to employ and support members of the extended family.

But it didn't. The new store struggled. Most people bought their electronics at department stores, so Sights and Sounds just wasn't attracting enough shoppers. By 1971, it was in debt and close to bankruptcy, but Eddie was certain he could turn the business around. So Sam bought out Cousin Ronnie, gave his son Eddie two-thirds of the business, and put him in charge.

Eddie was a born salesman. As a teenager, he'd cut school to hawk T-shirts and cheap electronics near the Manhattan Port Authority Terminal. Charming and aggressive, Eddie had once gone so far as to block a customer's exit, pleading with her not to leave until they made a deal. Sales tactics like that earned him the nickname

"Crazy Eddie." Now he applied those shrewd techniques to his store. He slashed his prices and guaranteed that he would beat any competitor's price. He changed the store's "boring" name to Crazy Eddie. Then he launched one of the most famous ad campaigns to ever assault New Yorkers.

EDDIE GOES INSAAAANE

Antar wanted an ad campaign that would bring in customers, and late one night on the radio, he heard the voice that could do it. WPIX disc jockey Dr. Jerry (real name: Jerry Carroll) ad-libbed a Crazy Eddie commercial on his show, and he put an extra bit of oomph in it. He didn't just say that Crazy Eddie's prices were "insanely" low—he shouted that they were "IN–SAAAANE!"

Eddie immediately hired Carroll to do all of his radio ads, and when Crazy Eddie expanded into television, Jerry Carroll played a fast-talking, hyperactive "Crazy Eddie" who shouted about his deals…while jumping up and down, waving his arms, and tearing at his clothing. He might be dressed as Santa Claus or Superman, but he always acted like a lunatic. The ads made such a splash that they were parodied by Dan Aykroyd on *Saturday Night Live*. And in a memorable scene from the popular 1980s film *Splash*, Darryl Hannah plays an overwhelmed mermaid who visits Bloomingdale's and watches in terror as "Eddie" goes through his schtick on dozens of TV sets.

The ads did the trick. Customers flocked to Eddie's stores searching for deals, and were often talked into buying "better quality merchandise" at a regular markup. Antar expanded his store to a chain of 43, fulfilling his father's dream of employing his relatives. And during that time, he pulled in about $350 million in sales…or did he?

EDDIE'S SECRET TO SUCCESS

It was true that Crazy Eddie sold electronics at lower prices than the competition. But how could Antar do that and still make so much money? The solution: tax fraud. He hired family members (and others) under the table to avoid payroll tax, and when there were cash sales, he kept the sales tax and hid the profits in overseas banks so he wouldn't have to pay income tax on them.

Then Eddie realized he could make much more if he inflated the value of Crazy Eddie, made it a public company, and sold its high-priced stock. So in 1980, Eddie and some of his family members started hiding fewer of the cash sales. They did that for three years, gradually adding more cash to the books and making it seem like their profits were increasing enormously each year. Then, in 1984, they turned the stores into a public company and sold stock shares.

Crazy Eddie stock climbed in value because the company appeared to be so profitable. But in fact, the company was running up deficits of $3 million to $12 million. Eddie's younger cousin, Sammy Antar, was hired as the chief financial officer, specifically to hide the deficits and create false profits. So he falsified the inventory and used the cash hidden in overseas banks to make phony sales payments to the stores. On paper, it looked like sales were booming. And according to court documents, Eddie Antar raked in about $75 million from the stock sales; his brothers, Mitchell and Allen, made $4 million and $3 million, respectively. But times were changing. Eddie was facing more competition, his stores were losing money, and his scheme was falling apart.

THE FALL OF CRAZY EDDIE

Crazy Eddie's scheme collapsed when a company from Houston decided to take over Eddie's stores by buying up controlling shares of Crazy Eddie stock. They went over the books and realized that the numbers didn't match what was in the stores—about $80 million in inventory was missing. They tried to turn the company around, but by 1989, the Crazy Eddie electronics chain was bankrupt, with investors holding worthless stock and creditors pressing for repayment.

In 1990, Crazy Eddie, Sammy, Eddie's brothers, and another cousin were all facing charges of stock fraud. Sammy made a deal with prosecutors and gave up all the details, which spelled the end for Eddie. Instead of showing up for trial, he went on the run with his millions. In 1992, authorities caught up with him in Israel, where he was using the alias David Cohen. Eddie Antar returned to the United States and served seven years in prison. Now a free man, Eddie doesn't like to talk much about the experience. He says, "It doesn't enter my realm of thought. It's so disturbing I don't even like to think about it. I'm just glad I'm back with my family."

The term "cops" comes from the copper badges first worn by NYPD officers in 1845.

FLUSH WITH PRIDE

What exactly flows under the streets that New Yorkers
walk on every day? Read on (and flush twice).

FLUSHING, NEW YORK
New York became America's largest—and, some say, most civilized—city in 1835, but its sanitation system was way behind the times. Most homes, even the most expensive ones, had privies out back. That meant waste fell into a hole in the ground, and when the hole was full, someone covered it with dirt and dug another hole. Pigs roamed Manhattan, eating up garbage and sewage on city streets. By the late 1800s, after several outbreaks of water-borne diseases, it became obvious that something needed to be done about all the sewage.

The city's first two wastewater treatment facilities were located in Brooklyn and Queens, and in 1906, the city established the Metropolitan Sewerage Commission to handle municipal waste. But the system was overwhelmed by New York's ever-growing population. By 1910, about 700 million gallons of raw sewage flowed into the city's rivers every day, and *Sunday Magazine* reported, "the Hudson River was so dirty that it could barely support fish."

The Sewage Commission responded by adding new treatment plants and upgraded others, and today, New York City's wastewater treatment plants handle more than a billion gallons of sewage per day through almost 7,500 miles of sewer pipes.

Still, it's not enough. As New Yorkers know, when it rains, raw sewage often threatens to back up through storm drains and into the subway. When that happens, the city's wastewater system does what it was built to do: It still discharges overflow into the East River, the Hudson River, and New York Harbor.

AW, RATS!

But aside from the obvious, what's really down in the sewers?

• One recent report estimated that there are 500 rats per mile of sewer pipes. (Another thought there were more rats in New York City than people, but that's never been proven.) Most of them are *rattus norvegicus*, or the common brown sewer rat, which can grow to weigh about two pounds and has been known to attack humans, even in broad daylight.

• Despite the number of urban legends, officially, there are no alligators in the city's sewers. But during the 1920s and '30s, the *New York Times* was full of stories about alligators running wild in the city. Still, only one of the stories actually reported an alligator near a sewer. It's more likely that any 'gators found in New York City or its surrounding waterways came from some above-ground source: aquarium escapees, lost shipping cargo, and so on. Alligators are warm weather creatures, and New York winters are too cold for the animals to survive.

• Animals fall into the sewer all the time, and smaller animals undoubtedly get flushed down. Most of them are dead before the whoosh, but some make it out alive, including turtles, fish, and at least one small and extremely lucky dog.

• Sewer workers have fished out guns, knives, game pieces, mattresses, Christmas decorations, electronics, jewelry, telephones, silverware, auto parts, tires, dead bodies, and a glass eye.

*   *   *

THE FIGHTER

Born in California, James "Gentleman Jim" Corbett— famous for knocking out boxing champ John L. Sullivan in 1892—lived the second half of his life in Bayside, Queens. Corbett moved to Bayside in 1902 at the age of 36, and lived there until his death in 1933. After his boxing career ended, Corbet performed in vaudeville, some low-budget movies, and wrote his life story, which was later turned into a movie that starred Errol Flynn. A *Bayside Times* writer once described Corbet's elegant style, which contributed to his nickname: "In the winter, he would have on a long black Chesterfield coat with a velvet collar, a derby hat, white shirt with a beautiful tie, a gleaming diamond stickpin, grey fawn gloves, a white scarf and, of course, grey spats, which were in vogue in those days."

WEIRD NEWS

New Yorkers do the darndest things.

SAY IT WITH INSECTS

Valentine's Day took a strange turn in 2011, when the Bronx Zoo offered (for a limited time) a unique gift for the man or woman who has everything: Doting partners could name one of the zoo's bugs after their sweeties. What kind of bug? "A Madagascar hissing roach, the biggest and loudest of these stalwart insects," said the museum's Web site. Each naming cost $10 and included an official certificate sent to the lucky recipient. According to the zoo, more than 5,800 people took them up on their offer.

PENNEY PINCHER

In early 2011, police charged postal worker Thomas Tang of Queens with grand larceny after he allegedly stole more than 7,000 discount coupons for JCPenney. According to police, between October 2009 and January 2011, Tang lifted the coupons from circulars meant for customers on his Long Island postal route, then bundled and sold the coupons on eBay. Said one resident, "I think it's terrible. He should go to jail." The prosecutor just seemed puzzled: "I'm not going to minimize it, but it is a little strange, not your typical case." At last check, the judge had set bail at $10,000, and Tang was headed for trial.

TURNING A BLIND EYE

In November 2010, NYU art professor Wafaa Bilal had a two-inch-wide digital camera implanted under the skin in the back of his head as part of an art project called "The 3rd I." Its goal: to raise "important social, aesthetic, political, technological, and artistic questions." He planned to wear the camera for a year as he went about his daily activities and the images were streamed live to a museum in Qatar. Unfortunately for Bilal (and the museum), the camera lasted only three months; it was removed in February 2011 after the skin around it became inflamed. No matter. Bilal just wore the camera on a cord around his neck and continued the project.

RIDING IN A HOLE IN THE GROUND

New York, New York, it's a wonderful town; the Bronx is up and the Battery's down. And how do people travel between them? On the IRT.

BEFORE THE IRT

Traffic in New York City today is a walk in the park compared to what it was in the mid-19th century. Back then, there were no bike lanes, and no bus lanes, no Walk/Don't Walk lights at every corner. Instead, the streets (especially in lower Manhattan) were chaos—pedestrians, pushcarts, horse-drawn streetcars, wagons, and carriages fought for position on streets that had no traffic signals. Overhead, the elevated trains clattered. The pandemonium (and the fact that London had built an underground railway in the 1850s) got *Scientific American* publisher Alfred Ely Beach thinking about new transportation systems for New York.

DIGGING DEEP

The governor had already vetoed a bill permitting a subway for moving *people*, however, so Beach started the Beach Pneumatic Transit Company. And in 1868, he got the state legislature to grant him a charter to build a pneumatic tube for shipping *packages*. But that's not what he built. Secretly, he had his workmen bore a 312-foot tunnel under Broadway near City Hall—the one block from Warren Street to Murray Street. The tunnel was just large enough for a 22-passenger subway car. The men dug for 58 nights, 21 feet below street level, using wagons with muffled wheels to haul away the dirt. Once the walls of the tunnel were bricked, the plush car would be pushed back and forth over the track by compressed air produced by a steam-powered, high-speed fan. Beach furnished the station with chandeliers, paintings, and even a fountain. It opened to the public on March 1, 1870, and by the end of that year, more than 400,000 people had paid a quarter each for a ride. The subway's popularity did not, however, convince the politically powerful merchants of lower Broadway that an underground railway was in their interests. They feared damage to their buildings and a decrease in street traffic

---

Laid end-to-end, all of NYC's subway track would reach to Chicago.

(in other words, customers). Beach kept trying until 1873, when he finally gave up and rented his tunnel first as a shooting gallery, then for storage, and finally just closed it.

By the late 1870s, it was clear that New York City needed better public transportation. Steam-driven elevated trains seemed to be a more practical solution than underground trains, and for the next two decades, the Second Avenue, Third Avenue, Sixth Avenue, and Ninth Avenue Elevated Railways, run by private companies, dominated "rapid" transit. But subways were appearing in other cities (like Glasgow, Budapest, Boston, Paris, and Berlin), and support for an underground rail system in New York was growing.

LAYING THE TRACKS

In 1894, the state legislature appointed a Board of Rapid Transit Railroad Commissioners to figure out the best route for a new subway and to decide whether the state should build it or contract it out to a private company. The powerful merchants again shot down the under-Broadway option, so planners chose a route from City Hall, north on today's Lafayette Street (then called Elm Street) and Lexington Avenue all the way to 42nd Street. At 42nd, the train would make a sharp turn west to Longacre Square (the precursor to Times Square, at the intersection of 42nd Street, Broadway, and Seventh Avenue). At Longacre Square, the train would turn north again and run all the way up to Harlem, a nine-mile ride in total.

But perhaps the engineers' most stunning concept was to lay four tracks instead of two: an uptown express track *and* an uptown local track, plus a downtown express track and a downtown local track. In other cities, the subways ran on just two tracks, with no distinction made between local and express stops. And New York's elevated trains often ran on single tracks, reversing direction with the daily commute. The new four-track IRT subway system allowed trains to run continuously all day long—more passengers could go more places at any time, and they could get where they were going much faster. Plus, the local trains also stopped at the express stations, making it easy for passengers to switch from express to local or vice versa. Today, commuters are so used to this system that it seems as if all subways were always meant to be that way, but the New York City subway system employed this versatile and convenient set up from the very beginning.

From 1777 to 1797, the first capital of New York State was Kingston.

BREAKING (A LOT OF) GROUND

Ultimately, the city gave the subway contract to August Belmont Jr., an extremely rich (and reputedly nasty) banker who could raise enough money to build the underground system—officially called the Interborough Rapid Transit (IRT) Company. The city kicked in $35 million for construction costs and another $1.5 million to buy the land for the stations. Belmont paid for the cars, rails, and other equipment, and when the system opened, he would pay an annual rent equal to the interest on the construction bonds. The IRT was, in essence, an incorporated private company with a 50-year lease to run the trains.

The method of building the subway was called "cut and cover": workers tore up the street, dug down one story below ground, laid the track, and then covered the top of the excavation with an iron-and-steel roof that could be paved over. In this way, the IRT avoided deep, difficult tunneling and also made it possible for passengers to access the station platforms via only one flight of stairs.

The stations were designed to be well lit and beautifully decorated with tile mosaics in motifs that reflected their locations—for example, the beaver mosaics at Astor Place reminded riders of John Jacob Astor's fur trading past. Many stations also featured different colors (white for Spring Street, blue for Bleecker, etc.), and the station names were clearly displayed on panels. Although it was certainly beautiful, the ornamentation had a practical purpose—it was there to help passengers recognize their stops if they missed the conductor's announcement.

OPENING DAY

The IRT opened on October 27, 1904, an event celebrated all over the city and glorified in local newspapers. The crowd at City Hall, where the first ride began, numbered about 7,000, and more than 1,000 people crowded onto each of the two eight-car trains that would make the inaugural trip. In the lead train, Mayor George B. McClellan Jr. took the controls (with the IRT general manager at his elbow, his hand on the emergency brake lever) and off they went. McClellan refused to give up the driver's seat until he had taken the train all the way to its last stop in Harlem.

IRT expected to carry 350,000 passengers a day, but the riding public took to the trains in even larger numbers. By the end of the

---

The U.N. Headquarters stands on the former site of NYC's oldest slaughterhouse.

IRT's first year of operation, more than 600,000 people were riding the subway every day. By 1914, that number had doubled. Less than a decade after opening, the subway system was carrying almost a billion riders per year. Now New Yorkers could commute to jobs that were beyond their own neighborhoods, traveling the length of Manhattan in half an hour. And they could visit families and friends, parks and playgrounds, theaters and colleges. And as the system expanded, they could even move to the outer boroughs, which developed as quickly as the subway could reach them.

The IRT (followed by the Independent Subway System and the Brooklyn-Manhattan Transit Corporation) soon turned New York into the most cosmopolitan city in the world. And until 1948, the fare was only a nickel. (That year, it went up to a dime.)

* * *

SUBWAY FACTS

• The New York City subway is the largest subway system in the world, with 659 miles of track, 468 stations, and 6,290 subway cars.

• Riding the subway reduces carbon emissions by 80 percent per mile, compared with a single occupancy car.

• About 4.5 million people ride the subway every weekday.

• Busiest subway station: Times Square, with 58 million passengers each year.

• Subway tokens were introduced on July 2, 1953. The iconic Y-cut was designed to make them identifiable by touch in your pocket. The Y-cut in subway tokens was removed in 1980 because lint caught in it was clogging machines.

• The Metrocard was introduced on January 6, 1994. The last token machines were removed on December 11, 1997.

• In 1985, the MTA started the Arts for Transit program, which has commissioned 125 works of art (murals, mosaics, and sculptures) for subway stations. The Music Under New York program also pays about 100 professional musicians to play in the subway stations, and yes, they have to audition—the ones who are there officially, at least.

Washington Irving gave NYC its first nickname: Gotham.

STREET TALK

We combed the Internet and let BRI correspondents loose in New York to find out what people were saying on the streets. Here's what we heard.

"I don't think he's working now. All he ever talks about is monkeys and robots."

"It was the saddest thing ever—almost as sad as watching a baby cough."

"Facts are such a distraction from the essence of what's really happening."

Tourist: "Do you know a place where I can get real New York pizza?"
New Yorker: "Lady, I'm looking at you, and you don't need no stinking pizza."

"So, like, I couldn't believe what happened to [a friend], but, like, I think she'll be OK. I mean, she's gonna marry some guy who went to Penn instead of some guy who went to Princeton, and she'll have a country house in South Hampton instead of, like, East Hampton, but I think she'll be OK."

"And that's when the firefighter threw me out the window."

"We're thinking of putting the baby in the closet. It's small, but we can fit a crib in there and keep the door open."

"I'm not even gonna try applying for a Gap card; they'll never give it to me. I don't know what it is about Gap; they always know if you have bad credit."

"I find the suburbs to be extremely frightening. I know they all have air conditioning, but still."

"This is an express, uptown C train. You heard right: an express C train. Next stop: 125th Street. If you need local service on the Upper West Side, please transfer across the platform to the D, as in 'Daddy done did it,' or B, as in 'bad boy Bobby Brown,' train."

Tourist: "Everyone has been so nice in New York, not what I expected."
New Yorker: "We are nice, just self-absorbed."

THE SKINNY ON SKYSCRAPERS

New York's decision to build skyward was based on necessity and technological invention...and driven by a heavy dose of ego.

FIVE-STORY LIMIT

By the 1820s, New York was the economic capital of the country. The city's growing businesses needed office space, but even back then, midtown Manhattan real estate was pricey. So owners wanted taller buildings—one way to get more useable space onto a small, expensive lot. But building high presented several problems.

The most obvious was gravity. Climbing up and down more than five or six flights of stairs made everyday business tasks—or just getting to the office—difficult. Plus, many of the practical needs for a skyscraper hadn't been developed yet: reliable central heating, indoor plumbing, and lighting systems.

And then there was the problem of the foundation. In the early 19th century, anyone who wanted to construct a building more than 10 stories high had to use the same technology that was around during the time of the pyramids: They'd need a huge foundation with thick walls to support the weight of the building. A 16-story building built of brick or stone, for instance, required walls that were at least six feet thick. To soar 20 stories or more, a building would have needed an enormous foundation that might not fit into a narrow midtown lot. And its walls would have to be so thick that they'd take up most of the square footage on the lower floors—there would be hardly any room left in it for office space. Tall commercial buildings seemed completely impractical, so in the mid-1800s, the Manhattan skyline boasted very few buildings more than five stories high.

UP, UP, AND AWAY

That didn't last long. In 1852, inventor Elisha Graves Otis from Yonkers created the first safety brake for elevators. The elevator had been around for centuries, evolving from crude pulley systems

---

"Skyscraper" is an old sailors' term for the uppermost sail on a ship.

to ones that worked with hydraulics, but they carried mostly freight because they were dangerous and difficult to control. Otis's brake, which prevented the elevator from falling if a cable snapped, made them safe for passengers. Five years later, Otis installed New York's first elevator in a department store on Broadway. It worked so well that its architects began to think vertically. By 1875, New York developers had begun constructing 10-story office buildings with elevators. The late 1800s also saw improvements in the electric light bulb, central heating, plumbing, and the telephone. Together, these amenities made it at least possible to construct an extremely high building.

But the foundation was still a problem—one that an Englishman named Henry Bessemer and an American, William Kelly, were trying to solve. Steel was a strong, light metal that could eliminate the need for thick walls, but during the mid-19th century, making steel required an enormous amount of coal to heat the metal. The process was extremely costly and time-consuming, and steel was so expensive at the time that forks and knives made of the metal cost more than ones made of gold.

But then, in 1856, Bessemer (who later bought out his competitor Kelly) figured out how to mass-produce steel: by using a furnace that blew air through molten iron. The air added oxygen to the burning process, and oxidization removed impurities from the iron; all that remained was high-quality steel. The Bessemer process needed less fuel, and tons of steel could be produced quickly. Prices tumbled, and steel suddenly became available for building projects.

THE FIRST SKYSCRAPERS

By the 1880s, New York's buildings were being constructed in an entirely new way. Much of Manhattan rests on granite rock, so crews dug down to that bedrock, which wouldn't shift. On that solid foundation, builders set *footings*—large concrete and steel pads that spread out to absorb the weight of an enormous structure.

Vertical steel columns then were attached to the footings, connected to each other by horizontal steel girders. Diagonal beams could be riveted to the girders and columns for extra support. The columns, girders, and beams formed a rigid steel cage that was strong but also lightweight. To keep that light cage from swaying in the force of strong winds, vertical concrete cores were installed.

Sometimes the cores anchored the center of the building around the elevator shafts; other times, concrete was poured around the vertical columns near the building's perimeter. Either way, the heavy concrete helped stabilize the structure and anchor it against wind pressure.

These steel frameworks were so strong and absorbed so much of a building's weight that there was no longer a need for thick outer walls. Instead, their outer walls became known as "curtain walls," because they weren't supporting the structure and hung like curtains on the inner frame. They would then be fitted with glass that brought in light and views.

THIS MEANS WAR!

Most people agree that the first skyscraper was the 100-foot tall Tower Building, which opened in 1889 on a narrow lot at 50 Broadway. A decade later, the Park Row Building became the tallest office building in the world, rising to 391 feet. In those early days, many New Yorkers worried about skyscrapers toppling—especially when the triangular-shaped Flatiron Building opened on Fifth Avenue in 1902. The Flatiron was 285 feet high and only six feet wide at its narrowest point. Its shape seemed so unstable that gamblers placed bets on when it would fall. (It's still there.)

As the city got used to skyscrapers—and they proved to be safe— "height wars" pushed buildings skyward. Owning one of the world's tallest buildings wasn't just a great advertising tool—it was also a status symbol. Discount store millionaire F. W. Woolworth decided that he wanted to own the tallest, most beautiful skyscraper in the world. In 1910, he commissioned the Woolworth Building. It opened three years later and rose to a staggering 760 feet, designed in a Gothic style that gave it the nickname the "cathedral of commerce."

In 1931, the Woolworth Building was eclipsed by the even taller Empire State Building. At more than 1,200 feet high, the Empire State Building remained the world's tallest building for more than 40 years until the World Trade Center climbed 100 feet higher. Since the 1970s, other cities have built skyscrapers even taller—today, the world's tallest building is the Burj Khalifa in Dubai (2,717 feet). But it all started in New York.

NEW YORK FOOD FROM "A" TO "P"

A smorgasbord of some of New York's favorite edibles and grazing grounds.

AMY'S BREAD: When your upscale bistro's breadbasket has a black-olive twist or a raisin-fennel roll in it, it's from Amy's. In 1992 Amy Scherber and her five employees started selling handmade specialty breads from a storefront on 9th Avenue. Today she has 150 workers and three retail locations—one of them in Chelsea Market, where the bread baking is done behind a glass wall. Wave to the bakers!

BUFFALO WINGS: These chicken wings prepared with spicy sauce, served with celery sticks and blue cheese dressing were invented by Teressa Bellissimo at the Anchor Bar in Buffalo in 1964. Since then, they've become essential bar food all over the country.

CHOPPED LIVER: New York didn't invent it—so what? From Brooklyn to the Bronx, chopped liver is as New York as the Yankees. Ingredients: sauteed chicken livers, schmaltz (chicken fat), hard-boiled eggs, salt, pepper, and onions.

DANISH: Actually danish *pastry*, but in New York it's just plain "danish" with a lowercase "d." Cheese danish, prune danish, maybe cherry, pecan, or cinnamon raisin. With a paper cup of coffee, the breakfast of New York champions.

ENTENMANN'S BAKED GOODS: In 1898, William Entenmann opened a bakery in Brooklyn and delivered door-to-door. Locals loved his layer cake, doughnuts, pies, and crumb coffee cake—but it wasn't until 1951, when the bakery started supplying supermarkets, that *all* New Yorkers had the opportunity to get hooked. Entenmann's is still going strong, with more than 100 products.

FAIRWAY MARKET: The grocery chain opened in 1976 on the Upper West Side, undercutting the competition with great prices

---

Before it became an immigration center, Ellis Island was an ammunition dump.

on produce, cheese, and baked goods—and won a following so de-voted that the place was (and is) jam-packed night and day. More branches have opened in Manhattan, Brooklyn, Long Island, and Westchester; more stores in the works.

GOD'S LOVE WE DELIVER: This service was founded in 1986 by Ganga Stone and Jane Best to take nutritionally appropriate meals to AIDS patients. Restaurants contributed food, volunteers helped cook and deliver, and philanthropists gave funds. By 2009, the group had delivered its 10 millionth meal.

HEBREW NATIONAL KOSHER MEATS: In 1905 Isadore Pinckowitz began making high-quality kosher franks and sausages on the Lower East Side, first selling to delis and the (Jewish) Wald-baum's grocery chain, then to supermarkets. His meats contained no by-products and no artificial colors or flavors, and the 1965 slo-gan said it all: "We Answer to a Higher Authority."

ICE CREAM, HÄAGEN-DAZS: Despite the "Danish" name, this is a born-and-bred New York product. In 1960, Bronx resident Reuben Mattus took his popular "superpremium" homemade ice cream (which he'd been selling to local restaurants), gave it an ex-otic foreign name, packed it in fancy cartons, and started a multi-million-dollar company. Back then, he offered only vanilla, chocolate, and coffee, but the company carries 34 flavors today.

JUNIOR'S CHEESECAKE: The signature dessert of Junior's Restaurant in Brooklyn. In the 1950s, people traveled from all over the city for a slice; it was as famous as the Brooklyn Dodgers. In 1973, six judges unanimously chose it "Champion Cheesecake" in *New York* magazine's cheesecake contest.

KOREAN GROCERIES: By the 1970s, Korean-run groceries were well established in most neighborhoods, open 24/7, selling everything from fresh produce and flowers to soda and snacks. They became convenient alternatives to supermarkets, but it was their lavish "salad bars"—the first ones in a deli setting—stocked with everything from salad to dumplings to mac and cheese that really pulled in the customers.

LI-LAC CHOCOLATES: New York's oldest handmade choco-lates, still prepared with the same recipes used by original owner

George Demetrious when he opened his shop on Christopher Street in Greenwich Village in 1923. The store is still in the Village, and there's another one in Grand Central's Market Hall.

MAYONNAISE, HELLMANN'S BLUE RIBBON: After Richard Hellmann opened a deli in Manhattan in 1905, his customers begged to buy tubs of his wife's homemade mayo. Finally, in 1912, he began to manufacture and bottle it in Astoria, Queens. He gave up the deli in 1917 to plunge full-time into mayonnaise biz.

NESSELRODE PIE: Nineteenth-century Russian Count Nesselrode lent his name to this pie that was popular in New York City in the 1940s and '50s, especially at Christmas. Now as rare as baked Alaska, it featured candied fruits folded into light, fluffy, rum-flavored Bavarian cream that was spooned into a piecrust and topped with chocolate shavings.

ONION BOARD (PLETZEL): A sort of Eastern European focaccia made of yeast-raised dough flattened to about 12" by 15", topped with sautéed onions and poppy seeds, and baked until golden brown. New York's pletzel mecca is Kossar's bakery on Grand Street in Manhattan, which has handcrafted its bagels, bialys, and pletzels since 1936.

PRETZEL, SOFT: The authentic New York soft pretzel, bought from a street vendor, is about eight inches across and is usually topped with a squiggle of neon-yellow mustard. It's New York City road food, grabbed on the run, guaranteed to tide you over until your next meal.

For more foods, turn to page 280.

*   *   *

ATTENTION, LIBRARY SHOPPERS

During the Great Depression, the New York Public Library ran a store in its basement, offering groceries, food, tobacco, and clothing at reasonable prices. (The lions outside the library were named Patience and Fortitude by Mayor Fiorello La Guardia to remind New Yorkers that they could survive the Depression.)

GIVE OUR REGARDS TO BROADWAY

Jazz hands at the ready! Can you answer these questions about the Great White Way? (Answers are on page 363.)

1. When *Carousel* opened on Broadway in 1945, the top ticket price (even higher than *Oklahoma!* across the street) was...
a. $5
b. $6
c. $10
d. $12

2. Which of these shows did not win a Tony for Best Musical?
a. *Rent*
b. *Hairspray*
c. *A Chorus Line*
d. *West Side Story*

3. The British are coming, the British are coming! Which of these playwrights (who had at least one show on Broadway) is not British?
a. Peter Shaffer
b. Alan Ayckbourn
c. Harold Pinter
d. John Guare

4. Sometimes things work backward, and a movie becomes a Broadway show. Three of these shows were films first. Which one wasn't?
a. *Mary Poppins*
b. *Chicago*
c. *The Color Purple*
d. *Billy Elliot*

5. When Broadway (or Off-Broadway) plays and musicals become Hollywood films, the leading actress from the Broadway production is often passed over in favor of a more bankable Hollywood star. That's what happened with these pairs of stars. Which show was at stake? (Remember: The Broadway star comes first here.)

a. Mary Martin, Julie Andrews
b. Julie Andrews, Audrey Hepburn
c. Jill Haworth, Liza Minnelli
d. Carol Channing, Barbra Streisand

6. Broadway has a fondness for one-word titles, like *Amadeus* or *Evita* or *Camelot*. Which of these wasn't actually the name of a Broadway play?

a. *Ballroom*
b. *Wicked*
c. *Annie*
d. *Sherlock*

7. Every once in a while there's a year when Broadway produces a bumper crop of memorable shows. In what year did all these hits open on the Great White Way: *Bus Stop, Cat on a Hot Tin Roof, The Diary of Anne Frank, A View from the Bridge, Inherit the Wind, A Hatful of Rain, Silk Stockings,* and *Damn Yankees?*

a. 1935
b. 1945
c. 1955
d. 1965

8. What's the longest running show on Broadway (so far)?

a. *Les Miserables*
b. *Oh, Calcutta!*
c. *The Phantom of the Opera*
d. *Mamma Mia!*

WHODUNIT?

*A young woman is murdered on her wedding night. Her lover is
charged with the crime, and the people and newspapers of New
York convict him before the trial even begins. Here's a murder
mystery that's ripped from the headlines...of 1799.*

A SENSATIONAL MURDER

On the evening of December 22, 1799, Gulielma "Elma"
Sands got dressed up and left her home—a boarding house
at 208 Greenwich Avenue, owned by Elias and Catherine Ring.
She was never seen alive again. According to Catherine Ring,
Elma's cousin, the young woman was planning to get married that
night. Instead, 11 days later, her body was pulled out of the Manhattan Well, which stood near the intersections of Greene and
Spring Streets in what is now SoHo, just a short carriage ride from
the boarding house.

Elma's tragic death was the talk of New York. It was the city's
first big murder mystery, and the press and public speculated over
who might have killed her. Soon, suspicion fell on a young carpenter named Levi Weeks, who worked for his brother Ezra Weeks, a
prominent, wealthy builder. Levi lived in the same boarding house
as Elma and had been courting her for some time; the two were
said to be lovers, a scandalous situation in the 18th century. After
Catherine Ring claimed that Levi was the man Elma had planned
to elope with on the night she disappeared, an inquest was held—
and Levi Weeks was indicted for murder.

The newspapers, of course, weighed in with their own version of
the story, speculating that Levi had seduced an innocent girl and
murdered her because he didn't want to get married. Then fellow
boarder Richard Croucher publicly declared that Weeks had an accomplice in New Jersey who'd confessed to the murder. By the time
the trial began in 1800, the public already considered Weeks a
guilty man. Elma's sympathizers packed the courtroom, and those
who couldn't get in milled around outside, yelling, "Crucify him!"

LEVI'S LAWYERS

The U.S. legal system was only 11 years old when the Levi Weeks trial began, and the idea that anyone accused of murder deserved more than torture or a quick hanging was still new. Trials ran all day—sometimes until well after midnight. Requests for breaks from exhausted lawyers on either side were frowned upon and often denied. Fortunately for Levi, his wealthy brother Ezra rounded up the most brilliant lawyers of the day—Alexander Hamilton, Aaron Burr, and Henry Brockholst Livingston—to defend him.

Hamilton, America's first Secretary of the Treasury, was one of the Founding Fathers and had been a trusted advisor to President George Washington. Burr was a hero of the Revolutionary War and former New York Senator who would go on to become the third vice president of the United States. Livingston was one of the nation's most prominent attorneys, and in 1802, he would become a justice on the U.S. Supreme Court.

LOOKING BAD FOR LEVI

The trial began at 10 a.m. on March 31, 1800. *New York Evening Post* editor William Coleman wrote a transcript of the proceedings, making the Weeks spectacle America's first recorded murder trial. After the jury was chosen, the prosecutor presented his case: Weeks had come to live at the Greenwich boarding house in July 1799 and seduced Elma Sands. He became secretly engaged to her sometime in the fall, promising to elope with her on December 22. On that evening, however, Weeks actually took his fiancée to the Manhattan Well, where he killed her. To back up his argument, the prosecutor presented testimony from a long string of witnesses.

Boarders at the Rings' home testified that Levi had been in Elma's room overnight several times, and that they appeared to be lovers. Catherine Ring testified that on December 22, Elma believed she was eloping with Weeks, and the two had exited the house within a short time of one another—Catherine heard them talking on the porch before they left. More witnesses said they'd seen a horse and sleigh near the crime scene that resembled one belonging to Levi's brother Ezra. There was even testimony from a witness who'd seen Levi measuring the Manhattan Well about a week before Elma disappeared. A medical expert testified that Elma's body showed signs of being badly beaten and strangled, and Levi was said to have returned to the boarding house looking "pale and nervous" the night Elma disappeared.

By the time the prosecution rested, things didn't look good for Levi. Many in the courtroom believed that even the great triad of Hamilton, Burr, and Livingston wouldn't be able to save his life.

THE DEFENSE TO THE RESCUE

Hamilton and Burr did most of the defense work for the trial. Burr gave a stirring speech, asking the jury to set aside their anger toward Weeks and portraying the carpenter as "an injured and innocent young man" who'd never treated Elma badly. Then the defense brought in its own string of witnesses.

First, the defense established that Levi had an alibi—several people had seen him at Ezra's house on the evening of December 22, placing him far from the Manhattan Well area at the time Elma disappeared. Other witnesses asserted that Ezra's horse and sleigh never left the barn. Character witnesses spoke of Levi's "goodness." Defense medical experts declared that the marks on Elma's body could have come from her autopsy rather than from a deadly beating. (The autopsy had been carried out to determine whether Elma was pregnant; she wasn't.)

The defense also brought in boarders from the Rings' house on Greenwich Street. But these people contradicted the prosecution's version of Elma as a happy innocent girl until Levi seduced her. They claimed that Elma used a drug called laudanum—a powerful opiate—and that she'd talked of killing herself with an overdose. One man, who lived in the room next to Elma, said Levi Weeks wasn't her lover at all. According to him, Elias Ring, the owner of the boarding house, sometimes spent the night with Elma when his wife was away. Levi's defense team painted the Ring boarding house as a place of sexual intrigue—a kind of 18th-century Peyton Place with Elma as a key player. And as for the prosecution's star witness, boarder Richard Croucher, the defense showed that he hated Weeks and implied that he might have lied on the witness stand.

A VERDICT AND A CURSE

The trial of Levi Weeks lasted two days—longer than most criminal trials of the time. It broke for recess at 1:00 a.m. the first night, after some jurors nodded off. The next night, it ended after 2 a.m. At that point, the judge bluntly informed the jury that the prosecution's collection of circumstantial evidence was a flimsy basis for conviction. Five minutes later, the jury returned its verdict: not guilty.

As the defense team congratulated each other, it's said that a furious Catherine Ring—whose dead cousin, marriage, and boarding house had all been dragged through the mud—cursed Alexander Hamilton. She supposedly shouted, "If thee dies a natural death, I shall think there is no justice in heaven!" And eerily, her curse came true five years later, when Hamilton and Burr, by then bitter political enemies, met on the dueling grounds at Weehawken, New Jersey, and Burr shot and killed Hamilton. Burr was eventually acquitted of murder, but his political career was over.

As for Levi Weeks, most New Yorkers disagreed with the jury's verdict and the young carpenter was run out of town. Sentiments eventually began to change when, less than a year after the trial, Richard Croucher was found guilty of raping a young girl in the Ring boarding house. Levi finally settled in Natchez, Mississippi, where he became a successful architect, married, and had a family.

Today, the Manhattan Well where Elma Sands met her end still exists—it's in the basement of Manhattan Bistro in Soho. From time to time, employees say, an eerie vapor rises in the kitchen, and Elma's ghost causes glasses and wine bottles to go flying.

* * *

YANKEE FACTS

• In 1929 the Yankees were one of two teams to put numbers on the backs of players' uniforms. (The Cleveland Indians were the other.) Originally the Yankee players' numbers corresponded to their positions in the batting order. That's why Babe Ruth was #3, Lou Gehrig was #4, and so on.

• In 1937 fan David Levy sustained a skull fracture during a scuffle with Yankee Stadium ushers as he tried to retrieve a ball hit into the stands. Levy sued and won $7,500...a decision that led to all baseball clubs allowing fans to keep balls hit into the stands.

• In the 1960s, catcher and outfielder—and the first African-American Yankee player—Elston Howard invented the "batting donut," the weighted ring that all on-deck players now use to warm up.

BEDBUGS, BEDBUGS

Whatcha gonna do when they come for you?

• According to entomologists at the American Museum of Natural History, 20 percent of New Yorkers had bed bugs in their homes during the 2009–11 infestation epidemic.

• Latin name for bedbugs: *Cimex lectularius.*

• Bedbugs are most active at night. Why? Because they live off of human blood, and that's when people are easiest to bite.

• Bedbugs are only a few millimeters long and as thin as a business card. So even if walls look sealed, bedbugs can usually find a way in.

• With hundreds of thousands of apartments so close together in New York City, an infestation can spread quickly as bugs travel through cable conduits, heaters, drop ceilings, or simply by scurrying across hallways.

• Notable locations infested with bedbugs: former president Bill Clinton's Harlem offices, the Metropolitan Opera House, the Waldorf-Astoria hotel, Fox News headquarters, Time Warner headquarters, *Elle* magazine, the Empire State Building, and flagship stores of Nike, Victoria's Secret, and Abercrombie & Fitch.

• Number of New York City bedbug complaints in 2006: 4,600. Number in 2009: more than 9,200.

• The bugs can live and breed for weeks without water, and for months without food.

• A University of Massachusetts study found that New York City bedbugs are 250 times more resistant to standard pesticides than Florida bed bugs. One theory: The New York variety may boost their natural defenses by generating more of an enzyme that cleanses the body of poisons.

• According to a poll by *Glamour*, 57 percent of guys would go home with a girl who admitted to having bedbugs.

...Her manager urged her to appear on the *Dick Cavett Show* instead.

- In 2011, the Animal Planet cable network began soliciting stories for a show about people with harrowing bedbug-related stories. The prize: free extermination.

- Protesting Teamsters used to picket union-unfriendly businesses while carrying a giant inflatable rat. In 2010, some protestors switched to a giant bedbug.

- Estimated cost of fumigating an apartment building for bedbugs: $70,000.

- Bedbug bites start out painless but eventually turn into large, itchy welts. Unlike a flea bite, they lack a red center spot (that's how you know what bit you). On the bright side, bedbugs are not known to spread disease from human to human.

- Removal and prevention tip: Steam killers and liquid nitrogen treatments kill only the bed bugs they come into direct contact with. Common, over-the-counter aerosols don't work, either—experts say those mostly just make the bugs scurry elsewhere. Exterminators typically have to use pesticides or extreme heat to kill bed bugs.

- If you think you're at risk for bed bugs, seal all cracks and crevices, including cable conduits; vacuum your carpets, mattresses, and other cloth furniture thoroughly; and wash all your clothes, towels, and linens in hot water, and then dry them on the highest setting.

- Despite the widely covered 2009–11 bedbug epidemic, New York City isn't the most afflicted place in the United States. According to the extermination company Orkin, Cincinnati is #1. New York is seventh.

*   *   *

"No good, sensible working bee listens to the advice of a bedbug on the subject of business."

—Elbert Hubbard

NY 'ZINES

Rolling Stone was founded in San Francisco, Look started in Des Moines. So what magazines came from New York City?

NEW YORK MAGAZINE

New York magazine's roots were in a newspaper: It began in 1963 as a Sunday magazine supplement in the *New York Herald Tribune*. When the paper folded in 1967, former *Trib* editor Clay S. Felker and graphic designer Milton Glaser turned the supplement into a hip, glossy magazine that focused mostly on city culture and style. Felker and Glaser also put together a group of cutting-edge contributors: feminist activist Gloria Steinem on politics, former *Trib* film critic Judith Crist on movies, and journalist Tom Wolfe on pop culture, to name a few.

The Felker/Glaser days lasted less than a decade. In 1976 both men were forced out when media mega-mogul Rupert Murdoch bought *New York* in a hostile takeover. Since then, the magazine has changed hands several times, with each owner bringing in a new editor and a new approach. Adam Moss, the current editor, was hired in 2003 by the most recent purchaser, financier Bruce Wasserstein. Moss has been criticized for being too Manhattan-centric and also for publishing too many non-New York–related stories (like pieces on national politics). But under his leadership, *New York* magazine's Web site has flourished: Today the site gets more than 5 million visitors a month.

Fun fact: Milton Glaser—graphic designer of the original *New York* magazine—may not be a name every New Yorker knows, but every New Yorker does know his most famous logo: I ♥ NY. He created it in 1975 as part of an ad campaign to boost tourism in the city, and it's been ripped off for everything from dry cleaners' hangers ("We ♥ our customers") to T-shirts ("I ♥ spreadsheets").

MS.

The first issue of the feminist *Ms.* magazine was a one-time sample inserted into the December 1971 issue of *New York* magazine. This was an act of bravery for its founders—Gloria Steinem, author and activist Letty Cottin Pogrebin, and several other prominent feminists—and for Clay Felker, the editor of *New York*. Back in 1971, feminism was controversial, denigrated, and dismissed in the national media; a new women's magazine that wasn't about marriage, babies, recipes, and window treatments, but instead covered the politics of equal pay, reproductive rights, and sexism, was a shocker.

The first stand-alone issue of *Ms.* went national in July 1972, and 300,000 copies sold out in eight days. From then on, the magazine was a strong voice for women of all classes, ages, and ethnicities who wanted to read about serious issues from a feminist viewpoint. (For instance, *Ms.* was the first national magazine to advocate for the passage of the Equal Rights Amendment.) The magazine often upset advertisers—both because of its outspoken feminist politics and because it ran a monthly feature called "No Comment," which called out ads that the editors considered offensive to women. In 1977, the magazine slammed an ad that showed a gray-haired man (clothed) and a much-younger woman (in a bikini) on a yacht; the ad's copy read, "57-ft. yacht for charter…for whatever you have in mind."

Advertisers weren't flocking to *Ms.*, so the best solution seemed to be to make it a nonprofit. From 1978 to 1987, *Ms.* was published through the nonprofit Ms. Foundation: Founded by Gloria Steinem and others, it was the first group that offered money and services to women who wanted to "elevate [their] voices." But the money problems didn't go away, and the magazine changed ownership four more times. In 1998, Gloria Steinem and other feminist investors bought back the struggling magazine for $3 million—only to face bankruptcy in 2001. Finally, on December 31, 2001, a group called the Feminist Majority Foundation—also cofounded by Gloria Steinem and dedicated to women's equality, women's reproductive health, and nonviolence—stepped in to rescue the magazine. The group moved the operation to the foundation's Los Angeles headquarters and has been publishing *Ms.* quarterly ever since.

Fun fact: When *Ms.* first appeared on the 'zine scene, no one knew how to pronounce its name—or even what the term really meant. Back then, there were two honorifics for women: Miss and Mrs., both of which indicated marital status—unlike Mr., which could be used for all men. Women who were unmarried or who had kept their maiden names had no honorific to use. As early as 1901, an editorial in *The Sunday Republican* addressed the problem and suggested Ms. as "a more comprehensive term, which does homage to the sex without expressing any views as to their domestic situation." But it didn't catch on.

In 1961, Sheila Michaels, a civil rights worker in New York City, noticed a typo on a letter sent to her roommate: "Ms." instead of "Miss." Unmarried and a feminist, she liked the ambiguous term and mentioned it on a feminists' radio show about eight years later. A friend of Gloria Steinem's heard the program and suggested it as a title for the magazine. Steinem liked it and decided to use it, but neglected to give credit to Michaels. The pronunciation we know today—"mizz"—was made popular by the magazine.

COSMOPOLITAN

Today, *Cosmo* is a sexy mag for twenty-something women, but it began in a much less salacious format: as a family magazine in the 1880s. Then, for a few years, it changed its focus to include articles about domestic and foreign policy, with book reviews, color illustrations, and fiction by famous writers like Willa Cather, H. G. Wells, and Edith Wharton. In 1905, media mogul William Randolph Hearst bought *Cosmo*.

In the 1950s, Americans began buying fewer magazines—television and cheap paperbacks became the new "in" things. *Cosmopolitan* struggled into the 1960s—until Helen Gurley Brown, who had never run a magazine but had written the popular book *Sex and the Single Girl*, became *Cosmo*'s editor-in-chief in 1965. Instead of following the serious path of the old publication, Brown set out to revamp it into a women's magazine unlike any other. She was convinced that her own experiences as a single woman (men, career, independence) were the perfect material for a magazine that would appeal to a growing market of young women. She put sexy women on the cover, added titillating lines, and filled the magazine with articles that were open about sexuality. Her *Cosmo* dealt with relationships, fashion, beauty, health, and single life. When Brown finally retired in 1997, she'd been the magazine's editor for 32 years and had turned *Cosmo* into the best-selling young women's magazine in the world.

Fun fact: For all its salacious covers and content, *Cosmo*'s offices are fairly plain—editors typically keep a low profile. That tone likely comes from Helen Gurley Brown herself. In 2000 she published *I'm Wild Again*—an autobiography that chronicled some of her sexual adventures as a young woman, but also revealed a more sedate side of her: Brown didn't drink, smoke, or ever cheat on her husband of 35 years. She also exercised fanatically and poured her considerable energy and passion not into sex, but into her work.

LIFE

In 1883, an illustrator named John Ames Mitchell took a $10,000 inheritance and started a weekly magazine of humor, commentary, and pictures. From the get-go, *Life* published up-and-coming illustrators such as Gibson girl creator Charles Dana Gibson (*more about him on page 138*); Rea Irvin, who later became the art director of *The New Yorker*; and Norman Rockwell, who painted his first *Life* cover in 1917. But Mitchell died in 1918, and without his leadership, the magazine lost money through the 1920s and '30s. But by then, Henry Luce was looking to buy the magazine.

Luce and his business partner Briton Hadden were already publishing *Time* and other magazines. After Hadden's death in 1929, Luce began to conceptualize a new type of magazine, one that was news-centered, published weekly, and used photojournalism to tell stories. In 1936, he bought *Life* for $92,000, strictly to acquire use of its name. Volume 1, Number 1 of the new *Life* was dated November 23, 1936, and the cover photograph (of the Fort Peck Dam in Montana) was taken by Margaret Bourke-White, who would later become the first American woman to work as a war correspondent. With Luce's vision and a slew of talented photojournalists—including Bourke, Robert Capa, W. Eugene Smith, and Gordon Parks—circulation boomed. Weekly circulation jumped from 380,000 to 1.5 million within a year. *Life* reached its high point of 8.5 million readers in 1969, but by then, profits were already declining. *Life* ended weekly publication in 1972, came back as a monthly magazine in 1978, and ceased publication completely in 2000.

Fun fact: The first Luce/Hadden-published issue of *Life* featured the birth of a baby named George Story, with a caption that read, "Life Begins." Over the years, *Life* reported on Story's progress as he grew up and had a family of his own. In March 2000, Time, Inc. announced the demise of *Life*—George Story died of heart failure a month later.

For the history of The New Yorker, *turn to page 175*.

DESTROYING NEW YORK

Whether blowing it up, burning it down, or covering it in marshmallow goo, the movies really seem to have it in for New York City.

ESCAPE FROM NEW YORK (1981)

Plot: The United States is awash in crime, and Manhattan is a wasteland and maximum-security prison isolated from the rest of the country. When a hijacking lands the U.S. president there, a convict and former soldier known as Snake (Kurt Russell) is given 22 hours to find the president and earn his freedom.

GHOSTBUSTERS (1984)

Plot: New York City is being overrun by poltergeists after a gateway to another dimension opens up in Manhattan and threatens the world. A quartet of ragtag exorcists (Dan Aykroyd, Bill Murray, Harold Ramis, and Ernie Hudson) goes on the hunt and battles, among other beasts, an enormous Stay Puft Marshmallow Man who stomps the Holy Trinity Lutheran Church on Central Park West into sticky rubble.

INDEPENDENCE DAY (1996)

Plot: Alien spaceships blow up the Empire State Building and then attack other major cities. Governments around the globe join forces to fight the alien menace. (Fortunately, Will Smith is on their side.)

ARMAGEDDON (1998)

Plot: Flaming meteorites flatten the Chrysler Building and Grand Central Station in the opening sequence, and a *really big* meteorite is on track to destroy Earth in 18 days unless Bruce Willis and his drilling crew can intervene in time.

THE DAY AFTER TOMORROW (2004)

Plot: In this movie about climate change and its aftermath, rising tides swamp the city, which then freezes over. A small group led by a young man named Sam (Jake Gyllenhaal) survives by burning books in the main branch of the New York Public Library.

In 1997 the *Utne Reader* named Ithaca, NY, "America's most enlightened town."

THE GRUMPY TOURIST

"I am sick to death of the life I have been leading here—worn out in mind and body—and quite weary and distressed." —Charles Dickens, during his first visit to New York

COMING TO AMERICA
In 1842, New Yorkers were thrilled to hear that English author Charles Dickens was about to visit their city. Dickens was a superstar by then—his novels *Oliver Twist*, *Nicholas Nickleby*, and *Barnaby Rudge* crusaded for the poor and the oppressed, making him the most read author in the United States. Americans wanted to go all out for Dickens, and as the nation's wealthiest city, New Yorkers felt sure they could wow him. They also hoped the author's next work would teach the world how modern and cosmopolitan New York was. Unfortunately, things didn't turn out that way.

On January 22, 1842, Charles Dickens arrived in Boston, where cheering crowds lined the streets. Artists, literati, and city officials all vied for his attention, and Dickens basked in the adulation. But the longer he stayed, the more Dickens found to criticize. For one thing, the thrill of having a nation in love with him got old fast. Without bodyguards or an entourage, Dickens had to face the jostling crowds on his own. He visited New York from February 12 to March 5 and during that stay, he wrote, "I can do nothing that I want to do, go nowhere where I want to go, and see nothing that I want to see. If I turn into the street, I am followed by a multitude. If I stay at home, the house becomes, with callers, like a fair...I am so enclosed and hemmed about with people...I am exhausted."

Aside from being mobbed by adoring New Yorkers, Dickens also had problems with the city's publishers and newspapers. Although his books were bestsellers in the States, Dickens never saw a cent of their sales profit because American publishers (based mainly in New York) simply reprinted his books without paying him any royalties. Dickens tried to rally support for establishing a fair international copyright law, but the American publishers wouldn't budge—they used free copy from England to save money. Even some Dickens fans resented his ideas, declaring that foreign guests shouldn't lecture Americans on what laws to pass.

LET'S PARTY

While Dickens struggled with too much fame and the theft of his royalties, New Yorkers continued to try to impress him. On February 14, in the Park Theatre (on what is now Park Row), 3,000 of the wealthiest New Yorkers gathered to honor Dickens at the Boz Ball. ("Boz" was the pseudonym under which many of Dickens's early works were published.) The theater glittered with lights, and decorations included flowers, drapery, and a large portrait of Dickens. The dancing throng was entertained in between sets with *tableaux*, life-size scenes from Dickens novels that included live models posing as characters. The Dickens-crazed crowd guzzled down champagne, 38,000 oysters, 10,000 sandwiches, 2,000 mutton chops, and 300 quarts of ice cream. New Yorkers lucky enough to attend the Boz Ball were overwhelmed by its glamour and fondly called it "the party of the decade."

But the guest of honor wasn't so thrilled. He wrote that he and his wife, Kate, were "paraded all 'round the enormous ballroom twice for the gratification of the many-headed. That done, we began to dance—Heaven knows how we did it, for there was no room." Dickens felt he'd been made into a moneymaking spectacle—Boz Ball tickets sold for $5 at a time when most events charged 25¢. So when theater management tried to sell even more tickets by throwing a second, cheaper Boz Ball a few days later, Dickens told them he was too sick to attend. In fact, he refused to be "honored" with any more public receptions during his trip.

THE "OTHER" NEW YORK

If New York's high society failed to notice Dickens's frustrations while he was in the city, they got an eyeful of his dissatisfaction when he published the book *American Notes* later that year. An entire chapter was devoted to New York, which Dickens described as dirty. He also emphasized the city's unique garbage collectors—pigs that strolled through the city, eating up the refuse. It wasn't quite the image cosmopolitan New York had hoped for. There were compliments to the city—Dickens really enjoyed the excitement of Broadway—but some of them were backhanded...like finding the fire department "admirable (as indeed it should be, having constant practice)."

As an author who crusaded for social justice, Dickens also spent

---

Last Republican presidential candidate to carry NYC: Calvin Coolidge (1924).

a lot of time discussing the suffering and downtrodden in New York. He exposed the misery of the insane asylums on what is now Roosevelt Island, where inmates suffered in bleak, unsympathetic conditions. He introduced readers to the "dismal" horrors in the Tombs prison, where he found convicts as young as 10 years old. Dickens also exposed America's wealthiest city as the site of one of the nation's worst slums. He describes the Five Points' "hideous tenements, which take their name from robbery and murder: all that is loathsome, drooping, and decayed is here."

New York fared no better in Dickens's next novel, *Martin Chuzzlewit*, published in installments from 1843 to 1844. When the hero Martin arrives in New York, he finds it riddled with rogues and fools. Dickens's New York characters lack compassion, especially for slaves, and the book featured a fictional newspaper called *"The New York Sewer."*

THE PRODIGAL AUTHOR RETURNS

The rest of America didn't fare much better in Dickens's writings than New York did, and the nation's bad feelings toward the author festered for some years. But in 1867, Dickens decided to return to New York on a reading tour.

This time, he and the city got along famously. Five thousand New Yorkers stood in a mile-long line for tickets to Steinway Hall, where Dickens gave 22 readings…making about $3,000 per performance (more than $200,000 in today's money). He enjoyed sleighing in Central Park and eating at fine restaurants. During his last dinner at Delmonico's in April 1868, a grateful Dickens promised to put a postscript on every new edition of *American Notes* and *Martin Chuzzlewit*, apologizing for his unkind descriptions of the States. Dickens told New Yorkers that he'd missed much of the greatness of the city during his first visit—and now he praised it with "love and thankfulness."

To read excerpts of Dickens's descriptions of New York City in the 1840s, turn to page 119 and 331.

YOU'RE MY INSPIRATION

It's always interesting to find out where pop-culture architects get their ideas.

LADY GAGA
Manhattan-native Stefani Germanotta wanted to be an entertainer, but she needed a catchier name to break into the business. Enter music producer Rob Fusari, who, after listening to a song Germanotta had written around 2005, proclaimed, "That's so Queen! You're so 'Radio Ga Ga.' Very theatrical." ("Radio Ga Ga" is a 1984 song by the British rock band Queen.) Fusari started calling Germanotta "Gaga," and the name stuck.

IN THE HEIGHTS
In 1999, Lin-Manuel Miranda was a sophomore at Wesleyan University in Connecticut when he began writing a musical set in his home neighborhood of Washington Heights, New York. According to Miranda, he often strolled the streets of Washington Heights looking for ideas: "I would go for walks when I got stuck for inspiration...I think I was on 181st Street walking around...and I saw a Chinese delivery guy riding his bike with a boom box strapped to the front of his bike. It wasn't a little radio; it was a two-speaker boom box blasting music...I always thought that was a classic New York thing: Of course the Chinese delivery guy has got a subwoofer on his bike!" The scene made it into the play, which moved from the Wesleyan theater to Off-Broadway and then finally to Broadway, winning four 2008 Tony Awards, including Best Musical.

DONKEY KONG
In the 1981 Nintendo video game *Donkey Kong*, the hero (named Jumpman) had to rescue a damsel in distress from the clutches of a giant ape. Game designer Shigeru Miyamoto turned to the movies for inspiration, modeling some of the story after another monstrous ape gone mad: King Kong, who first terrorized New York City from atop the Empire State Building in the 1933 film. The game was a huge hit for Nintendo and spawned an even more popular video game character: In 1983, Jumpman began appearing in his own series of games. He got a new name, too: Mario.

BOTTOMS UP

*When you say "wine country," New York isn't the place most people think
of first. But the state is home to some world-famous wineries...
and it's mostly thanks to a janitor from Cornell.*

THE ROOTS OF AN INDUSTRY

Long before California's Napa Valley flourished with vineyards, New York State had a wine industry of its own. Settlers had been planting grape vines all over the state since the 17th century, primarily Native American grape varieties like Concord and Catawba. These created sweet, fruity wines that were pleasant enough, but unremarkable.

That began to change in 1951, when a wine expert named Konstantin Frank arrived from the Ukraine. A renowned viticulturalist in his home country, Frank was unknown in the United States and unable to find work in his field. So he took a job as a janitor at Cornell University's Geneva Agricultural Experiment Station. In his spare time, Frank tried to persuade his colleagues that what they needed to catapult New York wines to world-class recognition were European vines. He especially liked the *vitis vinifera* species, which had long been used to produce quality Riesling, Chardonnay, Pinot Noir, Gewurztraminer, and Cabernet Sauvignon wines. But Cornell's researchers had been trying *vitis vinifera* for years. The vines always failed, and most people believed that a combination of insect infestations and the cold climate in New York did too much damage for the plants to thrive.

Frank disagreed. He thought the rootstock that Cornell had been using (the original plants from which all the working vines came) had been weak to begin with. What New York vintners needed to do, he said, was go back to Europe, get some healthy starter vines, and try again.

VITAL VINE

The Cornell researchers were skeptical, but champagne maker Charles Fournier, who headed a nearby vineyard, took interest and hired Frank to experiment with the *vitis vinifera*. The first thing

---

First and last entries in the *Encyclopedia of New York City*...

Frank did was to import hardy rootstocks from Europe and vinifera clones that he'd developed back in the Ukraine.

Frank's approach took time. With the financial backing of Fournier, he founded a small vineyard in the Finger Lakes region and spent several years working on his vines. His breakthrough came when he grafted the European *vitis vinefera* vines onto the roots of the *vitis labrusca*, the North American grapevine that was the foundation for the Concord variety. The resulting vine could not only withstand the cold, but was impervious to the aphid-like bugs that plagued the area. Finally, Frank's rootstock started to thrive, and by 1962, he'd produced New York's first commercially successful Chardonnay and Riesling wines.

Other winemakers continued to doubt Frank's work, and he had trouble finding distributors. But slowly their resistance gave way as his New York wines began collecting international awards. Eventually, even the researchers at Cornell had to admit that Frank's grafting techniques were a success. The vines that Frank created formed the rootstock that many of today's New York vineyards still use.

NEW YORK WINE COUNTRY

The state is now home to more than 240 wineries, as well as the largest wine company in the world: Constellation Brands. New York produces more than 200 million bottles of wine every year, with production concentrated in four regions: eastern Long Island, the Hudson River, the Finger Lakes of west-central New York, and the Lake Erie/Niagara region. These "wine countries" draw an estimated 4 million tourists annually, and to help them find their way, the state publishes a "wine map." In the Finger Lakes region, the Keuka Lake Wine Trail leads past eight wineries, including the Vinifera Wine Cellars... founded by the man who put New York wines on the map—Konstantin Frank.

*   *   *

NEW YORK CITY FACT

America's first car crash occurred in New York City in 1896, when a car collided with a bicycle and killed its rider.

...A&P (the grocery store) and Louis Zukofsky (a poet).

UNCLE JOHN'S PAGE OF LISTS

Some random information from the BRI's trivia files.

4 BODIES OF WATER THAT BORDER NEW YORK STATE
1. Atlantic Ocean
2. Lake Ontario
3. Lake Erie
4. Lake Champlain

3 HUSBANDS OF JENNIFER LOPEZ
1. Ojani Noa
2. Cris Judd
3. Marc Anthony

7 ORIGINAL SNL CAST MEMBERS
1. Dan Aykroyd
2. John Belushi
3. Gilda Radner
4. Chevy Chase
5. Jane Curtin
6. Laraine Newman
7. Garrett Morris

2 IVY LEAGUE UNIVERSITIES IN N.Y. STATE
1. Cornell
2. Columbia

3 STADIUMS WHERE THE N.Y. JETS HAVE PLAYED
1. The Polo Grounds
2. Shea Stadium
3. The Meadowlands

4 NICKNAMES FOR DONALD TRUMP
1. The Donald
2. DJT (Donald John Trump)
3. The Don
4. The Trumpster

1 OFFICIAL STATE MUFFIN
1. Apple

5 BOROUGHS IN NEW YORK CITY (FROM THE MOST TO THE LEAST POPULOUS)
1. Brooklyn
2. Queens
3. Manhattan
4. Bronx
5. Staten Island

1 CONEY ISLAND ROLLER COASTER STILL IN OPERATION
1. The Cyclone

2 ITEMS OF CLOTHING REQUIRED AT THE GREAT NEW YORK STATE FAIR IN SYRACUSE
1. A shirt
2. Footwear

"A sewer filled with all the depravities of human nature." — Thomas Jefferson on NYC

FOUND IN THE GROUND

Uncle John thought there was nothing under New York's cities and towns besides dirt and old subway tokens. But as these three stories prove, you never know what's under your feet.

GROUND ZERO'S WOODEN SHIP

In July 2010, construction workers at Ground Zero were clearing an area between Liberty and Cedar streets to build an underground security center when they hit more than mud and rock. To their surprise, they ran across a 30-foot section of a ship—a very *old* ship. As soon as the mud-encrusted pieces of hull were exposed to the air, they began to fall apart. So construction stopped, and archaeologists rushed to the site to gather whatever artifacts they could before it disintegrated.

What they found were wooden beams that had made up the vessel's prow or stern (no one could say for sure which end of the ship they'd found), an anchor, a leather shoe, and a metal and brick object that might have been part of an oven or boiler. But their most stunning discovery was the age of the ship: It was more than 200 years old. The scientists couldn't say if all of the items had actually traveled on the vessel, and they theorized that the ship probably didn't sink there. More likely, it was part of the landfill used to extend lower Manhattan's shoreline in the 18th and 19th centuries.

THE CARDIFF GIANT

In 1869, workers digging a well on a farm in Cardiff, New York, uncovered something amazing—the petrified remains of a 10-foot-tall giant. Geologists and archaeologists immediately labeled the creature a fake, but the farmers who owned the land and their friend George Hull put the giant on display in upstate New York and charged 50¢ a head to see it. The spectacle drew huge crowds.

The "Cardiff giant" was an especially big hit with religious New Yorkers. The Bible's "Book of Genesis" talks about a race of giant men who once roamed the Earth. (Goliath was one of them.) So, local Christians believed the Cardiff creature proved the giants' existence. But after about a year—and after making more than

$30,000 off the venture—Hull admitted that the Cardiff giant was a hoax. He'd created it in 1868, after a heated theological argument with a local minister. Hull, an atheist, wanted to prove that the minister's unwavering faith in religion was misguided, so he hired craftsmen to make the giant out of a mineral called gypsum and rough it up to make it look old. Then he had it buried on his friend's farm in Cardiff. A year later, he hired the well-diggers to exhume it.

Hull got some flak for duping the public, but the idea of buried giants remained a huge draw. Circus tycoon P. T. Barnum even created his own giant, claiming that his was the real thing and the Cardiff one was the fake. Eventually, though, audiences became more savvy and both giants' appeal waned. By 1901, when the Cardiff giant appeared at the Pan-American Exposition in Buffalo, only a handful of people were willing to pay to see it. It changed hands a few more times and eventually ended up in the Farmer's Museum in Cooperstown. It's still there today, under the name "World's Greatest Hoax."

THE BURIED TREASURE

In August 2010, two anonymous Brooklyn artists and puppeteers announced a treasure hunt on their Web site, WeLostOurGold.com. They'd buried a wooden chest, they said, filled with $10,000 in golden dollar coins somewhere in New York City's five boroughs. The "treasure map" they offered was in the form of eight Web video shorts (starring three puppet pirates and a ninja) with clues about where the money was hidden. But there were a couple of caveats: They insisted that the treasure was not in Central Park, writing, "We may be stupid enough to bury all our money, but we're absolutely not stupid enough to encourage people to start digging up Central Park." They also maintained that all the clues needed to find the coins could be found in their Web videos.

The guys had been saving the dollar coins for five years, and they hoped that the stunt would bring publicity to their puppet videos. And for all skeptical New Yorkers who doubted whether there really was a treasure chest, one of the creators promised, "You can punch me in the nose if I'm lying to you...which I'm not.'"

As of press time, no one had yet unearthed the treasure, so technically it's not "found in the ground" just yet. But Uncle John loves a good story...and a good treasure hunt. Happy digging!

Only street names to appear in all five boroughs: Broadway, Clinton, King, and Park.

IT'S PUZZLING

It isn't the only crossword puzzle in America, but the New York Times crossword has a certain snob appeal; a lot of people would be embarrassed to be seen solving anything else.

ACROSS AND DOWN

By the time the *New York Times* published its first crossword puzzle on Sunday, February 15, 1942, crosswords had already been around for 30 years. They'd reached their height in the 1920s, when they became a nationwide craze, and the fad had faded somewhat. The *Times* crossword didn't become a daily feature until 1950, when the paper began publishing smaller puzzles on Monday through Saturday. And yes, if you've heard that the puzzles get progressively harder as the week goes on, it's mostly true: Saturday is the hardest, and Sunday is about as tough as a Thursday puzzle, but bigger.

It's a common misconception that the editors write the puzzles. They do not. Here's how it works: A constructor (which is what a puzzle maker is called in the biz) submits a puzzle to the editor whose job it is to select or reject the puzzle. If it's selected, it's edited and slated for publication. In its 50-plus years of publication, there have been only four editors of the *New York Times* crossword puzzle, beginning with Margaret Petherbridge Farrar, who edited the first puzzle in 1942.

STYLE SETTERS

Farrar held that position for 27 years. She set the style and conventions of the puzzle, cautioning her constructors to "avoid things like death, disease, war, and taxes—the subway solver gets enough of that in the rest of the paper."

After Farrar died in 1969, the editorial baton was passed to Will Weng, a reporter who had worked his way up to chief of the *Times'* metropolitan news copy desk. He often quipped that he took the job because no one in upper management did crosswords, so they would leave him alone. A constructor himself, Weng added his own flair to the *Times* puzzles, which became famous for their whimsical clues. And he gave "advice": His reponse to a solver who asked if it was OK to use reference books to solve puzzles was, "It's your puzzle. Solve it any way you want." Weng retired on his 70th birthday in 1977, at which time one of *his* constructors, Eugene T. Maleska, was named editor.

Unlike Weng, Maleska stressed knowledge instead of humor—and fairly obscure knowledge at that. And no wonder: He'd spent his life as an educator in the New York school system, and it showed. Maleska's puzzles were sprinkled with cultural references, with a heavy emphasis on opera, a favorite interest of his. He treated his constructors as he might have treated his students, sending them scathing letters in response to submissions he considered inferior. One constructor got a letter that began, "I'm sick and tired of your puzzles." Maleska called another highly regarded puzzle writer a "hack." But the paper's crossword fans hardly noticed.

A SHORTZ HISTORY

The current editor, Will Shortz, took over the job on Maleska's death in 1993. Shortz rejuvenated the puzzle by attracting a younger audience with clues and themes that were more timely and modern, while mollifying the older crowd by bringing back the type of witty and innovative clues that editors Farrar and Weng would have appreciated. Shortz's advice when asked how to improve at solving crosswords: "Practice, practice, practice. The more crosswords you do, the better solver you'll become."

Under Shortz's editorship, the puzzles have gotten more innovative, too, with clever (sometimes complicated) themes or shapes that evolve as the puzzle is solved to reveal objects such as a sailboat, a Christmas tree, and even the Eiffel tower.

Every crossword editor has a favorite puzzle. Shortz's favorite appeared on Election Day in 1996, with this elegant twist: The clue at 39 Across referred to a "MISTER PRESIDENT" entry elsewhere in the puzzle. The two possible answers were —CLINTON or BOB DOLE; the words that crossed them were clued vaguely enough to allow for either possibility. Both answer grids appeared in the *Times* the next day. Today, the *Times* puzzle is syndicated in more than 300 newspapers and journals all over the world.

For some New York Times *crossword puzzle bloopers, turn to page 209.*

In the 1880s, when the Brooklyn Bridge was being built, its 275-foot towers...

WAS THERE EVER AN ORCHARD ON ORCHARD STREET?

Some things are pretty clear: Riverside Drive runs beside the river, Queens Boulevard extends through Queens, and the Grand Concourse still looks pretty grand. But how other city streets earned their names isn't quite as obvious.

BIG APPLES

Once upon a time, there really was an orchard on Orchard Street, or at least where Orchard Street stands today. It was part of the vast farm belonging to James DeLancey, chief justice of the New York Supreme Court and a two-time lieutenant governor of New York State. In the 18th century, the DeLanceys were the largest single-family landholders in Manhattan, with an estate that extended from the Bowery to the East River and from Rivington Street to Division Street—an expanse that also included the tract that later became (surprise) Delancey Street.

GOING DUTCH

There was once a wall on Wall Street too. The Dutch built it in 1653 to defend against attack by their archrivals in world domination, the British. The wall never was put to the test, though, and the Dutch eventually ceded New Amsterdam to the British in exchange for the South American colony of Suriname. After that, the British proceeded to anglicize the spelling and pronunciation of all the Dutch street names in Manhattan. Case in point: Broadway, which comes from the Dutch *breede weg*, or "wide street."

The Bowery also comes from a Dutch word—*bouwerij*, or farm. In the 17th century, Dutch governor Peter Stuyvesant had the largest one—around Third Avenue and Thirteenth Street, encompassing present-day Stuyvesant Street—and the route known as the Bowery ran from his farm to the city's business district.

WATER EVERYWHERE

As the name implies, Water Street *is* pretty close to the East River—but not as close as it used to be. Originally, the street on the East River shoreline was Pearl Street, named for the tens of thousands of oyster shells found there. In the late 1600s, landfill was brought in to expand lower Manhattan, and with it came a new street—Water Street—which remained the waterfront until 1780, when more landfill created Front Street. In 1800 even more landfill led to the creation of South Street.

A few blocks away, Canal Street traces the path of a 40-foot-wide canal built in 1805 to drain the fetid water of Collect Pond (situated around Leonard Street between Lafayette and Centre, where Collect Pond Park now stands) into the Hudson River. Once that giant open sewer channel had done its job, it was filled in and Canal Street was built. Farther north, Spring Street was named for an underground spring discovered there when the land belonged to Aaron Burr in the 1700s. And Minetta Lane comes from a Native American word that meant "devil's water."

MORE ABOUT N MOORE

No one paid much attention to N Moore Street (no period after the N) until the 1980s, when the "triangle below Canal"—TriBeCa—evolved from a collection of former manufacturing loft buildings into the trendy neighborhood of choice. You could argue that actor Robert DeNiro raised Tribeca's profile more than anyone; his production company is called Tribeca Productions, he's part owner of the Tribeca Grill restaurant, and he helped found the Tribeca Film Festival.

Once people took notice of N Moore, it was natural to wonder where the street's name came from. That's when the plausible explanation arose that N Moore Street was named for Nathaniel F. Moore, president of Columbia College from 1842 to 1849. Plausible, but a myth.

In reality, the street was named for Benjamin Moore, Nathaniel's uncle, who was also president of Columbia College (from 1801 to 1811), rector of Trinity Church, and the Episcopal bishop of New York. The N stands for North, to distinguish it from Moore Street in the Financial District. (That Moore Street was named for the place where ships were moored in the East River.)

IT AIN'T TEXAS

Some out-of-towners like to claim that Houston Street is a tribute to Sam Houston, the Texas patriot for whom the city of Houston was named. But as any New Yorker knows, it's not pronounced "Hyew-ston"—it's "How-ston."

William Houstoun, the true source of the street's name, was a delegate from Georgia to the Continental Congress from 1783 to 1786. (The Congress met in New York in 1785 and 1786.) In 1788 he married New Yorker Mary Bayard, whose family's New York roots went back to the 1600s. Mary's father Nicholas Bayard constructed the street through his family's land and named it for his son-in-law. The route appeared on official maps as *Houstoun* Street until 1811, when the second "u" was dropped for reasons that remain unclear.

LOST IN NEW YORK

In the 1992 film *Home Alone 2: Lost in New York*, young Kevin McCallister (Macaulay Culkin) gets lost in New York City and ends up staying at the Plaza Hotel (the only New York hotel he knows the name of). Here's some trivia about the movie:

• All shots inside the Plaza were filmed in an actual suite at the hotel, and the phone number given for the Plaza in the movie was one of the hotel's working numbers at the time.

• Real estate mogul Donald Trump makes a cameo: Kevin stops him in the Plaza's lobby to ask for directions. (Trump owned the hotel at the time.)

• The movie's director, Chris Columbus, also has a cameo: He walks by when Kevin goes into the toy store.

• Twelve-year-old Macaulay Culkin made $8 million for his work on this film, the largest salary ever paid to a child actor at that time.

• In the original film, Kevin visits many New York City landmarks, including the World Trade Center. But since the 2001 terrorist attacks, the scene at the World Trade Center has been removed from TV broadcasts.

Mayor Fiorello La Guardia worked as an interpreter on Ellis Island from 1907 to 1910.

STRANGE STATUES

Instead of the Statue of Liberty, wouldn't you rather visit the Cement Sphinx?

WHITE ANGUS
Near the entrance to the Discovery Center, a hands-on children's museum in Binghamton, sits a 20-foot-tall fiberglass Black Angus bull named Blossom. But he isn't black. The giant animal is painted white and covered with orange, red, yellow, and purple flowers. (The imposing bull, who stands watch over the parking lot, started his career atop a steakhouse in the nearby town Vestal, until he moved to the Discovery Center in 2004.)

THE STATUE OF...RALPH
In 1999, the TV Land cable channel paid tribute to Ralph Kramden of the 1950s series *The Honeymooners* by erecting an eight-foot statue of the fictional bus driver in Kramden's place of business: the New York–New Jersey Port Authority Bus Terminal in Manhattan.

FALLEN MAN
On March 12, 1888, Senator Roscoe Conkling was walking to the New York Club, a bar on 25th Street. It began to snow on the way, and the snow turned into a blizzard. Conkling collapsed and fell to the ground in Union Square. He never recovered and died a month later. His family asked the city to erect a Conkling statue in Union Square, but were turned down—Conkling wasn't a popular politician. But five years later, after repeated requests, a Conkling statue was built in Madison Square.

TO CLIMB OR NOT TO CLIMB?
The official mascot of the Fontana Cement Company in Bayport, Long Island, is a 10-foot-tall goofy-faced replica of the ancient Egyptian Sphinx...made entirely of cement. It's been on Fontana's grounds since 1974. Before that, it sat in front of the Anchorage Inn in Blue Point. Guests aren't allowed to climb on the Sphinx, but curiously, an inscription on it reads, "She who climbs to the Sphinx's head, a millionaire will surely wed."

GHOST STORIES

New York is a city where even the dead never sleep.

GHOSTS: Gertrude and Seabury Tredwell
HAUNTED SPOT: The Merchant's House Museum, Manhattan
STORY: During the 19th century, this building at 29 East 4th Street (near Washington Square) was the home of the wealthy Tredwell family. The house was built in 1832, the family moved in a few years later, and at least one Tredwell lived there for nearly 100 years, until the youngest daughter, Gertrude (born in 1840), died in the house in 1933. Since 1936, the home has been open to the public as a museum.

When Gertrude Tredwell was a young woman, her Anglican father (Seabury) forced her to end a romance with a Catholic medical student. That was the end of her dating days. Gertrude lived the rest of her life as a spinster, spending many solitary years in the Merchant's House…both while she was alive and, according to witnesses, even after she died. The sightings of Gertrude's ghost began in 1934—first, someone reported seeing her in the front doorway, and then neighbors said they'd seen her appear on the porch, angrily waving her arms at a group of noisy children. In the years since, Gertrude has supposedly glided through hallways and up and down the staircase, and played the piano.

People also claim to have seen Seabury Tredwell, Gertrude's father. During a 2006 séance, conducted by paranormal investigators, Seabury ordered the visitors to get out of his house.

GHOSTS: A wronged parishioner and others
HAUNTED SPOT: Most Holy Trinity–St. Mary's Church, Brooklyn
STORY: The strangest haunted building in New York may be this Brooklyn church. In 1897, a bell ringer, George Stelz, was murdered in the church's vestibule. The main suspect was a parishioner who was later executed for another murder, but Stelz's murder was never solved. Legend has it that the victim rings the bells at odd hours and that bloody handprints appear on the tower's stairway.

...nights in spring and fall so as not to confuse migrating birds.

But that's just the beginning of the church's haunted tales: A school on the church grounds was built over a former cemetery. Its hallways are reportedly filled with ghostly footsteps and lights sometimes flicker off and on in the gymnasium.

Perhaps the most mysterious aspect of the church, though, is its underground network of bricked-up tunnels, subbasements, and hidden rooms. In the 1800s, amid violent, anti-Catholic prejudice in New York, the tunnels were probably used by priests and church members so they could attend mass without being harassed. The tunnels might have also been part of the Underground Railroad for runaway slaves. Whatever their purpose, there have been so many reports of footsteps and other noises coming from inside the tunnels that New Jersey Paranormal Research investigated. The researchers say they found ghostly "hot spots" of energy and a surprisingly clear digital recording of an entity's voice saying, "I am Michael." (Michael May was the church's second pastor, who died in his rectory room in 1895. That room has long gone unused because of the many odd voices and footsteps that later occupants have reported.)

GHOSTS: Edna Crawford Champion and Charles Brazelle
HAUNTED SPOT: The penthouse of the Medical Arts Building, Manhattan
STORY: Albert Champion was a wealthy former French cyclist who won several races before he moved to the United States, changed his focus from bicycles to automobiles, and opened an auto-parts company that sold a spark plug he invented himself. In the early 1920s, he met and married a much younger American woman named Edna Crawford, and the two settled in New York. But Edna wasn't satisfied with just one man—while the couple was visiting Paris, she began an affair with a handsome Sorbonne graduate named Charles Brazelle. Albert Champion suspected the affair, and when he confronted the couple at a nightclub on October 25, 1927, the younger Brazelle beat him so badly that he died a few hours later. However, the coroner (who'd probably been bribed by Edna) declared that Albert had died from a heart attack—in other words, natural causes. So, with Albert's millions and her new lover in tow, Edna headed back to New York.

She bought the Medical Arts Building on West 57th Street,

and the new couple settled into the penthouse. Edna remodeled the place in elaborate fashion—including a 40-foot mural of a Venetian carnival that featured Edna wearing only a mask and high heels. But Charles Brazelle turned out to be abusive, and the pair's constant partying led to squandered millions, drug abuse, and drunken fights.

In 1935, during a vicious fight, Charles threw a telephone at Edna's head. Bodyguards hired by her family escorted him out of the penthouse, but he managed to sneak right back in...so the bodyguards hurled him out the bedroom window. Edna and Charles both died soon afterward of their injuries. When it came time to settle Edna's estate, her relatives expected to find Albert Champion's millions in a bank or investment somewhere, but they never found a dime. Edna and Charles were broke...or, as one paranormal investigator theorized, Charles Brazelle had hidden all of Edna's money.

Some years later, newlyweds Carlton Alsop and his wife moved into the penthouse with their four Great Danes. Within a few months, the Alsops started hearing the sound of high heels clicking across the floors and arguments emerging from empty rooms. Within a year, they'd split up and Carlton was living alone in the penthouse. Meanwhile, the Great Danes were so frightened they often lapsed into fits of barking, and Carlton had a nervous breakdown. After the two unhappy endings, the apartment was converted to a commercial space...but its haunted reputation remains.

For more spooky stories, turn to page 160.

*　　*　　*

THE EGG

Architect Wallace Harrison helped to design everything from Lincoln Center to LaGuardia Airport, and in 1966, he began work on one of his most ambitious projects—the Egg in downtown Albany, a flat-topped, round-bottomed masterpiece that looks like half of an enormous, silver, hardboiled egg balanced on a platform. (It's actually held upright by a support beam that reaches six stories underground.) It took Harrison's team 12 years to build the structure, and today, it's a performing arts center.

Macy's Herald Square store has more than 2 million square feet of floor space.

WHERE THE WILD THINGS ARE

If you want to see exotic animals in their natural habitat, you could take a trip to Africa or Asia…or you could just catch a train to the Bronx.

THE WILD BRONX

With 256 acres and about 2 million visitors a year, the Bronx Zoo is the largest metropolitan zoo in the United States. It opened in 1899 and over the years has pioneered conservation techniques that benefit not only its 4,000 animal residents, but countless others across the globe. The Bronx Zoo was the first in the United States to let visitors donate to animal-conservation projects of their choice, and the first to house predators (lions) where they could see and smell their natural prey (antelope), which helped the animals keep their natural instincts sharp. The zoo was also among the first to design enclosures that resembled natural habitats instead of cages. Because of the zoo's conservation efforts and dedication to building realistic habitats, it was also one of the first to display species rarely found in captivity. Here are just a few of the animal species that made a name for themselves at the Bronx Zoo.

CONGO GORILLAS

One of the largest groups of western lowland gorillas in North America lives in New York. The Bronx Zoo's 6.5-acre Congo Gorilla Forest, which opened in 1999, is the largest artificial African rain forest ever built and one of the most productive: It's the birthplace of at least six baby gorillas, the first of whom was Suki ("beloved" in Japanese) in 2000. Some gorillas that never produced offspring in other facilities are able to do so at Congo Gorilla Forest, presumably because the surroundings are so similar to their native Africa.

SNOW LEOPARDS

In 1903, the Bronx Zoo was the first zoo in the western hemisphere to exhibit snow leopards, an exotic animal found in remote mountains of Central Asia. Today, the animals live in the Himalayan

Highlands exhibit, which includes trees, plants, caverns, and streams. Over 80 snow leopard cubs have been born at the zoo, more than at any other facility in the world. Bronx leopards have been sent to many other zoos, including the Central Park Zoo, which received three when it opened its snow leopard exhibit in 2009.

The Himalayan Highlands exhibit is also the site of important research. Snow leopards are notoriously elusive, making it difficult for scientists to study them in the wild. So in 2004, World Wildlife Conservation used the exhibit to test ways to photograph snow leopards to count and identify them in the wild. Thanks to another study at the Bronx Zoo, cameras are now stationed in Asia.

MALEO BIRDS

Maleo birds are about the size of chickens and have bony faces and orange hooked beaks. They're also rare, endangered, and live only on the Indonesian island of Sulawesi…and at the Bronx Zoo. One reason the birds are so rare is their unusual nesting habits. A mother lays only one egg…and it's enormous, five times bigger than a chicken's. She buries it in warm sand or soil, and then takes off. When the chick hatches, it's on its own. Unlike other birds, newborn maleos can fly and defend themselves almost immediately. But the eggs are often attacked by wild dogs, pigs, and poachers, and their habitat is threatened by human development, so in 2006 there were fewer than 5,000 left in the world. The Bronx Zoo staff has been working with scientists in Sulawesi to restore the maleos' numbers. So far, they've helped the Indonesians hatch 4,000 maleo chicks successfully in the wild.

BISON

In the early 19th century, an estimated 50 million bison roamed the plains of North America. But by 1900, only about 1,000 remained—they'd been nearly wiped out by over-hunting and habitat destruction. So the Bronx Zoo established its own bison herd and, in 1907, sent 15 zoo-born bison by wagon and railroad to Oklahoma—the first time in American history that captive animals were purposely reintroduced into the wild. At the Wichita Mountains Wildlife Refuge, the Bronx bison helped to diversify the wild bison's gene pool, an important factor in revitalizing the species. Today, between 15,000 and 20,000 bison roam wild in North America.

WHO PUT THE LIGHTS OUT?

On a sizzling hot July night in 1977, the unthinkable happened—the entire city of New York went dark in a massive blackout. And for the city's residents, that was just the start of a memorably scary night.

THE CITY THAT SLEEPS?

Try to imagine this: At 9:36 on the night of July 13, 1977, with temperatures in the 90s, the entire Con Edison power system that serves New York City shut down—and without warning, all five boroughs and part of Westchester were plunged into darkness. Everything stopped—subways, elevators, TVs, air conditioners. From across the river, New Jersey residents watched the New York skyline flicker out. From above, pilots gaped as runway lights disappeared. There were no streetlights, traffic lights, or neon signs. Lamps flickered off in every room in every apartment building on every street in the city, and indoors, every room went dark. Water pumps stopped, so there was no running water in sinks, showers, tubs, or toilets. Refrigeration in supermarkets and restaurants shut down. Hospitals abruptly flipped to emergency power, and the city morgue had to be cooled by an NYFD portable generator. And no one knew what had happened.

THREE ACTS OF GOD

That wasn't the first time a blackout had happened. On the evening of November 9, 1965, the lights in New York State, along with half a dozen other northeastern states and a chunk of Canada, went out when the demand for electricity produced an overload that shut down the Con Ed power system. The city was restored to power about 12 hours later. The 1965 blackout was attributed to human error, and officials took measures to make sure that another manmade blackout wouldn't happen. But what happened on that sweltering night in July 1977 was something they couldn't prevent: Between 8:37 p.m. and 8:55 p.m., lightning struck not one, but *three* Con Ed substations along the Hudson River. The improbable triple-strike caused a cascade of events: loss of transmission lines,

---

The Bronx High School of Science counts 7 Nobel Prize-winning physicists among its alumni.

power overloads, and voltage reductions that took too long to complete. The blackout may have started as a natural disaster, but it quickly got out of hand, compounded by inadequate facilities and poorly trained operators who panicked as the crisis escalated.

On top of that, even before authorities at neighboring electric utilities in New Jersey and Long Island could decide whether to help out the Con Edison grid, their automated equipment made the decision for them: It shut off its ties to Con Edison and cut off New York City from surrounding sources of power. Finally, at 9:27 p.m., three supplemental Con Ed power lines blew, and Big Allis—the biggest generator in New York City—shut down.

Most residents carried on as best they could, helping their neighbors, listening to transistor radios for updates, and eating by candlelight. But some took the opportunity to go on a rampage. What shocked and frightened New Yorkers more than the power loss was the eruption of violence and looting that came on the heels of the lights-out.

RUNNING RIOT

That summer the mood in New York was already tense, with the city teetering on the brink of bankruptcy. Public services like trash collection were failing, housing in poorer neighborhoods was deteriorating at an alarming rate, jobs were scarce, and desperation was in the air. Fear was, too: A serial killer named David Berkowitz, who called himself "Son of Sam," was still at large, prompting the newspapers to dub this the "Summer of Sam." On the night of the blackout, the city was also suffering from a heat wave and overwhelming humidity. Fans and air conditioners were running full force all over town, and people fled their broiling apartments for the streets, stoops, and fire escapes.

Soon after the start of the blackout, the Brooklyn neighborhoods of Crown Heights, Flatbush, and Bushwick, as well as parts of Harlem and the South Bronx, were overrun by marauding looters breaking into stores and businesses. They grabbed anything they could—boxes of diapers, food, drugs, television sets, furniture, and even cars. Within hours, there was little that the police force could do to control it. The cops arrested so many people by the end—more than 3,700—that the jails couldn't hold them all and they spilled over into precinct basements, vans, and other makeshift jails.

NYPD BLUE

But in spite of all the chaos, only two people lost their lives that night: a robber who was shot and killed by a pharmacist and a burglary suspect who died of natural causes in the Brooklyn Criminal Courthouse. The police made it through the night with no fatalities. There was a good reason for this relatively positive outcome: After the 1967 Detroit race riots—which lasted five days and took 43 lives—a government committee argued that police use of firearms had aggravated the situation and caused what they termed "police riots." The NYPD heard the message loud and clear, and by 1972, they'd been trained in crowd control and "tactical shooting," which meant, among other things, knowing when not to shoot. Police Commissioner Michael Codd later said, "If we had let the men shoot at looters at will, you would have had dead people littering the streets. A lot of dead people."

The dearth of fatalities is even more impressive when you remember that at the time of the blackout, cops in the neighborhoods where violence broke out were far outnumbered—and their vehicles had been flat-tired by broken glass and other debris in the streets. It was estimated that 80 percent of the arrested looters had criminal records, and many might have had handguns themselves.

In the end, it took almost 25 hours to restore full power to the city. Con Ed's chairman, Charles Luce, claimed that the blackout was due to an act of God; Mayor Abe Beame took aim at Con Ed and accused the company of "gross negligence." Many residents, however, blamed Mayor Beame for not responding quickly enough to the disaster. Beame lost the confidence of the public. In the mayoral primary later that year, he was voted out in favor of Ed Koch, who went on to win the November election and served for almost 12 years.

* * *

NEW YORK CITY FACTS

• Broadway is also called Highway 9.

• Montauk, Long Island, is home to Deep Hollow Ranch, the oldest cattle ranch in the United States.

The only Yankee with a retired number who did not win a World Series: Don Mattingly.

THEY WERE GLOBETROTTERS?

The high-energy and theatrical Harlem Globetrotters basketball team has been entertaining people since 1929, and over the years, they've employed dozens of big-name celebrities and sports stars as actual and honorary members. Here are five of the team's most surprising alumni.

1. BILL COSBY

Cosby began his affiliation with the Globetrotters in December 1972, when he appeared in the debut episode of *The Harlem Globetrotters Popcorn Machine*, a short-lived variety show that aired on CBS. The team made the most of his appearance by signing the Emmy Award-winning funnyman to a lifetime contract—at $1 per year. (Cosby's rate was later increased to $1.05 in 1986 "to account for inflation.")

2. WILT CHAMBERLAIN

It might not seem like such a stretch that the 7'1" NBA legend Chamberlain was once a Globetrotter, but he did it before becoming one of the world's most famous centers. A two-time All-American at the University of Kansas, "Wilt the Stilt" signed a one-year contract with the Globetrotters in 1958 (they paid him $50,000, a huge amount at the time) so he could play professional basketball—NBA rules prevented underclassmen from entering the league, but the Globetrotters were out of its jurisdiction. It proved to be money well spent because his signing generated headlines all across America and brought the team more fans (and ticket sales). Chamberlain joined the NBA the following year, but he never forgot his time with the Globetrotters, often calling it the most enjoyable part of his career. Chamberlain died in 1999, but was posthumously honored by the team in 2000, when the Globetrotters retired his jersey.

3. POPE JOHN PAUL II

The Supreme Pontiff of the Roman Catholic Church, Pope John Paul II, became an honorary Globetrotter on November 29, 2000, in a star-studded ceremony in St. Peter's Square in Vatican City.

Staten Island residents voted to secede from NYC in 1993, but they couldn't get state approval.

Members of the team commemorated the historic event by presenting His Holiness with an autographed basketball and a #75 jersey in honor of the team's 75th anniversary. It wasn't the first time the Globetrotters were granted an audience with a pope. The team also met Pope Pius XII in 1951 and 1952, Pope John XXIII in 1959 and 1963, and Pope Paul VI in 1968.

4. MAGIC JOHNSON

A 12-time NBA All-Star and a three-time NBA MVP, Earvin "Magic" Johnson first suited up for the Globetrotters in April 1997, during a college all-stars game. Johnson enjoyed the experience so much that he played for the team again in November 2003 in a game against his alma mater, Michigan State. Johnson tallied five points and four assists during the first 16 minutes of the 97–83 victory, helping the Globetrotters avenge a loss to the Spartans in 2000 that had ended the team's 1,270-game winning streak (which had begun in 1995). Johnson is currently signed to a $1-a-year lifetime contract with the team and has a standing invitation to return at any time.

5. BOB GIBSON

Although best known as an outstanding baseball player, Bob "Gibby" Gibson—then a talented athlete at Nebraska's Creighton University—helped a team of college all-stars defeat the Globetrotters in April 1957 in the World Series of Basketball, an annual three-week tournament. His performance was so impressive that the Globetrotter's owner, Abe Saperstein, signed Gibson to a one-year contract for the 1957–58 season…thereby delaying the start of his Major League Baseball career with the St. Louis Cardinals. Gibson enjoyed the experience so much that he might have continued to play with the Globe trotters the next year if the Cardinals hadn't offered him a $3,700 bonus to join the team. Gibson went on to appear in nine All-Star games and capture two World Series titles over his 17-year Hall of Fame career.

* * *

First rookie NFL quarterback to throw two 2-point conversions in one game: Mark Sanchez of the New York Jets, in 2009

In 1859 French acrobat Charles "the Great" Blondin crossed Niagara…

SAY WHAT?

Sometimes New York politicians are witty; sometimes they're wise. And sometimes well...they say things like this.

"I haven't committed a crime. What I did was fail to comply with the law."
— **David Dinkins, after being accused of not paying taxes**

"It's no fun to protest on an empty stomach.
— **Michael Bloomberg**

"My truest disability has been my ability to overcome my physical disability."
— **David Paterson**

"Freedom is about authority. Freedom is about the willingness of every single human being to cede to lawful authority a great deal of discretion about what you do."
— **Rudy Giuliani**

"We don't windsurf in Harlem."
— **Charlie Rangel**

"Life is indeed precious, and I believe the death penalty helps affirm this fact."
— **Ed Koch**

"I've said that I'm not running [for president] and I'm having a great time being pres...being a first-term senator."
— **Hillary Clinton, 2004**

"Get action. Seize the moment. Man was never intended to become an oyster."
— **Theodore Roosevelt**

"I'm thinking about governing as the governor of this state, and that's what I'm going to do."
— **George Pataki**

"Not only is New York City the nation's melting pot, it is also the casserole, the chafing dish, and the charcoal grill.
— **John Lindsay**

"And still the question, 'What shall be done with our ex-Presidents?' is not laid at rest, and I sometimes think [journalist Henry] Watterson's solution of it, 'Take them out and shoot them,' is worthy of attention."
— **Grover Cleveland**

THERE GOES THE NEIGHBORHOOD: MANHATTAN

The island of Manhattan is home to dozens of neighborhoods, each with its own name and history. Here are the stories behind some of them.

- **Manhattan** comes from an Algonquin word, but nobody is sure what the original word was. Because of different Algonquin dialects and accents—plus hundreds of years of Europeans mispronouncing it—"Manhattan" could mean "island," "place for wood gathering"…or "place of general inebriation."

- **The Battery** was named for a *battery* (or grouping) of cannons placed at the southern tip of the island to defend the city during the 17th century.

- Not surprisingly, the **Flatiron District** is named for the iconic Flatiron building, which took *its* name from the triangular plot of land on which it was built, shaped like a 19th-century iron.

- **Greenwich Village** was originally a small town north of the main settlement of New Amsterdam. The origin of the name "Greenwich" is disputed, however. Some historians think it was named after Greenwich, England, but others say that it's actually a corruption of a Dutch term, *Greenwijck* (or "Pine District"), which was the name of a now long-gone section of Long Island that was dotted with pine trees. In the 1670s, a wealthy land owner named Yellis Mandeville moved from Greenwijck, Long Island, to the area that's now Greenwich Village, Manhattan, and many people believe he named his new neighborhood after the old one.

- No one's sure exactly where the term **Hell's Kitchen** came from, but during the 19th century, the West side of Manhattan was a notorious slum, with different areas sporting monikers like Battle

Row or House of Blazes. Some historians suggest that "Hell's Kitchen" might have originally referred to a specific tenement; it also might have been borrowed from a similarly named slum in London. Despite the area's gentrification and the best efforts of real estate agents, the name has stuck.

• The term **SoHo** was coined in 1968, an abbreviation of "South of Houston Industrial Area." At the time, the neighborhood was becoming known for its artsy scene, and the sobriquet was inspired by the SoHo neighborhood in London, which stands for "South of Holborn." It also spurred the creation of several other abbreviated place names in Manhattan: NoHo, "North of Houston"; NoLIta, "North of Little Italy"; and TriBeCa, "Triangle Below Canal."

• The **Tenderloin District** was a notorious red-light district in the 19th century, but its name doesn't have anything to do with prostitution. It actually refers to the quality of bribes a corrupt policeman could expect in this neighborhood. In 1876, when police inspector Alexander Williams (later nicknamed "Czar of the Tenderloin") began to oversee the area, he proclaimed, "I've been having chuck steak ever since I've been on the force, and now I'm going to have a bit of [better-quality] tenderloin." The name stuck.

• **Times Square** was known as Longacre Square until 1904, when the *New York Times* opened its headquarters there. That year, Times Square hosted its very first New Year's Eve party. Fireworks were replaced by the iconic ball drop three years later.

• During the Revolutionary War, the area that's now **Washington Heights** was home to Fort Washington, built on the highest point of Manhattan to defend it from the British. The fort gives both the neighborhood and the George Washington Bridge their names.

* * *

"They say life is what happens when you're busy making other plans. But sometimes, in New York, life is what happens when you're waiting for a table."

—**Carrie Bradshaw,**
Sex and the City

TEN LITTLE RESTAURANTS

Ah, nostalgia...and food! Here are the stories behind 10 of New York City's favorite restaurants, past and present.

1. SHAKE SHACK, MANHATTAN

Shake Shack is a small chain of high-quality fast-food joints invented by Danny Meyer, guru of fancier fine food meccas like Union Square Café and Gramercy Tavern. The first Shake Shack appeared in 2004 in Madison Square Park, and as of 2010, there were five Shacks scattered throughout Manhattan and Queens, and more were planned. Shake Shacks serve up burgers and fries the Danny way: Items are cooked to order and made with antibiotic- and hormone-free ingredients. Blanketing the world with standardized Shake Shacks is *not* a Danny Meyer goal; he prefers to expand slowly and to make sure that each new Shack maintains quality and reflects its neighborhood (like displaying the Mets logo on the shack at Citi Field). The strategy has worked: Each of the five Shacks averages sales of about $4 million per year—more than the city's average McDonald's.

2. P.J. CLARKE'S, MANHATTAN

Many of New York City's great saloons have disappeared, but this one has been serving drinks in a small building on the corner of 55th and Third since 1884. Patrick Joseph Clarke owned and ran the place for decades. In 1943, his family sold it to a buyer who, three months later, sold it to the Lavezzos, antique dealers who owned the building and loved the bar. The Lavezzos hung on until 1967, when they sold the building to a developer who wanted to build a skyscraper on the site. But the Lavezzos included a caveat in the sale: P. J. Clarke's had to be allowed a 99-year lease. The skyscraper went up, but the bar remained. There P. J. Clarke's sits today, just as full of memories (and devoted customers) as ever. Some of its legendary patrons include Frank Sinatra, Jackie Kennedy Onassis, Nat King Cole, Marilyn Monroe, George Steinbrenner, Mel Brooks, Cary Grant, and Martina Navratilova.

New York State is home to more than 70,000 miles of rivers and streams.

3. SYLVIA'S RESTAURANT, HARLEM

Sylvia Woods, the self-proclaimed "Queen of Soulfood," started her culinary career as a waitress at Johnson's Luncheonette on Lenox Avenue in Harlem. In 1962, the owner sold her the place—a 10-seat counter and a few booths—and 36-year-old Woods was on her way to what is today a small empire that includes Sylvia's Restaurant of Harlem, Sylvia's Also (a bar and lounge with sizzling hot DJ's), Sylvia's Catering Corporation, and a line of her own food products. The Harlem restaurant, which takes up most of an entire block, seats 450 and offers a Jazz Brunch every Saturday and a Gospel Brunch every Sunday. Customer favorites: barbecued ribs, sweet potato pie, smothered chicken, collard greens, okra and tomato gumbo, and banana pudding.

4. MANDUCATIS, LONG ISLAND CITY

Vincenzo and Ida Cerbone got married in 1960, had kids, and in 1977 opened Manducatis (Latin for "you all eat") in an unassuming gray-brick-faced building in a working-class section of Long Island City. But once inside, patrons step into the warm, friendly dining rooms, complete with a fireplace, and can order such delicacies as veal piccata, fresh pasta, stuffed peppers, and dozens of other homemade Italian specialties. The restaurant started with neighborhood customers, but soon, news got around and serious foodies (as well as artists from a nearby art center, MOMA P.S. 1) were beating a path to Manducatis's nondescript door. Today, Vincenzo runs the front, Ida (a self-taught cook) runs the small kitchen, and son Anthony is the wine expert.

5. LÜCHOW'S, MANHATTAN

In the late 1800s, immigrant August Lüchow was working as a waiter at a German restaurant on East 14th Street. In 1882, with the help of a loan from patron (and piano mogul) William Steinway, he bought the place from his boss. Over the years, he purchased surrounding properties and expanded Lüchow's until it was large enough for almost 1,000 customers to dine at once, eating Wiener schnitzel and bratwurst, drinking beer, and listening to musicians playing Strauss waltzes. The 14th Street area was a theater and music hall district back then, and Mr. Lüchow's customers included actors, musicians, and writers as well as politicians from nearby Tam-

The Chrysler Building was built at an average rate of four floors per week.

many Hall. Lüchow's lasted for an entire century, closing in 1982. The building was demolished after a fire gutted it in the late 1980s.

6. ROBERTO RESTAURANT, BRONX

The Arthur Avenue neighborhood is often called the Little Italy of the Bronx. People go there especially for the Italian markets and bakeries—and for Roberto Paciullo's cooking. He came to America from Salerno in the late 1960s, when he was 17 and began cooking in the Bronx—first at a social club and then at a restaurant he opened with his brother Tony. Tony bowed out, and the place became Roberto's. It's moved around a few times (as of 2011, it was located at 603 Crescent Avenue), but that hasn't deterred the fans: Roberto's policy is "no reservations," so on Saturday nights, customers line up and wait...and wait...for as long as it takes to get a table, competing for space with celebrities, politicians, and occasional New York Yankees.

More restaurants on page 228.

*   *   *

MIND YOUR MANNERS

In the 1930s and '40s, New Yorkers were getting a reputation for being rude and messy, especially on the subway. They threw trash on the floor, put their feet up on seats where people wanted to sit down, and generally paid little attention to the needs of other passengers...or so said the MTA, which hired an artist named Amelia Opdyke "Oppy" Jones to create a series of posters reminding riders to be polite. What Jones came up with was a fake newspaper called *The Subway Sun*, whose "front page" (the face of the poster) included a quippy tip (like "Seats are for people, not packages") and an accompanying illustration (a well-dressed woman with shopping bags strewn about, as an elderly man searched for a place to sit down). Jones drew dozens of posters between 1935 and 1966. She also claimed to have coined the term "litterbug," which she said derived from "jitterbug." She first used it on a poster that stated, "Nobody loves a litterbug." Over the years, the *Subway Sun* posters also promoted fun places that New Yorkers could get to on the subway and fare increases.

Chuck—NYC's official Groundhog Day groundhog—resides at the Staten Island Zoo.

IT'S AN ART-I-FUL TOWN

Even in a city packed with artists, some pieces stand out as...different.

TRASH IN A BOX
Artist: Justin Gignac
Medium: Authentic New York City garbage

The art: Around 2003, when Gignac was working as an intern at MTV, he got into a debate with a coworker who claimed that a product's packaging was unimportant to its success; what really mattered was the product inside. Gignac disagreed—packaging, he said, was everything. To test that theory, he went around New York City collecting trash (ticket stubs, plastic forks, scraps of subway maps, and so on), and then artfully arranged the pieces inside small, sleek plastic cubes. He called the creations "Garbage of New York City" and started selling them on the street for $10 each. To make the garbage "exclusive," Gignac signed each cube and attached a sticker with the date the garbage was collected. It worked. He eventually raised the prices...to $50 (for regular trash) and $100 (for "limited edition" trash—garbage from Opening Day at Yankee Stadium, or a Times Square New Year's Eve celebration). By 2008, he'd proven his point by selling more than 1,000 cubes. What kind of trash worked best? Gignac says, "I only pick up dry trash. Wet trash would rot in the cubes and, besides, I'm a bit squeamish."

THE BROKEN ANGEL HOUSE
Artists: Arthur and Cynthia Wood
Medium: A brownstone

The art: In 1979 the Woods bought a brownstown at #4 Downing Street in Bed-Stuy. The building had once been the headquarters of the Brooklyn Trolley, and by the time they bought it, it was old and run down. The couple spent the next 27 years turning that building into a work of art. They installed stained glass windows made of old bottles, put concrete angel statues on the roof, painted flame designs on the front door, and added dozens of other quirky touches. (The house's name derived from a porcelain angel Cynthia found in the gutter of a Staten Island street.) Over the

First person executed by the electric chair: murderer William Kemmler of Buffalo, in 1890.

years, the brownstone became their home, and the Woods raised two kids there.

In 2006, a rooftop fire brought the house to the attention of the New York City Department of Buildings. Firefighters had refused to go inside the top-floor room during the fire because they worried the floor wouldn't hold them. According to a city spokesperson, "A lot of the building is open to the elements...the walls are not complete, the floors are not there." The Building Department condemned the property and evicted the Woods.

Ever since then, the Woods have been battling to keep their house. For a while, the couple lived in their car, parked outside the building; eventually they moved in with friends. Cynthia Wood died in January 2010, but Arthur and his son continued trying to return to the building. They removed the dicey top floor and even offered to turn the building into a community center, but there was never enough money for all the needed renovations. Today the house is still standing, and the Wood family continues to try to make enough improvements to satisfy the Building Department.

BIG BAMBÚ

Artists: Mike and Doug Starn

Medium: Bamboo

The art: In 2010, the Metropolitan Museum of Art commissioned twins Mike and Doug Starn, best known as award-winning photographers, to create a sculpture for its rooftop garden. What the brothers came up with was a giant trellis-like web of interlocking bamboo poles that stood 50 feet high and stretched 100 feet long. Their purpose: They hoped to "awaken us to the fact that individually we are not so big."

The exhibition lasted for six months, from April through October, and was constantly changing. The brothers hired 20 rock climbers to scale the poles in bare feet and add new pieces daily. Some lucky museum-goers also got to experience Big Bambú's heights: Every day, guides (trained to recognize and assist people suffering from acrophobia, fear of heights) escorted groups of 10–15 people up bamboo paths and through the sculpture to its tiptop, where they got incredible views of both the structure and the city.

Q: What do civil rights pioneers Frederick Douglass and Susan B. Anthony have in common?...

NEW YORK Q & A

We had a lot of questions about New York...let's get started.

Q. Where did all the brownstones come from?
A. New York's brownstones—predominantly found in Brooklyn and on the Upper West Side—have become a city trademark, showing up in everything from *Sex and the City* to *Sesame Street*. This style of architecture prevailed in the late 19th and early 20th centuries, and the row houses were built for wealthy owners who didn't want to live in crowded apartments but still wanted to be close to the city. "Brownstone" refers to the building material—a brown sandstone with red and purple hues that was quarried mostly in Connecticut.

Q. Which professional New York sports team was founded by two bartenders?
A. What was to become the New York Yankees began in 1903 when city bartenders Frank Farrell and William "Big Bill" Devery bought the struggling Baltimore Orioles for $18,000, transplanted them to New York, and renamed them the Highlanders. That gave the city two teams: the National League's Giants and the American League's Highlanders, who lost their first game, but made steady progress over the years. The team also started wearing pinstripes and took on the interlocking "NY" logo that was already being used as an honorary symbol for police officers killed in the line of duty. That logo has since become one of the most recognizable in sports...especially after 1913, when the Highlanders changed their name to the Yankees.

Q. What's the oldest building in the Big Apple?
A. New York City has a lot of old buildings, but a farmhouse built in 1652 takes this title. The Pieter Claesen Wyckoff Farmhouse (now museum) in East Flatbush-Flatlands, Brooklyn, was built by Pieter Claesen, a Dutch indentured servant who worked his way to freedom after arriving in New Amsterdam. (After the British took control of New Amsterdam and named it New York, Claesen adopted the more English-sounding last name Wyckoff.) The

...A: Both were long-time residents of Rochester, NY.

Dutch-colonial home Claesen and his wife, Grietje Van Ness, built on Clarendon Road is now a National Historic Landmark.

Q. What was Rutherford Stuyvesant's claim to fame?

A. Rutherford Stuyvesant was a descendant of the famous Peter Stuyvesant, the last head of the Dutch New Amsterdam colony and the namesake of Manhattan's Stuyvesant High School, the Bed-Stuy area of Brooklyn, and many other places. In 1869, Rutherford built the city's first luxury apartment building based on Parisian flats, which were common in France. Tenements for the poor had been around since the 1830s, but the idea of "good" families living in similarly close quarters brought out many critics who called the plan "folly." But Stuyvesant pressed on, spending $100,000 on a five-story apartment building that replaced his fruit orchard on 18th Street, between Irving Place and Third Avenue. There were 16 apartments on the first four floors, and a top floor with space for four artist studios. The apartments, which were the first in America to offer private bathrooms and running water, rented from $1,800 a year for a ground floor apartment to around $1,000 for a fourth-floor suite. (Why cheaper at the top? No elevators.) Stuyvesant's building was occupied for 87 years and changed the way New Yorkers thought about apartments.

Q. Are there any farms left in New York City?

A. Yes, in Queens. The Queens County Farm Museum—a 47-acre patch of farmland in the Glen Oaks section—serves as the last tangible reminder of the agriculture that once characterized the borough. The farm has been operating since 1697, making it the oldest in New York State.

For more Q&A, turn to page 146.

*   *   *

The Rockefeller Center Christmas tree is usually 75 to 90 feet high and more than 50 years old. Every year, technicians use a five-mile-long string of lights to decorate it.

Long Island is the largest island in the continental U.S.

THE GREAT MAPLE SYRUP MYSTERY

Hey, New York—what's that smell?

SWEET EMERGENCY

Manhattan is full of smells—the stale scent of subway cars, the asphalt of road repairs, the waft of cigarettes, the hot, dirty water on hot dog carts. But on October 28, 2005, the city got a whole new smell: maple syrup. Residents from Lower Manhattan to Harlem started picking up the odor, but it seemed particularly strong on the Upper West Side.

Calls flooded in to 311, the city's information hotline. A few residents even called 911, fearing a biochemical terrorist attack. The Office of Emergency Management conducted extensive tests and concluded there was nothing harmful in the aroma.

BACK ON THE AIR

The incident might have just passed as another of those "only in New York" moments, but the maple syrup kept coming back—it was reported five more times between 2005 and 2009, and each occurrence spurred a new wave of frantic calls and another round of inconclusive testing.

After the first few incidents, the city created specific protocols so it could respond swiftly to "maple syrup events." Finally, in February 2009, the culprit was found: The sweet smell came from New Jersey, specifically, from a company in Hudson County that makes food additives. On each of the days in question, the factory was processing pungent fenugreek seeds, a spice often used in curries. Mayor Michael Bloomberg said, "Given the evidence, I think it's safe to say that the 'Great Maple Syrup Mystery' has finally been solved."

An investigation concluded that the factory hadn't done anything wrong, and city officials in the city closed the case. So it's fairly safe to say that, on future processing days, if the wind is blowing just right, New Yorkers will just have to live with a little unexpected sweetness.

"No other American city is so intensely American as New York." —Anthony Trollope

MUSEUM MANIA

You think that because you're from New York you've seen it all?
You haven't. Take a look at some of the weirdest museums
and roadside attractions from around the state.

SING SING PRISON MUSEUM
Where: Ossining (in the Joseph G. Caputo Community Center)
What you'll see: A replica of an electric chair (the real "display" chair is on loan at the Newseum in Washington, D.C.), two Sing Sing cells (one that you can actually sit in), confiscated prison weapons, pictures of prisoners being flogged, and other gruesome items.

JELL-O MUSEUM
Where: Le Roy
What you'll see: Le Roy in Upstate New York is the birthplace of Jell-O, and at this museum, you can see old TV commercials, print ads, and even a "gelometer" that was once used to measure the "gel quality" of the product. If you want to actually buy some Jell-O, though, you're out of luck; the gift shop doesn't sell any.

THE LUCILLE BALL–DESI ARNAZ CENTER
Where: Jamestown
What you'll see: Lucille Ball was born at 69 Stewart Avenue in Jamestown, and Lucymania reigns in her hometown. At the museum, visitors can see her wedding dress, one of Little Ricky's outfits, and sets from the *I Love Lucy* TV show.

HAVERSTRAW BRICK MUSEUM
Where: Haverstraw
What you'll see: It's basically...bricks.

AMERICAN MUSEUM OF CUTLERY
Where: Cattaraugus
What you'll see: Eventually, this museum hopes to "establish itself

as an important research and educational facility," but for now, visitors can edge up to swords, knives, scissors, and weapons in a funky storefront in a town where cutlery companies used to flourish.

CROSS ISLAND CHAPEL
Where: Oneida
What you'll see: On a wooden platform in the middle of a pond is the 29-square-foot (nondenominational) world's smallest church. The simple white wooden structure and steeple seats just two and is accessible only by boat.

NEW YORK STATE OLD TYME FIDDLERS HALL OF FAME AND MUSEUM
Where: Osceola
What you'll see: Fiddles made of wood and metal—one even has a scroll (the top part) shaped like an old man's face—pictures, and other memorabilia of old-time fiddlers...fiddling.

MUSEUM OF SEX
Where: Manhattan
What you'll see: Are you over 18? OK, then you're permitted to visit these exhibits about everything from fetishes to pin-ups.

MUSEUM OF THE EARLY AMERICAN CIRCUS
Where: Somers
What you'll see: This museum's exhibits are constantly changing, but they focus on the beginnings of the circus in America. It's housed in the Somers Town Hall, which is inside the Elephant Hotel, which is named for Old Bet, an actual elephant who lived in Somers in the early 1800s.

HOUSE OF FRANKENSTEIN WAX MUSEUM
Where: Lake George
What you'll see: Fifty-two exhibits of dummies being tortured, including an electrocution where visitors flip the switch, all to the sounds of piercing screams being played on a constant loop. (Around the corner is Dr. Morbid's Haunted House, where live actors scare you by jumping out from dark corners.)

HIPSTER SPOTTING

Of all the creatures native to New York, one of the most curious is the "hipster," found in Brooklyn and Manhattan. Here's our guide to spotting one.

If you answer "yes" to at least three of these questions, you have, in fact, found a hipster. Proceed with caution, don't mention that you use PCs, and keep quiet about your love of instant coffee.

• Does he have a mustache that was grown "ironically" because mustaches are out of date and uncool if grown to look cool?

• Ask her about her favorite rock band. If you have heard of the band, this person is *not* a hipster.

• Is he rail-thin, and the only thing skinnier than him is the pair of skinny jeans he's wearing?

• Does she wear earmuffs, a fur cap, or a scarf when it's not winter?

• Does he have a job in either the arts or at an espresso bar?

• Is she perpetually staring at an iPhone, Macbook laptop, or iPad, which she uses to blog or post pictures of herself in fur caps on Tumblr?

• Do a disproportionate number of her sentences begin with the words, "This reminds me of something Malcolm Gladwell says"?

• Does she have bangs?

• Do her clothes look like they were purchased at Goodwill or a thrift store, but when you ask, you find out that her sweater cost $250?

• Does he say he lives not in New York or Brooklyn, but in a specific, tiny neighborhood?

• When you ask him what he watched on TV last night, does he respond, "I don't own a TV"?

• Does she participate in an adult league of a children's sport (such as kickball) or a retro sport (such as roller derby)?

Opera most frequently performed at the Met: *La Bohème*.

OPENING LINES

Here are some great openings from some quintessentially New York books. How many have you read?

"Serene wasn't a word you could put to Brooklyn, New York. Especially in the summer of 1912. Somber, as a word, was better."

—Betty Smith, *A Tree Grows in Brooklyn*

"On the first day of my teaching career, I was almost fired for eating the sandwich of a high school boy."

—Frank McCourt, *Teacher Man*

"On a January evening of the early seventies, Christine Nilsson was singing *Faust* at the Academy of Music in New York."

—Edith Wharton, *The Age of Innocence*

"Amerigo Bonasera sat in New York Criminal Court Number 3 and waited for justice; vengeance on the men who had so cruelly hurt his daughter, who had tried to dishonor her."

—Mario Puzo, *The Godfather*

"I was leaning against the bar in a speakeasy on Fifty-Second Street, waiting for Nora to finish her Christmas shopping, when a girl got up from the table where she had been sitting with three other people and came over to me."

—Dashiell Hammett, *The Thin Man*

"On some nights, New York is as hot as Bangkok."

—Saul Bellow, *The Victim*

"My biggest problem is my brother, Farley Drexel Hatcher. Everybody calls him Fudge. I feel sorry for him if he's going to grow up with a name like Fudge, but I don't say a word. It's none of my business."

—Judy Blume, *Tales of a Fourth Grade Nothing*

"In those days, cheap apartments were almost impossible to find in Manhattan, so I had to move to Brooklyn."

—William Styron, *Sophie's Choice*

The Indians who sold Manhattan to Peter Minuit in 1626 were from what's now Brooklyn.

"I first met Perkus Tooth in an office. Not an office where he worked, though I was confused about this at the time. (Which is itself hardly an uncommon situation for me.)
—Jonathan Lethem, *Chronic City*

"Those who saw him hushed. On Church Street. Liberty. Cortlandt. West Street. Fulton. Vesey. It was a silence that heard itself, awful and beautiful. Some thought at first that it must have been a trick of the light, something to do with the weather, an accident of shadowfall. Others figured it might be the perfect city joke—stand around and point upward, until people gathered, tilted their heads, nodded, affirmed, until all were staring upward at nothing at all, like waiting for the end of a Lenny Bruce gag."
—Colum McCann, *Let the Great World Spin*

"Ok, don't panic. Don't *panic.* It's simply a question of being organized and staying calm and deciding what exactly I need to take. And then fitting it all in my suitcase."
—Sophie Kinsella, *Shopaholic Takes Manhattan*

"It was a queer, sultry summer, the summer they electrocuted the Rosenbergs, and I didn't know what I was doing in New York."
—Sylvia Plath, *The Bell Jar*

"If you really want to hear about it, the first thing you'll probably want to know is where I was born, and what my lousy childhood was like, and how my parents were occupied and all before they had me, and all that David Copperfield kind of crap, but I don't feel like going into it, if you want to know the truth."
—J. D. Salinger, *The Catcher in the Rye*

"Sometimes, it seems like all I ever do is lie."
—Meg Cabot, *The Princess Diaries*

"I am always drawn back to places where I have lived, the houses and their neighborhoods. For instance, there is a brownstone in the East Seventies where during the early years of the war, I had my first New York apartment."
—Truman Capote, *Breakfast at Tiffany's*

NYC borough with the most park acreage: Staten Island.

NYC: THEN AND NOW

1964 was a big year: President Lyndon Johnson delivered his first State of the Union address, the Beatles made their live TV debut on the Ed Sullivan Show, *and Jack Ruby was convicted of killing Lee Harvey Oswald. What was life like in New York City then, and how have things changed?*

THEN: A subway token cost 15¢.
NOW: Tokens have been replaced by Metrocards—the fare is $2.25...and rising.

THEN: A taxi ride from Midtown to LaGuardia Airport was about $4, not including tip or tolls. There was no partition between driver and passenger; you just reached over the front seat to hand your cash fare to the cabbie.

NOW: It costs about $30 to take the same ride. That includes the starting fare (called the "drop") of $2.50—just for getting into the cab. It doesn't include the night surcharge of 50¢ between 8 p.m. and 6 a.m., a peak-hour weekday surcharge of $1 after 4 p.m. and before 8 p.m., and a New York State surcharge of 50¢ per ride. And now there's a heavy-duty partition between passenger and driver, and you can pay your fare with a credit card.

THEN: If you wanted info on traffic, school closings, or other official city happenings, you dialed (dialed!) 999-1234 and got a recorded announcement.

NOW: Punch 311 into your cell (or go online) to navigate through dozens of options: Get the latest on traffic conditions and school closings, report a bad landlord, find a public beach, complain about a yellow cab, find out where to get a flu shot, carp about a New York City agency, or check up on just about anything else regarding the city.

THEN: At Barbetta, a swanky restaurant on West 46th Street, a full dinner ran you about $12 per person.
NOW: A full dinner at Barbetta costs upwards of $60 each.

Number of executions in NYC between 1639 and 1890 for "horse stealing": 5.

THEN: A double room at the Algonquin Hotel on West 44th Street cost between $14.50 and $20.50. The rooms were small and cozy, with large closets and modern bathrooms.

NOW: A double room at the Algonquin starts at $459.00. For this you get air conditioning, room service, bottled water, phones, high-speed Internet and WiFi, TV with remote, premium movie channels, radio, CD stereo, and an iPod dock.

THEN: At National Bowling on Eighth Avenue (open 24/7) the charge per game was 50¢. Bowling shoes were free on weekdays before 4 p.m. and 20¢ a pair at other times.

NOW: At Bowlmor Lanes at 110 University Place in Manhattan (hours vary), the charge per person per game is $12.95. Shoe rental: $6...all the time.

THEN: The White Horse Tavern on Hudson Street at West 11th was a bit of Britain in New York, and very famous as the former hangout of hard-drinking Welsh poet Dylan Thomas. A Black-and-Tan, an ale, or a porter ran you 30¢. And sandwiches were about 50¢.

NOW: Same tavern, same address, but a Black-and-Tan is $6.50, an ale is $6.00, and the sandwiches cost between $6.25 and $7.95.

THEN: The Bronx Zoo charged 25¢ admission on Tuesdays, Wednesdays, and Thursdays; it was free the rest of the week and on holidays.

NOW: Admission is $16 for adults, $12 for children, and $14 for seniors—every day except Wednesday, when admission is donation-based.

THEN: At Canine Styles on Lexington Ave., your pooch got a basic grooming (including shampoo and pedi) for $13 and up, depending on FiFi's size and the condition of her hair.

NOW: At Biscuits & Bath on the Upper East Side, a full grooming includes bath, brushing, blowout, ear cleaning, and pedi. And it all costs about $85...for a small dog.

For more NYC: Then and Now, *turn to page 241.*

Four of the five tallest buildings currently standing in NYC were built in the 1930s.

WILD WEATHER

New Yorkers—whether they live upstate or in the city—aren't strangers to extreme weather. But these storms tested the mettle of even the hardiest Empire State residents.

THE GREAT WHITE HURRICANE, 1888
On March 11, 1888, a light rain began to fall in New York City. The temperature had been in the 50s for several days, unseasonably warm, and the forecast called for some cloudiness and then clearing skies. Forecasters couldn't have been more wrong: Over the next 24 hours, the temperature dropped more than 30 degrees, and 10 inches of snow fell. By March 13, the city was buried under more than three feet of snow. And it wasn't just the city that got socked, either: Albany recorded four feet, and Saratoga Springs nearly five.

In New York City, the heavy snow knocked down power lines and telegraph cables throughout the boroughs. Drifts rose to the third stories of some houses—one man from Long Island told an incredible tale of snowshoeing to a nearby store on drifts that were 60 feet high. Some residents even claimed that the snow drifts were so high they didn't fully melt until July. In another legendary story, a man said he'd fallen into a snowdrift and hit his head on the hoof of a frozen horse. The gash on his temple was proof, he said, that he was the only man ever to be "kicked by a dead horse."

Transportation all along the eastern seaboard came to a stand-still, stranding 15,000 people, and about 400 people died by the time the two-day storm was over. But New York and other eastern cities learned some valuable lessons: Many rebuilt their telegraph lines underground, started thinking about subways, and began using weather balloons to help make forecasting more accurate.

THE GREAT FLOOD, 1913

The winter of 1913 was warmer than usual all across the United States. In New York, the towns of Albany and Troy saw many January and February days with highs at least 10 degrees above normal...the upper 30s and 40s, even some 50s. That meant rain fell instead of snow. The result: clogged rivers.

New York's police officers were first issued guns in 1887.

By late March, the ground across the eastern United States was saturated, and much of Ohio and Pennsylvania had already seen severe flooding Then from March 23–27, rain fell nonstop across much of New York State. River towns from Olean to Albany found themselves under 10 feet of water. Powerlines snapped, and rescuers faced the daunting challenge of reaching stranded people via boat because so many roads had washed away. In all the affected areas, more than 300 people died and nearly 65,000 were displaced.

THE GREAT NEW ENGLAND HURRICANE, 1938

In the fall of 1938, a junior meteorologist with the U.S. Weather Bureau (now the National Weather Service) tracked a storm out of the eastern Atlantic for more than a week and became sure it was headed for New England. But popular thinking at the time was that hurricanes "never" hit New England—the water in the northern Atlantic was supposedly too cold to sustain a tropical storm. So when the junior weatherman brought his concerns to his boss, he was told not to bother sending out an alert. Big mistake: The Category 3 hurricane crashed into Long Island without warning at about 2:30 p.m. on September 21.

Forty-foot waves slammed into the south shore, winds roared at 120 mph with 180 mph gusts, and nearly 50 houses were immediately washed away. The stormed moved fast; by late afternoon, it had blown into Connecticut and then on to Massachusetts. By the time it ended later that night, more than 700 people had died and 23,000 homes were destroyed or damaged. Clean-up estimates reached $300 million (more than $4 billion today), making the September 1938 hurricane, according to the History Channel, "the most destructive storm to strike the region in the 20th century."

* * *

TRINITY CHURCH CEMETERY

Some of the world's most famous people are buried in the Trinity Church Cemetery at Broadway and Wall Street, including naturalist John James Audubon, Founding Father Alexander Hamilton, writers Ralph Ellison and Clement Clarke Moore, actor Jerry Orbach, and industrialist John Jacob Astor. There's also a headstone ready for a future "resident": former mayor Ed Koch.

THE BORSCHT BELT

The Jewish Alps, the Sour Cream Sierras, the Borscht Belt—those were just a few names for a stretch of upstate New York that, every year, turned into one big summer vacation spot…just for Jews.

HEAD FOR THE HILLS

From the 1920s through the 1960s, a Jewish summer community of resort hotels, bungalow colonies, camps, and boarding houses flourished about 100 miles northwest of New York City, in the foothills of the Catskill Mountains. Fleeing the hot, humid city, some families went for a week or two to be wined, dined, and entertained at the fancy hotels. Others rented inexpensive bungalows—small cottages where mothers, children, and grandparents usually stayed for the whole summer and fathers traveled up from the city for the weekends. Even working-class families could vacation in the Catskills, renting simple rooms in a *kuchalein* ("cook by yourself")—a boarding house with a communal kitchen. The families were usually of Eastern European descent, all were Jewish, and because *borscht* (a kind of cold beet soup) was popular with Jews from that part of Europe, the whole area became known as the Borscht Belt.

The Catskills, beautiful and easily accessible by train or car, were a complete contrast to the city: You could see the stars, breathe fresh air, swim, and play on real grass. But most important, the Borscht Belt was free of the anti-Semitism that was common in American society at that time. Jews owned and ran the hotels, and Jewish vacationers could feel safe, comfortable, and relaxed. There were no signs saying "No Hebrews Accommodated," as there were in other parts of the state. Jews went to the Borscht Belt because they knew they'd be welcome there.

BOOK ME A ROOM

The cottages in the bungalow colonies were usually single-floor, white-painted boxes, with one or two bedrooms, one bath, a kitchen that also served as a dining/living room, and a front porch. Bungalows were clustered around oval plots of grass or laid out in a street-like grid that gave them the feel of the suburbs, complete

---

First American to make his living solely as a writer: Washington Irving.

with lawn furniture in the tiny front yards. By the 1950s, most colonies had day camps, swimming pools, and a small store, but not much else. The residents made their own entertainment—birthday parties, dances, barbecues, and card games.

BETTER BORSCHT

The hotels were another story entirely. A list compiled in 1991 by the *Sullivan County Democrat* documented more than 900 hotels that dotted the Borscht Belt over the decades, many full of amenities. But it's the grand hotels like the Nevele, the Concord, the Tamarack Lodge, and Grossinger's that are most remembered for their kosher feasts, fantastic facilities, and stellar entertainment.

At its height, Grossinger's in Liberty, New York, spanned 1,200 acres with 35 buildings and housed 150,000 guests per year. It had an indoor pool, an outdoor pool, a lake, a golf course, bridle paths, tennis courts, a softball diamond, a nightclub, several dining rooms, a social director, an athletics director, and the Eddie Cantor Playhouse. Grossinger's also had its own airplane landing strip, its own post office, and in 1952 it became the first hotel to offer artificial snow for skiing.

The food served at Grossinger's was legendary. Adhering to strictly *kosher* guidelines—meaning that dairy and red meat or products never appeared in the same meal—Grossinger's required two separate kitchens with separate cleaning equipment, dishes, and silver. Breakfast (16 kinds of smoked fish) and lunch (cheese blintzes were the favorite) came from the "dairy" kitchen; dinner came from the "meat" kitchen. And guests who didn't like any of the evening's offerings could always ask for something special. Mrs. Grossinger's mantra was "Never let anyone go hungry."

As for the entertainment, it was different each night, starting with "casual" Mondays, when the staff and guests performed in talent shows and played raucous games. The rest of the week featured productions from traveling theater groups, variety shows put on by New York performers, and sports competitions against teams from other hotels. Saturday night brought special "star-studded extravaganzas," often with big show business acts. And there was always dancing to the house band.

TRAGEDY TOMORROW, COMEDY TONIGHT

Entertainment was always one of the big draws in the Borscht Belt. In the early days, a resort's social director (called a *tummler*) was expected to write and produce shows, as well as to sing, dance, act, stage-manage, do lighting and scenery, and emcee.

By the 1940s, though, customers were more demanding, and the hotels hired pros to write and produce shows starring professional singers, comedians, and chorus girls. The bigger hotels had nightclubs and small orchestras. But comedy was king at most of the Borscht Belt resorts, and the list of famous comedians who got their start in the Catskills is long and impressive: Sid Caesar, Jerry Lewis, Joan Rivers, Jonathan Winters, Jackie Mason, Milton Berle, Phyllis Diller, Carl Reiner, Mel Brooks, Robert Klein, Woody Allen, Billy Crystal, and dozens more.

When they performed in the Catskills, these comedians catered specifically to their audiences: Their humor was full of Jewish cultural references and punctuated with Yiddishisms. They riffed, often self-deprecatingly, about nagging wives, stingy husbands, misbehaving children, dodgy business deals, physical ailments (gastrointestinal problems loomed large), and a host of injustices that Jews suffered in mainstream America. Few of the performers referred openly to anti-Semitism, but much of their humor alluded to it. Ironically, as these Borscht Belt comedians became more and more popular and began to do their acts in mainstream venues, Jewish humor became part of American humor—and helped non-Jews to better understand and empathize with the Jewish experience.

THE LAST DANCE

By the end of the 1970s, the Borscht Belt was fading into history. Air travel had become more affordable and vacationers could go wherever they wanted: Las Vegas, Mexico, or Europe. Many women had jobs by then, too, and fewer moms could (or wanted to) spend whole summers stashed away in an upstate bungalow. And with the grip of anti-Semitism loosening, there was less demand for safe, separate vacation spots.

By the 1980s, most of the hotels had gone out of business. A few were sold, but many were abandoned and simply fell into

---

...the Civil War Draft Riots of 1863, with more than 120 civilian deaths.

disrepair. Eventually the land and buildings were bought for use as rehab centers, special-needs schools, college dorms, ashrams, and new housing developments. But some Orthodox Jews began to move into the area, taking over the old bungalow colonies for summer or year-round communities. Still, it's a far cry from the prosperous, thriving resort area it once was. The Borscht Belt, it seems, is gone for good.

*For quotes by some of the Borscht Belt comedians,
turn to page 296.*

* * *

GOVERN-MENTAL

Until the mid-1980s, New Yorkers could tell what borough they were in based on the colors of the street signs:

- **Manhattan and Staten Island:** Yellow background with black lettering.
- **Brooklyn:** Black background with white lettering.
- **Queens:** White background with blue lettering.
- **Bronx:** Blue background with white lettering.

But in 1985, the federal government said that green was the easiest color for the eye to see, so by law, all American street signs had to be green with white lettering. New York City made the change. Then, in 2010, the city embarked on yet another street-sign initiative, this time converting any signs currently in all capital letters into lowercase with initial caps for each new word. With more than 250,000 street signs in the five boroughs, each costing $110 to replace, the expense is estimated at over $27 million. New Yorkers who think that's a waste of money can thank the federal government, which passed a law requiring that all American street signs be changed again. According to the Department of Transportation, the lowercase letters are easier to read, so they will decrease the number of accidents. New York and other cities protested, saying "While the mixed-case words might be easier to read, the amount of improvement in legibility did not justify the cost." The feds refused to relent but did give cities until 2018 to make the change.

Average number of costume changes a Rockette makes during the annual Christmas show: 9.

CITY CINEMA

Lots of movies are set in New York, but they aren't all shot there. Here's a sampling of those real city movies.

King Kong (1933, 1976, and 2005)

The Lost Weekend (1945)

Kiss of Death (1947)

Miracle on 34th Street (1947 and 1994)

Cry of the City (1948)

The Sleeping City (1950)

Sweet Smell of Success (1957)

The Apartment (1960)

Breakfast at Tiffany's (1961)

Barefoot in the Park (1967)

Midnight Cowboy (1969)

The Panic in Needle Park (1971)

Plaza Suite (1971)

The Godfather (1972)

Serpico (1973)

The Taking of Pelham 1 2 3 (1974 and 2009)

The French Connection (1971)

The Lords of Flatbush (1974)

Dog Day Afternoon (1975)

Taxi Driver (1976)

Annie Hall (1977)

Saturday Night Fever (1977)

An Unmarried Woman (1978)

All That Jazz (1979)

Manhattan (1979)

Fame (1980 and 2009)

The King of Comedy (1982)

The Cotton Club (1984)

Brighton Beach Memoirs (1986)

Moonstruck (1987)

Wall Street (1987)

Coming to America (1988)

Crossing Delancey (1988)

Working Girl (1988)

Do the Right Thing (1989)

New York Stories (1989)

When Harry Met Sally (1989)

Goodfellas (1990)

A Bronx Tale (1993)

The Usual Suspects (1995)

You've Got Mail (1998)

Big Daddy (1999)

Autumn in New York (2000)

Maid in Manhattan (2002)

The Royal Tenenbaums (2001)

The Producers (2005)

The Squid and the Whale (2005)

Night at the Museum (2006)

Inside Man (2006)

Doubt (2008)

Pride and Glory (2008)

Sex and the City (2008)

City Island (2009)

The Extra Man (2010)

The Adjustment Bureau (2011)

New York has been the most populous city in the U.S. since 1810.

THE GREAT STATEN ISLAND GAMBLE

Fact or fiction: The borough of Staten Island belongs to the state of New York because of a boat race in the 17th century. Well...

THE LEGEND

The story is told as often as the one about Dutch settlers buying Manhattan for $24 (which isn't true). It goes like this: In 1667, England's King Charles II and his warships had just booted the Dutch from their colony of New Netherlands (now Manhattan), ending the Second Anglo-Dutch War. To mark the occasion, the king gave the territory to the Duke of York to govern. But squabbling broke out between English settlers in the new colony and those who lived in New Jersey. The topic: Who owned Staten Island? Both sides claimed the 60-square-mile gateway to the Hudson River.

To settle the matter, the Duke suggested a bet: One of the king's ships would sail around the island. If it could circumnavigate the 35 miles of waterfront within 24 hours, the island would belong to New York. If not, it would go to New Jersey.

ROUGH WATERS

By modern standards, sailing around the island might not seem difficult, but stiff Hudson River currents, shifting winds, and tidal forces from the ocean—plus the fact that ships were slower back then—made it a true challenge. Determined to win, the Duke tapped Captain Christopher Billopp, a distinguished officer who commanded a small sailing ship called the *Bentley*, for the job. Billopp realized that he was up against the odds, so he made some modifications to his ship—in particular, he mounted empty barrels on the deck to catch the breeze and harness more wind power, giving the vessel a little boost.

At the appointed time (a specific date is never given), Billopp and the *Bentley* set off and, in just over 23 hours, completed the circumnavigation. New York had won Staten Island.

STATES' RIGHTS

Nowadays, most historians consider the story to be nothing more than a tall tale repeated by Staten Islanders in need of a local legend to boost their standings among the five boroughs. Carlotta DeFillo of the Staten Island Historical Society says, "It's a lovely, persistent myth, but it is a myth...apparently, we were never part of New Jersey. Jersey tried to claim [Staten Island] but never succeeded."

The office of Mayor Michael Bloomberg did a little research, though, and discovered that the story had appeared in print as early as 1873. And in the 140 years since, several reputable newspapers and authors has repeated it. Still, no one could say for sure that it happened...or didn't. So Bloomberg decided to end all the speculation. On June 2, 2007, the city held the "unofficial Staten Island Decision Race." Ten sailboats (five from New York and five from New Jersey) sailed from the North Cove Marina in lower Manhattan's Battery Park, around a buoy near Staten Island, and back again (seven miles total) in an effort to determine once and for all whom the island really belonged to. Fortunately, no one in the borough had to shift allegiance to the Garden State—a boat called the *Exuberance*, which hailed from the Bronx, took first place.

THE CAPTAIN'S PART

Regardless of whether or not the original race ever happened, Captain Christopher Billopp was very real, and he played a huge part in the history of New York City. An officer with the 17th-century Royal Navy, he built a 1,163-acre estate on the southern tip of Staten Island, in what is today the Tottenville section, and named it the Bentley Manor after his ship.

Almost a century after the supposed Staten Island sailing race, Billopp's great grandson—also named Christopher Billopp—owned Bentley Manor in the days before the American Revolution. The younger Billopp was a loyalist who renounced the Americans and maintained ties to Great Britain. On September 11, 1776, Benjamin Franklin, John Adams, and Edward Rutledge rowed across the Hudson to the manor at the invitation of Lord Richard Howe, commander-in-chief of British forces in North America. Howe hoped to bring the American Revolution to a quick end by brokering a deal with the three delegates. (The Continental Congress had voted to break away from England the previous July.) Negotiations lasted for three hours, but the rebels ultimately declined the offer and rowed back to the mainland. As a result, the American Revolution lasted another seven years.

After the war, the new state government seized Bentley Manor. In 1926, a developer sought to tear down the stone house, but a nonprofit organization stepped in to save it. The renamed "Conference House" became a National Historic Landmark in 1966. Today, it is the southernmost point on New York State.

* * *

TOO CLEVER FOR WORDS

The *New York Times* crossword puzzle has long been famous for its clever clues. Here are six of our favorites—the question mark is a clue that the answer is a pun, and the number tells you how many letters are in the answer. Can you puzzle them out?

1. Northern hemisphere? (5)

2. Army threats? (6)

3. Pat on the buns? (4)

4. Life preserver? (3)

5. Jam ingredients? (5)

6. Sentence structure? (4)

Answers

1. Igloo: It's shaped like a hemisphere and, obviously, appears in the north. 2. Octopi: They have a lot of arms. 3. Oleo: "Oleo" is margarine; you put a pat of it on a bun. 4. Bio: A "bio" tells the story of someone's life and preserves it for posterity. 5. Autos: These make traffic jams. 6. Cell: A "cell" is where a criminal goes after sentencing.

ANDREW WHO?

*If not for Andrew Haswell Green, the five boroughs
might never have become one city.*

THE ROBERT MOSES OF THE 19TH CENTURY
According to Manhattan Borough Historian Michael Mis-
cione, lawyer and city planner Andrew Haswell Green was
a "forgotten visionary [who] didn't have just one moment of glory.
He was literally the Robert Moses of the 19th century." Green not
only had a vision of what New York City could be, but—like New
York's "master builder" Robert Moses in the 20th century—he
championed and oversaw projects that changed the face of the city.
Yet even though Green did so much for New York, he's mostly unknown. In fact, until the recent decision to turn a section of Manhattan along the East River into a park named in his honor, Green
was commemorated only by a portrait in City Hall and a stone
bench on a hill in the upper reaches of Central Park.

WHO WAS THAT MASKED MAN?
Green was born into a prominent family in Worcester, Massachusetts, in 1820. He came to New York in 1835 and joined the law
firm of the up-and-coming Samuel Tilden, a reform-minded and
politically connected man who became governor of the state in
1874 and ran for president in 1876. As for Green, he never married. Instead, he poured all his energy into improving New York
City. In 1857, he got a job that launched the career he would be
known for: He was appointed president of the commission that
would oversee the construction of Central Park.

In 1859, the Central Park Commission became the city's first
comprehensive planning group, a perfect fit for Green. He believed
in looking to the future, and in his view, the best future for New
York lay in consolidation: merging Manhattan with the surrounding counties and unincorporated lands—southern Westchester
(the Bronx), Queens, Kings (Brooklyn), and Richmond (Staten Island)—to form one Greater New York City. He first proposed this
consolidation in 1868, but three decades passed before it actually
happened.

The first gold tooth in the U.S. was developed and used by a dentist in Rochester.

THE GREENING OF NEW YORK

During the 30 years that passed before consolidation, Green was busy with other projects that reflected his wide-ranging ambitions for the city. Under his leadership...

• Riverside Park, Fort Washington Park, and Morningside Park were created.

• The city implemented an improved street grid above 155th Street so the Bronx would be more accessible (Green was thinking ahead to consolidation).

• A bridge was built over the Harlem River.

• The American Museum of Natural History and the Metropolitan Museum of Art opened.

• The New York Public Library opened.

Green also served as chairman of the board of directors of the New York Society for the Prevention of Cruelty to Children. There was hardly a New York pie he didn't have a finger in, but the one he cared about most was consolidation.

WELCOME TO GREATER NEW YORK

Green saw a consolidated Greater New York as a way for the city to get more economic and cultural power. The upstate politicians saw it exactly the same way—but they didn't like it. They worried that a downstate stronghold might turn out to have an intrusive amount of influence on state politics. Still, Green forged ahead. In 1894, he polled voters in Manhattan and its surrounding areas. A few places (like Flushing, Queens, and some parts of Brooklyn) voted against, but most people were overwhelmingly in favor of becoming boroughs (self-governing townships) of the new New York City.

In the face of all this support for consolidation, the state legislature voted it into law. On New Year's Day 1898, New York became one city comprising five boroughs. It was now the second largest city in the world, with a population of 3 million. Only London—with 4.5 million people—topped it.

NO GOOD DEED GOES UNPUNISHED

President Theodore Roosevelt called Green "the Father of Greater New York," but not everyone held such a high opinion of him. On

November 13, 1903, the 83-year-old civic leader was shot to death in front of his home at 91 Park Avenue by Cornelius M. Williams, a 43-year-old African American. *The New York Times* headline read "Andrew H. Green Murdered by Negro…Assailant Probably Insane…Believed His Victim Had Caused Him to Be Dispossessed—Fired Five Times, and Death Was Instantaneous."

Williams claimed that Green was protecting a woman who had slandered him and caused him to be expelled from his church. Williams also insisted that Green had ordered Williams to be thrown out of his home. None of it appeared to be true, and friends and reporters speculated that Williams might have been gunning for an entirely different Andrew Green. Flags were lowered to half-mast at City Hall, and the whole city mourned.

BURIED TREASURE

Andrew H. Green was buried in his hometown of Worcester, Massachusetts. His fortune was distributed among at least 18 relatives, but his possessions were put away at the family estate. When the estate was sold in 1905, Green's nephew Nathan transferred the boxes of his uncle's belongings into storage, where they remained until 1947, when Nathan's son tried to sell the items to Yale University. Apparently, he told curators at the school's archive, "I have an enormous pile of trash here that might be of interest to you." Yale didn't want it, though, so the boxes went to another family member, Nathan's granddaughter Julia, who never opened them.

After Julia Green died, the boxes went to her nephew and niece—who *did* open them and discovered that Andrew Green had been quite a collector. The boxes included thousands of items— valuable American paintings, rare books, Tiffany silver, antique toys, stamps, coins, and pieces of correspondence, including a collection of presidential letters. One of the rarest items was a copy of George Washington's will, printed in Worcester in 1800; only 14 copies are known to exist.

* * *

The narrowest house in New York is located in Greenwich Village—it's only 8 feet, 7 inches wide and was once the home of poet Edna St. Vincent Millay.

THE DONALD SPEAKS

Deep thoughts from Donald Trump.

"As long as you're going to be thinking anyway, think big."

"I could never have imagined that firing 67 people on national television would actually make me more popular, especially with the younger generation."

"Everything in life is luck."

"I try to learn from the past, but I plan for the future by focusing exclusively on the present. That's were the fun is."

"Anyone who thinks my story is anywhere near over is sadly mistaken."

"I wasn't satisfied just to earn a good living. I was looking to make a statement."

"If you're interested in 'balancing' work and pleasure, stop trying to balance them. Instead make your work more pleasurable."

"In the end, you're measured not by how much you undertake but by what you finally accomplish."

"Money was never a big motivation for me, except as a way to keep score. The real excitement is playing the game."

"Part of being a winner is knowing when enough is enough. Sometimes you have to give up the fight and walk away, and move on to something that's more productive."

"It's tangible, it's solid, it's beautiful. It's artistic, from my standpoint, and I just love real estate."

"Sometimes your best investments are the ones you don't make."

"If you have to lie, cheat, and steal, you're just not doing it right. My career is a model of tough, fair dealing and fantastic success—without shortcuts."

"The final key to the way I promote is bravado. I play to people's fantasies. People may not always think big themselves, but they can still get very excited by those who do. That's why a little hyperbole never hurts."

New York Harbor is the world's southernmost fjord.

TAKE 'EM TO BELLEVUE

For a hospital whose name became synonymous with big-city healthcare, Bellevue came from humble beginnings. Here's the story of New York's oldest public hospital.

WHAT'S SO SPECIAL ABOUT IT?

New York City has 11 "municipal hospitals," meaning ones that are run by the city and open to the public. Bellevue Hospital Center, a 25-story mega-facility at 462 First Avenue on Manhattan's East Side, is the go-to hospital for residents of the official Bellevue district—from the East River to Sixth Avenue; from East Houston Street to 42nd Street. No one who lives in the district can be denied medical treatment there—unlike at private hospitals, Bellevue is free if you can't pay, and your ability to pay is investigated *after* you've been admitted. The hospital has an attending physician staff of 1,200, and more than 500 residents and interns. Each year, those doctors treat a staggering 600,000 people.

Bellevue is the place where injured police officers and firefighters are taken, and the designated medical facility for dignitaries visiting New York, including the president of the United States. And after 9/11, Bellevue became the primary center for treating survivors and for identifying those who had lost their lives. It also has a center for brain and spinal cord injuries, a Level 1 trauma center (the highest level of surgical care for trauma patients), a heart station for cardiac emergencies, and a center that specializes in limb reattachment.

BELLEVUE BEGINNINGS

Bellevue's history goes back to 1736, when it was founded on the lot that City Hall now stands on. It started as the city's first almshouse and a six-bed infirmary for its neediest people—orphans, the elderly, the blind and disabled, the insane, and the sick. In 1816, the almshouse moved to new buildings at the site of a former farm called Bellevue (French for "beautiful view"). The spot was on 27th Street near the East River, alongside the city's "pesthouse," or fever hospital. The whole complex became known as the Bellevue

---

In 1949 Syracuse became home to the country's first drive-through bank.

Institution. By the mid-1800s, it also included a penitentiary, a school, and the city's first morgue. Gradually over the next 25 years, everything but the medical facilities were moved to other locations; all that remained was Bellevue Hospital.

Public hospitals were required to accept the poor (private hospitals were allowed to turn them away), so it wasn't long before Bellevue was overrun with sick patients...mostly destitute immigrants from Europe who lived in Lower East Side tenements where disease ran rampant. Bellevue itself was infested with rats and lice, afflicted with epidemics, and short of beds, but by the mid-1850s, it was handling 4,000 to 5,000 patients a year. Still, it was Bellevue's mission to serve the needs of the public: In 1867 it opened one of the nation's first outpatient departments and, in 1874, the country's first children's clinic. In 1876 Bellevue established the nation's first emergency pavilion, an area removed from the main building that functioned like a modern emergency room.

AT HOME AND AWAY
When World War I broke out, Bellevue was one of only three city hospitals (the others were New York Hospital and Presbyterian Hospital) asked by the American Red Cross to send teams of doctors and nurses overseas to treat soldiers. Bellevue put its teams together and got them in the field so quickly and efficiently that its unit was awarded the name Base Hospital Unit #1.

At the same time, Bellevue was coping with a terrible disaster at home: the influenza epidemic of 1918–19. The outbreak killed 33,000 New Yorkers in six months. Every hospital in the city was inundated with flu victims, but Bellevue bore the heaviest load since it had to accept every patient who came to its doors. The facility was so overcrowded that cots filled all available space—in the pediatric ward, three children lay in every bed. And even the dedicated staff couldn't hold off the inevitable deaths—sometimes more than 60 per day.

AHEAD OF ITS TIME
In the early 20th century, very few women worked in hospitals in the United States, but Bellevue, always short of staff, became a pioneer in hiring women. In 1913, four female graduates of Cornell Medical College applied for internships. The young women not

In its 7,485 performances, the Broadway musical *Cats*...

only scored high on their exams, they also actively lobbied support, personally visiting doctors at Bellevue and attending social activities where they could meet city leaders and hospital board members. All four were awarded internships, and by 1920, Bellevue had 12 women on staff. It was almost 10 more years before any other major New York hospital even accepted female interns.

VISITING THE LOONY BIN

Before the early 20th century, psychiatric wings in hospitals, known as "lunatic asylums," were usually crowded, dirty places where patients were treated like prisoners, often starved, and sometimes tortured. One of the things that always set Bellevue apart were its psychiatric facilities. In the 1930s, the hospital opened a brand-new, eight-story red brick building on First Avenue between 29th and 30th Streets to house its own lunatic asylum. According to a 1939 guide to New York City, behind the building's iron gates, "the alcoholics, the sexually unbalanced, the hysterical, and the alleged insane are under care…The 'disturbed,' or violent, wards utilize none of the old-fashioned, inhumane methods that some hospitals still employ for pacifying psychotics." That facility became famous—and infamous—in the lore of New York City: Mark David Chapman (John Lennon's assassin) and playwright Eugene O'Neill were both committed there, and in the 1947 movie *Miracle on 34th Street*, it's the psychiatric hospital where the cops took Kris Kringle (after he claimed he was the real Santa Claus).

In spite of—or perhaps because of—its stellar reputation, within months of Bellevue Psychiatric Hospital's opening in the 1930s, it was bursting at the seams with patients, and that led to problems. By the mid-1960s, a former hospital attendant revealed that only four nurses cared for 800 patients at a time and that abuse of inmates was routine. In October 1966, the *World-Journal Tribune* published an article detailing the horrible conditions in the psych ward, called "A Night at Bellevue: They Scream Behind Bars." Still, anyone who couldn't pay and "went crazy" in Manhattan—whether freaking out from drugs or alcohol, threatening to harm themselves or someone else, hallucinating, or just acting too weird for others to handle—was sent to Bellevue Psych.

The allegations of abuse continued through the 1970s. In 1984, the psych ward was moved to 462 First Avenue, where patients had access to better facilities, more staff, and more space, and the psychiatric services steadily improved. The old building became a shelter for the homeless, a move that was extremely unpopular with the neighborhood residents. Finally, in 2008, the city put out a call for redevelopment proposals. Officials wanted to shut down the shelter and turn the old Bellevue building into a hotel—and proposed moving the shelter facilities to Crown Heights, Brooklyn. Bellevue's local community loved the plan, but the Crown Heights community hated it. Crown Heights won the round: The city gave up the plan, and the shelter remained—fitting, some say, for an old hospital building that made a name for itself by treating the poor.

* * *

THE INSIDE SCOOP ON 30 ROCK

• The sitcom *30 Rock* tells the story of Liz Lemon, the head writer of a sketch comedy TV show...just like Tina Fey, the show's creator, writer, and star, who used to work as a head writer on *Saturday Night Live*.

• Although the show is set at 30 Rockefeller Plaza—the site of the *Saturday Night Live* studios—most of its interiors are filmed at Silvercup Studios in Queens.

• When she came up with the idea for the show, Tina Fey didn't intend to star in it herself. She changed her mind because NBC insisted that she take the part.

• Like Liz Lemon, Fey's first name is Elizabeth—Elizabeth Stamatina Fey. Her mother is Greek, and Stamatina is a traditional Greek name, meaning "one who stops."

• Fey's husband, Jeff Richmond, composes all the music for the show.

• In 2009 *30 Rock* received 22 Emmy nominations, the most for a comedy show in a single year.

BETWEEN THE LIONS

*Climb the steps between "Patience" and "Fortitude," and you'll
find yourself in one of the most famous, important, and
comprehensive libraries in the world.*

A TALE OF TWO LIBRARIES

In the late 19th century, New York was the second-largest city in the world (London was first), and many people realized that soon it would be a cultural capital, too. One of them was former New York governor Samuel J. Tilden, who left a $2.4 million trust to "establish and maintain a free library and reading room in the city of New York." The city already had two major libraries—the Astor and the Lenox—but both were research libraries, both were having financial difficulties, and only the Astor was open to the public. Seeing an opportunity, Tilden's trustees came up with a plan to combine the Astor and Lenox Libraries and the Tilden Trust to form what would become the New York Public Library (NYPL, or "nipple" to devoted users). The plan was finalized on May 23, 1895, and Dr. John Shaw Billings, an eminent librarian and surgeon, became the new director.

HOUSE OF BOOKS

Billings was a visionary too—he wanted a spectacular building that could house the riches of the Astor and Lenox Libraries, while offering comfortable facilities for scholars and ordinary readers alike. The chosen site was the former Croton Reservoir, a two-block area on Fifth Avenue between 40th and 42nd Streets that had once held most of the freshwater used in the city. The new library would have seven floors, a huge reading room, and 30,000 reference books. It would also have the world's fastest book-to-user delivery system: A patron would send a call slip to the "closed stacks," or storage rooms, downstairs via a pneumatic tube, and in a matter of minutes, the book would be sent up to the reading room via dumbwaiters.

For two years, 500 workers dismantled the old reservoir and prepared the site. Construction finally began on May 1902, and the official dedication took place on May 23, 1911. Total cost: $9 million. On May 24, when the library first opened its doors, more than 30,000 New Yorkers rushed in.

NYPL FACTS AND FIGURES

Over the years, NYPL has racked up an impressive list of stats. Here are some of the most important.

- In-person visits per year: 18 million
- Online visits per year: 24 million
- Only boroughs not included in the NYPL system: Brooklyn and Queens. (They have their own independent library systems.)
- Total items in the branch and research libraries: 51.6 million
- Items in the Photography Collection: 500,000
- Items in the Map Division: 433,000 sheet maps, and 20,000 books and atlases published between the 15th and 21st centuries
- Historic menus: 26,000
- Historic U.S. postcards: more than 100,000
- Categories the online and phone reference system ASK NYPL will not answer questions about: crosswords or contests, children's homework, and philosophical speculation

GIMME SHELTER

Anyone who has visited a branch library on a sweltering day (or a frigid one) knows that the NYPL is a haven. Libraries, as former head of NYPL Paul LeClerc said in 2008, "are the only indoor communal spaces left in New York." People with no air conditioning cool off there; homeless men and women warm up. But there are rules. Anyone who visits a NYPL branch is expected to adhere to the following:

- You may not wash your clothes or bathe in the restrooms.
- No loud talking on your cell phone.
- Don't bring knives, guns, or any other weapons to the library.
- No obscene gestures, abusive language, or lewd behavior.
- No shopping carts, bicycles, or scooters.
- No napping in the library or sleeping in the entryway.
- No dropping your kid at the library and forgetting to pick her up.
- No hacking or using the Internet for any illegal activity.
- You must wear clothes and shoes, and you can't smell bad.

THERE GOES THE NEIGHBORHOOD: STATEN ISLAND

Before Staten Island became known for its landfill,
it was known for its trees. (Yes...really.)

• The Lenape Indians who originally lived in the area that's now **Staten Island** called it *Monacnong* ("Enchanted Woods"). And in 1776, a British soldier referred to the future borough as the "paradise of the world" because its forests were so beautiful. But the Dutch who settled there in the 1600s had already called it *Staaten Eylandt*, after the name of the Dutch parliament (the Staaten-Generaal). And that's the name that stuck.

• In 1872, the American Linoleum Manufacturing Company moved into Travisville and changed the community's name to Linoleumville. ("Travis" was the last name of a man who owned a lot of land in the area.) By the time the factory closed in 1931, residents were tired of—and embarrassed by—their town's name, so they voted on another name change—to **Travis**. Only four people (out of more than 300) voted to keep Linoleumville.

• The neighborhood of **Bulls Head** gets its name from the Bull's Head Tavern that stood at the intersection of Richmond Avenue and Victory Boulevard. During the Revolutionary War, British supporters used the tavern as a base of operations.

• **Arthur Kill** is the name of the tidal strait that separates Staten Island from New Jersey. It comes from a Dutch term, *achter kill*, which means "back channel," because the waterway is essentially "behind" Staten Island. (*Kille* is Dutch for "water channel" or "riverbed.") When the English moved into the area, they kept the term but anglicized the spelling.

...is 600 Madison Avenue in Manhattan, between 57th and 58th Street.

SHOP TILL YOU DROP

Once upon a time, no self-respecting New York lady went shopping without donning white gloves, a fancy chapeau, and her nicest dress…while the stores duked it out for her money.

IN THE BEGINNING

In 1856, an Irish immigrant named Alexander Turney (A. T.) Stewart opened the first department store in New York City…A.T. Stewart at 280 Broadway. Inside the building—nicknamed the "Marble Palace" because of a showy exterior that featured expensive marble and Italian architecture—shoppers could find all kinds of European goods at decent prices. Best of all, everything was in one place, so they didn't have to run around town to dozens of shops.

Within a few years, A.T. Stewart was joined by several new department stores, and the section of Broadway between Eighth and 23rd streets became known as "Ladies' Mile" because so many of the stores catered to women. Shopping on the Ladies' Mile was a fantastic and fancy affair: Stores lured women with marble floors, personal shoppers, and high tea on mezzanines overlooking the stores.

AND STEWART BEGAT…

The owners of the stores on the Ladies' Mile soon realized, though, that uptown was where the money was. The city's most fashionable families lived closer to Central Park, so New York's high-class shopping hub gradually shifted north, until it centered around Fifth Avenue between Midtown and the park. The quintessentially New York department stores that lined the streets helped make Fifth Avenue (and Park, Melrose, and Lexington to the east) some of the "most expensive streets in the world":

• **Lord & Taylor** was the first store on Fifth Avenue to install an elevator and the first to set up grand Christmas displays in its windows each holiday season. Technically, this store opened before A.T. Stewart, but it sold only a handful of specialized things: mostly clothing and lingerie in the 1820s. What became Lord & Taylor wasn't technically a "department store" until 1861, when it varied its merchandise. To this day, the Fifth Avenue store starts each morning with the "National Anthem."

• Opened in 1892, **Abercrombie & Fitch** originally catered to men by selling mostly hunting, fishing, and outdoor gear. Before the company sold its brand in the 1980s and the new owners switched over to casual wear for men and women, the store outfitted such adventurous celebrities as Teddy Roosevelt, Ernest Hemingway, and Howard Hughes. Abercrombie & Fitch's original Manhattan store (which closed in 1977) even had a shooting range in the basement.

• **Bloomingdale's** opened in 1872 on the Lower East Side but moved uptown in 1886. By the 1920s, the store covered an entire city block at 59th and Lexington. Bloomie's execs mastered the use of direct-mail catalogs, and the store marketed itself as being "fashion-forward," with its avant-garde designer clothing. In 1961, Bloomie's also became the first department store to design its own shopping bags.

• The first **Saks** store opened in 1902 on Ladies' Mile as Saks and Company. In 1923 Saks merged with Gimbel Brothers Inc. (but kept the name of Saks). Finally, in 1924, Saks Fifth Avenue—founded by Horace Saks and Bernard Gimbel—opened on 5th Avenue near St. Patrick's Cathedral. Merging the two huge department store families (the Saks and the Gimbels) was supposed to create a megastore that had a reputation for offering only the most lavish and upscale merchandise. It worked.

• The first **Macy's** store—a small Sixth Avenue emporium that sold dry goods—opened in 1858. The first day, it netted $11 in sales; the second was a little better…$51 worth of merchandise was sold. But thanks to savvy merchandising and good business sense, Macy's sold almost $100,000 by the end of the next year—an amazing amount for the times—and things just got better from there. Within four years of opening, Macy's was a New York City destination, particularly at Christmas. It was the first New York department store to invite Santa in for annual visits, and in 1867, it was the first store to stay open until midnight on Christmas Eve. In 1902 Macy's opened a much larger store on 34th Street near Herald Square. It boasted 33 elevators, four escalators, and that cool pneumatic tube system that sent payments to invisible clerks in an upstairs office. The building eventually grew to 11 stories of retail heaven.

First manufactured in 1870, chewing gum is a NYC invention.

GONE, BUT NOT FORGOTTEN

Not every fancy department store that opened in New York City managed to stick around. These three fought the good fight but lost:

• **Altman's** (also known as B. Altman's) opened in 1865 and became Fifth Avenue's first large-scale department store in 1906. Altman's was famous for its lavish Christmas window displays and its in-house restaurant, which was built to look like Scarlett O'Hara's house in *Gone With the Wind*. In 1989, the corporation filed for bankruptcy; it closed the next year.

• Opened in 1895, **Bonwit's** (originally Bonwit Teller) was known for high-end merchandise and the higher-than-average salaries paid to its upper-management employees. Located on Fifth Avenue, the store merged and morphed over the years until its parent company went bankrupt in 1989. But in the store's heyday, Marilyn Monroe, Audrey Hepburn, and Jacqueline Kennedy Onassis all shopped there.

• Not originally a New York store (the first ones opened in Indiana, Wisconsin, and Pennsylvania), **Gimbels** opened in 1910 near Macy's in Herald Square. The first Manhattan store to sport a bargain basement, Gimbels boasted that they would not be undersold. Giant enough to be considered Macy's main competitor for many years, Gimbels bought out Saks and Company in the 1920s. But by 1987, Gimbels was no longer making enough to stay afloat and had to close its doors.

* * *

WHEN NIAGARA FALLS SHUT DOWN

Park rangers get a lot of silly questions, including "When do they turn off the water at Niagara Falls?" But in 1969, the answer was an astounding, "In June." For five months that year, the U.S. Army Corps of Engineers diverted the water that typically flows over American Falls so that they could figure out how much the rocks underneath had eroded and repair any damage.

STATE HODGEPODGE

Quick! Some facts about the state of New York.

- One quarter of New York State is farmland. The most common "crop": dairy production.

- New York achieved statehood on July 26, 1788. It was the 11th state admitted.

- One of the world's longest expressways is the New York State Thruway (officially called the Governor Thomas E. Dewey Thruway), which stretches 559 miles from Yonkers to the Pensylvania state line by way of Albany, Syracuse, and Buffalo.

- About 25 percent of the state's labor force belongs to a union—double the national average.

- Highest point: Mount Marcy (5,344 feet), Essex County, part of the Adirondack range. (The lowest point is the bottom of Seneca Lake in the Finger Lakes region; it's 196 feet below sea level at its deepest point.)

- "Uncle Sam," the iconic white-haired, patriotic personification of America, was modeled after Samuel Wilson, a meatpacker from the town of Troy. Wilson supplied beef to the U.S. Army in crates stamped with the initials "U.S." to show they belonged to the government. When someone asked what the letters stood for, a worker at Wilson's plant jokingly responded, "Uncle Sam," a nickname for Wilson. As time went on, other products marked the same way were linked to Wilson, and "Uncle Sam" became a nickname for the United States as well.

- State motto: "Excelsior" ("Ever Upward").

- New York was the first state to officially call a piece of property a historic site: Washington's Headquarters in Newburgh—the small stone house that served as George Washington's headquarters during the Revolutionary War—was designated in 1850.

DYING TO VISIT

*There are some spots in New York that you might like to
visit, but you wouldn't want to live there because…
well…nobody actually "lives" there.*

THE AFRICAN BURIAL GROUND
Where: At the corner of Duane and Elk streets, lower
Manhattan

The story: In 1991, workmen constructing a new office building dug
20 feet below the surface and discovered a nearly six-acre, 300-year-
old burial ground for African slaves and freedmen. In the 1600s,
New York City was the largest port for slave trading in the American
colonies. In fact, the very first sales tax in New Amsterdam—later
New York—was levied on "human cargo," and in 1709, the British
set up a slave market on Wall Street.

At the time, the local government made little distinction between free and enslaved Africans (all were referred to as "slaves")
and refused to bury Africans in cemeteries alongside whites. So the
city set up a separate African burial ground about a mile outside of
what was then the city limits.

The U.S. government outlawed new slave importation in 1807,
and by then, New York's African burial ground had filled in with
debris and was developed. By the time slavery ended for good in
1865, the burial ground was largely forgotten—until that day in
1991. In all, an estimated 10,000 people were buried at the site, including 21 men executed after a slave rebellion in 1712. After the
burial ground's discovery, work on the office building was halted to
allow for a proper excavation, and the building was redesigned to
accommodate a memorial at the site. In 2006, President George W.
Bush declared the burial ground a national monument, and a visitor's center (located at 290 Broadway) opened in 2010.

HARTSDALE PET CEMETERY
Where: Westchester County

The story: It's fitting that a veterinarian founded the largest pet
cemetery in the world. Dr. Samuel Johnson was a veterinary sur-

---

The NYC subway system is 81 miles longer than the state's thruway system.

geon in New York City and the state's first official veterinarian. In 1896, a distraught pet owner visited him with a delicate problem—where to bury her beloved, but recently deceased, dog. Johnson volunteered a spot on his Westchester property, in his apple orchard.

Not long afterward, Johnson told the story to a friend, who was a reporter. Within a few days, the story was in print...and Johnson was inundated with requests from bereaved pet owners. He couldn't turn them away, so the apple orchard became a cemetery. In 1914, Johnson officially formed the Hartsdale Canine Cemetery, though it was open to animals of all kinds.

Today more than 70,000 animals are interred there...along with about 700 people who wanted to be buried with their pets. "Residents" include rabbits, birds, Westminster Kennel Club ribbon-winners, dogs belonging to Diana Ross and Elizabeth Arden, a lion cub, monkeys, and many everyday—but no less special—animals.

Some of the epitaphs at Hartsdale:

- "For You I Wait, At Heaven's Gate"
- "Our Beloved Pudgy"
- "Thor: Good Boy"
- "My dear little true-loving hearts, who would lick the hand that had no food to offer."

THE NEW YORK CITY CEMETERY (POTTER'S FIELD)

Where: Hart Island, western edge of Long Island Sound, the Bronx

The story: Over the years, New York City has had several potter's fields—cemeteries where people are buried when they can't afford a private funeral. Bryant Park, Madison Square Park, and Washington Square Park all started as potter's fields. But today, the most famous one is located on Hart Island, a 101-acre stretch of land in Long Island Sound.

Hart Island got its start in New York history as a Civil War prison camp for Confederate soldiers. It also housed an isolation area for yellow fever patients, a charity hospital, an insane asylum, a boys' workhouse, a missile base, and disciplinary barracks for wayward servicemen during World War II. Through its many incarnations, the island was often used by the city as a burial ground, but it didn't become New York's official indigent cemetery until 1991.

Today, the New York Department of Corrections operates the Hart Island potter's field, and inmates from Riker's Island perform the burials as part of their work details. (Each prisoner is paid about 35 cents an hour.) Coffins are placed in large, common burial plots, and the location of each one is recorded. More than 850,000 bodies rest there today, making Hart Island the largest public (i.e., tax-funded) cemetery in the world. Hart Island isn't open to the public, but family members can usually get permission to visit their relatives' graves.

* * *

NEW YORK'S "X FILES"?

When it comes to rumors of strange happenings, the old military base at Camp Hero—at the eastern tip of Long Island—may have some of the weirdest. Established in 1942 during World War II to protect against the very real threat of a German submarine attack on the United States, the base closed after the war...or so says the U.S. military. Conspiracy theorists tell a different tale. According to them, soldiers at Camp Hero worked on an experiment during World War II, in which the U.S. Navy teleported a destroyer, the USS *Eldridge* from Pennsylvania to Virginia and back again. Supposedly the ship transported successfully, but the sailors on board suffered a terrible fate: Some became fused to the ship during the teleportation. Others went insane after seeing what had happened to their shipmates. After the war, say the conspiracy buffs, Camp Hero expanded into a vast underground city of tunnels and research labs where scientists studied time travel, teleportation, aliens, mind control, and wormholes hyperspace.

The state of New York isn't buying it (and neither are we). Officially, Camp Hero is just a park—415 acres of trails and greenery open to the public 365 days a year. There are still some abandoned military buildings on the grounds, and the park service hopes to eventually convert some of them into a museum telling the story of Camp Hero's role in World War II. Whether the museum will include teleportation devices or reconstructions of alien spaceships remains to be seen.

WHAT IN THE DICKENS?

*In 1842, celebrated author Charles Dickens visited New York City
for the first time and later wrote about the sights, sounds, and
smells of the Big Apple in his book* American Notes.
Here are a few of his observations.

ARRIVING IN NEW YORK HARBOR
"There lay stretched out before us...confused heaps of
buildings, with here and there a spire or steeple, looking
down upon the herd below; and here and there, again, a cloud of
lazy smoke; and in the foreground a forest of ships' masts, cheery
with flapping sails and waving flags. Crossing from among them to
the opposite shore, were steam ferry-boats laden with people,
coaches, horses, wagons, baskets, boxes: crossed and recrossed by
other ferry-boats: all travelling to and fro: and never idle. Stately
among these restless insects, were two or three large ships, moving
with slow majestic pace, as creatures of a prouder kind, disdainful
of their puny journeys, and making for the broad sea."

FIRST IMPRESSIONS
"The beautiful metropolis of America [New York] is by no means
so clean a city as Boston, but many of its streets have the same
characteristics; except that the houses are not quite so fresh-
coloured, the sign-boards are not quite so gaudy, the gilded letters
not quite so golden, the bricks not quite so red, the stone not quite
so white, the blinds and area railings not quite so green, the knobs
and plates upon the street doors not quite so bright and twinkling."

THE NEW YORK LUNATIC ASYLUM, ROOSEVELT ISLAND
"One day, during my stay in New York, I paid a visit to the different
public institutions on Long Island, or Rhode Island: I forget which.
One of them is a Lunatic Asylum...The whole structure is not yet
finished, but it is already one of considerable size and extent, and is
capable of accommodating a very large number of patients.

I cannot say that I derived much comfort from the inspection
of this charity. The different wards might have been cleaner and

---

"If man can live in Manhattan, he can live anywhere." —Arthur C. Clarke

better ordered; I saw nothing of that salutary system which had impressed me so favourably elsewhere; and everything had a lounging, listless, madhouse air, which was very painful...In the dining-room, a bare, dull, dreary place, with nothing for the eye to rest on but the empty walls, a woman was locked up alone. She was bent, they told me, on committing suicide. If anything could have strengthened her in her resolution, it would certainly have been the insupportable monotony of such an existence."

THE PIGS THAT CLEAN THE STREETS

"Here is a solitary swine lounging homeward by himself. He has only one ear; having parted with the other to vagrant-dogs in the course of his city rambles. But he gets on very well without it; and leads a roving, gentlemanly, vagabond kind of life...He leaves his lodgings every morning at a certain hour, throws himself upon the town, gets through his day in some manner quite satisfactory to himself, and regularly appears at the door of his own house again at night...He is a free-and-easy, careless, indifferent kind of pig, having a very large acquaintance among other pigs of the same character, whom he rather knows by sight than conversation, as he seldom troubles himself to stop and exchange civilities, but goes grunting down the kennel, turning up the news and small-talk of the city in the shape of cabbage-stalks and offal, and bearing no tails but his own: which is a very short one, for his old enemies, the dogs, have been at that too, and have left him hardly enough to swear by. He is in every respect a republican pig, going wherever he pleases, and mingling with the best society, on an equal, if not superior footing, for every one makes way when he appears, and the haughtiest give him the wall, if he prefer it. He is a great philosopher, and seldom moved, unless by the dogs before mentioned. Sometimes, indeed, you may see his small eye twinkling on a slaughtered friend, whose carcase garnishes a butcher's door-post, but he grunts out 'Such is life: all flesh is pork!' buries his nose in the mire again, and waddles down the gutter: comforting himself with the reflection that there is one snout the less to anticipate stray cabbage-stalks, at any rate."

For more of Dickens' observations about
New York, turn to page 331.

Yonkers is named for Dutch settler Adriaen Van Der Donck...

SCOOP THE POOP

In the early 1970s, dog poop had reached critical mass on the sidewalks of New York City—an estimated 125–250 tons were deposited per day. Some citizens were sick of it and the Sanitation Department couldn't cope with it. It was time for action.

LORDS OF DOGTOWN

New York has always been a doggie town, but for many years, dog owners were accustomed to letting their dogs do their business and walking away, leaving the poop on the sidewalks for other people to step in and around. There was a longstanding city ordinance against letting dogs poop on public property, but dog owners generally ignored it. As far back as the 1930s, the Department of Sanitation—trying to take a practical approach—began posting "Please Curb Your Dog" signs, meaning that dogs should be made to poop in the gutters. A few dog owners complied; most protested that it was unsafe to make their dogs go in the street, where they might be hit by cars. So the poop problem got worse with each passing decade. Since New York City didn't have the manpower to police the delinquent dog owners, there was no real incentive to obey the law.

LENIENT LINDSAY

By the early 1970s, the city's level of dog-poop tolerance had changed, and the filthy sidewalks and parks sparked tempers everywhere. Mayor John Lindsay recognized the poop problem but refused to address it...except to express his opinion that dogs should relieve themselves in their owners' apartments, not on the streets.

But complaints about the dog droppings and the law-breaking dog owners were flooding the city's Environmental Protection Administration (EPA) and the City Council. Something had to be done. On May 16, 1972, EPA official Jerome Kretchmer proposed a new ordinance: Dog owners would have to pick up their dogs' droppings, or pay a $25 fine. Dog owners were convinced that this was just the first step down a slippery slope that would end with dogs being banned from nearly everywhere in the Big Apple. Local politicians were caught in the middle—they were afraid to support

---

...who was informally known as *De Jonkeer*, or "young gentleman."

the law because they'd been warned that they wouldn't be re-elected if they did, but they were also tired of hearing the dog-doo complaints from environmental groups, civic groups, block associations, and private citizens. Kretchmer viewed his proposal as a simple compromise: Pet owners could keep their dogs, but the poop would cease to be a problem. The ordinance didn't pass.

BEAME'S B-LIST

The next mayor, Abe Beame, inherited the poop problem from Lindsay, but by the time he was elected in 1974, the city was mired in a financial recession and the new mayor didn't consider dog poop to be an A-list issue. In fact, the city's EPA was downsized almost out of existence in 1977. But complaints about dog poop kept coming. The city's First Lady, Mary Beame, tried to lead an anti-poop campaign—complete with posters reading "Parks are for recreation, not defecation"—but it didn't have much impact on a city teetering on the edge of bankruptcy. Sanitation Commissioner Anthony Vaccarello proposed another impractical solution: a city tax on dog food. If dog food were more expensive, he reasoned, owners would feed their dogs less food: less food in, less poop out. That law also failed to pass.

KOCH'S CLEANUP

It fell to Mayor Ed Koch, elected in 1978, to cope. Unable to get action from a City Council afraid to go head-to-head with dog owners, Koch went straight to the state government in Albany, where he presented the canine waste problem as a statewide issue. But in order to circumvent the New York City Council and override "home rule" (a constitutional issue), the state legislature had to make the proposed pooper-scooper law apply to more cities than just New York.

So State Senator Franz Leichter and State Assemblyman Edward H. Lehner cowrote the Canine Waste Law, which called for the "removal of canine wastes in cities with a population of 400,000 or more persons." Dog owners who failed to pick up their dogs' poop would be fined $100. In June 1978, the law passed by a narrow margin. Aside from New York City, only Buffalo met the population criterion, so New York was now the first major American city to have such a law.

NYC was the first U.S. city to pass housing regulations.

ENFORCEMENT BLUES

Enforcing the law was going to be just as hard as passing it had been, but since it wouldn't go into effect for a full year, Mayor Koch had time to get people used to the idea.

These days, New York sidewalks are significantly cleaner and the fine has been raised to $250. But that doesn't mean the problem has been solved completely. In 2009, there were 4,443 dog-poop calls to the city's complaint line—the highest number in three years. So the saga continues.

* * *

THE POOPER-SCOOPER LADY

Fran "Pooper-Scooper Lady" Lee (1910–2010) started her career as an actress, but her passion was consumer activism. From the 1940s through the 1990s, she regularly appeared on TV and radio giving advice on household how-tos, public health, and consumer safety. She was loud, strident, insistent, and often a pain in the neck to public officials. But Lee is best known and remembered for her crusade against dog poop. In the early 1970s, she founded Children Before Dogs, a group that wanted to have dog waste removed completely from the city's streets, sidewalks, and parks. The *New York Times* called her "New York's foremost fighter against dog dirt."

Lee insisted that *Toxocara canis*, a tiny roundworm found in dog feces, was a serious health risk to children: *T. canis* eggs could accumulate in soil where dogs defecate, she said, be transferred onto the hands or under the fingernails of anyone who touched that soil, and then be ingested. The disease that results from ingesting *T. canis* ranges from inflammation of certain organs all the way to blindness. Experts disputed Lee's claims about just how great the risk might be: Alan Beck, director of the city's Bureau of Animal Affairs in the 1970s, said that dog feces on sidewalks and in parks were not specifically a public health problem, although he did agree that they were "very much a psychological and aesthetic problem."

Fran Lee was enraged by Beck's stand, and she opposed the city's early attempt to pass a pooper-scooper law; she felt it wasn't tough enough. But Lee was as practical as she was passionate. In the end, she supported the proposed Canine Waste Law and was reported to have been thrilled when it finally passed in 1978.

All of the Bronx was originally a sprawling plantation.

WEIRD NEWS

City people do the darndest things.

EXCESS BAGGAGE

In January 2011, Columbia University researcher Edward Hall III arrived at JFK Airport to catch a flight to the West Coast...and realized he'd forgotten his picture ID. He tried to get help from one of the United Airlines desk agents, explaining that he "really needed to get to San Francisco." When she refused to allow him to board without his ID, Hall took matters into his own hands: He jumped over the ticket counter and dove onto the baggage conveyor belt...which carried him through the airport and deposited him on the tarmac. Airport personnel detained him, and when police arrived to take him into custody, he explained, "I just wanted to make my flight."

TRASH PILE

After the blizzards of 2010–11, trash sat on city streets for weeks and irritated everyone from Staten Island to the Bronx. But it turned out to be a lucky break for Vangelis Kapatos of Manhattan, who, in January 2011, tried to kill himself by jumping out of a window on West 45th Street. Fortunately, about 100 bags of trash at the curb below broke his fall. "He landed on a garbage pile," said one city official. "That's the only reason he's alive." Kapatos wasn't injured, and his family took him to Bellevue for psychiatric evaluation.

GIVE HIS REGARDS TO BATHROOMS

In 2008 Irish playwright Paul Walker staged an unusual production: His play *Ladies & Gents* was performed in a bathroom in Central Park. Why? According to Walker, he wanted to take the audience "out of their comfort zone." The play was a thriller about a sex scandal in 1950s Ireland, and it was performed in two 20-minute parts: one in the ladies' room, and one in the mens'; audience members switched bathrooms to see how the story ended. (Portable, working toilets were stationed outside, since the facilities were occupied.) In its review of the show, the *New York Times* said, "The cast members sell the gimmick perfectly."

Along with St. Moritz, Switzerland, and Innusbruck, Austria, Lake Placid is...

SEARCHING FOR UTOPIA

You probably think "utopia" is somewhere else—like in the Himalayas, or maybe Hawaii—and not in your own backyard. But from the late 1700s to the early 1900s, many utopian communities sprang up around the country—three of them in upstate New York.

THE GIFT OF BEING SIMPLE

The first Shakers—members of the United Society of Believers in Christ's Second Appearing—came from England with their leader, Mother Ann Lee, in 1774 and settled near Albany, New York. Shakers are usually remembered for their religious rituals of dancing and shaking, and for their finely made handcrafts and furniture. But Shaker doctrines also included communal living (common ownership of all property and goods), celibacy, and productive labor, as well as equality of the sexes and pacifism. By 1830, there were 19 Shaker communities from Maine to Kentucky, but it was the community called Mount Lebanon in Columbia County, New York, that became the spiritual and ideological center of the entire movement.

Mount Lebanon was founded in 1785 by Father James Whittaker, who envisioned it as a model for all Shaker communities. Since worship was the most important thing to Shakers, Whittaker built the "meetinghouse" (church) first, and Mount Lebanon expanded from there to include more than 100 buildings on 6,000 acres. It was so large that in 1861 the federal government awarded the settlement its own post office. The community supported itself by selling high-quality seeds (Shakers invented the seed packet in 1816), herbs and herbal medicines (some 100,000 pounds of dried herbs were sold each year in the 1850s), and those distinctive Shaker-style handmade chairs.

Mount Lebanon was the biggest and most successful of the Shaker communities and lasted longer than almost all the others, but by the 1930s, even it was failing—partly because of the sect's emphasis on chastity, which meant they had to replenish their numbers solely by recruiting converts. And with cheap manufactured products available, few people still wanted the handmade Shaker goods—and during the Great Depression, most couldn't afford to buy them anyway. The last seven residents left in 1947, and today only a small part of the Mount Lebanon compound remains. Mount Lebanon Shaker Village was designated a National Historic Landmark in 1965.

TOWARD A MORE PERFECT UNION

You can't get much more utopian than thinking it's possible to achieve perfection on Earth, and that's what John Humphreys Noyes, founder of the Oneida Community, believed. He called his unorthodox doctrine simply "Perfectionism," and—since it defied prevailing Christian belief in the earthly sinfulness of man—it got him kicked out of Yale Divinity School. In 1840, with a group of about 35 followers, Noyes went to Putney, Vermont, to start a religious commune run on his strict principles. "Mutual Criticism" required all members (except Noyes) to endure organized sessions of criticism of any "bad traits" that threatened the community, and "Complex Marriage" held that every man in the commune considered himself married to every woman (and vice versa) and that no couple was allowed to form a lasting attachment. Monogamy, Noyes asserted, was a "tyrannical institution."

Noyes also advocated what he called "stirpiculture," a kind of selective breeding that he believed would produce ever more perfect children. Members who wanted children were carefully matched, and all other couples were expected to use birth control to avoid producing unwanted (less perfect) kids.

These unorthodox ideas outraged the local citizens of Putney and their religious leaders, who persecuted the members of the commune and even had Noyes indicted for adultery. So Noyes fled Vermont and bought 23 acres of land in Oneida, New York. In 1848 he and 45 followers established a new community there. Noyes laid out strict rules for every aspect of life in the Oneida Community: In particular, everyone was expected to work, and even though women did most of the domestic jobs, they were considered to be equal to men. The community didn't attract many members (by 1878, there were only 306), but it did manage to launch a profitable business—Oneida Community Limited, a corporation that started out making tin-plated spoons and graduated

---

The first town to be established in Queens: Astoria (1837).

to making inexpensive Oneida flatware and silverware.

Noyes did not fare well with critics outside his community. In 1879, he was forced to flee to Canada, just ahead of an arrest warrant for statutory rape. He never returned to the U.S., and the commune didn't survive long without him; it dissolved in January 1881. However, Oneida Community Limited continued to make silverware and cutlery into the 21st century. It stopped manufacturing in 2005.

WORKING FOR THE MAN

In the late 1800s, Elbert Hubbard was a marketing genius with a lucrative job at the Larkin Soap Company in Buffalo, New York, but he longed for more than soap salesmanship—he wanted success (and fame) as a writer and philosopher. When commercial publishers rejected his work, he took matters into his own hands. In 1895, he moved to East Aurora, New York, and founded the Roycroft Press to produce hand-printed, hand-bound books—including his own. Around the press, he shaped his own little kingdom, an idealistic artisan community called Roycroft.

Hubbard was deeply influenced by the English Arts and Crafts Movement, whose members believed that even everyday objects should be beautiful. The craftspeople and artists Hubbard gathered at Roycroft soon branched out from printing to leatherwork, copperwork, and furniture-making. "The Roycrofters," Hubbard said, "are a small band of workers who make beautiful books and things—making them as good as they can." And good work translated into good sales—the compound made a lot of money for Hubbard.

But Roycroft was more than just a factory. The Roycrofters (almost 500 of them by 1910) lived communally, sharing meals, meetings, and games, but Hubbard was definitely the leader and decision-maker. He provided housing and jobs for his followers, organized farming so they could be self-sufficient, encouraged their artistic expression, and entertained them with concerts, festivals, and lectures. On Sunday nights, he preached to the community on the principles of clean living...even though he'd carried on an affair with a younger woman (a suffragette named Alice Moore) while he was still married, got her pregnant, and wound up in a scandalous divorce.

An 1897 fire on Ellis Island destroyed all immigration records dating back to 1855.

Hubbard married Moore in 1904, and in 1915, both drowned in the sinking of the *Lusitania*. The ship was torpedoed by a German U-boat, an event that eventually pulled the United States into World War I. The Roycrofters struggled along without them until the Great Depression finally finished them off in the 1930s. Today, 14 of the original buildings still exist on the original site, and the "Roycroft Campus" was designated a National Historic Landmark in 1986. Elbert Hubbard's most famous descendant: his nephew L. Ron Hubbard, of Scientology fame.

*　*　*

WELCOME TO MUNCHKINLAND

Emerald green hills surround the small, central New York town of Chittenango where L. Frank Baum was born. In 1900 Baum published *The Wonderful Wizard of Oz*, a children's book that became 13-book series and, in 1939, a world-famous movie. Baum was just four years old when he moved the 15 miles to nearby Syracuse, but Chittenango still takes honoring its most famous native son—or at least the books he wrote—very seriously.

In Chittenango, the sidewalks of Genesee Street are paved with yellow concrete stamped to look like brick. (They used to be real yellow bricks, but over time, snow, rain, and ice ruined them.) Oz fans can stop for a bite to eat at the Emerald City Grill, grab dessert at Oz Cream, or buy a souvenir at the Land of Oz and Ends. And every year, during the first week of June, the town holds an Oz-Stravaganza with parades, costumes, rides, and a tribute to the 124 actors who played Munchkins in the famous 1939 film.

During the 1980s, actor Meinhardt Raabe—he played the Munchkin coroner who sang that the Wicked Witch of the East was "really, most sincerely dead"—often came to the celebration. Raabe died in 2010 at the age of 94, but other Munchkin actors still show up and sign autographs in "Glinda's Royal Tent." The 2010 festival included appearances by 90-year-old Jerry Maren (Lollypop Kid), 91-year-old, Karl Slover (Soldier), and 86-year-old Margaret Pelligrini (Sleepyhead). Pelligrini even wore a copy of her original costume...featuring a flowerpot on her head.

FASHION WARS

When it came to being the crème de la crème of the fashion world, New York was the little city that could.

THE RAG TRADE'S ALL THE RAGE

Today, thanks to the Style Channel and shows like *Project Runway*, most people with a remote control can catch a glimpse of New York's "fashion weeks," when renowned designers preview their newest collections. In September, they show off the styles for the following spring, and in February, the newest fashions for fall. New York Fashion Week is known around the world for its superstar models, world-class designers, and the international celebrities, debutantes, and otherwise well-to-do who attend the fashion shows. But how did these glitzy fashion celebrations find their way to big, boisterous, decidedly un-Parisian New York?

It all began in 1825 with the opening of the Erie Canal. Before the canal, New York City was one of several American ports competing for a share of the luxury fashion goods being imported at the time from design houses in Paris and London. But the Erie Canal connected New York to the Great Lakes region, and suddenly the city was the port with the cheapest access to the rest of the country. European fashion imports flooded its waterfront. As a result, the Big Apple became the center of the "rag trade," America's distribution hub for the luxury clothing, hats, furs, and jewels that wealthy people all over the country wanted…especially the fancy goods that came from Europe.

WELCOME TO THE MILE

These changes brought wealth to the city, too, and as more New Yorkers gained the means to buy the latest European fashions, shopping became big business. In 1846, clothing retailer Alexander T. Stewart opened the city's first department store at 280 Broadway. (*More about that on page 112.*) A. T. Stewart and Co. was one of the first to offer goods targeted specifically at wealthy women. Stewart also believed that "you must make [the customer] happy and satisfied, so she will come back." So many women emptied

their pocketbooks in Stewart's store that other retailers copied his marketing ideas, until department stores filled the area along Broadway and Sixth Avenue from Eighth Street to 23rd Street, a shopping district that was called "Ladies' Mile."

But with all those department stores in one area, competition was tough. So the Ehrich Brothers developed a unique sales gimmick; they created an American version of the Parisian "fashion parade." In the great fashion houses of France, live models paraded through the showrooms, wearing a designer's creations. Ehrich Brothers modified that concept and, in 1903, produced what they called a "fashion show," with live models strutting on runways right in the store, where the clothes were also for sale. New York's first runway event was a solid hit, and suddenly fashion shows were the newest American mania.

PARIS IS CLOSED

At first, New York was the only city to host fashion shows, but by the 1920s, the events had become so popular that they were everywhere—in stores, hotels, and restaurants in cities all across the country. That was a problem for New York's designers: If you didn't need to go to New York to see the most stylishly clad models gliding down the runway, how could the city maintain its exclusive hold on fashion? Another complication: The clothes featured in the shows didn't come from American designers; they still originated in Europe. American fashion editors and department store buyers traveled to Paris to view the newest collections and decide what to bring back to the States. Wealthy socialites knew the names of Parisian designers like Coco Channel, but the only truly famous American designer of the day was Chicago native Mainbocher...and he was famous because he worked in Paris. As far as fashion went, Paris was in and New York was out—until Adolf Hitler gave the Yanks an unexpected shove forward.

In 1940, the Nazis invaded France and occupied Paris. For the next five years, the world's fashion center was completely cut off from its allies; there were no more trips to France for America's fashion elite. But American shoppers were still looking for new inspiration, so New York City seized the opportunity to become the new capital of artsy clothing. "Paris is dead. Long live New York!" became a local rallying cry.

DESIGNING NEW YORK

And thankfully, when it came to making New York the focus of *haute couture*, the Big Apple had an ace up its puffed sleeves: Eleanor Lambert. Press director of the New York Dress Institute (a group created by the garment workers' union to boost manufacturing in the city), Lambert was a marketing dynamo. She produced an annual "Best Dressed List" that highlighted American designers, and started a biannual event called Press Week, where she invited journalists from around the world to New York to see the city's fashion designers exhibit their spring and fall collections.

Only about a third of the invited journalists showed up for the first event in 1943, even though the New York Dress Institute offered to cover their expenses. But Lambert kept at it, enticing reporters with social events that included dinners at her Fifth Avenue apartment. Her work soon paid off, and by the 1960s, Press Week had evolved into Fashion Week...and everyone who was anyone in fashion journalism showed up. Lambert's concept worked so well that today the world's four major fashion cities—New York, Paris, Milan, and London—all hold their own "fashion weeks" twice a year.

A PERMANENT HOME

Before New York Fashion Week became the celebrity-studded event it is today, though, it endured growing pains. In particular, it lacked a permanent home. Designers showed their work during the same week, but they chose to do so in different locations around the city: clubs, hotels, even lofts.

The need for one central location suddenly became critical in 1990, when designer Michael Kors held a show in a Manhattan loft. As the models walked down the runway, the ceiling began to crumble. Plaster pelted the models and dropped into the laps of journalists as people rushed for the exit. One member of the audience was Fern Mallis, the executive director of the Council of Fashion Designers of America and the head of Fashion Week, at the time. Given the safety concerns (and, no doubt, the embarrassment), Mallis decided to search for a venue where all designers could hold their shows in one place. By 1994, she had settled on Bryant Park, where fashion shows could be held in large white tents—with no plaster ceilings.

Fashion Week continued to grow, though, and eventually, Bryant Park became too small to hold all the shows and invited guests. By 2010 the event (now called Mercedes Benz Fashion Week) had moved to the larger Damrosch Park at Lincoln Center. Today, Fashion Week attracts more than 230,000 spectators and generates more than $770 million in revenue each year for the city of New York.

*   *   *

DEAR, MR. LINCOLN...

In 1860 a young Westfield, New York, resident named Grace Bedell wrote to then-presidential candidate Abraham Lincoln, expressing her enthusiasm for his candidacy and offering some advice for his campaign. Bedell wrote:

> I am a little girl only 11 years old, but want you should be President of the United States very much, so I hope you won't think me very bold to write to such a great man as you are. Have you any little girls about as large as I am? If so give them my love and tell her to write to me if you cannot answer this letter. I have got four brothers and part of them will vote for you any way, and if you let your whiskers grow I will try and get the rest of them to vote for you. You would look a great deal better for your face is so thin. All the ladies like whiskers, and they would tease their husbands to vote for you, and then you would be President.

She addressed the envelope "Abraham Lincoln, Springfield, Illinois" and dropped it in the mail. Lincoln actually got the letter and, taken with the little girl's precociousness, responded:

> Your very agreeable letter of the 15th is received. I regret the necessity of saying I have no daughters. I have three sons—one seventeen, one nine, and one seven years of age. They, with their mother, constitute my whole family. As to the whiskers, having never worn any, do you not think people would call it a piece of silly affectation if I were to begin it now?

But he took her advice...and won the presidency that November. Then, in February 1861, during his inaugural train ride from Illinois to Washington, D.C, Lincoln stopped in Westfield to meet Bedell. Today, a statue memorializing the event stands in the town's Lincoln–Bedell Statue Park.

ROADSIDE ATTRACTIONS

Next time you're on a road trip and need a break,
consider one of these New York pit stops.

The Upside-Down Traffic Light (a.ka. Green on Top): Syracuse

World's Largest Kaleidoscope: Mount Tremper

The 300-Pound Concrete Foot: Manhattan

World's Largest Dead Shark: Vanderbilt Museum, Centerport, Long Island

The 50-Foot-Tall Teepee: Cherry Valley

Carousel Capital of the World: Binghamton

The Hello Kitty Fountain: Manhattan

Metal T-Rex: Duanesburg

Giant Roll of Pep-o-Mint LifeSavers: Gouverneur

Elephant Rock: Hague

The Pink Elephant Statue: Owego

The Big Duck: Flanders

House Shaped Like a Boat: Morehouse

Giant Bronze Alice in Wonderland Statue: Manhattan

Paul Bunyan's Golf Bag: Clayton

The Two-Story Brick Outhouse: Phelps

The Sword-in-the-Stone: Rochester

The Dog Bone Memorial: Manhattan

The Mountain Man (and Bear): North Hudson

The Mushroom House: Pittsford

The Headless Horseman Statue: Sleepy Hollow

World's Second-Largest Garden Gnome: Kerhonkson

Neil Diamond was considered for the lead role in *Taxi Driver*.

PUNKED, PART II

A few more famous New York hoaxes. (For Part I, turn to page 10.)

THE "DATING A BANKER ANONYMOUS" HOAX
Perpetrator: Dating a Banker Anonymous (DABA)
Story: On January 28, 2009, the *Times* ran a story about several women who had formed a support group called Dating a Banker Anonymous (DABA) to "help women cope with the inevitable relationship fallout from, say, the collapse of Lehman Brothers or the Dow's shedding 777 points in a single day." The women met, said the *Times*, once or twice a week to help each other deal with the problems of morose, financially strapped former-banker boyfriends and the difficulties of being "Wall Street widows." The women talked all about their disappointments (fewer vacations, no fancy restaurants, etc.) and their support group's coping strategies: "Slip into a dress and heels. Sip a cocktail and wait your turn to talk. Pour your heart out. Repeat as needed."
Exposed! Whoops. The *Times* admitted on February 25 that it had been duped. There was no support group at all, just a blog called "Dating a Banker Anonymous." One of the blog's founders described it as a "satire that embellishes true experiences for effect."

THE *NEW YORK TIMES* HOAX
Perpetrator: The Yes Men
Story: On Wednesday, November 12, 2008, George W. Bush was on his way out of office, and Barack Obama had just been elected. But on a New York street corner, a guy handed out copies of the *New York Times* with some unexpected headlines: "Iraq War Ends," "Maximum Wage Law Succeeds," "Ex-Secretary Apologizes for W.M.D. Scare," "USA Patriot Act Repealed," "Court Indicts Bush on High Treason Charge." Times readers paged through the edition. What had happened?

Before long, the truth came out: The papers—1.2 million perfectly reproduced copies of the *Times* distributed on the streets of New York and Los Angeles—were the work of a group identified as the Yes Men, hoaxers whose pranks also included posing as federal housing officials and as National Petroleum Council reps. The Yes

Men claimed it had taken six months to create the bogus *Times*, six presses to print it, and thousands of volunteers to hand it out.

Exposed! "It is fake and we are looking into it," said *Times* spokesperson Catherine Mathis.

THE HOWARD HUGHES HOAX

Perpetrator: Writer Clifford Irving

Story: Howard Hughes (1905–76) was an aviator, a Hollywood producer and director, one of the richest men in the world, and, later in life, a mentally disturbed recluse suffering from obsessive-compulsive disorder and multiple drug addictions. In the late 1960s, everyone wanted to know more about him, and that's where New York author Clifford Irving saw his big chance.

In 1970, he and friend Richard Suskind decided to write Howard Hughes's autobiography...without Hughes. Since they figured the isolated Hughes would never come forward to challenge them. Suskind did the research, while Irving forged letters he later claimed Hughes wrote to him. He convinced his New York publisher, McGraw-Hill, that Hughes was on board and would be interviewed for the book. (Irving later faked the interviews.) He also got his hands on a manuscript written by James Phelan, who was (legitimately) ghostwriting the memoirs of Hughes's former business manager. Plagiarizing the Phelan pages, Irving put together his "autobiography" and delivered it to McGraw-Hill in 1971. *Life* magazine signed on to publish excerpts; the forged "Hughes" letters were even examined and declared to be real. McGraw-Hill paid an advance of $765,000.

Exposed! On January 7, 1972, Howard Hughes did the unimaginable—he came out of seclusion and told the world that he'd never heard of Clifford Irving. To make matters worse, James Phelan identified the parts that Irving had stolen from his book. And the Swiss bank where Irving's wife, Edith, had deposited the McGraw-Hill money turned her in.

Irving confessed on January 28. He, his wife, and Suskind were indicted for fraud, tried, and found guilty. McGraw-Hill canceled the book, and Irving returned their money. He spent 14 months in prison, but had at least two last laughs—in 1981, he published *The Hoax*, a book about the events, and in 2007, a film based on that book was released, starring Richard Gere as Clifford Irving.

Previous names for Roosevelt Island: Hog Island, Blackwell Island, and Welfare Island.

NEW YORK I.Q. QUIZ

Yeah, yeah, yeah, you think you know everything about New York, but fuggedaboudit, you don't. (Answers on page 363.)

1. What was the first capital of the USA? (Duh.)
a. Albany
b. Buffalo
c. New York City
d. Syracuse

2. In 1803, Alexander Hamilton started a newspaper that is today the longest-running paper in the country. Which is it?
a. *New York Times*
b. *New York Post*
c. *Daily News*
d. *Wall Street Journal*

3. Bowling Green in downtown Manhattan was once a parade ground and cattle market. In 1733, a trio of enthusiasts turned it into a park with shaded walks and…a bowling green. What annual rent did they pay to the city?
a. $2
b. One bale of beaver furs
c. £1 sterling
d. One peppercorn

4. The New York Lottery is one of the oldest government-run lotteries in America. What year did it begin?
a. 1955
b. 1967
c. 1972
d. 1980

Midtown has more office space per acre than any other central business district on Earth.

5. Which ballplayer was not born in New York City?
a. Whitey Ford
b. Sandy Koufax
c. Phil Rizzuto
d. Joe DiMaggio

6. How many millions of gallons of water flow over Niagara Falls in one minute?
a. 3
b. 30
c. 300
d. 3,000

7. Which of these is not currently a New York State political party?
a. Rent Is Too Damn High Party
b. Working Families Party
c. Marijuana Reform Party
d. Peace and Freedom Party

8. In the late 1940s and early 1950s, one midtown-Manhattan street was world-famous for jazz clubs. Which was it?
a. 42nd Street
b. 47th Street
c. 52nd Street
d. 57th Street

9. These are all Brooklyn neighborhoods, right? Wrong. One of them is an impostor.
a. Bayside
b. Bushwick
c. Bensonhurst
d. Bay Ridge

The Bronx is home to the country's oldest golf course: Van Cortland Park (est. 1895).

GIBSON'S GIRLS

If you think that the American obsession with a media-defined standard of beauty is a new thing, think again. Long before supermodels and movie stars told us all how to look, think, and act, American women turned to magazine illustrations to decide what "beautiful" was.

AMERICAN GIRL

Throughout much of the 19th century, the social values of Victorian England set the standard for what a "good" woman was: chaste, subservient, destined to play the role of wife and mother, and given virtually no legal rights. If a Victorian woman worked outside the home (something she did only as a prelude to marriage), she was a teacher...nothing more. She certainly had no time for makeup, independence, or mischief. And like their counterparts across the Atlantic, women in the United States also adhered to this standard. But as the 1800s wound down and a new century dawned, American magazines began to feature pen-and-ink illustrations of a new kind of woman: whimsical and willowy, with her hair piled loosely on her head, her neck bare, her tiny waist corseted, and a mischievous glint in her eyes. But who was this maverick woman, and who was daring enough to draw her?

THE ILLUSTRATIVE MAN

Charles Dana Gibson moved from Massachusetts to Flushing, Queens, in 1875, when he was eight years old. He spent some time at Flushing High School, but proved to be a talented artist early on, so his parents saved up and sent him to the Art Students League, a prestigious art school in Manhattan. He spent about a year there before the money ran out. Gibson specialized in line art, so he shopped his pieces around, hoping to sell his work to help support his family. Finally, in 1886, he sold his first illustration to *Life* magazine: a dog chained to a doghouse, baying at the moon. He made $4. That led to more sales—and more money—and by 1889, he'd saved enough to take a trip to Europe to study art.

It was there that the image of a spunky, independent women

began to take shape in Gibson's head. In London, he spent time with a French-born artist and cartoonist named George du Maurier, who was known for his whimsical art. Du Maurier encouraged Gibson to make his sketches more fun and to add more life to them. When Gibson got back to the United States, he sketched his first girl.

GIBSON MANIA

By then, Gibson had already established himself as a go-to artist for the popular magazines of the day: *Harper's Monthly*, *Collier's*, *Life*, and others. And before long, the girls started appearing in his work and earning a following of their own. They came to be called "Gibson Girls," and they were more than just art. Gibson created entire stories around them: In 1899, he did a series of drawings, complete with captions, that documented the "life" of one of the girls from birth to old age.

Pretty soon, Gibson's drawings came to represent a new kind of American woman: She was beautiful, tall, independent, and mysterious. According to one historian, a Gibson Girl "would smile, but was never seen laughing, further adding to her enchanting persona of self-assurance." The Gibson Girls went to college (many drawings showed them on campus), and they participated in activities typically restricted to men: ice skating, bicycling, and golf. And they did it all while keeping their hair and makeup perfect.

The public loved them. Women started styling their hair in swept-up dos, with a few tendrils hanging loose for that carefree effect. Images of Gibson Girls appeared on everything from pillowcases and spoons to fans and ashtrays. Young men decorated their rooms and apartments with Gibson Girl wallpaper, and famous models and actresses of the era—including Evelyn Nesbit, Gibson's own wife, Irene Langhorne, and theater star Camille Clifford—posed for Gibson Girl drawings.

One thing a Gibson Girl wasn't, however, was political. Women's voting rights were a hot topic in the late 19th and early 20th centuries. But in most circles, suffrage was a touchy subject. Much of the population—men *and* women—was against it...or at least wary of it. So Gibson was very careful never to risk alienating the buying public by associating his spirited girls with the cause.

END OF AN ERA

The Gibson Girl craze began to wane in the 1910s. When the United States entered World War I in 1918 and young men started dying in Europe, Americans lost interest in the whimsy the girls represented. Gibson himself seldom drew any during the war, focusing more on patriotic and heroic images. By the time the war ended, flappers—with their fitted skirts and sleek hairstyles—had become the public's new "It Girls."

That was fine with Gibson. He went on to become editor and owner of *Life* magazine and turned his attention to oil painting instead of line art. By the time he died in 1944, flappers were out, too, having been replaced by conservative, proper fashions inspired by the Great Depression. But women still combed the pages of magazines (and flocked to movie theaters) to learn how they should dress and act, and what they should want. The names changed over the years—Vivien Leigh, Katherine Hepburn, Twiggy, Angelina Jolie, Heidi Klum—but the idea that beauty could be determined by a picture in a magazine remained, thanks to Charles Dana Gibson and his playful girls.

* * *

LOW TURNOVER

The New Yorker has no masthead (the list that most magazines include up front, calling out the names of all the people who work there), a tradition since its early days. So it's hard to track the comings and goings of the staff. Maybe it's also because there is so little turnover: In its more than 85 years in print, *The New Yorker* has had only five chief editors. Cofounder Harold Ross edited the magazine for its first 26 years. He was a whirlwind of energy, working at least 10 hours a day. Sometimes he was pessimistic, grumbling, and prone to temper tantrums, but he was still considered a brilliant editor—idiosyncratic and well-liked. His death from cancer in December 1951 at the age of 59 was a terrible blow to the staff and writers. But by then, *The New Yorker* was so well established that its managing editor, William Shawn, could step right into the editor-in-chief's job in January 1952. Shawn edited the magazine until 1987—he was followed by Robert Gottlieb (until 1992), Tina Brown (to 1998), and the current editor, David Remnick.

THERE GOES THE NEIGHBORHOOD: BROOKLYN

Nearly 15 percent of all Americans can trace their family history back to Brooklyn, one of the most ethnically diverse areas in the country. Here are just a few of the histories of some of the borough's neighborhoods.

• **Brooklyn** comes from the town Breukelen, in the Netherlands. When the Dutch settled New Amsterdam, they gave the name to a small village near what's now Brooklyn Heights. When the Dutch lost New Amsterdam to the British in the 1660s, the new colonizers kept the name and the pronunciation, but changed the spelling.

• **DUMBO** is an acronym for Down Under the Manhattan Bridge Overpass, and even though the name is relatively new (the area has only been called DUMBO since the late 1970s), there's already debate about how it started. Some people say that David Walentas, a New York developer, coined the term—as he was buying up properties in the area, he wanted a cool-sounding acronym for the new neighborhood...like SoHo in Manhattan. Others say that residents actually started calling the area DUMBO to discourage gentrification (a silly sounding neighborhood was more likely to put off trendy residents). Either way, DUMBO stuck. Before that, the area was known as Rapailie, Olympia, Fulton Landing, and Gairville.

• The Dutch originally called **Red Hook** "Roode Hoek": *roode* for the red clay soil, and *hoek*, "point," because part of it "points" into the East River.

• **Flatbush** also comes from two Dutch words: *vlacke*, or flat, and *bosch*, woodland. East Flatbush, though, had a more colorful name—during the 1800s, it was called Pigtown, because it was full of shanties and pig farms.

• Around 1670, farmers in Flatbush started moving out of town in search of open land. Many of them settled in an area near Jamaica Bay, called the "east woods." But as more people moved in, the area became a small town in its own right...**New Lots**, for all the new parcels of land those farmers had settled.

• **Weeksville** gets its name from a former slave named James Weeks, who bought some land on the outer edges of Brooklyn in 1838 and created a self-sufficient community for free, professional African Americans. (New York City's first black police officer, Wiley Overton, lived in Weeksville, and the city published the *Freedman's Torchlight*, one of the first black newspapers in the United States.) By the mid 20th century, though, the town had been absorbed into Crown Heights and mostly forgotten. That is, until a historian named James Hurley rediscovered the town, which led to an archaeological dig to unearth important artifacts. Many of the buildings were later added to the National Register of Historic Places.

• When the Dutch first visited the area that became **Coney Island**, there were rabbits everywhere...so many that the settlers named the penninsula *Konijn Eiland* (Rabbit Island). When the British took over, as usual, they anglicized the spelling.

• Before the 1920s, the water in **Sheepshead Bay** teemed with marine life, in particular a flatfish with stubby teeth called the *sheepshead*. But as developers moved in and started building houses along the water and polluting the bay, the sheepsheads and many other marine animals left or died off.

*   *   *

"Brooklyn was a lovely place to hit. If you got a ball in the air, you had a chance to get it out. When they tore down Ebbets Field, they tore down a little piece of me."
— **Duke Snider, centerfielder,
Brooklyn Dodgers (1947–58)**

CROOKED AS A DOG'S HIND LEG

Elected or appointed, some politicians always seem to be dipping their paws into money they shouldn't be anywhere near. Bad dog...bad dog!

REDEFINING NONPROFIT
Who: State Senator Pedro Espada Jr. (Democrat, the Bronx)
What he did: The unraveling of State Senator Espada began in 2009, when he and fellow senator Hiram Monserrate defected to the Republican side of the aisle, taking majority control of the State Senate away from the Democrats. A five-week legislative deadlock ensued, after which Espada agreed to rejoin the Democratic fold...but only in exchange for being named Majority Leader.

This kind of coercion doesn't play well in Albany and runs the risk of retribution. New York Attorney General Andrew Cuomo investigated Espada, and there was plenty to find. Cuomo filed a civil suit accusing Espada of draining $14 million from a group of nonprofit health clinics that he owned in the Bronx and using the money for personal expenses (including $20,000 worth of sushi delivered to his Westchester home). Another lawsuit accused Espada of running a bogus job-training program that let him pay janitors at the clinics only $1.70 per hour, far below the minimum wage. He was also being investigated by the federal government and the IRS for his connection to a consulting firm allegedly involved with tax fraud and money laundering. And the Bronx district attorney was after him too...for not actually living in the Bronx.

Result: In the September 2010 Democratic primary, a 34-year-old unknown named Gustavo Rivera defeated Espada. Rivera said that the choice between the two candidates was between "ethics or indictments...[and] the people of the Bronx made the right choice." Rivera went on to win the November election.

THE CONSULTANT
Who: State Senator Joseph L. Bruno (Republican, Rensselaer and Saratoga Counties)

The Staten Island Ferry fleet carries more than 60,000 passengers a day.

What he did: In 1995, Bruno became majority leader in the Republican-controlled State Senate. He was a powerful force who channeled billions of public dollars to the Albany region. It all went bust in 2008, though, when he resigned in the face of a federal investigation into his business dealings. Bruno was charged with several crimes, including receiving lucrative consulting fees from companies that were either seeking business from the state or in need of assistance with state regulators, and for failing to disclose his conflicts of interest. The investigation probed into 15 years of Bruno's activities as a consultant for more than a dozen firms, during which he earned about $3.2 million in fees.

Result: In January 2009, Bruno was indicted on eight felony counts of corruption, including mail and wire fraud. In December, he was convicted on two of the counts, acquitted on five, and got a hung jury on the last count. A federal judge sentenced him to two years in prison, and Bruno had to pay $280,000 in restitution to the State of New York, the amount of money he made in the two felony counts on which he was convicted. "I can say to you honestly," he insisted, "as honestly as I can: In my heart, and in my mind, I did nothing wrong."

RETIREMENT PLAN

Who: State Comptroller Alan Hevesi (Democrat, Queens)

What he did: Hevesi had a Ph.D (his doctoral dissertation: "Legislative Leadership in New York State"), and had been a professor of political science at Queens College and a 20-plus-year veteran of the State Senate. He aspired to higher office, and was elected New York City's comptroller in 1994. He tried for the mayoral nomination in 2001, but that was a no-go, so in 2002, he ran for state comptroller and won. He then decided to run for a second term. But in September 2006, just before the election, his Republican opponent called in a tip (to the hotline Hevesi himself had set up for citizens to report fraud and corruption) revealing that Hevesi had been using a state worker as chauffeur and errand boy for his ailing wife.

What started as a minor infraction turned into a very big deal, apparently, because the inquiry sparked a much wider investigation that revealed a pattern of fraud, bribery, and what State Attorney General Andrew Cuomo called a "culture of corruption."

Result: Hevesi still won that 2006 election, but was forced to resign almost immediately, pleading guilty to charges of defrauding the government. The state's pension fund (third largest in the country) was worth $125 billion, and it had apparently become a money maker for Hevesi—his top political consultant had been acting as a middleman, steering pension-fund investments to Hevesi's friends and political associates—and getting kickbacks for his efforts. By the time the investigation was over in 2010, Hevesi pleaded guilty to directing $250 million in state pension funds to an investment company that gave him $75,000 for travel expenses for himself and his family, $380,000 for other expenses, and $500,000 in campaign contributions.

HELPFUL COP?

Who: Bernard Kerik (Republican)

What he did: In 1994, Bernie Kerik was an NYPD detective assigned to Mayor Rudy Giuliani's "protective detail" as bodyguard and driver. The mayor liked Kerik so much that he appointed him as head of the Department of Corrections and then, in 2000, promoted him to NYPD commissioner. Kerik was the commissioner on 9/11, and happened to meet (and impress) President George W. Bush at the disaster site. In 2004, Kerik was tapped by the Bush administration to be the next Secretary of the Department of Homeland Security.

Kerik, a highly decorated police officer, had always been a tough guy and a bit of a loose cannon, but when he was vetted by White House officials about his career, he assured them he was squeaky clean. He wasn't: A New Jersey construction company had paid for $255,000 of renovations on Kerik's Bronx home in the hope that Kerik would help them get a New York City building license, and Kerik had contacted city officials on the company's behalf.

Result: Kerik was convicted and sentenced to prison after pleading guilty to eight felony charges, including tax fraud and lying to White House officials. His plea agreement recommended a maximum of 33 months in jail, but the angry judge slapped him with 48, calling him a "toxic combination of self-minded focus and arrogance."

MORE NEW YORK Q & A

Our list of New York facts and oddities continues.
(Part I appears on page 81.)

Q. Who ensured public safety on the city's Death Avenue before 1934?
A. "Cowboys." Until the 1930s, the thoroughfare known as Death Avenue (Tenth Avenue) on Manhattan's West Side was home to numerous factories serviced by railroads. The tracks posed a deadly hazard to cars, carriages, and pedestrians, who often strayed into the path of oncoming trains. In fact, the avenue was so hazardous that railroads employed men on horseback—who came to be called the Westside Cowboys—to ride ahead of the trains, waving flags and warning the public that they were coming. By the 1930s, the tracks had been replaced by an elevated line that remained in use until 1980.

Q. Of the five boroughs that make up New York City, which is the only one with a freshwater river running through it?
A. The Bronx. In fact, it has two: the Bronx River, which bisects it, and the smaller Hutchinson River, which passes through the northeast section of the borough and empties into Eastchester Bay.

Q. Why are the entrances to Central Park named for generic groups of people?
A. Central Park's 843 acres are accessed by 20 entranceways, or "gates," cryptically named the Inventors' Gate, Artists' Gate, Engineers' Gate, Hunters' Gate, Explorers' Gate, Warriors' Gate, Women's Gate, and so on. When the park was built in the 1860s, the landscape architects who designed it—Frederick Law Olmsted and Calvert Vaux—wanted to ensure that the greenbelt was welcoming to visitors and accessible to everyone. So, even though many people wanted the city to install ornate, iron gates—some even wanted the park to be locked at night—Olmsted and Vaux protested, insisting that the "gates" consist only of open pathways and low walls. They also named the entrances after types of people who might use the park. There was never a formal naming process,

---

William Randolph Hearst and Norman Mailer both ran for mayor of NYC. (And lost.)

though, so for more than 100 years, most New Yorkers just referred to the entrances by their cross streets. It wasn't until 1999 that the names were etched in sandstone at each entrance.

Q. Why do the avenues get closer together near the rivers?
A. In 1811, surveyors working for the State of New York unveiled the Commissioners Plan, which laid out the street/avenue grid pattern that Manhattan is now famous for. The surveyors theorized that real estate close to the rivers would be more valuable than that in the center of the island because the waterfronts were the city's import/export hubs. So surveyors crimped the acreage into smaller parcels along the rivers to make more money. East Side avenues are spaced at 680 feet, while West Side avenues are separated by 800 feet. The avenues in the middle of Manhattan have the widest spacing: 920 feet.

Q. What solved New York's Great Horse Manure Crisis?
A. You've never heard of the Great Horse Manure Crisis? Here's what happened: Like many large cities in the 19th century, New York depended on horses for city services, and those animals generated a lot of waste. By the start of the 20th century, more than 100,000 horses lived in New York, and they produced about 2.5 million pounds of manure every day. In 1898, a group of urban planners convened, with the goal of finding a solution to New York's waste-clogged streets. After three days, the planners gave up, convinced that there was nothing that could be done—horses were a necessity, and as the city grew, even more horses would move in. Residents would just have to learn to live with the mess. A few years later, a businessman in Michigan came up with an invention that inadvertently solved New York's crisis. Henry Ford introduced the Model T in 1908, and within 10 years, automobiles had replaced horses for most city services. Pollution problem solved! (Well, one of them.)

Q. Why is Broadway the only diagonal street in Manhattan?
A. Because it follows the route of a Native American footpath across Manhattan Island. Broadway is New York City's oldest avenue—the Indians called it *Wickquasgeck* and used it to cross the thick forests, fields of wild strawberries, and fishing inlets that

existed before the Dutch built their settlement. The rest of New York City grew up around Broadway and was laid out in the grid pattern favored by Europeans. But Broadway remained a diagonal arrow across the Big Apple.

Q. Where, or what, is the "Boogie Down"?
A. It's a reference to the Bronx, the birthplace of hip-hop music. On August 11, 1973, Clive "DJ Kool Herc" Campbell hosted a "back-to-school" party in a rec room at 1520 Sedgewick Avenue in the west Bronx. His sister Cindy came up with the idea—she wanted to raise enough money to buy some new school clothes. The teenagers charged admission (25¢ for "ladies," and 50¢ for "fellas") and invited as many people in their neighborhood as they could find. Hundreds of kids showed up. Campbell put together the music by taking two copies of the same song and playing them side-by-side on separate turntables, repeating different beats that he thought sounded good. That party led to others, and eventually to huge events in a nearby park. (Campbell hot-wired street lamps to power his collection of massive speakers.) He used a microphone to "rap" over the music and encouraged break dancers (whom he nicknamed "b boys," for "break boys") to perform as well. Campbell went on to become a well-respected DJ, and the Bronx earned the nickname "the Boogie Down" for all the music that came out of the borough.

Q. What's the oldest bridge in the five boroughs?
A. The High Bridge, built between 1837 and 1848. Connecting Manhattan and the Bronx, the bridge was a way to move water from the Croton Aqueduct to other parts of New York. It was just a pedestrian walkway (no road), but that closed in 1970 after someone tossed a brick onto a boat in the Harlem River. Rumor has it that the High Bridge will reopen to foot traffic sometime in 2013.

* * *

"People say that money is not the key to happiness, but I always figured, if you have enough money, you can get a key made."
—Joan Rivers

THE LANDLORD OF NEW YORK

*Before Donald Trump took over New York City
real estate, there was John Jacob Astor.*

THE MAKINGS OF A MILLIONAIRE

John Jacob Astor grew up poor in 18th-century Waldorf, Germany. His father was a butcher, and his mother was incredibly frugal, a trait her son inherited. By all accounts the family was happy, but Astor wasn't content to be happy and poor. He wanted to be happy and rich.

As a teenager, Astor moved from Germany to London, where he lived with his older brother George and learned how to make musical instruments. He'd heard stories of great opportunity in North America, though, so in 1784, he boarded a ship bound for the New World. Along the way, he met a fellow German immigrant who told him that there was a lot of money to be made in buying and selling furs. In the late 1700s, wealthy Europeans were crazy for fur hats, especially ones made of beaver. The animals had been hunted almost to extinction in Europe, but American forests were full of them...and otter, ermine, and mink. Native American and frontier trappers sold merchants pelts that they then sold to Europeans for huge profits. (Ten beaver pelts might cost a merchant $3, but he could sell them in Europe for $30.) So by the time the 21-year-old Astor arrived in Baltimore Harbor, he'd decided to make it big in the fur trade.

BUY, BUY, BUY!

But he couldn't just jump into the business. He had no contacts, no money for investment, and no idea how to get started. So in the meantime, he made and sold wooden flutes. He used the money he made to travel to New York City, where he held a variety of jobs—including peddling baked goods on the street and selling more flutes. He also made sure to work for furriers whenever he could, and saved every penny to buy fur pelts.

A year later, Astor had enough furs to go back to London and

..."The Angel of the Waters" (in Central Park's Bethesda Fountain) by Emma Stebbins.

sell them...and made a killing at it. He used some of the profits to buy muskets and pots and pans—goods that he could trade to Native Americans and other trappers for more furs. Astor also made deals with makers of musical instruments so he could sell their wares in New York. By 1785, he'd established himself as an international merchant.

INTO THE WILD

That same year, Astor returned to New York City and married Sarah Todd, the daughter of his landlady. She turned out to be an excellent business partner and shrewd manager. She also brought a free place to live in her mother's boarding house and plenty of good connections through her influential family. Thanks to all that, Astor was able to open a shop on Little Deck Street (now Water Street) in lower Manhattan that sold furs and musical instruments.

Every spring for the next few years, he left the shop in Sarah's hands and took off for the "wilds" of upstate New York to buy furs directly from trappers. In the earliest years, Astor traveled by horse and on foot, following Native American trails through the Adirondack Mountains. The trips rarely went smoothly—the young man often had trouble navigating through the wilderness, and he once lost all his goods in a swamp. But the money he made was worth it.

Astor soon realized that he could make even more money if he set up trading posts along the way, where both white and Native American trappers could meet with buyers, making it easy for them to trade in their furs. He also offered the Indians the goods they wanted—blankets, kettles, and rifles—at high quality and low prices. That made the trappers flock to Astor's posts. He had competition in the fur business—most notably Britain's Hudson Bay Company, the Canadian North West Company, and the United States government, which had set up its own trade network—but because he offered the best goods for the best prices, his American Fur Company became the one most trappers preferred to do business with...and it was the leading U.S. exporter of furs. Astor's first trading post was in Schenectady on the Mohawk River, and by 1808, his agents were operating as far away as Mackinaw, Michigan. But Astor still wasn't satisfied.

GO WEST, YOUNG RICH MAN

Astor wanted his American Fur Company to reach all the way to the West Coast, and that ambition altered the course of American history. In 1810, he organized and financed the overland Astor Expedition, only the second American expedition (after Lewis and Clark) to cross the continent. Astor hired pioneer William Price Hunt to lead the group, and after having some trouble finding "quality" men to join the party (Hunt said that most of the men he tried to hire were "drinking in the morning, drunk at noon, and dead drunk at night"), he set off for Oregon to establish a fort and a center for buying furs. Hunt's expedition discovered the South Pass, a crossing point in the Rocky Mountains that was later used by thousands of pioneers traveling to Oregon and California along the Oregon Trail.

In 1811, while his overland expedition was still heading west, Astor also sent ships up the Columbia River from the Pacific Ocean to set up his new outpost, Fort Astoria, on the Oregon coast. His settlement was established six weeks before the Canadians from the Northwest Company arrived to claim the area for Canada.

Astor had big dreams for Fort Astoria: Ships would drop off trade goods for the trappers and pick up furs, then sail to China, where the furs would be traded for teas, silks, and other exotic Asian goods. Those goods would be carried to Europe and traded for European goods to sell in New York. With each trade, Astor would make a substantial profit. It was a grand scheme...and a great failure. Shipwrecks, Native American uprisings, and the War of 1812 derailed his plans in Oregon. By 1813, Fort Astoria had to be sold off.

SLUMMING IT

When the war ended, Astor went back to his fur business, and by the early 1820s, he once again dominated the trade. But the times were changing: European fashions were evolving, and they didn't use as many furs as before. As a result, Astor started looking into even more profitable ventures. Since he already had an export company established, he used it to become a weapons dealer, supplying English guns to South American revolutionaries. He also entered the opium trade in China, bringing back the addictive drug along with his furs. But these ventures didn't last long. By then, he'd found another, even more profitable, business.

The 1927 Yankees were the first team to occupy first place for every day of the regular season.

The main offices for Astor's trading company were in New York, and he'd noticed that the city was growing…and growing…mainly because of the influx of immigrants like himself. But Manhattan was a small island; space was running out, even as the people kept coming, which would certainly run up prices. So in 1803, he began buying up property. He also took land as payment for debts. Then he subdivided the land, leasing it long-term to tenants who were required to build on it themselves. Astor's gamble paid off as the value of land in New York continued to rise. By the 1830s, he was concentrating exclusively on real estate. His annual income from rents was more than $1,250,000…earning Astor the nickname "the landlord of New York."

Many of the buildings on Astor's land became slums, and he wasn't known for being a generous landlord. His rental agents were known to put poor families out on the street for not paying up, and he soon earned a reputation for being heartless and greedy.

A MELLOWER MILLIONAIRE?

But as he got older, Astor's priorities seemed to shift. From about 1838 to his death 10 years later, he lived quietly and became more interested in education and culture than in making money. He helped to encourage and support artists and writers like John James Audubon, Edgar Allan Poe, and Washington Irving. When Astor died in 1848, he left $400,000 to establish a public library in New York City.

Despite all that, Astor is remembered today for his incredible wealth and for leaving so much of New York City's land in the hands of his descendants. All over New York, the family left its stamp: the Waldorf-Astoria Hotel in Manhattan; the neighborhood of Astoria, Queens; Astor Row in Harlem; and Astor Avenue in the Bronx. Still it never seemed to be enough for Astor. In his later years, when asked what he might have done differently in his life, the old man replied, "I would buy every foot of land on the island of Manhattan."

*   *   *

First MLB player to have a hairdryer in the clubhouse: Joe Pepitone, New York Yankees (1962–69).

Staten Island's Fresh Kills was opened in 1947 as a "temporary landfill"…

IN THE BIG HOUSES

In most of New York's prisons, inmates are known for the single worst crime they've committed...or been caught for. But a few prisoners also made names for themselves for what they did while they were doing time.

INMATE: Lil Wayne, Grammy winner and self-proclaimed "Best Rapper Alive"
LOCKED UP IN... Rikers Island
WHILE IN PRISON... In 2010, Lil Wayne released the album titled *I Am Not a Human Being* (which shot to #1 on the Billboard charts), collaborated on a song with rappers Drake and Jay-Z, was sued by a record producer, and posted regular blog entries. The last month of his incarceration was spent in solitary confinement because he was caught with contraband—not drugs or weapons, but an iPod charger and earphones.

INMATE: John Colt, brother of revolver inventor Samuel Colt
LOCKED UP IN... The Tombs
WHILE IN PRISON... The day before Colt's execution in 1842, he married his housekeeper. Hours later, he committed suicide in his cell by stabbing himself through the heart. At the same time, a candle (or lamp) ignited a fire that swept through the prison and destroyed part of the roof. Several prisoners escaped, and Colt's bride was never seen again, sparking a rumor that she had set the fire while Colt faked his death, substituted another body for his own, and escaped.

INMATE: Drifter Eddie White
LOCKED UP IN... Rikers Island
WHILE IN PRISON... By 1994, White had broken out of Rikers Island three times. (He'd been locked up for the murders of two people and sentenced to 200 years to life.) The breakouts earned him the respect of inmates, who dubbed him "Rabbit Man" for his quickness. In one escape, he allegedly killed two more people, but those charges were dismissed when the judge noted that he was already going to die in jail.

INMATE: Con artist Tuvia Stern
LOCKED UP IN... The Tombs
WHILE IN PRISON... In June 2009, Stern threw a lavish bar mitzvah for his son...behind bars. Held in the prison gym, the gala had 60 guests, catered kosher food, and a band. Attendees were even allowed to keep their cell phones, a big no-no in prison, and the jail paid officers overtime for the event. Four months later, Stern threw another party, this time for his daughter's engagement. When the city's corrections commissioner found out about the parties, he suspended the prison rabbi who'd overseen the bar mitzvah and took away vacation benefits for four corrections officers who'd been in on the event.

INMATE: Robber Ronald Tackman
LOCKED UP IN... Rikers Island
WHILE IN PRISON... In October 2009, Tackman donned a suit for his trial and walked out of prison by posing as a lawyer—he asked, "Which way is out?" and a guard escorted him. (Two days later, he was re-apprehended.) That con worked because Tackman was a crafty master of disguise. During stick-ups, he wore a fake nose or a big-rimmed gangster hat. And in jail, Tackman once took over a prison van using a "weapon" carved out of soap.

*   *   *

LOST AND FOUND

In 2008 people in the five boroughs left about 19,000 items on New York City's subways and buses—42 percent of those things were returned to their owners. Unsurprisingly, some of the most frequently lost (and found) items include IDs, cell phones, iPods, wallets, keys, shoes, and toys. But on the informational posters the MTA puts up in the city's buses and subway cars, the pictures of "suggested" lost items include a crutch, a set of false teeth, a computer mouse, and a cobra. And maybe those possibilities aren't so far-fetched: According to the *New York Post*, in 2008 the MTA found (among other things) "a fake limb, a used cooking pot, and a trumpet."

Amount of wire rope strung across the Brooklyn Bridge: 14,000 miles.

THE APOLLO

If you want the best in black entertainment in the best theater in the best city, check out the Apollo.

IT'S SHOWTIME

Harlem's Apollo Theater opened in 1914 as a burlesque hall, and even though it was located in the heart of New York City's most prominent African American neighborhood, blacks were not allowed to attend the shows. They didn't even perform at the theater until 1925, when, with the Harlem Renaissance in full bloom, whites began to recognize the value of black entertainment. But even as African American acts appeared on the playbill, the audience remained whites only.

The theater stayed that way until the early 1930s, when Mayor Fiorello La Guardia began a campaign to clean up New York City's vices and inadvertently created the most famous black theater in the United States. One of the "low-class" entertainments La Guardia wanted to get rid of was burlesque. (Another was organ grinders; he blamed them for causing traffic congestion and had them banned in 1936.) So in 1934, the Apollo's owner, Sidney Cohen, decided that instead of getting in the mayor's way, he'd change what kinds of shows played at his theater. In setting up the new playbill, Cohen also decided to cash in on the large, potential audience that lived in the neighborhoods surrounding the theater. That year, the Apollo "home of burlesque shows" became the Apollo "the center of African American entertainment." For the first time in New York's history, blacks and whites attended the same shows and cheered for the same (black) entertainers: Billie Holiday, the Count Basie Orchestra, Bill "Bojangles" Robinson, and Bessie Smith, among others.

BEWARE THE EXECUTIONER

Since 1934, one of the most popular shows at the Apollo has been Amateur Night. Held every Wednesday, new singers, dancers, and comedians climb onto the theater's big stage to compete for prizes and, hopefully, to wow the audience. A good performance can

The first year NYC had traffic lights: 1916.

make a career; a bad performance can kill it. And at the Apollo, it's the audience that decides good from bad. If the crowd doesn't like a performer on Amateur Night, they make it known—by yelling, jeering, heckling, stomping their feet, and, in the old days, occasionally throwing things. Then it's the job of a man known as "the Executioner" to chase the unsuccessful contestants from the stage. Stagehand Norman Miller created the character in the 1930s. Today, the Executioner is played by singer and comedian C. P. Lacey.

Many Amateur Night performers have gone on to great careers. Seventeen-year-old Ella Fitzgerald made her singing debut on Amateur Night in 1934. She'd originally planned to dance, but was so intimidated by a group that went before her that she chose to sing instead. The Executioner didn't come for Ella, and she went on to win first prize: $25. Other Amateur Night performers include Pearl Bailey, Dionne Warwick, James Brown, Sarah Vaughan, Jimi Hendrix, Gladys Knight, and the Jackson 5.

FAMOUS FANS
Tourists and Harlem residents aren't the only people who love the Apollo. The theater has some famous fans too.

• In the 1930s and '40s, comedian Milton Berle used to take in shows at the Apollo, gauging crowd reaction so he could apply jokes and the comedians' timing to his own performances.

• In the 1970s, when Aretha Franklin performed at the Apollo, the marquee read, "She's Home," because in the 1950s, long before she'd recorded any hit records, Franklin hung out at the theater. She came to watch and support her friends, like the Motown group the Four Tops.

• In 1964, on their first trip to the United States, the Beatles came to New York. When asked what they wanted to see in the city, the first thing they came up with was "a show at the Apollo."

EQUAL OPPORTUNITY
Although the Apollo is known for nurturing black entertainers, many white performers have played on its stage too. Among them: Buddy Holly, Rod Stewart, Boy George, and Joe Cocker.

PELTED

Whether as a gesture of contempt or of celebration, throwing
stuff is a universal form of expression. And over the years,
New Yorkers—always an expressive bunch—have put
on some noteworthy displays of public pelting.

MESSY DEBUT

Through much of the history of theater—since medieval times at least—a well-established form of critical insult was to pelt lousy performers with rotten food. (Eggs and, later, tomatoes were typically the rotten foods of choice.) One of the first recorded instances of this in the New World happened in Hempstead, Long Island, in 1883, when a hometown performer named John Ritchie took the stage before a full house in Washington Hall. According to a *New York Times* article published at the time, Ritchie was an "aspiring actor and lecturer" who had just begun his act with some tumbling and somersaults when the tomatoes started flying. He then tried to perform on a trapeze, but a tomato thrown from the gallery "struck him square between the eyes, and he fell to the stage just as several bad eggs dropped upon his head." Ritchie tried to escape, but the stage door was locked, so he fled through the audience amid a flurry of rotten tomatoes. What became of Ritchie's acting and lecturing career is unknown, but the article did note that he vowed never again to perform in Hempstead.

LEAVING A PAPER TRAIL

Ticker-tape parades represent the other king of public pelting: the positive kind. And New York, where the tradition began, has hosted more than 200 of them over the past 125 years. These paper-strewn celebratory marches down lower Broadway through Manhattan's financial district—a stretch of road known as the "Canyon of Heroes"—have honored everyone from visiting kings to returning astronauts, army generals, and Super Bowl champions.

The first ticker-tape parade took place on October 28, 1886, during a procession marking the official dedication of the Statue of Liberty. Huge crowds—by some estimates nearly a million people—lined the streets of Manhattan to see President Grover

Cleveland pass by, followed by bands and marching groups. When the procession reached the financial district, stockbrokers threw ticker tape—ribbons of paper churned out by machines that gave them up-to-date market prices—out of overhead brokerage firm windows in celebration. "Every window appeared to be a paper mill spouting out squirming lines of tape," reported the next day's *New York Times*. Ticker-tape machines are now obsolete, so modern parades include showering recipients with shredded office paper and confetti.

TRICK AND TREAT

Baseball legend Reggie Jackson once declared—while still a member of the Oakland A's—"If I played in New York, they'd name a candy bar for me." Jackson's statement proved to be prophetic. After leaving Oakland, and following a brief stopover with the Baltimore Orioles, Jackson signed with the New York Yankees for the 1977 season and led them into the World Series. In the series-clinching Game 6, "Mister October" slugged three home runs on three consecutive pitches, earning a World Series MVP title.

The next season, at the Yankees' home opener against the Chicago White Sox, all 72,000 in attendance were given free "Reggie!" bars—a circular chocolate treat, filled with nuts and caramel—in recognition of Jackson's achievements the previous October. In the first inning, with two Yankees on base, Jackson belted another one of his trademark home runs. As he rounded the bases, candy bars came raining down out of the stands and the crowd chanted, "Reggie! Reggie! Reggie!" Play resumed after the groundscrew cleaned up the mess, and the Yankees went on to win 4–2. Afterward, Jackson was appreciative, calling the shower "a nice gesture." But the White Sox manager Bob Lemon wasn't impressed: "People are starving all over the world," Lemon griped, "and 30 billion calories are laying on the field."

*   *   *

"I feel that the most important requirement in success is learning to overcome failure. You must learn to tolerate it, but never accept it."

—Reggie Jackson

CELEBRITY 101

Get to know your New York celebrities.

• CNN anchor **Anderson Cooper** was once a child model. At 10 years old, he had a contract with the Ford Modeling Agency.

• In 2004, **Jennifer Lopez's** mother, Guadalupe (a Westchester County teacher), won $2.4 million at an Atlantic City casino.

• Before becoming an Academy Award–winning actor, **Adrien Brody** did magic shows at children's birthday parties. His stage name: the Amazing Adrien.

• **Humphrey Bogart's** mother, Maud, worked for many years as a commercial artist and illustrator, and around 1900, she submitted a drawing of her infant son to Mellin's Baby Food. The company's execs liked the little boy's chubby cheeks and put him in all of their ad campaigns. Bogey said later, "There was a period in American history when you couldn't pick up a goddamned magazine without seeing my kisser on it."

• As a kid, **Tom Cruise** wanted to be a priest. He even enrolled in a seminary, but dropped out after a year.

• **Robert De Niro** and **Martin Scorsese** grew up within just a few blocks of each other in Manhattan's Little Italy in the 1950s, but they didn't actually meet until 1972, when they were introduced at a party.

• **Taye Diggs's** real first name is Scott. "Taye" comes from his childhood nickname, "Scottaye."

• **Rosie O'Donnell's** senior classmates at Commack High School on Long Island voted her "Most Popular."

• In 1936, as a favor to her grandfather, **Lucille Ball** joined the Communist Party. Fast-forward to the 1950s: When the House Un-American Activities Committee began investigating entertainers with Communist ties, Ball appeared on their list. But ultimately, the committee decided that she wasn't a Communist after all (she'd never contributed any money or attended any meetings) and dropped the investigation.

GHOST STORIES, PART II

More spooky tales from the city where even the
dead never sleep. (Part I is on page 63.)

WHO: Various specters
WHERE: #12 Gay Street, Manhattan
Built in 1827, this West Village brick townhouse is considered one of the most haunted buildings in New York City. The ghosts date back to the 1920s, when a speakeasy called the Pirate's Den—frequented by socialites, celebrities, and politicians of the day—operated in the basement. On the upper floors, the building's owner, Mayor Jimmy Walker, kept his mistress, a showgirl named Betty Compton.

Fast forward to 1956. That's when puppeteer Frank Paris (famous as the creator of the *Howdy Doody Show*) bought the house. Paris lived upstairs, and he turned the basement into a studio where he crafted marionettes and gave puppet shows. He had some strange experiences in the home: He and his friends sometimes heard footsteps going up and down the stairs or people making loud noises on the upper floors. Working very late at night in the basement, the puppeteer reported smelling violets at least once. In other rooms, he smelled onions frying (a phenomenon that the house's later owner also experienced). Paris also claimed to have seen a dark-haired ghost, whom he called the "Gay Street Phantom." The Phantom was a man dressed in a cape, top hat, and tails, as though he were heading out for a night on the town. And although his face was shadowed, Paris thought he looked like a youngish man with "sparkling eyes." He seemed so friendly and ordinary that Paris's dog ran to greet him...just as the ghost vanished.

Some "supernatural historians" note that a cemetery once occupied the land where Gay Street is now, and they question whether "lost spirits" made their way to #12. But others believe that the Phantom of Gay Street is Mayor Jimmy Walker himself, who was famous for looking the other way when it came to enforcing the rules of Prohibition and for making it legal for New Yorkers to play sports and go to the movies on Sundays (previously forbidden because it was the Sabbath). Many people wonder if the other ghosts traipsing through the townhouse are the spirits of speakeasy customers returning to revisit the good times they once had there.

WHO: Mary Parrish
WHERE: The Old Stone House, Bronx
In 1851, Scottish immigrant Alexander Diack built a stone house in a small Bronx village that was then called Pelhamville (now just Pelham). Today, the Old Stone House at 463 First Avenue in the Bronx is a well-known landmark because it's been haunted for more than 100 years.

James and Mary Parrish bought the house in 1855, and Mary continued to live there alone after James died. She had a considerable income from stock shares and was known to carry around as much as $600 in her purse. In July 1879, three burglars broke into the elderly widow's home, ransacked the house, and stole at least $100. (Mary said that the burglars also tied her up, but she could never explain how she escaped to alert the neighbors.) Mary hid all her money after that, and legend said there was a pot of gold hidden on her property. About 100 small coins were found, but some people say that, after she died, Mary returned for the rest of it. Supposedly, her spirit still searches the property, apparently unable to remember where she hid her money. When residents of the house described the ghost to one of Mary's descendants—actor Edward Everett Horton—he showed them an old daguerreotype of his relative that fit the apparition's appearance exactly.

WHO: Edward Kreischer, his wife, and various others
WHERE: The Kreischer mansion, Staten Island
This home was built by Balthazar Kreischer, a German brick mason who made a fortune in the late 19th century. (His bricks can still be seen in many Staten Island buildings.) In 1885, Balthazar decided to build two mansions for his sons, Edward and Charles, on Arthur Kill Road in Charleston. Edward's home burned down in the 1930s, but Charles's home—a looming Victorian structure with a wrap-around porch and iron gates—still stands. Supposedly, it's one of the most haunted buildings on Staten Island.

Over the years, the mansion eventually was turned into a

restaurant, and employees and patrons reported hearing scratching noises in one of the closets, doors that slammed for no reason, footsteps in empty rooms, the sound of a woman crying, and vaporous apparitions that appeared and disappeared in the house and on the grounds. Although the mansion belonged to Charles, the ghosts are believed to be Edward and his wife, who came back "home" after their deaths. And Edward may have been the victim of foul play—in 1894, he was found dead at the family's brick factory with a revolver beside his body. Authorities assumed he'd committed suicide after fighting with his father or brother (or maybe even a foreman in the family brick business), but no one ever investigated the possibility of murder. Many supernaturalists believe that the crying woman is Edward's wife.

These days, some people wonder if the house is cursed too. In 2005, ex-marine Joseph Young began looking after the Kreischer mansion for its absentee owner-investor. Soon after he moved in, though, Young stabbed a man and drowned him in a pond on the property. Young had friends in the Bonanno crime family, and one of them was owed money by a man named Robert McKelvey. Young was offered about $8,000 to murder McKelvey. Afterward, with help from mob pals, he chopped up the corpse to burn in the furnace. Young was convicted of the murder in 2009 and sentenced to life in prison.

* * *

N.Y. BUMPER STICKERS

- No, this is not a taxi.

- Smile if you love Wall Street.

- I'm from New York, and you talk too slow.

- This vehicle is protected by an anti-theft sticker.

- Keep New York beautiful. Dump your trash in Jersey.

- Support bacteria: It's the only culture some people have.

As the first player to use a bat with a knob at the end of the handle...

ONLY IN ALBANY

*Every state has a capital, but only New York has
Albany and these unusual claims to fame.*

1. "YANKEE DOODLE." In 1758 (probably, though some historians cite the date as 1755 or '56), British army surgeon Richard Shuckburgh and his unit were stationed at Fort Crailo, just over the Hudson River from Albany. As he prepared to take on the French (who were allied with the colonists during the French and Indian War), Shuckburgh penned a catchy little tune that he called "Yankee Doodle," in which he made fun of the American soldiers gathering across the river. Those soldiers had been ordered to stay out of Albany (to keep them from being distracted by the city's brothels and taverns), and their ragtag platoon was the laughingstock of the British redcoats. In those days, a "doodle" was slang for a simpleminded person. "Macaroni" was a sophisticated, trendy style of dress—so a "Yankee doodle" who stuck "a feather in his cap and called it macaroni" was a bumbling bumpkin passing himself off as a well-dressed gentleman.

But Yankee soldiers were nothing if not adaptable, and they adopted Shuckburgh's song as their own. (Legend says that Americans just liked the tune.) By the 1770s, when the Revolutionary War was in full swing, colonial militias were singing "Yankee Doodle" as a proud battlecry against their English counterparts.

2. ERASTUS CORNING II. Albany's "grandest son," Corning served as the city's mayor from 1941 until his death in 1983—an astonishing 42 years—making him the longest-serving mayor of a major American city.

3. MODERN TOILET PAPER. In 1871, Albany resident Seth Wheeler received a patent for his new invention: perforated toilet paper. Individual sheets of toilet paper had been around for a few years, but Wheeler was the first to offer a long, single sheet from which you could tear off pieces. His company—with the unwieldy name of the Albany Perforated Wrapping Paper Company—started selling the paper in drugstores as a means of preventing hemorrhoids: It was, according to ads, "free of all deleterious substances." Eight years later, he patented the toilet paper roll, combined the two, and a modern bathroom staple was born.

4. THE PINE BUSH. This stretch of land along I-87 near Albany is one of only about 20 inland pine barrens in the world. What's a "pine barren"? It's a region covered with prairie grass, wildflowers, pitch pines, and shrubs that grow in sand dunes. During the last Ice Age thousands of years ago, a glacial lake covered the area between the modern-day towns of Glen Falls and Newburgh. When the ice melted and the lake drained, it left behind about 40 square miles of sandy soil. Today, only 20 percent of the Albany Pine Bush remains—the rest has been gobbled up by highways and shopping malls.

5. A SINKING CAPITOL. In 1867, construction began on the state capitol building in Albany (one of only 10 state capitols in the U.S. that do not include a dome). But workers soon discovered that they were constructing the building on quicksand. Visitors today don't need to worry about losing their footing, though. The builders dug up the quicksand (by hand) until they reached solid ground and then replaced the foundation with clay and concrete.

6. THE SUNY WEATHERVANE. Perched atop the State University of New York Central Administration Building is the largest working weathervane in North America—it's 8'10" tall, weighs 400 pounds, and is a replica of the *Half Moon*, the ship Henry Hudson took to sail up the Hudson River and into Albany.

7. THE BEGINNING OF THE END FOR ABRAHAM LINCOLN. On February 18, 1861, president-elect Lincoln was traveling by train to Washington, D.C., for his inauguration and he stopped in Albany to give a speech at the New York State Legislature. He was greeted by thick crowds of protesters, many of whom disagreed with his stance on slavery and shouted insults and obscenities. Most were nameless, but one of them would later determine Lincoln's fate: John Wilkes Booth joined in the protests. Four years later, he assassinated Lincoln at Ford's Theatre in Washington, D.C.

The geographic center of New York State is the village of Pratts Hollow.

THE GANG'S ALL HERE

"I would rather risk myself in an Indian fight than venture among these creatures after night."—*Frontier hero Davy Crockett, describing the gangs of Manhattan's Five Points*

GANGS OF NEW YORK

In the 1800s, one of the worst slums in the United States was in lower Manhattan, centered at the intersection of what are now Park, Worth, and Baxter streets. Called the Five Points (because the neighborhood used to be at the intersection of five streets), its tenements were damp, unhealthy, and built on landfill so their foundations were sinking into unstable ground. The people who lived there, mostly destitute Irish immigrants who'd come to America seeking a better life, couldn't afford to live anywhere else.

Typically, entire families in the Five Points were shoehorned into one small room, so many people spent a lot of time outside…and young men spent a lot of time in the streets. They had little education and few prospects for work, but the neighborhood had plenty of opportunities for drinking, gambling, brawling, and crime, making the Five Points one of America's first breeding grounds for powerful street gangs. Eventually, these gangs gained political clout and a public following, and when they went to war, it sometimes took the military to restore peace.

THE FORTY THIEVES

Leader: Edward Coleman

Turf: The neighborhood in and around Centre Street

Claim to fame: The Irish gang called the Forty Thieves was America's first known street gang, and it introduced organized crime to New York. The Forty Thieves met at a grocery store on Centre Street, but they never bought the rotting vegetables that the owner, Rosanna Peers, sold out front. Instead they gathered in the back room to drink rotgut liquor, and founding leader Edward Coleman used the store as his headquarters. From there, he kept track of the pickpockets, hold-up artists, and muggers that he'd sent out to terrorize the neighborhood.

Placed end-to-end, the 9,000 benches in Central Park would stretch 7 miles.

Gang members were required to turn over their cash or stolen goods to Coleman. Anyone who didn't bring in money was thrown out of the gang immediately. And Coleman expected big earnings from anyone who worked for him—which led to his downfall.

In the 1830s, Coleman married a "hot corn girl," one of the young women who sold roasted ears of corn on the streets. In 1838, when she didn't bring in enough earnings, Coleman killed her. The murder shocked New York City, and Coleman—the city's first street-gang leader—also became the first person executed in the newly completed Tombs Prison. The Forty Thieves continued for a while without Coleman, but its members gradually merged into newer, more powerful Irish gangs...like the Dead Rabbits.

THE DEAD RABBITS

Leader: John Morrissey

Turf: The entire Five Points

Claim to fame: The story of how the Dead Rabbits got their name is blurred with legends. One story says they began as part of the Roche (pronounced "roach") Guard Gang but, after a disagreement, split off into a group of their own. Supposedly that was when someone threw a rabbit corpse on the floor, and the new gang found its name. Another legend claims that the members carried a dead rabbit impaled on a pole when they battled other gangs. But in reality, it's probable that no bunnies were involved with the gang in any way. "Rabbit" likely came from the Irish term *ráibéad*, which meant a "rowdy" or a "battler," and the term "dead" was 19th-century slang for "extremely." And the Dead Rabbits were definitely extremely rowdy fighters—they used brickbats, paving stones, clubs, knives, and guns to attack their rivals. They also used them to win elections.

What made 19th-century gangs like the Dead Rabbits so dangerous and powerful was their alliance with crooked politicians. Dead Rabbits were "shoulder-hitters"—thugs who helped to rig elections by intimidating voters and tampering with votes, destroying any ballot boxes and polling booths that favored an opposing candidate. As payment, the politicians forced police to look the other way when Dead Rabbits broke the law.

The Dead Rabbits backed pro-Irish, pro-Catholic candidates and Mayor Fernando Wood, elected in 1854, who claimed to be tough on crime but really was allied with the gang. That year, an anti-Irish, anti-Catholic gang called the Bowery Boys (see below) was trying to rig the election in support of its own Protestant candidate. At the time, the Dead Rabbits were led by John Morrissey, a tough, bare-knuckle boxer, who—along with his men—waylaid the Protestant supporters at the polls and saved Catholic ballots from being dumped in the East River. It worked. Wood was elected mayor, and to show his gratitude, he allowed Morrissey and the Dead Rabbits to open a gambling hall protected by his corrupt police force.

THE BOWERY BOYS

Leader: Bill "the Butcher" Poole
Turf: The Bowery, just north of the Five Points
Claim to fame: In the 1860s, the Bowery was a working-class neighborhood, and unlike lower Manhattan's other nearly destitute gangs, most of the Bowery Boys had steady jobs as butchers or mechanics. Bowery Boys had money to spend at their neighborhood's saloons, beer gardens, and dance halls. They could also dress well in hip stovepipe hats, frock coats, black flared pants, tall black boots, and even silk ascots.

Like their arch enemies the Dead Rabbits, the Bowery Boys were also shoulder-hitters. They might wear fancy clothes, but they'd steal and murder in the service of their political allies—in particular, the Know Nothing Party. This Protestant, anti-immigrant political party worked to repeal any laws that benefited the new Irish, German, and Jewish immigrants. The Know Nothings resented the immigrants—especially the Roman Catholic Irish, whose large numbers were seen as a threat to their jobs and way of life.

The most famous leader of the Bowery Boys, William Poole (a.k.a. "the Butcher"), a native of Sussex County, New Jersey, was also a leader of the Know Nothings. Poole was, according to the *Brooklyn Eagle*, "a knock-down, gouging, biting, brutal savage." Once, in 1854, Poole confronted John Morrissey, his enemy from the Dead Rabbits, who was also a boxer. After exchanging insults, the leaders agreed to meet at a pier near Christopher Street for a bare-knuckle duel.

Morrissey arrived at the pier with a dozen of his friends...only to discover that Bill the Butcher had hundreds of supporters with him. According to the *Daily Times* newspaper, Poole threw Morrissey to the ground and then beat, gouged, and bit him until Morrissey was forced to yell "enough!" Morrissey and his pride were badly wounded. So in 1855, when Poole was shot to death, few people were surprised when Morrissey and his friends were accused of the murder. After three trials—all resulting in hung juries (rumors flew that political pals kept the Dead Rabbits out of jail)—the defendants went free. But the Bowery residents held a hero's funeral for Poole, whose last words were, "Goodbye, boys. I die a true American!"

THE END OF AN ERA

In 1863, the Bowery Boys and the Dead Rabbits put aside their Catholic vs. Protestant feud and united—in their opposition to the Civil War. Many poor and working-class New Yorkers opposed Abraham Lincoln's Emancipation Proclamation because they feared freed slaves might come north and take their jobs. In addition, Congress had passed a Conscription Law, which allowed drafted men to pay $300 to stay out of the army, ensuring that the rich didn't have to fight. It was a sum well beyond most people in the Bowery and Five Points. In July 1863, the Dead Rabbits, the Bowery Boys, and several other smaller gangs joined in the Draft Riots. Buildings were looted and destroyed, and many of New York's African Americans were murdered. It took federal troops five days to quell the riot, which ultimately failed—the government refused to change the law, and both Bowery Boys and Dead Rabbits were drafted into the Union army. Although no one knows for sure if they all actually went to war, the gangs' numbers (and power) were diminished. By the time the war was over, newer gangs had already formed, and the Bowery Boys and Dead Rabbits gangs gradually disbanded.

*   *   *

DID YOU KNOW?

The New York State Thruway introduced E-Z Pass in August 1993, the state's first automated toll-collecting system.

There are 6,374.6 miles of streets in NYC.

THE ART STUDENTS LEAGUE

Think you're the next O'Keeffe, Pollock, or Rothko? There's a way to find out—attend the same unconventional school they went to.

NOT YOUR TYPICAL ART SCHOOL

Most art schools in New York City—Cooper Union, Parsons, School of Visual Arts, Queens College, Pratt—have highly structured programs that require certain classes and award degrees. But the Art Students League, on West 57th Street between Broadway and 7th Avenue, is nothing like that. It was founded *by* artists, *for* artists. There are no entrance requirements or exams; anyone who wants to go may sign up, pay tuition, and attend classes in drawing, painting, printmaking, and sculpture. Students don't even have to have any prior art-making experience.

Since there's no set curriculum, each aspiring artist invents his own program by choosing classes (as many or as few as he likes) and following a course of study with whichever teachers he prefers. Not everyone who goes to the League turns out to be a genius, but the school does boast a galaxy of art stars who studied there: Georgia O'Keeffe, Jackson Pollock, Mark Rothko, Milton Avery, Romare Bearden, and Lee Krasner, to name just a few.

REBELLION ACADEMY

The Art Students League started in 1875 when a group of students broke away from the extremely traditional, strictly organized National Academy of Design in Manhattan. The National Academy's purpose was to train students to be professional artists, and its teaching methods included having them make drawings of antique sculpture and attend lectures on anatomy, perspective, architecture, and ancient history.

The League group felt that the National Academy was too boring, too conservative, and too resistant to new ideas about art. They wanted to get away from painting old-fashioned subjects (like scenes from mythology) and embrace more naturalistic subjects taken from life. And they wanted a very different kind of school, too—one based on the French *atelier* (or studio) system: Each room of the new school would function as an independent studio, where a class would be given by a teacher who was free to instruct his students however he saw fit, with no interference from an administrative body.

DECLARATION OF INDEPENDENCE

The Art Students League's first home was on the top floor of a building at 16th Street and Fifth Avenue. The school's only support came from its students' membership fees, so the League had complete independence and got right to work setting up the kind of school it wanted. Life-drawing classes became a cornerstone; League artists believed that drawing real life (especially human forms) instead of inanimate objects—the norm at the time—was crucial to developing one's artistic skills. This change especially benefited female artists, who had long been banned from life-drawing classes because the 19th-century art world felt it was inappropriate for women to draw nudes. The League held life-drawing classes every day of the week, the first art school in the country to do so. Then in 1878, the League's members voted to incorporate—they became a legal entity with a charter, mission statement, financial responsibilities, and so on, instead of just a loosely organized group. But they didn't lose their idealistic vision: The League's charter required that out of the 12 people who served on the committee that made decisions for the school, three had to be currently enrolled students. This guaranteed that students would have a say in the way the school was run—another first for the League...and for the art world. Finally artists were empowerd to direct their own education, a principle that still guides the League today.

As more and more students enrolled, the League outgrew its space and had to move several times. Finally it joined with a few other arts associations to form the American Fine Arts Society (AFAS), which had a building large enough to accommodate everyone. In 1892 the AFAS members moved into a new French-Renaissance-style building on West 57th Street, where the Art Students League remains today.

These days, the League isn't the avant-garde force it once was.

Last Dodger to pitch a game at Brooklyn's Ebbets Field: Danny McDevitt (1957).

Newer, hipper galleries and art schools (like Black Mountain College in North Carolina) opened in the mid-1900s, and new forms of art—abstract painting, photography, minimalism—took the spotlight, pushing figurative painting and drawing into the background. But in spite of the abstract leanings of some of its alumni, like Pollock and Rothko, the Art Students League continued to focus on figure, portraiture, landscape, and still life, and today still does what it always has: make classes accessible to anyone with the desire to be an artist.

* * *

DEEP THOUGHTS FROM JERRY SEINFELD

"Make no mistake about why these babies are here—they are here to replace us."

"Now they show you how detergents take out bloodstains, a pretty violent image there. I think if you've got a T-shirt with a bloodstain all over it, maybe laundry isn't your biggest problem."

"Sometimes the road less traveled is less traveled for a reason."

"Where lipstick is concerned, the important thing is not color, but to accept God's final word on where your lips end."

"It's amazing that the amount of news that happens in the world every day always just exactly fits the newspaper."

"The big advantage of a book is it's very easy to rewind. Close it and you're right back at the beginning."

"I was the best man at the wedding. If I'm the best man, why is she marrying him?"

"Dogs are the leaders of the planet. If you see two life forms, one of them's making a poop, the other one's carrying it for him, who would you assume is in charge?"

There's no college in College Point, Queens. Its namesake, St. Paul's College, closed in 1848.

SMARTER THAN THE AVERAGE BERRA

Former New York Yankees catcher Lawrence Peter "Yogi" Berra is just as famous for his tendency to mangle the English language as for his epic home runs. Here are some Yogi-isms.

"A nickel ain't worth a dime anymore."

"Always go to other people's funerals—otherwise they won't come to yours."

"Baseball is ninety percent mental, and the other half is physical."

"Even Napoleon had his Watergate."

"He hits from both sides of the plate. He's amphibious."

"I never said most of the things I said."

"If the world was perfect, it wouldn't be."

"I'm not going to buy my kids an encyclopedia. Let them walk to school like I did."

"If people don't want to come out to the ball park, nobody's gonna stop 'em."

"In theory, there is no difference between theory and practice. In practice, there is."

"The future ain't what it used to be."

"You can observe a lot by just watching."

"Nobody goes there anymore. It's too crowded."

BERRA FACTS

• Yogi Berra played for 18 seasons with the New York Yankees, from 1946–63. He played on more pennant-winning (14) and World Series-winning (10) teams than any other player in Major League Baseball history.

• He got his nickname, "Yogi," from a childhood friend who, while watching a movie about an Indian snake charmer, said, "That yogi walks like...Berra!"

NEW YORK'S FINEST... AND TALLEST

They're part of the New York City scene and photographed almost as often as any local celebrity—here's introducing the horses (and the men who ride them) in the New York City Mounted Unit.

BRING 'EM UP FROM DOWN ON THE FARM
If you're ever near Central Park or Midtown, you might come across members of the New York Police Department Mounted Unit. These police officers and their four-legged equine partners patrol the streets, looking for criminals, providing crowd control for large events, and generally keeping order. The unit was founded in 1871 to deal with criminals in Central Park, and at one time, it boasted more than 700 officers on horseback. Their numbers began to dwindle at the dawn of the automobile age, though, and the unit was nearly disbanded in the 1970s due to budget cuts. But the police department loved its horses—and considered the mounted unit a valuable asset—so a group called the Police Foundation stepped in and saved the day, creating a program that allowed the unit to save money by accepting donated horses. Texas millionaire H. Ross Perot gave the department 12 animals; local nightclubs and restaurants—including the 21 Club, the Four Seasons, and Sardi's—followed his lead. Broadway star Bernadette Peters donated two animals, and a group of theater owners and banks chipped in to help with the rent on a midtown stable.

These days, the department mostly buys its horses—from places like Arkansas, upstate New York, and Pennsylvania. (At least one of the animals currently in the unit used to pull a buggy in Amish country.) Most of the mounts are castrated thoroughbreds and quarter horses that weigh between 1,200 and 1,500 pounds, and they're typically dark-hued horses of one color.

NEW IN THE "NEIGH"BORHOOD

The unit's ideal horse is intelligent, fearless, and friendly. Officials immediately pass over horses that bite, buck, or spook. Those that make the first cut are then tested at a stable in a quiet corner of the

Bronx, where they're put through what's called "nuisance train-ing." Walking shoulder to shoulder with older horses, the new re-cruits and their riders have to gallop across a blue plastic tarp and then march against a "crowd" waving trash bags and firing off air horns. The idea is to simulate the scary things that can happen in a city: a gun battle, a mass protest, or even the loud aftermath of a sporting event. Other tests include the use of smoke bombs, clang-ing metal pots, hissing flares, and the most important…blanks fired a few paces from a horse's head.

If a horse makes it through the early stages of testing and train-ing (and only about one out of six does), then he is walked through the streets of quiet residential neighborhoods in the Bronx to get some low-key on-the-job training. Only after three to six months can the graduates leave the stable and make the 12-mile victory march to Manhattan, where they move into one of the unit's five stables and take up their assignments.

RIDER ATTACHED

The police officers who ride the horses find it nearly as difficult to get a spot in the unit. There are many more applicants than open-ings because once in, most officers stay until they retire. The de-partment has stringent prerequisites for its hopeful applicants: Five years of experience on the force, with at least two spent in high-crime neighborhoods. A cop who passes that particular hurdle then has to wait, sometimes years, for an opening. When it comes, the officer is paired with a horse and the two begin training together. It sometimes takes two or three pairings for an officer to find the per-fect equine partner (and vice versa), but once found, rider and horse often spend the rest of their careers together.

Today, the Mounted Unit employs about 60 horses and police officers. And although horses used to be named things like "Zeus" or "Cherokee," these days it's more likely that a horse will be named for an officer killed in the line of duty. Several of the horses in today's Mounted Unit sport the names of officers and firefighters who died on September 11. When Mounted Unit horses get too old to perform their duties, they retire to a farm in Orange County that the two-legged officers refer to as "horse heaven." Not bad for a life-time of service.

The first game of tennis in the U.S. was played in 1874 on Staten Island.

TALK OF THE TOWN

*New York magazines come and go, but the most prestigious
one of all,* The New Yorker, *remains.*

THE IDEA

Harold Ross was a high-school dropout with a vision. Originally from Aspen, Colorado, he worked as a journalist during World War I, editing the servicemen's newspaper *Stars and
Stripes*. In 1919, the 27-year-old visited New York and fell in love
with the city, so he stayed. The next year, he married his other
love—Jane Grant, a *New York Times* reporter. Soon, the couple
began to hatch an idea for a weekly magazine that would "capture
the spirit of New York." Such a great modern city needed a great
modern magazine, they thought, one that was sophisticated, literary, timely...and funny. "*The New Yorker*," Ross wrote in 1924, not
long before the launch of the first issue, "will be a reflection in
word and picture of metropolitan life." Whether readers actually
lived in New York or not, they would feel as though they were getting an insider's perspective on the most important happenings in
the world's most important city.

It was a big, expensive undertaking, though, so Grant and
Ross convinced their friend Raoul Fleischmann (who was heir
to the Fleischmann's Yeast fortune) to back the venture. Ross
and Fleischmann were poker buddies, members of the all-male
Thanatopsis Literary and Inside Straight Club—a poker-playing
gang that had grown out of the famous Round Table, a group of
Manhattan wits who ate lunch together daily at the Algonquin
Hotel. Fleischmann was an entrepreneur, and he agreed to match
the $20,000 that Ross and Grant had saved, never suspecting that
he was about to become publisher of a classic that he would ultimately pour most of his fortune into. The first 36-page, 15¢ issue
of *The New Yorker* appeared in February 1925...and it was a bust.

EARLY DAYS

That first issue sold only 15,000 copies (in a city of 7.8 million),
but it showed promise. The first cover, by cartoonist Rea Irvin,
was a drawing of a top-hat-wearing dandy whom Irvin named Eu-

---

stace Tilley. (Tilley adorns every anniversary issue to this day.) The layout began with two pages of clever gossip called "Of All Things," followed by "The Talk of the Town" (similar to today's "Talk" pages) and a page of cartoons. Other features included a profile of Signor Gatti-Casazza, the impresario of the Metropolitan Opera; short pieces about politics; a few poems; more cartoons; short reviews on what was current in theater, music, art, books, movies; "Goings On," a calendar of "events worth while"; and a section called "In Our Midst," a collection of short items about writers, playwrights, publishers, movie people, stage folks, and rich people.

It looked a lot like the *New Yorker* we know today, but the tone was more coy and playful; the magazine didn't seem to take itself seriously. The content was also almost entirely focused on New York living—Ross approached it as something written *by* his friends *for* his friends, and it captured the attention and imagination of New York writers and artists. Many agreed to work on the project: E. B. White (author of the children's book *Charlotte's Web*) anonymously wrote most of the first "Talk of the Town" pieces. Journalist Janet Flanner signed on as the magazine's Paris correspondent, a job she performed for almost 50 years. A cartoonist known for his wit, James Thurber became a regular humor writer. But even with all that talent, circulation fell. In the magazine's first two years, Raoul Fleischmann invested more than $700,000 to keep it going.

Harold Ross wasn't discouraged, though. He firmly believed that the magazine just needed to find its footing…and its audience. He was selling a lifestyle, and from the beginning, *The New Yorker*'s revenue depended more on advertising than on subscriptions. As more issues came out, the magazine began to get a reputation for glamorous ads that appealed to the upwardly mobile readership it courted: white, liberal, well-educated, upper-middle-class professionals. It was shamelessly snobbish, and advertisers loved that. In 1928, *The New Yorker* finally started making a profit.

IN (AND OUT OF) TROUBLE

The New Yorker may have started out as a lighthearted, entertaining New York–centric magazine, but by the late 1940s, it had taken on another role, more like the one it has today: committed to reporting on larger political, scientific, and social issues in America and around the world. And the magazine took risks. In 1946, Ross devoted an entire issue to a piece by Pulitzer Prize winner John Hersey. In 31,347 words, "Hiroshima" was a frank and detailed description of the horrors of nuclear war, told through the eyes of six victims of the bombing. For most readers, it was their first exposure to the event from the Japanese point of view. During the McCarthy years of the 1950s, *The New Yorker* was one of the few media outlets that spoke out against the red-baiting and constitutional-rights violations of the House Un-American Activities Committee. Over the years, the magazine also published stories on race, the environment, and the trial of Adolf Eichmann, one of the major organizers of the Holocaust.

RUFFLING FEATHERS

The risk-taking has continued into more recent times, too. For the Valentine's Day 1993 issue, artist Art Spiegelman created an extremely controversial cover that showed an African-American woman kissing a Hasidic Jewish man. The image alluded to the tensions between the two ethnic groups that had erupted in riots in Crown Heights, Brooklyn, in 1991, and the city's African-American and Hasidic Jewish communities were furious. In answer, editor Tina Brown insisted that the cover was meant to encourage the two sides to "replace their animosity with love."

A recent uproar came during the 2008 presidential campaign season, when a *New Yorker* cover showed then-candidate Barack Obama as a Muslim and his wife Michelle as a terrorist, fist-bumping in the Oval Office in front of a portrait of Osama bin Laden. Angry letters and e-mails inundated the magazine's offices. "Tasteless and offensive" were the words Obama's staff used to describe the cover. But the magazine never backed down, maintaining that the intention was to caricature the right-wing's accusations about Obama's loyalties. "Satire is part of what we do," said current editor David Remnick, "and it is meant to bring things out into the open, to hold up a mirror to prejudice, the hateful, and the absurd. And that's the spirit of this cover."

QUALITY WRITERS, QUALITY READERS

In its long history, *The New Yorker* has attracted some of the most respected journalists, humorists, commentators, poets, and fiction writers of the 20th and 21st centuries: Alice Munro, Philip Roth, Margaret Atwood, Henry Louis Gates, Jr., Joyce Carol Oates, John O'Hara, J. D. Salinger, Shirley Jackson, Seymour Hersh, Susan Sontag, E. L. Doctorow, John Updike, John McPhee, Ved Mehta, and James Merrill, among others, have all appeared in *The New Yorker.*

And the formula continues to work. Today *The New Yorker* has more than a million subscribers, 85 percent of whom are so loyal that they renew their subscriptions every year—one of the highest renewal rates in the typically fickle magazine world.

To read about other New York magazines, turn to page 43.

* * *

COVERED BRIDGES

New York State is home to many historic covered bridges—old, wooden structures built between 1823 and 1912. Here are some of our favorites:

• The **Hyde Hall Bridge,** the oldest surviving covered bridge in the United States, can be found in Gillmerglass State Park in Otsego County. Built in 1923, the bridge spans a small body of water called Shadow Brook on the Hyde Hall country estate, which belonged to George Clarke, son of New York's colonial governor (also named George Clarke).

• The New York State Covered Bridge Society calls the 232-foot long and 26-foot wide **Blenheim Bridge** (1855), which crosses Schoharie Creek, the "longest single span wooden bridge in the world."

• Just north of Albany, between the towns of Buskirk and Salem, are three covered bridges that span the Battenkill River. The **Eagleville** (built in 1858) and **Rexleigh** (1874) bridges still let vehicles pass, but the **Shushan** (1858) is only for pedestrians. A sign on the Shushan reads, "Five-dollar fine for riding or driving on this bridge faster than a walk."

WOW...WHAT A RECORD!

New York's people and places have been instrumental in setting some of the world's most amazing (and wacky) records.

- **Record time for traveling the entire New York subway system:** 22 hours, 52 minutes, 36 seconds—set by Manhattan-based financial analysts Chris Solarz and Matthew Ferrisi in 2010.

- **Most continuous upright spins on ice skates...on one foot:** 115, by Swiss skater Lucinda Ruh at the Sky Rink at Chelsea Piers, Manhattan, in 2003.

- **Oldest tennis ballboy at the U.S. Open:** Manny Hershkowitz (from Virginia), who was 82 when he worked at the 1999 tournament.

- **Smallest guitar:** 10 micrometers long (about 1/20 the width of a human hair), created by scientists at Cornell University in 1997.

- **Largest cup of hot chocolate:** 480 gallons, or about 8,000 cups, (before marshmallows) created by the American Dairy Association & Dairy Council and displayed in Manhattan in 2010.

- **Most times jumping rope in an hour...underwater:** Ashrita Furman, from Queens, at the Gurney's Inn pool in Montauk, in 2001.

- **Highest score in the video game *Guitar Hero III*:** 973,954. The highlight: seven minutes of the game's hardest song, "Through the Fire and Flames," by heavy-metal group DragonForce. Fourteen-year-old Danny Johnson from Texas set the record at a Best Buy in Midtown Manhattan in 2009.

- **Smallest centipede:** the Hoffman's dwarf, which is 0.4 inches long and has 41 pairs of legs. Researchers from the American Natural History Museum collected 10 of them in Central Park in 1998.

- **Most expensive omelette:** the Zillion Dollar Lobster Frittata appeared on the menu at Norma's Restaurant at Le Parker Meridien Hotel in Manhattan in 2004. Ingredients: six eggs, a roasted Maine lobster tail, and 10 ounces of caviar. Price: $1,000.

Number of performances tenor Enrico Caruso had with the Metropolitan Opera: 861.

POISONOUS NEW YORK

A little info on the five poisonous spiders and snakes that call New York home.

NORTHERN BLACK WIDOW SPIDER. A relative of the more common Southern black widow, these spiders live throughout the state, though very rarely in the upstate region. The females can be distinguished by their unorganized webs (no patterns), and the distinctive red hourglass mark on their otherwise jet-black abdomens. (The smaller males are usually grayish, with markings that look like white bands.) A bite can result in intense pain, nausea, unconsciousness, and, very rarely—death.

Extra New York Note: In 1998, a family in Niskayuna found a black widow in their home—and kept it as a pet. Over the next several months, the spider produced three egg sacs and hundreds of baby black widows. The family finally donated the creatures to the New York State Museum in Albany, where entomologist Jeffrey Barnes said it was the "first naturally occurring black widow I have seen in upstate New York."

BROWN RECLUSE SPIDER. These spiders are not native to New York, but are found in many parts of the state nevertheless. They also weave unorganized webs and are light to dark brown, with a violin-shaped marking on the front section of their bodies. Effects of brown recluse bites are similar to those of the black widow, but they also cause *necrosis*, or cell death, of tissue around the bite, which can take many months to heal and can cause severe scarring.

Extra New York Note: In September 2010, a woman found a spider in the kitchen sink of her Manhattan apartment. (The spider was stuck in some pesto.) Scientists confirmed that it was a brown recluse. She went on to find 11 more. She moved.

TIMBER RATTLESNAKE. Found mainly in forests in southern New York, these thick, stocky snakes can grow to be five feet long. They're light to dark brown, with several darker bands across their bodies. Timber rattlers are very dangerous snakes, due to the large amount of venom they're able to inject. Symptoms after a bite can include pain, swelling, rapid pulse, nausea, slurred speech, convulsions, loss of consciousness, and sometimes death.

Extra New York Note: For many decades, New York State paid a bounty for timber rattlesnakes. One legendary snake hunter, Art Moore, of Whitehall in northeast New York, collected bounties of up to $5...on the more than 9,000 timber rattlers he killed starting in the 1950s. The bounty system—and Art Moore—are credited with nearly wiping out timber rattlesnakes in the state. Killing the creatures for sport was finally outlawed in 1971, and timber rattlesnakes are now a protected species in New York.

MASSASAUGA RATTLESNAKE. These are found only in wetland regions south of Lake Ontario. They grow to be about 24–28 inches long, and are gray or tan with roundish brown spots. Bite symptoms are similar to the timber rattlesnake, though the massasauga can't inject as much venom. (You should still go to a hospital if bitten, though.) The name *massasauga* comes from the Chippewa Indian language and means "great river mouth."

Extra New York Note: In October 2008, Emanuele Tesoro of Waterdown, Ontario, was arrested in Niagara Falls, New York... with 33 massasauga rattlesnakes hidden in the door panels of his van. The animal smuggler was convicted of several charges in 2009, and the massasaugas were released in his prison cell. (Kidding! The snakes were kept at the Toronto Zoo until they could be released into the wild.)

COPPERHEAD. Found mainly in the Lower Hudson Valley, these snakes can reach 40 inches in length, are tan or pinkish with striking, chestnut-colored bands, and have distinctive copper-colored heads. Bite symptoms are similar to rattlesnake bites, but are known for being extremely painful.

Extra New York Note: In August 2009, New York City resident Richard Petti was cleaning a septic tank in Orangetown when he was bitten on the arm by a copperhead. Initially, he thought it was a nonpoisonous snake, but then his entire arm swelled up and turned black. Petti was rushed to Jacobi Medical Center in the Bronx, the snakebite center for New York City and the surrounding region, where he spent the next few days before being released.

I SEE SPACE PEOPLE

*A visit to Pine Bush, New York, a place that's become
synonymous with things not of this Earth.*

WE MADE THE ENQUIRER! For at least 90 years, people in the tiny town of Pine Bush, 30 miles southwest of Poughkeepsie, have been witness to some strange phenomena: White orbs appear in the night sky amid a red mist. Mechanical rumblings emanate from deep underground. Strange lights illuminate farmers' fields. Gusty, warm winds blow out of the woods on freezing nights. And according to one observer, swirling lights hang suspended in the darkness "like a Ferris Wheel on fire." In fact, there were so many eyewitness accounts in the 1980s—more than 2,000—that *The National Enquirer* proclaimed Pine Bush the world capital of UFO sightings.

In 1992, a geologist named Bruce Cornet initiated an investigation…and concluded that several transmitters beneath Pine Bush send "photon beams" into space. Five years later, he recorded a strange boomerang-shaped object flying through the air accompanied by a stream of bright, white light. Cornet insisted it was an alien UFO.

BRING IN THE EXPERTS

But, the skeptics wondered, why not a more ordinary explanation…like an airplane? Pine Bush is only about 82 miles outside of New York City, one of the busiest air travel hubs in the world, and an airplane seemed logical. Cornet was ready to answer his critics:

• Lights from airplanes usually move in straight lines—the light from the boomerang swirled and jerked in a circular path.

• The boomerang was flying lower and slower than a conventional aircraft.

• In 2008, researchers from the History Channel examined Cornet's photos and interviewed him about the methods he used to capture them. Most important, they wanted to know if his camera could have been moving while he took the pictures, maybe *creating* those jerks and swirls. But Cornet assured them that the camera

---

Most common cockroach found in NYC: the German cockroach.

had been secured on a tripod and that he'd controlled it with an electronic shutter release. After much investigation and study, they concluded that they couldn't determine what Cornet's photos actually showed.

SPACE TOURISTS

These days, reports of strange lights and happenings in Pine Bush have declined, and some locals worry that they're losing their thunder to Wanaque, a town in northern New Jersey, where mysterious lights, flying discs, and other "interdimensional phenomena" have been reported since the 1960s. But Pine Bush still wears the title of New York's UFO capital proudly, and local businesses welcome terrestrial visitors hoping to find evidence of extraterrestrial. The Chamber of Commerce hosts an annual "Pine Bush Area UFO Festival and Parade" and encourages "aliens and Earthlings alike [to dress in] UFO, alien, ET, space, and galactic-related costumes." T-shirts sporting images of big-headed, bulbous-eyed purple aliens are optional.

* * *

WOODSTOCK EXPOSED

The Woodstock Music Festival—which ran from August 15–18, 1969, in Bethel, New York—remains one of the most iconic events of the 1960s hippie counterculture movement in America. But the event actually began as a capitalist venture, a way for four local music promoters to make enough money to open a music studio. John Roberts, Joel Rosenman, Artie Kornfield, and Michael Lang managed to line up some of the most successful musical acts of the time—Jimi Hendrix, The Who, Jefferson Airplane, Janis Joplin, and others—and entice hundreds of thousands of young music lovers to pay between $18 and $24 each ($108 to $144 today) to see them perform. And don't think those artists played the show for free: They were paid anywhere from $10,000 (Credence Clearwater Revival) to $26,000 (Jimi Hendrix)...and several of them—like Janis Joplin, The Grateful Dead, and The Who—refused to take the stage until they'd gotten their checks.

Most points scored in a game by a member of the NY Knicks: 60 (Bernard King, 1984).

STEINWAY VILLAGE

"Company towns" were only for Ohio steelworkers or West Virginia miners, weren't they? Not at all—once upon a time, there was a bustling one in Astoria, Queens.

PIANO MEN

In the northwest corner of Astoria, Queens, not far from LaGuardia Airport, there's a Steinway Place, Steinway Street, Steinway Reformed Church, Steinway Library, Steinway Playground...and nearly a century and a half ago, there was a whole Steinway Village. All were named for the Steinway family, the people who made the most famous pianos in the world.

Heinrich Engelhard Steinweg came to America from Germany around 1850 with three of his five sons (a fourth son followed later). When he arrived, he was already an accomplished piano builder and had trained his sons to build the instruments too. Once in New York, they Anglicized their name to Steinway (and Heinrich to Henry) and worked for established piano companies until they were able to start their own in 1853. With their superb craftsmanship and revolutionary techniques (such as a unique method of bending a single piece of maple to create a piano's rim), the Steinways' pianos quickly earned them national and international recognition.

GRAND SCHEME

The original Steinway workshop was on Varick Street in busy lower Manhattan. The company became so successful there that it had to move to a larger space at 81 Walker Street and then, in 1859, to an even larger factory at 53rd Street and Park Avenue. By the late 1860s, though, Henry's son William had become convinced that the future of the company lay outside of Manhattan—away from the influence of labor unions and "the machinations of the anarchists and socialists...who were continually breeding among our workmen, and inciting them to strike." In the early 1870s, William bought 400 acres of rural land across the East River in Queens and began to build—not pianos (yet), but a new piano factory and a town to go with it.

Washington Irving's 1809 satirical history of Dutch New York contains...

IT TAKES A VILLAGE

William's land was sparsely populated and mostly undeveloped, a perfect blank slate for his vision of the piano factory—a sawmill and a foundry to supply materials, housing for his workers to live in, stores, restaurants, and everything else needed for a Steinway Village. His plans included new streets with shade trees, good transportation, amusements, schools—and he watched over the progress of every phase of construction.

Steinway located the piano factory at #1 Steinway Place in the new town, near an inlet that was dubbed Steinway Creek. The wide, tree-lined main avenue of the new neighborhood was named Steinway Street; it became the main thoroughfare of the area. The two-story, red-brick Victorian row houses that would be rented to William's workers were completed between 1877 and 1879 on streets that today are called 20th Avenue, 41st Street, and 42nd Street, but were at that time named for Steinway family members: Winthrop, Albert, and Theodore Streets.

William also donated land for a public school: P.S. 84 (still called Steinway Elementary School), where German was taught as a second language. Steinway Village had its own post office, parks, and one of the first free kindergartens in America. The Steinway Library was stocked with William's private collection of books (it's now part of the Queens Library system). In 1886, to provide his (mostly German) workers with recreation, William and a brewer named George Ehret constructed the Bowery Bay Beach amusement park and beer garden—it was renamed North Beach in 1890 and lasted until Prohibition began in 1920, but today is the site of LaGuardia Airport. By 1879, Steinway Village even had its own Protestant Union Church, and when the congregation outgrew the building, a new one was built in 1891. William Steinway donated the pipe organ. The church (still in existence) has since changed its name to Steinway Reformed Church.

A MAN, A PLAN, AND A TUNNEL

William Steinway wanted to be close to the village he'd created, so in 1873, he moved his family into a four-story, 27-room granite mansion a few blocks from the piano factory. The grand house had been built in the 1850s as a country villa, a showplace on a knoll overlooking the East River. It was renamed Steinway House, and

---

...the first known reference to St. Nicholas as "Santa Claus."

the family occupied it until 1926. The building still stands at the end of 41st Street, between LaGuardia Airport and the Con-Edison Power Plant.

William Steinway was also passionately interested in public transportation, so he ran a horse-drawn rail line from his piano factory to the ferry that crossed the East River to Manhattan. William's interest in transit lines earned him a place on New York's transit commission, which soon became known as the Steinway Commission. In 1891, the commission released a plan for a new subway system, and looked for private financiers to build it. There were no serious bids, so William began constructing the Steinway Tunnel in 1892, an underwater trolley tunnel that ran between what is now Long Island City in Queens and Grand Central Terminal in Manhattan. Construction began in 1892, but was stopped in 1893 due to flooding and financial problems. Both of these projects—the subway system and the tunnel—came to fruition after William's death in 1896: In 1902, August Belmont, a rich financier, revived the Steinway Tunnel and also formed the Interborough Rapid Transit Company to build the subway that William Steinway had championed. The tunnel now carries the #7 IRT Flushing Line subway trains that connect Manhattan to Queens.

COMPANY TOWN NO MORE

Steinway pianos are still produced at the factory in Queens, but a series of other companies have bought out the Steinway line over the years. The area of Queens once called Steinway Village is still called Steinway, however, and many of the Steinway namesakes remain. And as of 2011, the 29 workers' row houses were still there, though some have seen additions over the years, such as metal awnings, iron gates, and brick stoops.

As for the Queens factory itself, it's still on the cutting edge of technology: In 2009, construction was completed on its new solar-powered rooftop dehumidifier and air-conditioning system, the largest in the world. The eco-friendly machinery became a model for similar systems around the Northeast.

GOT DIAMONDS?

New York has everything: great theater, great restaurants, great museums—and great diamonds…for cheap.

• Of all the diamonds entering the United States, 90 percent of them come in through Manhattan's Diamond District, a one-block stretch of West 47th Street (between Fifth and Sixth Avenues) that's lined with buildings full of diamond merchants. It's one of the six major centers of the world's diamond industry. (The others are London, Antwerp, Johannesburg, Mubai, and Ramat Gan, Israel.)

• About 2,600 independent businesses operate in the Diamond District. But not all of them are actual stores—most are just booths in the 25 jewelry "exchanges" (institutions organized for the trading of diamonds and gems) scattered throughout the buildings on the block. Each exchange can house as many as 100 separate dealers, all with their own selections of merchandise.

• When dealers in the District sell to each other, they usually complete the transaction with a handshake and the traditional Yiddish phrase *"mazel und broche,"* meaning "luck and blessing." Even in transactions that involve millions of dollars, there are rarely formal written contracts. In spite of the seemingly casual organization in the Diamond District, a single day's business can average $400 million.

• The diamond merchants sell to regular people, too, and according to many accounts, shopping in the Diamond District is like looking for a used car in a low-budget lot. According to one man who went there for an engagement ring, "The sellers—many of which have a thuggish quality to them—can be very upfront and aggressive…the salesmen are ubiquitous and will not simply let you browse. Some will even stand out on the street and openly solicit you for business if you so much as slow down near their door."

• So why shop there at all? Cost. In the Diamond District, buyers often pay half (or less) of what they would at a retail jewelry store.

• Buyers beware: A 2010 *New York Post* investigation found that booths in the jewelry exchanges can be rented for as little as a day, making it difficult for buyers to distinguish shady dealers from reputable ones. Still, some of the biggest names in the diamond industry do business in the District, including the Gemological Institute of America and the Diamond Dealers Club.

• Merchants sell other kinds of jewelry besides diamonds. Gold bracelets, gold earrings, pearls, rubies, and other precious metals and gems can all be bought there.

• Some tips for shopping in the Diamond District:

✓ Sellers expect buyers to haggle. Don't accept the first price offered.

✓ Many won't take a check or credit cards. Bring cash.

✓ The "handshake" system is only for merchants. As a buyer, you should always get a receipt.

✓ Buy either a diamond that comes with a certificate of authenticity or one that the seller will allow to be certified on the spot. The exchanges all have appraisers who will certify a diamond for about $50. All deals should be contingent upon the diamond being appraised and certified.

✓ Usually, the most reputable diamond dealers have shops not at street level, but on higher, more secured floors. So they can be hard to find. To locate them, you may need some sort of "in." (Basically, you have to "know a guy.")

✓ Watch out for trickery; disreputable merchants have been known to show a certificate for one stone while selling another. Others try to pass off synthetic stones as natural ones. According to one New York City blogger, buyers in the Diamond District need to remain alert and vigilant, do plenty of research before they go, and "know what they are doing!"

* * *

C-H-A-M-P-S

Every years since 1925, the E. W. Scripps Company has sponsored the National Spelling Bee in Washington, D.C. Only two New Yorkers have won: Tim Kneale of Syracuse, in 1976 (winning word: narcolepsy); and Rebecca Sealfon of New York City, in 1997 (winning word: euonym).

SHOT IN NEW YORK CITY

Rightly or wrongly, the Big Apple is well-known for its violence. Here are a few famous people who ended up on the wrong end of a New York gun.

THE FIRST "TRIAL OF THE CENTURY"
On a warm afternoon in June 1906, as famed architect Stanford White sat watching a show at the new Madison Square Garden (which he had designed), nobody thought much about the young man who approached him wearing a long black coat despite the heat. When the man, Harry Thaw, pulled a gun, the high-society audience initially thought it was a part of the show. But when White slumped over dead, panic ensued.

Thaw had been madly in love with the beautiful Evelyn Nesbit, a model and chorus girl whose looks had also caught the eye of White and actor John Barrymore, among others. Thaw repeatedly asked Nesbit to marry him, but she put him off, saying that she and White were having an affair.

The jealous Thaw was furious that White had "taken her honor," but he and Nesbit did eventually marry. Soon after, she told friends that Thaw was suspicious and abusive. He seemed obsessed with thoughts of his wife and Stanford White until, on June 25, his anger finally spilled over.

The case first went to trial in January 1907 amid a frenzy of media coverage in which the sensationalized case was referred to as the "trial of the century," but the jury ended up deadlocked. Thaw pleaded insanity at his second trial and was committed to the state hospital in Fishkill, New York. He escaped briefly to Canada, was extradited back to the U.S., and was finally released in 1915. Evelyn Nesbit had been granted a divorce while Thaw was still in prison, and they went their separate ways.

YOU'RE FIRED!
On August 9, 1910, New York mayor William J. Gaynor was boarding a ship at a dock along the Hudson River, in preparation for a vacation cruise. Photographer William Warnecke hung around after the other photojournalists left, figuring he could get a good, casual shot of Gaynor. But instead, he caught an assassination attempt:

Disgruntled ex-city employee James Gallagher stepped up to Gaynor and shot him in the throat…at the exact moment that Warnecke snapped a photo. Gaynor survived, but the bullet was never removed, and three years later, he died from the lingering effects of the bullet lodged in his neck. Gaynor remains the only New York City mayor to have been shot while in office.

YOU NEVER KNOW WHO'S IN THE AUDIENCE

Malcolm Little of Nebraska grew up to be one of the most controversial civil rights leaders in American history: Malcolm X. His admirers called him a great advocate for African Americans, but critics demonized him for advocating violence and racism. For many years, Malcolm had been an outspoken leader of the Nation of Islam, a religious organization whose mission was to raise the economic, social, and spiritual position of African Americans. But a 1963 falling out with the group's leaders led Malcolm to leave the group.

On February 21, 1965, Malcolm X attended a rally in Washington Heights. Just as he stepped onto the stage to speak, Thomas Hagan, a disgruntled Nation of Islam member, pulled a sawed-off shotgun from underneath his coat and shot the civil rights leader in the chest. Malcolm's supporters immediately rushed forward, tackling and attacking Hagan before he could be captured and arrested by police. Hagan and two coconspirators were taken to jail, but Malcolm X died immediately. It was reported afterward that the civil rights leader had been afraid for his life and had begun carrying a pistol for self-defense, but he was unarmed when he was killed.

I'M NOT A FAN, REALLY

In 1967, writer and feminist extremist Valerie Solanas met artist and filmmaker Andy Warhol outside his studio in New York City and handed him a script she'd written, hoping that he might produce it. Initially, Warhol was interested, but after reading the play (an angry, pornographic, man-hating story), he suspected that Solanas was working with the police—he'd been accused of producing pornography in the past and feared a setup, so he didn't contact Solanas about the play. Eventually, though, Solanas got in touch with him, and they began a shaky collaboration. Warhol gave her a role in two of his movies, but in the end, her extreme views and behavior ended the relationship.

Q: What do rapper Tupac Shakur and punk-rocker Sid Vicious have in common?...

On June 3, 1968, Andy Warhol arrived at the Factory, a New York art studio where he made his films...and Solanas was waiting for him. She pulled out a gun and fired three shots; two missed, but one hit Warhol in the chest. Then she shot another man (art critic Mario Amaya) before fleeing. Solanas later turned herself in. Warhol survived—but barely—and suffered health problems from the injury for the rest of his life. He died in 1987. Solanas was tried and declared criminally insane. After many years in mental hospitals, she died in 1988.

THE VOICES MADE HIM DO IT

As a teenager, Mark David Chapman loved the Beatles, especially John Lennon, but the admiration grew to obsession and disillusionment as he grew into adulthood. Twice, he left his home and his wife in Hawaii and flew to New York to kill Lennon, thinking that fans would someday mention his name along with those of the Fab Four. But he changed his mind both times. (Once he needed to buy bullets, and the second time, he had a brief change of heart.)

On December 8, 1980, Chapman met an unsuspecting John Lennon on the street, chatted with him, and got him to autograph a copy of an album for him. Chapman later claimed that "voices" were telling him to kill Lennon even during that meeting, but it wasn't until later that night that the "voices" won. As Lennon and his wife Yoko Ono returned home to the Dakota apartment building, Chapman fired five times...and four of the bullets hit the musician.

Chapman didn't run. He didn't even try to deny what he'd done. Police said afterward that he was polite and noncombative when they arrested him. Chapman eventually pleaded guilty to murder and was sent to Attica. John Lennon lived for half an hour after the shooting, but died on the way to Roosevelt Hospital.

IT'S A RAP

Many rap artists have been shot in New York City, but rapper Lloyd Banks might be one of the most incredible. Banks grew up in South Jamaica, Queens, and released his first album with the group G-Unit in 2003. But on September 10, 2001, Banks was shot at a nightclub in Queens, the victim of stray gunfire. Some accounts say he walked himself to a hospital, but Banks told MTV that he ran there...10 blocks. He woke up the next day to the devastation of 9/11.

IF THOSE BLEACHERS COULD TALK

From 1923 to 2008, the New York Yankees won 39 pennants and 26 World Series Championships—more than any other team. And before the original Yankee Stadium was demolished in 2009, it was home to four of the greatest moments in baseball history.

APRIL 18, 1923—OPENING DAY
The Yankees weren't always the winningest team in baseball. They began in 1901 as the Baltimore Orioles. After moving to New York two years later, they played at Hilltop Park as the Highlanders. They later changed their name to the Yankees and moved to the Polo Grounds in Manhattan, which they shared with (and rented from) another baseball team, the New York Giants. But for their first two decades, the Yankees couldn't catch fire. Most New Yorkers preferred the Giants, who'd already won the World Series once. The Yankees hadn't even won a pennant, and they'd even been known to come in dead last.

Then, in 1920, the team's owners, Jake Ruppert and Tillinghast Huston, bought the contract of a talented slugger called Babe Ruth from the Boston Red Sox. Ruth's home runs brought the Yankees winning games and thousands of new fans. Giants manager John McGraw (who didn't want to help out his successful competitors) evicted the Yankees from the Polo Grounds. So the Yankee owners bought 10 acres in the Bronx and built the biggest ballpark the country had ever seen…the first one to have three decks and the first to be called a "stadium."

Critics didn't think the Yankees had a chance of filling the stands—even with Ruth's help. McGraw predicted that the Yankees would starve because no baseball fan who could watch baseball in Manhattan would trek all the way to the Bronx— "Goatville." Yet when Yankee Stadium opened on April 18, 1923, "Goatville" was where the fans went. The grandstands were packed with 60,000 of them (most ballparks accommodated 30,000) who cheered as John Philip Sousa and the Seventh Regiment Band

---

Before refrigeration, NYC's annual consumption of ice was about 1,885,000 tons.

escorted the Yankees onto the field along with their archrivals, the Red Sox. And they watched Governor Alfred Smith throw the first pitch.

But most of the fans were really there to watch Babe Ruth. The stadium had already been nicknamed The House That Ruth Built, because the team had taken such a gamble on his home runs filling the bleachers. Ruth had said, "I'd give a year of my life to hit a home run in the first game in this new park." Sure enough, in the third inning, Ruth's bat connected with a pitch from Boston's Howard Ehmke. The ball went into stands, and Ruth scored the first home run in the first game at Yankee Stadium. (Sure, the ballpark had been built to favor left-handed hitters like Babe Ruth—the left-field pole was 281 feet from home plate, while the right-field pole was 295—but still.) Sports followers took it as a sign that the Yankees were no longer the "other baseball team" in New York, and the Yankees went on to win the game, 4–1. Instead of starving, the Yankees won the pennant and their first World Series that year—defeating McGraw's Giants.

SEPTEMBER 30, 1927—BABE RUTH'S 60TH HOME RUN

Babe Ruth slugged 54 home runs in 1920, his first year as a Yankees, shattering the previous record of 29—which he'd set himself while playing for the Red Sox. The next year, Ruth hit 59, breaking his record again. Then, for the next five years, Ruth pushed to take his home run record to 60.

In September 1927, that goal seemed out of reach. To get a record-breaking 60 home runs by the end of the season, Ruth needed to hit at least 17 in a single month—a number that was more than most players managed in a season. But Ruth wasn't most players. By September 29, he had racked up an amazing 16 home runs.

On September 30th, thousands watched as Ruth faced the Washington Senators at Yankee Stadium. It was the next-to-last game of the season, and Ruth was sitting on 59 homers—he needed only one more for a record-breaker. Seven innings passed, and no luck. Then, in the 8th inning, Ruth took a chance on a slow pitch from Tom Zachary and smashed a ball to far right field. The fans held their breath as the ball arced...and landed in the stands, just six inches inside the foul pole for a home run. As Ruth slowly circled the bases, fans danced, waved handkerchiefs, threw

---

Staten Island's Todt Hill is the highest natural point in the five boroughs.

homemade confetti (torn from newspapers), and tossed their hats into the air.

After the game, Ruth felt content with his new record. He'd hit more home runs than any other *team* that season. Ruth predicted that it would be tough for anyone to beat him—and he was right: It was 34 years before another Yankee slugger, Roger Maris, broke the record with 61.

JULY 4, 1939—LOU GEHRIG APPRECIATION DAY

As first baseman for the Yankees, Lou Gehrig was one of the best power hitters of his day, surpassed only by his teammate Babe Ruth. The native New Yorker set several batting records, but was most famous for playing in 2,130 consecutive games. After officially joining the team in June 1, 1925, he never missed a game…for 14 years. Broken fingers and other injuries didn't bench him—he even showed up to bat on his wedding day.

But early in the 1939 season, Gehrig became so weak that on May 2 he simply couldn't play. Doctors at the Mayo Clinic in Minnesota told Gehrig that he had a degenerative neurological disease called ALS, or amyotrophic lateral sclerosis—now commonly known as Lou Gehrig's Disease.

On July 4, 1939, between games of a doubleheader against the Washington Senators, the Yankees held a ceremony to honor the 34-year-old Gehrig. The crowd numbered 61,808—standing room only—and many people had come just to pay tribute to Gehrig. Yankees Manager Joe McCarthy, New York Mayor Fiorello La Guardia, Babe Ruth, and others delivered heartfelt speeches, and Gehrig himself gave one of the most famous and touching speeches in sports history. By the time he concluded, "So I close in saying that I might have had a bad break, but I have an awful lot to live for," many in the stadium were crying openly. Later that year, the Yankees also retired Gehrig's number (#4), the first time an MLB player ever had his jersey number retired.

JULY 2, 1941—JOE DIMAGGIO SETS A RECORD FOR CONSECUTIVE HITS

On May 15, 1941, with a run against the Chicago White Sox, Joe DiMaggio began scoring a hit in every single game he played.

Though he was already a Yankee superstar—who had led the team to four World Series titles between 1936 and 1940—it wasn't until DiMaggio got his 18th consecutive hit in a game against the Cleveland Indians a few weeks later that the *New York Times* began to keep track of the numbers. As his streak lengthened to 30 games, the public noticed too. In a year when most news was about Adolph Hitler's conquest of Europe, DiMaggio's hitting streak dominated headlines. The first question addressed by newspapers, radio announcers, and even strangers on the street was often, "Did Joe get a hit today?"

When the streak went to 44 games, it tied the MLB record that Willie Keeler had set in 1897. Many sports aficionados thought that Keeler's record couldn't be broken in the 20th century, due to tighter rules on foul balls being called as strikes, tiring night games, and long road trips that exhausted players. So on July 2, when the Yankee batters squared off against the Boston Red Sox pitcher Dick Newsome, the huge crowd in Yankee Stadium, along with the entire country, wanted to see if "Joltin' Joe" could accomplish the impossible and surpass Keeler.

In his first chance at bat against pitcher Dick Newsome, DiMaggio hit a line drive, but Boston outfielder Stan Spence made a spectacular catch, and DiMaggio was out. His next hit came in the third inning, but it was a ground ball fielded by third baseman Jim Tabor—another out. Finally, in the fifth inning, with a count of two balls and a strike, DiMaggio slugged a home run over the wall. The crowd jumped to its feet and erupted in cheers. Even the cynical press corps applauded. News went out over the radio that DiMaggio now held the major-league record for scoring hits in 45 consecutive games. In the end, Joe DiMaggio would have 56 hits that season before his streak ended, a record that still stands today.

* * *

JOLTIN' JOE WASN'T ALWAYS A HERO
In 1938, his third season with the Yankees, DiMaggio butted heads with the team's owners, insisting that he deserved more than the $25,000 salary he was offered. After that story hit the newspapers, angry Depression-era Yankees fans booed every time he stepped on to the field, and DiMaggio eventually gave in.

NEW YORK'S #1!

It's no wonder that New York State is sometimes called "the center of the universe"—the state is the birthplace of many American firsts.

FIRST PIZZERIA. Grocery store owner Gennaro Lombardi received the first American merchant license for a pizzeria in 1905. Back then, pizza was called tomato pie, and ingredients were piled upside down, with the cheese on the bottom, then anchovies (the only topping available), and the sauce last. A whole pie was 5¢, but Lombardi's would sell smaller pieces based on how much customers wanted to spend. The pie (or piece) was then wrapped in paper and tied with string.

FIRST SUCCESSFUL STEAMBOAT. Steamboats were invented in America in 1787, but they weren't successful until 20 years later, when Robert Fulton built one that traveled up and down the Hudson River—150 miles each way—without sinking. Although it traveled at only five miles per hour, it ferried guests from New York City to Albany...in about 30 hours, with an overnight stop. Passengers feared the new technology, though—the boats spewed smoke, and people thought their boilers might explode—so the cost was only $3 (the same as older, much slower sailing ships), and included a cabin and meals.

FIRST LOCOMOTIVE RAILROAD. In 1830, the Mohawk and Hudson Company started building a railway between Albany and Schenectady. It was America's first steam-powered railroad, though horses still pulled the train over certain parts of the track. Mohawk and Hudson conductor Billy Marshall made history when he got in a fistfight with the train's engineer and, upon winning, insured that the conductor would manage a train's operations and crew, instead of the engineer.

FIRST CHESS TOURNAMENT. Chess had been played in the New World since at least 1641, but it wasn't until 1843 that New York held the first chess tournament in America. Two years later, Charles Henry Stanley started America's first chess column, published in New York's *Spirit of the Times* newspaper.

Since the U.N. isn't part of any one country, items in its gift shop are duty-free.

FIRST COMMERCIAL 3D MOVIE SHOWING. In June 1915, audiences donned cardboard red-and-green glasses and paid to see three one-reel films that tested the new medium of 3D movies at the Astor Theatre on Broadway. They watched selected scenes from the crime drama *Jim the Penman*, shots of rural America, and scenes of Niagara Falls. The 3D action was blurry, though, and reviewer Lynde Denig panned the experiment in *Moving Picture World*: "Images shimmered like reflections on a lake...it detracts from the plot."

FIRST DAILY YIDDISH NEWSPAPER. Kasriel Sarasohn, a conservative rabbi in New York City, launched the *Tageblatt* ("Daily Page") in 1885 to serve the needs of the city's rapidly growing Jewish community. While most Yiddish newspapers were sold only in kosher stores, Sarasohn employed newsboys to peddle them on the streets alongside English-language papers, a move that got *Tageblatt* out to a wide audience and made it extremely popular.

FIRST STATE PARK. During the Industrial Revolution, mills and factories were built along the Niagara River. To protect the area from pollution and further exploitation, the Niagara Reservation—a park containing American Falls, Bridal Veil Falls, and some of Horseshoe Falls—was formed in 1885. Instrumental in its creation was landscape architect Frederick Olmsted, who also designed Central Park. Now part of Niagara Falls State Park, the Niagara Reservation protects endangered Peregrine falcons, lake sturgeon, bald eagles, and 14 rare plant species.

FIRST CAR REGISTRATIONS AND LICENSE PLATES. In 1901, New York mandated that all cars be registered with the state and display license plates. Vehicle registration numbers were issued by the state, but the plates were not—car owners made the plates themselves, out of everything from iron to leather.

FIRST SOCIAL FRATERNITY. Sometimes called the Mother of Fraternities, Union College in Schenectady is where Kappa Alpha began as the first general college fraternity. Other groups founded at Union College include Sigma Phi, Delta Phi, and Phi Beta Kappa.

For more firsts, turn to page 252.

The New York Botanical Garden is the world's largest Victorian glasshouse.

BIRDS OF A NEW YORK FEATHER

Helicopters and jets aren't the only frequent flyers in the city sky. New York is one of the world's best cities for birdwatching, and not just for pigeons.

BRING YOUR BINOCULARS
Experts calculate that between 300 and 400 different species of birds migrate through or inhabit New York City each year. On an ordinary day, without trying too hard, a birder can see 75 to 100 species; in a year, if you work at it, you can see 200 to 300. Fairly easy to spot are herons, doves, orioles, wrens, woodpeckers, falcons, owls, mockingbirds, and cardinals, to name just a few. And birders can track rarer species by checking out the New York Rare Bird Alert. For those who like to keep score, New York City Audubon organizes an annual Christmas Bird Count, in which teams count every bird seen in their assigned areas of the five boroughs—on a single day.

WHY NEW YORK?
New York City is situated along the Atlantic Flyway, the coastal north-south migration route for millions of birds. During their long flights, the birds must rest and feed, and millions of them land in New York City parks, gardens, and beaches. The city is also home to many year-round nesting and breeding species.

Habitat is the key: New York City has an astonishing number of habitats that are hospitable to birds. There are 1,700 public parks; fresh-water marshes, lakes, and streams; saltwater beaches and marshes; rocky shorelines; estuaries; small islands; manmade ponds; private lawns; and even woodlands. Central Park is an outstanding birdwatching spot, an oasis for migrating and nesting birds, in which at least 285 species have been observed in recent years. The best spots for watching: around the water of the Harlem Meer, and in the woods and glades of the Ramble.

LIFE ON THE LEDGE
Across from Central Park, on the 12th-floor ledge of a luxury

---

In 1984 the NY Knicks won the NBA's first draft "lottery"—they chose Patrick Ewing.

co-op building at 927 Fifth Avenue, is a large bird's nest made of twigs and sticks. Its builder and longtime tenant is a red-tailed hawk called Pale Male. He was first spotted in the park in 1991 and, as of 2006, had fathered 26 chicks with three different mates. He's been with his latest mate, Lola, since 2002, and they raised seven chicks between 2002 and 2004.

Then disaster struck: In December 2004, the co-op board of 927 Fifth Avenue removed both the nest and the row of iron spikes that anchored it because some of the residents had complained about the bird droppings and meal "leftovers" from the hawks' diet of rodents and pigeons. Bird lovers—especially the New York City Audubon—were outraged, sparking protests and political speeches; actress Mary Tyler Moore (who lived in the building) even came out to support the hawks. The board finally relented, and Pale Male and Lola were allowed to rebuild their nest on the same spot. But even though Lola has laid eggs every year since then, none of them have hatched. Still, devoted (and optimistic) New Yorkers continue to track the hawks with binoculars and through telescopes set up in Central Park, hoping to spy new chicks.

WATCH YOUR STEP

Each spring and summer, a mile-long stretch of Rockaway Beach in Queens is declared off limits to everyone except a few Urban Park Rangers. The rangers' mission is to keep New Yorkers away from the breeding ground of the piping plovers, a species that's considered threatened in the Atlantic coastal area. In order to live and reproduce, these plump little grayish-white shorebirds need sandy beaches where they can find marine worms, beetles, mollusks, and other delicacies and where they can make nests and lay eggs safely.

What complicates their survival around humans is how effectively plovers use camouflage: Their nests (called *scrapes*) are small, barely noticeable depressions in the sand, often lined with bits of shell. Their eggs are speckled like sand, and their tiny hatched chicks are almost indistinguishable from the pebbles and twigs around the nests. One wrong step by a careless jogger could wipe out an entire plover home and family. Plovers were first discovered on Rockaway Beach in 1995, and with careful protection by the Urban Rangers, the rare bird's population in Rockaway continues to increase.

The Empire State Buildings contains 1,860 steps from street level to the 102nd floor.

ROOMS FOR REBELS

The Chelsea Hotel has been a magnet for artists, writers, and other creative types for the last century, but it's in for some big changes.

WHAT'S IN A NAME?

Its *real* name is the Hotel Chelsea, but this New York landmark is better known as the Chelsea Hotel or just "the Chelsea." Twelve stories high, the red-brick building sits on 23rd Street, taking up a huge hunk of space between Seventh and Eighth Avenues in a neighborhood also called Chelsea. (The neighborhood came first and dates to about 1750, when a British officer bought the land and named it after...*something* in London. The "what" is disputed.)

The hotel has fallen on hard times lately, but it began life spectacularly in 1884 as the Chelsea Home Club, one of New York's first cooperatively owned apartment buildings, or co-ops...at a time when there were fewer than 300 apartment buildings in New York. At the time, most middle-class people lived in single-family homes (row houses, brownstones, and so on)—apartment living for the middle class was a new idea. Members of the club could purchase one of the Chelsea's 70 units of three to nine rooms for $7,000 to $12,000. Each unit had high ceilings, wood-burning fireplaces, fire- and soundproof walls; some even had private penthouses. There were also 30 rental units that were designed to produce income for the co-op; they went for $50 to $100 per month. Most of the building's 100 units didn't have full kitchens, so the ground floor had a restaurant and several private dining rooms. The top floor had artists' studios and a roof garden. An impressive interior stairway swooped 12 stories up, lit by a large skylight.

In those days, the neighborhood around the Chelsea was a bustling theater district: Proctor's Theater (for vaudeville) was across the street; the Grand Opera House and others were nearby. But by the early 1890s, two major changes hit the Chelsea hard: Theaters began to relocate uptown, and a financial panic resulted in a depression. The Chelsea Home Club might have survived as a co-op if there hadn't been *another* financial panic in 1903. But in the uneasy economic climate, the place went bankrupt, and by

---

Most Broadway theaters omit the row "I" to avoid confusion with the number 1.

1905, the building had been bought and renamed the Hotel Chelsea.

ARTISTIC LICENSE

The Chelsea's reputation for attracting artsy tenants began soon after: Painters, writers, actors, and musicians discovered it, and they brought a certain bohemian caché with them. (Sarah Bernhardt and Lillie Langtry, two of the most famous actresses of the 1920s, often stayed there.) But history repeated itself and the hotel went bankrupt, so in 1939 a trio of partners—Hungarian immigrants Julius Krauss, Joseph Gross, and David Bard—bought the building. For the next 65 years, the Chelsea was a residential hotel: Tenants moved in (and were tossed out) at the discretion of the manager. Some stayed for short periods of time, some for decades, in accommodations that varied from a tiny room with a sink in the corner to a four-room suite with kitchen and private bath.

David Bard was the first manager, and his son Stanley took over the day-to-day operations in the mid-1950s. Stanley was an ever-present figure in the lobby, schmoozing with the residents, and became legendary for letting tenants slide with their rent when they were broke or short of cash. Stanley Bard was said to have a sixth sense about who was going to become famous (and therefore, whom to welcome to the hotel), and he didn't run a tight ship. The building wasn't kept up well or renovated. Tenants were pretty much left alone to live their lives. Stanley Bard's Chelsea was full of struggling artists whom the loose management style suited just fine.

THE GLITTERATI AND THE VICIOUS

Probably the most notorious of the Chelsea Hotel's residents was Sex Pistols bassist Sid Vicious. On October 12, 1978, his girlfriend, Nancy Spungen, was stabbed in their room at the Chelsea, and Vicious was charged with the murder. He was later released on bail but died of a heroin overdose before the case could be tried.

Many other famous Chelsea residents also did famous things in the building:

• Welsh poet Dylan Thomas, 39, a longtime alcoholic and gravely ill with pneumonia, was staying at the Chelsea when he was rushed to the emergency room at nearby St. Vincent's and died there on November 9, 1953.

There are 578 miles of waterfront in NYC.

- Beat poet and author William Burroughs lived at the hotel in the 1950s and wrote some of his novel *Naked Lunch*, detailing the life of a heroin addict, at the Chelsea; it was published in 1959.

- After the 1960 breakup of his marriage to Marilyn Monroe, playwright Arthur Miller lived at the Chelsea for six years, during which time he wrote the play *After the Fall*.

- In 1966, Andy Warhol made a 3½-hour experimental "underground" film called *The Chelsea Girls*, using various rooms and locations in the hotel. The movie is supposedly about the Chelsea and its residents, but no one in the film except the poet Rene Ricard actually lived there at the time.

- Bob Dylan wrote his song "Sad-Eyed Lady of the Lowlands" at the hotel; it was released in 1966 as the final track on *Blonde on Blonde*.

- Writer Charles R. Jackson, author of the 1944 novel *The Lost Weekend* (about alcoholism), overdosed on sleeping pills at the Chelsea on September 21, 1968.

- In 1970, rocker Patti Smith and photographer Robert Mapplethorpe moved into Room 1017 (reputed to be the smallest in the hotel). That's where Mapplethorpe took some of his earliest photographs—with a Polaroid camera loaned to him by another Chelsea resident.

DOWNHILL SLIDE

By the 1980s, the Chelsea had become an unsavory place. According to rumors, it had an in-house heroin dealer who ran his business undisturbed; there was a brothel in one room; fires were a common occurrence, the result of passed-out occupants dropping lighted cigarettes; and more than one suicidal resident jumped into the 12-story well of the central staircase. But by the 1990s, gentrification was in full swing, and the rowdy crowds who had once flocked to the neighborhood were now drawn to cheaper apartments in other parts of the city and the outer boroughs. Unfortunately, this didn't do much for the future of the Chelsea. The hotel—despite being a beloved landmark—was shabby, run-down, and losing money. Things didn't get any better as the new century arrived.

On June 16, 2007, Stanley Bard turned 73 years old. It wasn't a happy birthday. He'd managed the Chelsea for more than 50 years and was expecting his own son to take over as manager after him. The Bards, after all, had been one of the Chelsea's original owner families. But out of the blue—or so says Stanley Bard—he was fired by the rest of the hotel's board members.

SELLING OUT

To some, the ouster wasn't a complete surprise—the board had long been pressuring Bard to make the hotel more profitable. That hadn't happened, so they decided to get rid of Stanley and bring in an outside management firm to run the Chelsea and to renovate, modernize, restore, and reinvigorate it. The new firm failed, and it was fired in less than a year. The next manager walked out after seven months, driven away in disgust by "incessant tenant harassment."

The board itself then assumed management of the hotel and stopped accepting long-term residents. Forty long-termers had already left after Stanley Bard was fired; about 90 were still in the hotel, and they claimed that the owners were trying to evict them by any means possible. The owners denied it, but rumor had it that the board was divided over how to run the hotel. Finally, on October 19, 2010, the board announced its intention to sell the Chelsea. Old tenants would be protected by New York City rent laws as long as their leases were in effect, but after that—no guarantees. The board's spokesperson said, "The history itself makes the hotel what it is...and there's nothing you want to do to change what the Chelsea is."

*   *   *

CHARGE IT

In 1949 businessman Frank McNamara hosted a dinner at a New York City restaurant called the Major's Cabin Grill. But when it came time to pay, McNamara realized he'd left his wallet at home, and he had to have someone go to his house and get it for him. That inspired McNamara and a business partner to create the first credit card: the Diners Club Card, in 1950.

...It's over the 59th Street Bridge. It's not over the Atlantic Ocean." —Cyndi Lauper

OUR TOWN

Welcome to New York, home of the Coney Island, the Catskills…and a lot of really strange town names.

Neversink	Hoosick
Big Flats	Beaver Dams
Busti	Podunk
Butternuts	Place Corners
Result	Chili
Coxsackie	Yaphank
Hicksville	Climax
Horseheads	Owls Head
Root	Flushing
Mooers	Hogtown
Pumpkin Hollow	Pound Ridge
Tuxedo	Shinhopple
Gayhead	Handsome Eddy
Cat Elbow Corner	North Pole
Painted Post	Looneyville

Only U.S. president buried in NYC: Ulysses S. Grant.

KNOW YOUR POLITICIANS

In this quiz, we list the "accomplishments" (good and bad) of five New York politicians. Can you name them all? (Answers are on page 363.)

1. Finished construction of the Brooklyn Bridge, built Manhattan's Old New York County Courthouse, and increased the city's debt by $47 million over 11 years. (Hint: He's best known as one of the most corrupt leaders in U.S. history.)

2. Redrafted New York's state constitution, enacted strict child-labor laws, and increased state aid to mothers and children. (Hint: He was the first Roman Catholic to run for president of the United States.)

3. Decreased overall crime rates in New York City by 65 percent, got more than 691,000 people off of welfare, and enacted policies that increased the city's property values. (Hint: Time magazine named him "Person of the Year" for 2001.)

4. Introduced the sales tax to New York (even though he'd opposed Herbert Hoover's earlier attempts to create a national sales tax), unified the city's subway system, and installed rent-control laws that remain in place today. (Hint: Among his many accomplishments, he was known for defeating the powerful political machine most often associated with Politician #1.)

5. Balanced New York City's budget for the first time in a decade, launched a ticker-tape parade to celebrate the Yankees' 1978 World Series win, rebuilt the Bronx after a series of fires and crime sprees, and installed a merit selection system for the appointment of judges. (Hint: He was well-known for his quips, which sometimes got him into trouble. Many people argue that he lost the 1982 governor's race after saying, "Living in rural areas is a joke...have you ever lived in the suburbs? It's sterile. It's numb. It's wasting your life...living in Albany would be a fate worse than death.")

The serrated knife, the dental chair, and the air-cooled engine were all invented in Syracuse.

THE KILLER PENNY

According to legend, a penny dropped from the Empire State Building will build up enough velocity to put a hole in the concrete below…or in your head. But is it true?

LOOK OUT BELOW!
The Empire State Building is 1,454 feet high. When it was built in 1931, it was the tallest skyscraper in the world. (Today, it's 15th.) Sometime after it went up, a rumor began: If you dropped a penny from the observation deck, it would pick up so much speed on the way down that it could put a hole in the sidewalk or kill a person walking below. No one seems to know who actually started the rumor, but it's circulated over the years. According to one tourist at the Empire State Building, a falling penny "could actually go through someone's skull." Oh, really?

DEADLY DROP?
Several scientists have tried to test the tale of the killer penny, but no one's actually dropped a coin from the Empire State Building's observation deck. A penny dropped from the deck would probably just land on a lower roof anyway, because the building's lower stories are much wider than the upper ones. Not only that, but when wind hits a building, it can bounce off and go straight up, creating an updraft so strong that it could carry the penny back to the observation deck. So experimenters have tried another route: simulations.

University of Virginia physics professor Louis Bloomfield recently theorized that the killer penny legend was a myth because of the coin's susceptibility to air resistance. According to Bloomfield, "Air resistance is a big deal for little things. It slows down leaves, it slows down raindrops, and it slows down pennies." Pennies weigh more than leaves or raindrops, but Bloomfield maintains that they still tumble and flutter as they fall, which slows their terminal velocity (the fastest speed reached during the drop).

In 2007, to prove his point, Bloomfield did an experiment on the TV show *20/20*. He attached a penny dispenser to a weather balloon, which he then launched 200 feet in the air. Using a remote control, he dropped pennies from the dispenser and stood below the balloon to catch them. Bloomfield wasn't a good catch, but he did manage to get hit by a penny or two, and though he felt a sting, he survived.

A PENNY FOR YOUR MYTH

One obvious problem with Bloomfield's experiment was that the weather balloon was only 200 feet above ground. Skeptics contended that such a short distance didn't really simulate a drop from the Empire State Building. But according to Bloomfield, "It doesn't matter. The penny will hit full speed after 50 feet or so, and it just coasts."

For those who still doubt the professor, there was another experiment: Adam Savage and Jamie Hyneman from the TV show *Mythbusters* put a penny inside a wind tube and used the swirling air current to find the fastest speed that a falling penny can reach—from whatever height. They established a penny's terminal velocity at 65 mph.

Next, using a modified staple gun, the pair shot pennies at concrete and asphalt at 65 mph. Neither was damaged. Next, they shot a penny at 65 mph at a gelatin dummy—the kind that ballistics labs use to test the results of gunshots on human bodies. When the penny didn't damage the dummy, the experimenters shot pennies at their own arms and legs. The pennies stung but didn't cut the skin.

DON'T TRY THIS ON THE OBSERVATION DECK

Still, debunking the penny myth doesn't mean that small stuff can safely be tossed from the top of tall buildings. As Bloomfield points out, aerodynamically streamlined objects—like ball-point pens—don't pick up wind resistance the way coins do. An object like that could reach top speeds of more than 200 miles an hour and could definitely be dangerous.

Heavier objects with less wind resistance could also be lethal. For example, a Milky Way candy bar falling from a great height could reach a speed of 250 mph. And even though the candy bar weighs only about 2.5 ounces, if it fell that fast and landed on someone's head, the result could be fatal.

So, come to think of it, the next time you're walking past a tall building, it might not be a bad idea to wear a hard hat after all.

NUDE YORK

*Need a place to get naked in New York? Here are
a few spots that aren't your bathroom.*

FIRE ISLAND. Since the 1960s, this barrier island just to the south of Long Island has had several clothing-optional beaches, including Lighthouse Beach, Kismet, and Cherry Grove. As for simply tossing aside your bathing suit top, in 1992, the New York State Supreme Court ruled that women had the right to be topless in public just like men do. It was the first state to do so.

FULL TAN SUN CLUB. This nudist club is in the town of Sprakers, on Interstate 90 just east of Albany. There's nude swimming in the club's pond, nude camping, nude fishing, nude trail hiking, and nude lawn games.

POTTER'S FALLS. Located on Six Mile Creek on Rt. 79 just southeast of Ithaca in central New York, this is a 25-foot waterfall where people have been skinnydipping for decades. But don't tell them we sent you: It's actually illegal to swim there, since the creek is part of Ithaca's water supply.

LAKEVIEW WILDLIFE MANAGEMENT AREA. Located on the eastern shore of Lake Ontario, this undeveloped and little-known beach is a popular spot for nude sunbathers and swimmers. There's also an area of protected sand dunes. Don't walk on them, though: The area has "Dune Stewards" who can give you a ticket for being (naked or dressed) on the dunes.

SKINNY DIP FALLS. This aptly named waterfall is found in western New York State, just north of the Chautauqua Gorge State Forest. (Look on the Internet for detailed instructions. You'll have to walk a bit and look for a rock that's painted with "Nudist area next one mile.") If you're not happy with Skinny Dip Falls, you can always go to Bare Butt Falls in nearby Zoar Valley.

EMPIRE HAVEN. At this 97-acre "family-oriented" nudist park in Moravia, in the Finger Lakes region, feel free to enjoy the park's pool, camping places, hiking trails…and "pickleball court."

He must not be a baseball fan: St. Patrick is patron saint of both Boston and NYC.

ACROSS AND DOWN BLOOPERS

Despite careful testing and fact-checking by a crack editorial team, about 20 errors make their way into the New York Times crosswords every year. (Not a bad statistic, considering that the other 345 are error-free.) Here are some offenders from the past few years.

Clue: Defense secretary Powell
Answer: COLIN
Wrong! Colin Powell was not the secretary of defense; he was secretary of state.

Clue: Most G.I.'s
Answer: PVTS
Wrong! G.I. is a general term for members of the U.S. armed forces. Only a small number of G.I.s are privates.

Clue: Backup singers in a 1960's R&B group
Answer: THE MGS
Wrong! The M.G.s (of Booker T. & the M.G.s) didn't sing; they were a band of backup musicians.

Clue: Tubular food
Answer: SALAMI
Wrong! A tube is hollow—salami isn't. The clue should have read "cylindrical food."

Clue: Beau's belle
Answer: CHERI
Wrong! The correct answer to the clue would be CHERIE, the feminine form of the masculine *cheri.*

Clue: "Raid on Entebbe" airline
Answer: EL AL
Wrong! The hijacked passengers who were held hostage at Uganda's Entebbe Airport and rescued by Israeli commandos hadn't been flying El Al. They were traveling to Paris on Air France.

Clue: Mate for "my friend" Flicka
Answer: MARE
Wrong! The horse first made famous by the 1941 novel *My Friend Flicka* was a mare, so her mate would have been a stallion.

"There are two million interesting people in NY, and only 78 in Los Angeles." —Neil Simon

Clue: University of Ohio athlete
Answer: BOBCAT
Wrong! There's an Ohio University, and its sports teams are the Bobcats, but there's no University of Ohio.

Clue: He's found in the Prado
Answer: DALI
Wrong! Madrid's Prado museum houses works by Goya, El Greco, and even Picasso, but nothing by Salvador Dali.

Clue: "___ chance!"
Answer: BON
Wrong! *Chance* is a feminine word in French, so "good" as in "good luck" would be spelled BONNE: *bonne chance.*

Clue: Mark Twain's hometown on the Missouri
Answer: HANNIBAL
Wrong! Twain's hometown was Hannibal, it's true, but Hannibal, in the state of Missouri, is on the Mississippi River.

Clue: Writer/director of *Spartacus*
Answer: MAMET
Wrong! David Mamet did not write and direct *Spartacus*. The puzzle editor must have been thinking of the movie *Spartan*, a Mamet thriller that was released in 2004. The 1960 film *Spartacus* was directed by Stanley Kubrick.

Clue: Southpaw's hit
Answer: LEFT JAB
Wrong! A left-handed boxer would probably jab with his right, or front, hand, saving his dominant left hand for the power punch. Boxers with a traditional, right-handed stance would jab with the left.

Clue: Bean source
Answer: COCOA
Wrong! The cocoa plant actually produces berries. Cacao plants produce beans.

Clue: Pierce portrayer on TV and film
Answer: ALDA
Wrong! It's true that Alan Alda played Hawkeye Pierce on the TV show M*A*S*H (1972–83), but it was actor Donald Sutherland who portrayed the character in the 1970 movie.

Clue: Dutch _____ (uncommon sights nowadays)
Answer: ELMS
Wrong! "Dutch elm" is a fungal disease...of elm trees.

TENEMENT TALES

*The only time a modern New Yorker is likely to encounter an
outhouse in America is on vacation at a campground. But
for 19th-century New Yorkers living in Lower East Side
tenements, an outdoor privy was the only option.*

A HOUSE DIVIDED

The South Bronx, Brownsville (Brooklyn), and Harlem all
have histories of substandard housing, but the 19th-century
tenements of Manhattan's Lower East Side have come to symbolize
the worst housing conditions in New York's history. Tenant-houses,
later called *tenements*, were multifamily rental dwellings for the
mostly immigrant urban poor—either apartment buildings or
houses divided into separate apartments. Most units (often only
three rooms for families of five or more people) had no windows, no
daylight, and no fresh air. Stairs and hallways were pitch-dark and
dangerous. There was rarely indoor plumbing, and the only water
came from pumps outside. Lice and vermin were rampant.

CHANGING NEIGHBORHOODS

Around 1800, the southern end of Manhattan was divided into a
grid of 25-foot by 100-foot lots, and typically, a single-family home
was built on each lot. By the 1840s and '50s, however, the wealthy
owners of those single-family homes had moved north, leaving
empty houses behind. To accommodate the influx of Irish and German immigrants—who helped the city's population double by
1860—many of the narrow old row houses were converted into
dwellings for 20 or more families. Others were demolished to make
way for "purpose-built tenements"—cheaply constructed apartment buildings designed to squeeze as many poor people as possible
into cramped housing for as much rent as the owner could get.
(The first custom-built tenement went up around 1824 at 65 Mott
Street, in today's Chinatown.) Greedy landlords did as little maintenance as they could in order to realize the greatest profit from
their overcrowded properties.

By the 1870s, the worst of the tenements were located in two
adjacent wards: the 10th (bounded by Rivington Street on the

north, Division on the south, Bowery on the west, and Norfolk on the east) and the 13th (bounded by Rivington on the north, Division and Grand on the south, Norfolk on the west, and the East River). Most residents were still Irish and German, with some Italians and Jews. Then, between 1880 and 1914, more than 2 million Eastern European Jews arrived in America, escaping widespread persecution and anti-Semitic attacks in their native countries. Many of the new arrivals settled in the 10th and 13th wards, where there was work, community, and often relatives. This area, which was part of what came to be called the Lower East Side, gradually evolved into a primarily Jewish enclave.

THE MORE THEY STAY THE SAME

Although some tenement building regulations had been enacted in the 1860s, there were too few inspectors and no incentive to enforce them, since politicians didn't want to go up against the city's powerful real-estate owners. It took until 1879 for the state legislature to enact the Second Tenement House Act, the most comprehensive and wide-reaching tenement law to date. It laid out rules for how new tenements should be constructed: They couldn't have any "dark rooms," interior spaces with no windows. So most new tenements were built according to a design called a "dumbbell": five to seven stories, wide at the front and back and narrow in the middle. The narrow section was supposed to create a "shaft," or open space, to allow in air and light, but the shafts usually remained small and dark, and light rarely reached the lower floors. The shafts were also convenient places to toss garbage, and since tenements were built only a few feet apart, there was no way to get down into the shafts to clean them—so the smell was atrocious.

The 1879 law also mandated that the building would have four apartments per floor, each with three or four rooms; two shared toilets per floor (but no running water in the apartments); and windows in all bedrooms (even though some inevitably faced the shaft). This new housing was marginally better than the old, but it deteriorated rapidly from overcrowding. Meanwhile, the older tenements got even worse as they aged.

LIFE IN A TENEMENT

Imagine an oppressive New York summer in an old tenement in

the 1880s: The masonry walls held heat that rose up through seven stories of small apartments with little ventilation or natural light. The stench of food, garbage, dirt, and unwashed bodies permeated the dark common stairs and hallways. The privies in the backyard stank and bred disease. Bathing and doing laundry were next to impossible: There were no bathtubs, no money for soap, and the only available water came from a pump or hydrant in the backyard.

In winter, life was even harder. Apartments were heated by one small coal stove in the kitchen—when the occupants could afford coal. Tenement dwellers had few warm clothes or shoes, and little bedding or blankets. In summer and winter, wages were meager and working hours were long—16 or 18 hours a day in dangerous, unsanitary, overcrowded factories. Conditions were no better for people doing "piecework" at home, working long hours in poorly lit rooms doubling as living quarters, making hats, leather goods, garments, cigars, jewelry, clocks, wigs, paper bags, and artificial flowers. Though children were supposed to be in school, they were often pressed into service to earn money for their families, putting finishing touches on those goods. Some families took in boarders or entire other families to bring in a little more money, packing them into the already crowded few rooms. Contagious diseases like influenza, typhus, tuberculosis, scarlet fever, and diphtheria were rampant; fires were common; and food was scarce.

In 1896, after a visit to the Lower East Side's tenements, William Dean Howells, a highly respected journalist and editor of *Harper's Magazine*, wrote: "I have tried to report simply and honestly what I saw of the life of our poorest people that day. One might say it was not so bad as it is painted, but I think it is quite as bad as it appeared; and I could not see that in itself or in its conditions it held the promise or the hope of anything better. If it is tolerable, it must endure; if it is intolerable, still it must endure."

SEEING IS BELIEVING

Meanwhile, reformers were trying to bring the tenement situation to the attention of New York's more fortunate citizens. Jacob Riis, an author and photographer, was prominent among the reformers. Riis came to America from Denmark in 1870, when he was 21, and lived in poverty until he stumbled into journalism. While making a career as a police reporter for the *New York Tribune* and the *New*

Only New York–born winner of the Nobel Prize for Literature: Eugene O'Neil (1936).

York Evening Sun, he also explored the slums and wrote about them, saying, "The sights gripped my heart until I felt that I must tell of them or burst."

His articles about tenements never managed to ignite the concern of his readers, though, so he turned to photography to tell the story. Camera in hand, he began documenting the crushing poverty, desperation, disease, hunger, and filth in the city's tenements. The shocking images were made possible by a new technology Riis learned about in 1887: the magnesium-powder flash. Using the flash wasn't easy—the powder explosion created a blinding flare (which sometimes frightened away the subjects of the photos) and could set fire to the buildings he was photographing (which happened twice). But the flash allowed Riis to take pictures in the city's darkest tenements and alleys.

The images were first printed in the *Sun* in 1888, as line drawings based on the photographs. Another article followed in 1889, and that was expanded to become a book called *How the Other Half Lives: Studies Among the Tenements of New York*, containing Riis's groundbreaking photos. The book forced middle- and upper-class New Yorkers—and local politicians—to acknowledge the scourge of the slums, though it took another 10 years to pass legislation that brought some reform.

ONE STEP FORWARD, TWO STEPS BACK

In 1901, New York's state legislature passed the Tenement House Act to regulate the design of the next generation of tenement buildings. "Dumbbell" designs were outlawed. Building lots now had to be 50 feet wide (instead of 25 feet), creating larger rooms in the apartments; indoor plumbing (including running water) was required; and every room had to have a window that offered at least a little bit of light and fresh air. Landlords were supposed to make some renovations to old buildings, too, but they mostly ignored the regulations. The old tenements remained just as bad as before, and very few of them were torn down.

World War I and the Immigration Restriction Act of 1924 slowed the influx of immigrants, and soon the Great Depression ended the need for cheap immigrant labor. The increasing power of labor unions also began to produce better wages for working people, who then moved out of the tenements. Unions also began to build

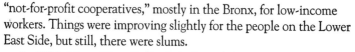

"not-for-profit cooperatives," mostly in the Bronx, for low-income workers. Things were improving slightly for the people on the Lower East Side, but still, there were slums.

In 1934, Mayor Fiorello La Guardia wrangled federal funding for urban renewal, and the New York City Housing Authority (NYCHA) was set up to provide public housing. Its first project was called First Houses, between First Avenue and Avenue A, from East Second Street to East Third Street. (The area is now part of the East Village.) NYCHA continued to build more public housing, but the rental requirements—in many cases, you had to have $100 in the bank to be considered—meant that many of the neediest people were turned away. La Guardia also insisted that all landlords bring their buildings up to code. It was a good idea in theory, but instead of complying, many landlords simply boarded up their tenement—at least 10,000 of them—and evicted the poor tenants.

SLOW TO CHANGE
As late as 1941, the Lower East Side was full of abandoned, closed-up buildings and vacant lots, and rents on the remaining apartments had skyrocketed because they were so scarce. Urban-renewal programs lasted well into the latter half of the 20th century, but even as late as 1997, an NYU Law School report still cited the Lower East Side as an area suffering from "owners or renters living in buildings which are dilapidated."

In some ways, the Lower East side hasn't changed much in recent years. Most of the buildings are still run-down, and many residents are people who can't afford to live in the more upscale parts of the city—mostly artists and young people. But the area is showing signs of gentrification: Trendy restaurants, hipster bars, funky shops, a few boutique hotels, and a huge club scene now dominate the Lower East Side, making it a hip, modern neighborhood—something that was unimaginable a century ago.

*　*　*

IT'S A FACT
The only New York City subway line that doesn't
run through Manhattan is the G Train.

One-third of the battles of the Revolutionary War took place in New York State.

THE STATUE OF LIBERTY: SEVEN FACTS

The Statue of Liberty has presided over New York Harbor since 1886. Most people know that she was a gift from France and that she's greeted millions of immigrants arriving in the United States. But here are a few facts that you might not know.

1. SHE WAS BORN AT A DINNER PARTY.

One night in the 1860s, French author Edouard de Laboulaye was entertaining some dinner-party guests when he came up with a grandiose idea: France and the United States should jointly build a monument honoring democracy and the friendship between the two countries. One of Laboulaye's guests, sculptor Frédéric Auguste Bartholdi, was so intrigued that he came up with the idea for the Statue of Liberty. Bartholdi officially named her *Liberty Enlightening the World* and hoped that the statue would enlighten his fellow Frenchmen about the importance of democracy in government.

2. SHE ALMOST HAD NO PLACE TO STAND.

The Statue of Liberty is regarded as a treasure today, but when she was first built, many Americans had no use for her. The people of France raised about $400,000 so that Bartholdi could complete the monument, and the United States then had to raise about $100,000 for the pedestal. But by the time Lady Liberty was finished in 1884, the U.S. was having trouble coming up with the money. During the late 1800s, the nation was in the midst of a financial depression, and many Americans didn't want to pay good money for a statue that hadn't even been made at home. *The New York Times* complained, "No true patriot can countenance any such expenditures for bronze females in the present state of our finances." (The newspaper was mistaken about the metal—the Statue of Liberty is covered in copper.) Meanwhile, Congress refused to pay for the pedestal because the statue seemed more like a gift to the City of New York than to the entire country. And New York's Governor Grover Cleveland vetoed a $50,000 state grant for the pedestal.

The Buffalo Bills are the only NFL team to lose 4 consecutive Super Bowls.

Finally, in 1885, Joseph Pulitzer—owner of the *New York World* newspaper—wrote, "It would be an irrevocable disgrace to New York City and the American Republic to have France send us this splendid gift without our having provided even so much as a landing space for it." Claiming that the *World*'s working-class readers could save the day, he promised to publish in his paper the names of people who gave even small contributors to the pedestal fund. It worked. Donations poured in—more than 120,000 readers gave nearly $102,000 to place the statue on her pedestal.

3. SHE WAS A "FIRST" LADY.

On October 28, 1886, the Statue of Liberty was installed on Bedloe's Island (now Liberty Island). There were fireworks and speeches from dignitaries, including President Grover Cleveland—who praised the statue that he'd failed to finance as governor. A month later, the Statue of Liberty became the country's first electric lighthouse when nine electric arc lamps were installed in her torch and five were placed around her star-shaped base. The torch, at 305 feet above sea level, was visible 24 miles out to sea. It acted as a navigational light until 1902.

4. SHE'S THIN-SKINNED.

Lady Liberty's outer copper coating is just 0.09 of an inch thick, thinner than two pennies. And her green color is the result of *patina*, tarnish on the copper.

5. SOMETHING'S DIFFERENT ABOUT HER FOOT.

Most humans have what experts call a "normal foot"—the "big" toe is the longest. But about 20 percent of people have what's called Morton's Toe—meaning the second toe is longer than the big toe. (The condition is named for American orthopedist Dudley J. Morton, who discovered in the early 1900s that a short big toe could cause painful foot disorders.) But long before it was called Morton's Toe, the condition was known as Grecian Foot—because in classical and Renaissance art, a long second toe was considered to be beautiful. Bartholdi had always found inspiration in the statues of the ancient Greeks and Romans, so he designed Lady Liberty with one of the classic features of ancient Greek art: the Grecian Foot.

The current NYPD uniform was adopted in 1853.

6. SHE ALSO WEARS A BIG SHOE.

Bartholdi had always been drawn to large works, and he decided that his statue would be the largest since ancient times. (The largest in the ancient world was the 100-foot-tall Colossus of Rhodes built during the 3rd century B.C. and was later destroyed in an earthquake.) The Statue of Liberty is just over 111 feet tall from her heel to the top of her head. Her face is 10 feet wide (Bartholdi used his mother as the model), her mouth is three feet wide, and her nose is 4½ feet long. Her bust measures 36 feet around, and her feet are 25 feet long, which, shoe experts say, makes her sandals the equivalent of size 879.

7. A POET CHANGED HER IMAGE.

Originally the Statue of Liberty was intended to be a simple symbol of democracy, but her proximity to Ellis Island also made her an icon of hope for new immigrants. Another reason for the symbolism is the poem "The New Colossus," which is inscribed on a plaque attached to the statue's pedestal. In the poem, Lady Liberty declares, "Give me your tired, your poor, your huddled masses yearning to breathe free."

But the poem didn't appear on the plaque until 1903. Its author, Emma Lazarus, worked with poverty-stricken Jewish immigrants who arrived in the United States after fleeing anti-Semitism in Eastern Europe. She wrote "The New Colossus" for them. Lazarus died in 1887, and her poem was forgotten until it resurfaced in a Manhattan used bookstore several years later. People found it so moving that, more than 20 years after it was written, it became part of the statue.

* * *

"People say New Yorkers can't get along. Not true. I saw two New Yorkers, complete strangers, sharing a cab: One guy took the tires and the radio; the other guy took the engine."

—David Letterman

BIENVENIDOS, FIDEL!

The United States has been snarling at Cuba's Fidel Castro for so long that it's hard to believe he ever visited our shores. But he did, three times—most notably, in September 1960. Where did he go? New York, of course.

NOT YOUR ORDINARY TOURIST

Cuba was (and still is) a permanent member of the United Nations, so in September 1960, Fidel Castro—just a year and a half after overthrowing the island nation's American-supported military dictator, Fulgencio Batista—chose to exercise his right to speak before the U.N.'s annual meeting at its headquarters in New York City. Castro was looking to legitimize himself in the world's eyes as the country's leader. Relations between the U.S. government and Cuba were already unfriendly, though—Castro hadn't yet officially declared himself a communist, but he had been busy nationalizing American-owned companies in Cuba like Texaco, Esso, and Shell, and foreign-owned banks, including the First National City Bank of New York and the Chase Manhattan Bank. The American government wasn't happy to have Castro on its turf, but there was nothing it could do to prevent him from going to the United Nations. The feds did, however, order the Cuban delegation not to leave Manhattan.

CASTRO WAS HERE

On September 18, Castro and his entourage of about 50 arrived at Idlewild (now JFK) Airport and drove through downtown Manhattan, waving at crowds of supporters. (Unfortunately, someone in the crowd roughly shoved Castro's waving arm, which prompted the Cuban president to file the first of many official complaints about his treatment in the city.) The cars finally made it to their destination, the Shelburne Hotel on Lexington Avenue.

Finding a hotel for the Cubans hadn't been easy: None of the hotels near the U.N. were willing to take them in, and it wasn't until the U.N. and U.S. State Department leaned on Edward Spatz, owner of the Shelburne, that Spatz agreed to let the Cubans stay there. But to demonstrate his displeasure, Spatz hung a big American flag outside the hotel...and refused to hang a Cuban

---

Dutch name for Cobble Hill, Brooklyn, in the 17th century: Punkiesberg.

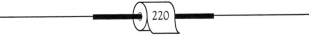

one. He also insisted that the Cubans pay for their rooms in advance, in cash, and he wanted them to put down a $10,000 deposit in case of damage. And to top it all off, according to the Cubans, their rooms at the Shelburne were tiny. Castro was furious.

To make matters worse, the press reported that Castro and his group had brought in live chickens to pluck and cook, that they were tossing burning cigars onto the rugs, and that they were generally trashing their rooms. The reports were unsubstantiated, but after just 24 hours, Castro decided that enough was enough. His entire Cuban delegation stormed out of the Shelburne and headed for the United Nations.

A STUNT IS BORN

When the Cubans appeared at U.N .headquarters, they went straight to the office of Dag Hammarskjöld, the U.N. Secretary-General. There, Castro complained about his treatment at the Shelburne and the lack of hospitality from New Yorkers, and threatened to sleep in Central Park.

Somehow Hammarskjöld managed to get the Commodore Hotel on 42nd Street to offer rooms—at no charge—but Castro refused to accept what he called "charity." In fact, he already had a backup plan: the rundown Hotel Theresa in Harlem, where he'd made arrangements with owner Love B. Woods for several rooms. As it turned out, the dramatic departure from the Shelburne had been planned—so that Castro could spurn the fancy midtown venue and install himself among the "common" people of Harlem, where he expected to receive sympathy and a warm welcome.

The Hotel Theresa on 7th Avenue (now Adam Clayton Powell Jr. Boulevard) was a Harlem landmark. From its opening in 1913 until 1940, it was a whites-only hotel that made exceptions for a few African-American celebrities. That changed in the 1940s and '50s, when it was taken over by new management, catered to a high-class African-American clientele, and became known as the "Waldorf-Astoria of Harlem."

By 1960, it was no longer at the height of its glory, but the Hotel Theresa's history and location suited the Cuban delegation perfectly. Thousands of black New Yorkers lined the streets around the building, hoping for a glimpse of the hero of the Cuban revolution. The move proved to be less convenient for the NYPD. The hotel was five miles from the U.N., and the long trip made it harder to protect the Cuban delegation.

THE OUT-OF-TOWNERS

Castro spent less than two weeks in New York, but he kept as busy as any tourist. He met with international leaders friendly (or at least somewhat friendly) to his cause—Nasser of Egypt, Nehru of India, Nkrumah of Ghana, and Gomulka of Poland, among others—but most important of the lot was Premier Khrushchev of the Soviet Union, who came to see him in Harlem. Khrushchev used his visit to Harlem to show solidarity with Castro and to highlight what he called "the discriminatory policies of the United States of America toward Negroes, as well as toward Cuba." But Khrushchev was also shocked by what he found when he arrived at Castro's suites: The Hotel Theresa's rooms were pretty shabby to begin with, and the Cubans had made them even worse, tossing old cigar butts (among other things) on the floors.

Khrushchev wasn't the Cubans' only visitor, though. Malcolm X, whose Organization of Afro-American Unity later had offices at the Theresa, visited Castro, and so did poets Allen Ginsburg and Langston Hughes.

THE GRAND FINALE

Annual sessions of the General Assembly were traditionally conducted with diplomacy, even when speeches got heated. Not in 1960, however. This was the year when Khrushchev pounded the table with his shoe, shouted at British Prime Minister Harold Macmillan, raged at Dag Hammarskjöld, and spoke to the U.N. delegates for more than two hours in October. But those two hours of Premier Khrushchev were nothing compared to the speech Castro delivered at the general session on September 26. After telling the gathered U.N. representatives and dignitaries that he would "endeavor to be brief," Castro launched into a speech that lasted for more than four hours.

Two days later, he was back in Cuba, telling his citizens that the United States was a cowardly place where Cubans were brutalized, blacks were persecuted, and everyone was motivated by money. They were lucky, he said, to live in a country where people recognized the truth and had something to fight for.

...Grover Cleveland, Theodore Roosevelt, and Franklin Delano Roosevelt.

The United States ended diplomatic relations with Cuba the next year and more than four decades of strained interactions between the two countries followed—including the extremes of the Cuban Missile Crisis and the failed Bay of Pigs invasion. Castro did come to the U.S. once more in 1979, again to address the United Nations, but that visit lacked the drama of the 1960 trip.

*　　*　　*

THE NEW YORK BOTANICAL GARDEN
In the late 1800s, Nathanial Lord Britton and Elizabeth Knight (husband-and-wife botany professors at Columbia University) went on a trip to England, where they visited London's Royal Botanic Garden. The pair was inspired to create a similar garden in New York City. With the help of the city and prominent financiers (like Andrew Carnegie and Cornelius Vanderbilt), they established the New York Botanical Garden in the Bronx on land that once belonged to a tobacco merchant named Pierre Lorillard.

Today the 25- acre site is a U.S. National Historic Landmark and houses 50 gardens and plant collections that contain more than one million plants, including...

• a 50-acre replica of the forest that once covered New York City.

• 30,000 trees, many more than 200 years old.

• an 11-acre azalea garden

• 3,500 rose plants, in over 600 varieties.

• more than 8,000 orchids.

• 90 different kinds of lilacs in colors from white to pale blue to deep purple.

• a greenhouse that includes an ecotour of the world, highlighting tropical rain forests, deserts, carnivorous and aquatic plants, and one of the world's largest collections of palm trees.

• 100-year old tulip trees averaging 90 feet high.

LOONY LAWS

Mot of the time, laws are important...they keep us safe and maintain order. But laws like these make us go, "Huh?".

Statewide, it's illegal for women to go topless in public...but only if they're doing it for "business." (At all other times, it's OK.)

In New York City, you may not purposely throw a ball at someone's head.

In Ocean City, eating while swimming in the ocean is against the law.

In New York City, honking a car horn in a non-emergency is illegal and subject to a $350 fine.

An old law still on the books says that it's illegal for men in New York City to "look at a woman in that way" (i.e., flirt). If caught, guys can get a $25 fine for a first offense. For a second offense, they can be made to wear horse blinders every time they go out.

It's illegal to carry around an open can of spray paint in New York City.

In Brooklyn, donkeys are not permitted to sleep in bathtubs.

The New York Department of Health forbids people from growing poison ivy.

If you want to take a bath in a pond in Sag Harbor, you must wear a bathing suit.

Within the New York City limits, people may not keep mountain lions, grizzly bears, or kinkajous as pets, and they may not dye their rabbits. (Cattle and pigs are OK, as long as they're fenced.)

Statewide, the only people allowed to put you in handcuffs or leg irons are the police.

People in Towanda may start fires in public parks, but only if they intend to cook something.

More than three unrelated people may not live in one apartment in New York City.

Milk sold in New York State may not contain pus, blood, manure, or vermin. (Maybe this one isn't so loony after all.)

RECLAIMING CENTRAL PARK

From above, Central Park looks like a big green rug lying in the middle of Manhattan Island. But from the ground, it's more complicated, with 843 acres of careful landscaping...and 150 years of history.

BIRTH OF A PARK

Until the mid 1800s, New York City had no great public park. People got away from the noise and chaos of city life by visiting the few quiet open spaces they could find. Among the most popular spots: cemeteries. On hot summer days, wealthy people could go to the country, but the poor were trapped in the sweltering city. Influential New Yorkers began to push for a centrally located park that would offer meadows, lakes, fountains, and woodlands for everyone to enjoy. Popular 19th-century journalist William Cullen Bryant wrote, "If the public authorities who expend so much of our money in laying out the city would do what is in their power, they might give our vast population an extensive pleasure ground for shade and recreation...which we might reach without going out of town."

In 1853, the state legislature agreed to let New York City acquire 700-plus acres (it later was expanded) in the center of Manhattan, an area that had been home to a cluster of small villages and settlements built on rocky, swampy soil. (Part of the reason the land was considered good for a park was that it wasn't suited for commercial use.) The Central Park Commission held a landscape design competition, and landscapers Frederick Law Olmsted and Calvert Vaux won. Their plan: to shape the natural scenery around a minimum amount of architecture. In 1873, Central Park was completed.

SHARE AND SHARE ALIKE

Unfortunately, the new park was still far away from where most poor people lived, and train fare was expensive. Work weeks were long—six days a week, usually—so they could get to the park only on Sundays. Two small but important things finally made the park more attractive to working-class people: regular Saturday afternoon concerts were moved to Sundays, and the first Central Park

To prepare for his role in *Taxi Driver*, Robert DeNiro...

playground was built in 1926. Soon the park was in constant use for strolling, picnics, sports, and other recreations—but with so many people using it, the park soon fell into disrepair.

THE GOOD MOSES YEARS

Robert Moses began his political life as an idealist. In 1920 his progressive ideas for getting rid of corruption in Albany brought him to the attention of Governor Al Smith and put him on the road to power in the state. Though Moses was never elected to office, he worked hard behind the scenes. And when President Franklin Delano Roosevelt's New Deal offered the city millions of dollars in the early 1930s, Moses was ready with plans to spend much of it on public works. Building parks, housing, highways, bridges, and tunnels in New York City and New York State became his life's work.

In 1934 he was appointed the New York City Parks Commissioner. By that time, Central Park was full of dead trees, untended lawns, broken benches, and litter. Moses changed all that: The park's purpose, in his view, was not to be a natural landscape (as Olmsted and Vaux had envisioned), but to be a playground for New Yorkers. He built ballfields; handball, croquet, and shuffleboard courts; a revamped zoo; bridle paths; and more playgrounds.

Moses also paid attention to park maintenance. His crews repaired bridges and walls, replanted lawns and flowers, and replaced trees. But he also implemented new rules for park behavior—for example, no bathing suits, no halter tops, and shorts had to come at least to mid-thigh. Moses liked things to be done his way, and the more power he had, the more autocratic he became.

THE BAD MOSES YEARS

One day in 1956, after Robert Moses had reigned over the park system for two decades, a group of mothers discovered that their children's playground on the west side of Central Park was about to be destroyed to build a parking lot for the ritzy Tavern on the Green restaurant. The mothers staged a protest that was soon dubbed the "Battle of Central Park." First, they wrote a petition against the bulldozing. When that had no effect, they held a rally in front of Tavern on the Green. That got Moses's attention—he promised a prompt reply, but instead sent bulldozers onto the playground a few days later. The mothers and their children stood in

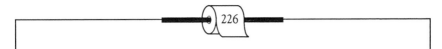

front of the bulldozers, and they halted the project. The same thing happened the next day and the next, but then Moses had his crew sneak into the park in the middle of the night, put up a fence around the play area, and start bulldozing trees.

The press was all over the story, and a judge ordered a cease-fire. Moses backed off. In one day, the mayor received 4,000 letters of protest against Moses. It ultimately took three months and a court battle but the playground was finally restored. The incident badly damaged Moses's reputation. And that was just the beginning.

In the late 1950s, Joseph Papp—the producer who later established the Public Theater—had been delighting audiences with free presentations of Shakespeare in the park. Funding the shows was always a problem, and Papp continued his efforts to raise the money from foundations—but he wanted Moses's Parks Commission to help fund the program. Moses, however, staunchly opposed the city subsidizing free theater in the park (or anywhere else). He also didn't like Papp and considered him to be something of a bully. Why? Those Shakespeare plays were performed near Belvedere Lake, and according to Moses, Papp "presumed the area was his."

In 1959, Moses demanded that Papp charge an admission fee to cover the cost of "grass erosion." Papp, who, by most reports, was as rigid as Moses, refused and took Moses to court. After a storm of negative publicity and a bitter legal battle, Moses agreed to withdraw his demand and to build Papp a proper amphitheater in the park. But Moses never recovered from the scandal. In May 1960, he resigned as commissioner.

FUN PARK IN FUN CITY

John Lindsay became mayor in 1966 and promptly dubbed New York "Fun City." To make Fun City even more fun, he appointed Thomas P. F. Hoving as parks commissioner. Although Hoving was commissioner for just a year, he managed in that short time to stage dozens of "Hoving Happenings"—band concerts, Halloween events, kite-flying, a "Central Park A-Go-Go" dance concert, and other spectacles that drew enormous crowds into Central Park. He even closed the park to traffic on Sundays—and when visitors loved that, he closed it to traffic on Saturdays, too. His successor, August Heckscher, kept the Central Park events coming.

The first Jews in NYC were 23 Sephardic refugees who arrived from Brazil in 1654.

But from the late 1960s through the early 1970s—while Commissioners Hoving and Heckscher were sponsoring happenings, performances, and parties—the crime rate in Central Park was on the rise. As more and more people used the park, more of them became victims of crime. In addition, upkeep had become a concern again. From 1969 until 1977, New York City suffered from the same recession that plagued the rest of the country. The city's financial woes got worse and worse, and if there wasn't enough money for police and schools, how could there be enough for parks? Central Park once again became a shambles: Gardens were neglected, meadows wore down to dusty ground, benches fell apart, statues deteriorated, and bridges were defaced by graffiti. By the end of the 1970s, concerned citizens felt it was time to step in.

PUBLICALLY PRIVATE AND PRIVATELY PUBLIC

In 1980, the Central Park Conservancy was formed, a unique partnership between the Parks Department and a group of civic leaders who saw that Central Park could not be restored to its original beauty and purpose without help from the private sector. Under a special agreement, the Parks Department retained control of park policy, while the Conservancy took responsibility for the park's day-to-day maintenance and operation—and for raising the money to do it. Today, 85 percent of the park's $27 million annual budget is controlled by the Conservancy, and 80 percent of the park staff is employed by it. The city pays for lighting, maintenance of park roads, 20 percent of the park staff, and the Central Park Police Precinct.

Since the Conservancy began, it has raised more than $390 million in private money that, added to the $110 million contributed by the city, has made it possible to restore the Great Lawn, Bethesda Terrace, and the Harlem Meer, and to create Strawberry Fields, named in honor of John Lennon. Conservancy crews tend 130 acres of woodland, 250 acres of lawn, and 150 acres of lakes and streams; maintain 9,000 benches, 26 ball fields, and 21 playgrounds; and preserve 36 bridges. They remove graffiti within 24 hours of finding it and dispose of 5 million pounds of trash each year. The park is now a beautiful and safe haven for New Yorkers and tourists. How safe? In the early 1980s, there were 1,000 crimes reported per year in Central Park; in 2005, there were fewer than 100.

Original home of the U.N., from 1946–51: Flushing Meadows Park, Queens.

TEN LITTLE RESTAURANTS, PART II

Our nostalgic look at some of New York City's most celebrated restaurants continues. (Part I is on page 76.)

7. CAFÉ DES ARTISTES, MANHATTAN

The Café des Artistes opened in 1917 on the lobby floor of the Hotel des Artistes (a building of artists' studios on West 67th Street) for the purpose of providing meals for the hotel's residents. The much-coveted studios had plenty of windows, but no kitchens, so the artists brought their own ingredients and the café's chefs prepared their meals. The café evolved into a beautiful restaurant with murals of nymphs (painted by resident artist Howard Chandler Christy in 1934), lush flower arrangements, and soft lighting. It became a destination for performers, musicians, and artists—a clientele that increased after Lincoln Center opened in the early 1960s. Famed restaurateur George Lang bought the Café des Artistes in 1975. Lang had managed the Four Seasons restaurant from 1967 to 1969, and then pioneered the field of international restaurant consulting, working with hotel corporations like Marriott and Sheraton. If anyone should have been able to keep the Café des Artistes going, it was Lang—and for many years it was a great success under his leadership. But by 2009, business was down, union-related costs were soaring, Lang was 85, and the curtain finally came down on one of New York's most romantic dining spots.

8. RATNER'S, MANHATTAN

In 1905, Jacob Harmatz and his brother-in-law Alex Ratner flipped a coin (so the story goes) to decide whose name would go on the kosher dairy restaurant they were about to open on Pitt Street, on the Lower East Side. Ratner won, but in 1918, he sold out to Harmatz, and the restaurant moved to a bigger space on Delancey Street. At its most popular in the mid-1950s, Ratner's served about 1,200 customers for brunch each day, dishing up cheese blintzes, potato pancakes, gefilte fish, borscht, and split-pea soup. Open 24 hours a day, it was a hangout for night people: Jewish performers like Al Jolson, Alan King, Groucho Marx, and Fanny Brice; gangsters like Meyer Lansky and Bugsy Siegel; and even politicians like John Lindsay, Robert Kennedy, and Nelson Rockefeller.

On Second Avenue there was *another* Ratner's, run by other family members, and during the late 1960s (when the area became known as the East Village), it was more popular than the original. The food concession at the Fillmore East, right next door, served Ratner's baked goods, and the restaurant was frequented by musicians like Janis Joplin, Jim Morrison, and the Grateful Dead. Ratner's of Second Avenue closed in 1974; Ratner's of Delancey Street closed in 2002.

9. LUNDY'S RESTAURANT, BROOKLYN
Sheepshead Bay, at the southern end of Brooklyn, was a longtime home to charter fishing boats and seafood restaurants, and Lundy's (or Lundy Brothers Restaurant) was the biggest and best. Owner Irving Lundy was born into a prosperous Sheepshead Bay family of seafood wholesalers. He started in the business as a young boy around 1900, selling clams from a pushcart, and in 1907 he opened a small clam bar. When government-funded waterfront development began in earnest in 1934, Lundy built a big new restaurant on Emmons Avenue, across from the bay. It was a success from the start, and by the 1950s, Lundy's was reported to be the largest restaurant in America, with seating for about 2,400 patrons and serving up to 15,000 diners on special holidays like Mother's Day. The customers came for the fresh fish, lobster, clam chowder, and hot biscuits. It was a sad day for Brooklyn when Lundy's closed after Irving's death in 1977. The building received landmark status in 1992, and hopes flared briefly when it reopened (at barely a third of capacity) in 1997—but it closed for good in 2007.

10. BENIHANA OF TOKYO, MANHATTAN
Long before there were two sushi restaurants per block in Manhattan, there was Benihana of Tokyo, a tiny four-table Japanese joint on West 56th Street. Benihana was the brainchild of 25-year-old Rocky Aoki, an enterprising Japanese Olympic wrestler who arrived in the United States in 1960 with the idea that New Yorkers might be ready for something new. Aoki had grown up in the restaurant business, and he wanted to offer food prepared *teppan-yaki* style:

beef, chicken, or shrimp grilled right at the table by trained chefs with swashbuckling showmanship. Diners would have the thrill of watching their food being sliced, diced, tossed in the air with a flash of knives, and dropped sizzling-hot onto their plates.

The restaurant opened in 1964, but almost no one came... until the *New York Herald Tribune* restaurant critic gave it a rave review. Suddenly, customers flocked to Rocky's place—the first of the national Benihana chain. Within a year, Aoki had opened a bigger restaurant down the block, and the New York passion for Japanese food was up and running.

* * *

MAD ABOUT *MAD MEN*

Few TV shows in recent history have made New York City look as sleek and sophisticated as *Mad Men* has. Here's some random trivia about Don Draper and the gang from the BRI's files.

• In 2008 *Mad Men* was nominated for (and won) an Emmy for Outstanding Drama Series, the first basic cable show ever to receive that distinction.

• In real life, Talia Balsam—who plays Mona, Roger Sterling's ex-wife—is married to John Slattery...who plays Roger Sterling.

• The actors on *Mad Men* smoke only nicotine-free cigarettes. In California, where the show is filmed, it's illegal to smoke real cigarettes indoors, including inside sound stages.

• Kiernan Shipka, who plays Sally Draper, isn't allowed to watch the show—she was just eight when it premiered in 2007. Her mother prescreens each episode and shows her only the scenes she's in.

• Although well-known for its realistic portrayal of the sexist 1960s, seven of the show's nine primary writers are women.

• In 2009, during the third season of *Mad Men*, President Barack Obama sent creator Matthew Weiner a letter saying how much he enjoyed the show.

NEW YORK INVENTORS

*If it weren't for the State of New York, the world
would be without many important products.*

GEORGE EASTMAN

A high-school dropout from Waterville, New York, George Eastman changed the way we see the world in 1885 when he invented rolled photography film. The creation did away with the delicate glass plates and messy gelatin emulsions used in photography at the time and made it easier for everyone to document the world around them. Eastman continued to take photography mainstream over the next decade with the invention of the hand-held, push-button camera.

LINUS YALE SR.

Linus Yale Sr. of Salisbury helped Americans feel more secure in 1848 when he invented the pin-tumbler lock, a cylindrical mechanism that employs rods of various lengths to prevent a lock from being opened without the appropriate key. The design was later modified in 1875 by his son, Linus Yale Jr., and remains popular today.

WILLIS HAVILAND CARRIER

Anyone who has ever used an air conditioner to cool off on a hot day has Willis Haviland Carrier to thank. This Angola engineer outsmarted Mother Nature in 1902 when he created the first air-conditioning unit to control the heat and humidity levels in a Brooklyn printing plant. Carrier continued to refine his invention, and by 1915 he was selling his "Apparatus for Treating Air" to grateful clients all around the world.

JONAS SALK

In 1948, New York City native Jonas Salk was the head of the Virus Research Lab at the University of Pittsburgh when he first began work on a way to eradicate the dreaded polio virus. Salk's experiments proved to be successful, and by 1952 he had created a safe and effective polio vaccine that he tested on his wife and three sons. Nationwide testing began two years later, and by 1955 America's "Polio Panic" had become a thing of the past. Salk's breakthrough made him a national hero and led to the creation of the Salk Institute, a leading independent scientific research center located in La Jolla, California.

GEORGE CRUM

The head chef at a resort in Saratoga Springs, George Crum unwittingly made history in 1853 when a notoriously hard-to-please patron sent back a plate of French fries, complaining they were too thick. Fed up with the patron's frequent complaints, Crum tossed several thin slices of potato into a pan, fried them to a crisp, and covered them with a generous helping of salt. To his surprise, the patron loved them, and Crum's "potato chips" soon became a staple on his menu. By the 20th century, potato chips had made their way into millions of American homes.

PIERRE LORILLARD IV

This wealthy tobacco magnate found himself on everyone's best-dressed list in October 1886, when he wore a tail-less black jacket and matching black tie to a formal ball at the Tuxedo Club in Tuxedo Park, New York. He may have heard about King Edward VIII of England wearing a similar outfit—some say as early as 1875. Regardless, after the Tuxedo Club's ball, news soon spread and it wasn't long before socialites were sporting "tuxedos" at formal functions all around the country.

JOSEPH C. GAYETTY

In 1857 New York City inventor Joseph C. Gayetty brought some much-needed relief to Americans when he created the world's first commercial toilet paper. Marketed as a means to cure sores and prevent hemorrhoids, Gayetty's Medicated Paper contained 500 individual sheets moistened with soothing aloe; each package sold for 50¢.

For more inventors, turn to page 301.

RUN, NEW YORK...RUN!

Think it's hard to get a hotel room in New York at Christmastime? Just try getting one during the Marathon.

MARATHON MAN

The New York City Marathon, run every November, is the largest in the world—in 2010, 45,344 runners participated in the race, cheered on by 2.5 million spectators lining the streets. Its 26.2-mile course takes the runners through all five boroughs: The race starts on the Staten Island side of the Verrazano Bridge and then snakes through Brooklyn, crosses the Pulaski Bridge into Queens, goes over the Queensboro Bridge into Manhattan, swings briefly through the Bronx, and then returns to Manhattan for the last five or so miles, ending in Central Park.

New York City owes its world-renowned feat of footwork to one man: Fred Lebow (born Fischel Lebowitz in Romania in 1932), who took up running in the late 1960s, hoping it would improve his tennis game. Running soon replaced tennis as his first love, though, and he agreed to become the (unpaid) president of the New York Road Runners, a running club that sponsors many races and events. Lebow organized the first New York City Marathon in 1970: a four-loop race in Central Park with only 127 starters, 55 finishers (Lebow finished 45th), and very few spectators. The entrance fee was $1, and the prizes were wristwatches that Lebow bought himself. But it was a beginning, and over time, the marathon became an annual—if modest—event.

OFF AND RUNNING

In 1976 Lebow convinced the city to allow a five-borough race, and he knew it had to be a major success if it was going to get enough support to continue. Lebow lined up a few sponsors (such as *New Times* magazine), a pair of American marathon stars (Bill Rodgers and Frank Shorter), and 2,000 runners. Crowds came out to cheer, the media covered the event, and Fred Lebow and the New York City Marathon were off and running. Each year, the race got more popular and received more press coverage.

In 1992 Fred Lebow, who had been battling brain cancer, ran

...A: Gene Simmons and Paul Stanley of the rock band Kiss.

his last race. He ran slowly—his finish time was 5 hours, 32 minutes, and 34 seconds—and was accompanied by nine-time marathon winner Grete Waitz. Lebow died two years later, on October 9, 1994. At his memorial service, Mayor Rudy Giuliani and the president of the New York Road Runners, which still sponsors the marathon, led 3,000 mourners in a march across the race's Central Park finish line.

WINNING THE LOTTERY

There are three main types of participants in the marathon, though everyone must be over 18: elite runners (proven world-class winners with top-level times from a variety of races); AWDs (athletes with disabilities like impaired vision or prosthetic limbs, or conditions requiring wheelchairs or handcycles); and everyone else. Each runner wears an identifying number and carries a computer chip in one shoe to record when he or she crosses the start and finish lines.

The famous runners—like world record-holding Ethiopian Haile Gebreselassie—are invited to participate; so are some special people like rescued Chilean miner Edison Peña in 2010. But for most people, getting into the race is tough. They're selected by lottery—more than 60,000 runners apply for spots, and about 45,000 get chosen.

But if you're not an invited runner and you don't want to depend on winning the lottery to secure a spot, there are some other ways you can be guaranteed an entry to the marathon:

• If you run a qualifying marathon a year before and your time is good enough to meet the official standards (published by January 1), even if you're not a world-class competitor.

• If you agree to raise money for one of the marathon's official charities.

• If you've gotten an entry before and had to cancel before the race.

• If you're a member of New York Road Runners, have completed at least nine qualifying races, *and* have volunteered for one event during the previous year.

• If you've completed 15 or more New York City Marathons.

• If you've been denied an entry for the last three years in a row.

What's included if you do get a spot, aside from the thrill of running with the pack? You get transportation to the starting line; a ticket to the "start festival" (breakfast, entertainment, and religious services); medical support; hydration; a goody bag; an official handbook; a medal, food, beverages, and a silver "heat sheet" at the finish to help you cool down; and an official finisher certificate.

MARATHON STATS

• Along the course, 24 official fluid stations dispense 62,370 gallons of water and 32,040 gallons of Gatorade in 2.3 million recyclable cups. (Eleven tons of trash are collected from the fluid stations after the race.) Portable toilets can be found every mile, starting at Mile 3. And "sweep" buses follow the runners to transport any dropouts to the finisher area in Manhattan.

• There hadn't been a marathon-related death since 1994, but in 2008, there were three: One runner had a heart attack at Mile 22 and died 11 days later; a runner with a preexisting heart condition had a fatal heart attack right after completing the race; and a third died of a heart attack several hours after the race.

• Slowest race time: In 2000, Zoe Koplowitz, who had multiple sclerosis and diabetes, finished in 35 hours, 27 minutes.

• Men's fastest time: 2:07:43, in 2001, by Ethiopian Tesfaye Jifar. Women's fastest time: 2:22:31, by Margaret Okayo of Kenya in 2003.

• Men's prize money: 2010 men's winner Gebre Gebremariam of Ethiopia (making his New York City Marathon debut) took home $170,000. Women's prize money: 2010 women's winner Edna Kiplagat of Kenya (also making a debut) took home $130,000.

*   *   *

"I think I bit off more than I could chew. I thought the marathon would be easier...That was without a doubt the hardest physical thing I have ever done."

—Lance Armstrong, after finishing the
New York City Marathon in 2006

Male and female sewer rats can mate as many as twenty times a day.

HEAR THEM ROAR

*A quiet town on the shores of Cayuga Lake may seem like
an unlikely place to start a civil rights movement, but
when it came to protecting women's rights, the
small village of Seneca Falls led the charge.*

MEETING OF THE MINDS

Early in the history of the United States, as in the rest of the Western world at the time, women had to take a backseat to men. They couldn't vote or own property. They weren't the legal guardians of their own children, they couldn't sign contracts, and they couldn't even cash their paychecks—their husbands had to do it. But by the middle of the 19th century, a group of women in upstate New York was challenging those social norms. Most of them were abolitionists and Quakers—a Christian sect that believed in equality of the sexes and adamantly opposed slavery. The leap from civil rights to women's rights wasn't difficult: If blacks should be free, the reasoning went, shouldn't women be afforded the same consideration? The 1848 Women's Rights Convention in Seneca Falls was the first organized event to answer that question with a resounding "yes."

The convention was led primarily by two women: One of them, Lucretia Mott, grew up in a Massachusetts Quaker family and worked as a teacher in a Quaker school, where she soon learned that female teachers were paid about 50 percent less than male ones. She later became a minister who, with the support of her husband, James, traveled all over New England giving speeches about the evils of slavery and the need for gender equality.

Elizabeth Cady Stanton was a rare non-Quaker in the 19th-century women's movement. Her father was a federal judge who introduced his daughter to the law. Early on Stanton noticed how differently the law treated men and women, and how few rights women had. She was also a rabid abolitionist who had seen slavery first-hand. New York State didn't outlaw the practice until 1827, when Stanton was 12 years old, and she and her siblings were partially raised by a black slave named Peter.

Mott and Stanton first met at an antislavery convention in

London in 1840. Even though Mott was a delegate at the convention (she'd become something of a celebrity among the abolitionist crowd), she and the other women in attendance weren't allowed to give speeches or participate in the convention's debates; they could listen only from a roped-off section out of the sight of the men. The affront infuriated both Mott and Stanton, and the two vowed to do something about it when they got back to New York.

TIPPING POINT

It took a while for the women to get their feminist movement going, though they continued to work with established civil rights organizations. The village of Seneca Falls, where Stanton lived, had become crucial to the antislavery movement: It was home to many Quakers, some of whom hid escaped slaves in their homes. And where there were abolitionists, there were often feminists. As time went on, two other important events motivated the growing Seneca Falls women's movement: One was the declaration by the Tennessee State Legislature that women didn't have souls and were, thus, unequal to men. The other was the publication of a book called *How to Rule Your Wife*. The activists in Seneca Falls were incensed.

Finally, in July1848, Mott and Stanton joined a group of women at the Waterloo, New York, home of Martha C. Wright (Mott's sister) to discuss a law recently passed by the New York State legislature. The Married Women's Property Rights Act gave women some rights to property, but it didn't go far enough, as far as Mott and Stanton were concerned. They, Wright, and the two other guests (Jane Hunt and Mary Anne McClintock) decided the time was right to take the next step. What they needed was a written document declaring their intentions and an official conference of their own. The conference would take place in Seneca Falls over two days—July 19 and 20. But who would write the declaration? The women decided on Stanton.

The document she drafted became known as the Declaration of Sentiments. It was extraordinarily harsh, so much so that when Stanton showed it to her husband, Henry, he vowed to leave Seneca Falls if she read it to the convention. (He made good on the threat, but eventually came home. Henry never agreed with her about women's rights.) Based on the U.S. Declaration of Independence, the document began, "We hold these truths to be self-evident: that all men and women are created equal." It went on to list the ways men suppressed women: forcing women to turn over any wages they earned to their husbands, reserving colleges for men, monopolizing the most profitable occupations for men, and denying women the right to vote, among others. The declaration closed with a broad denunciation of the male gender: "He has endeavored, in every way that he could, to destroy her confidence in her own powers, to lessen her self-respect, and to make her willing to lead a dependent and abject life."

A WHOLE NEW CONVENTION

The date was set, the declaration written. Hand-written flyers went out advertising the event and inviting people to attend the very first women's rights convention. Finally, on July 19, 300 people (including about 40 men, one of whom was the famed orator and former slave Frederick Douglass) filed into the Wesleyan Chapel—a red brick building often used by antislavery groups. Attendees participated in lessons on the law, heard speeches by Mott, listened to a reading of Stanton's Declaration of Sentiments, and discussed women's roles in society. At the end of the second day, the convention officially adopted the Declaration of Sentiments, and 100 of the people who attended—68 women and 32 men—signed the document.

In the days after the convention, the reaction in the press was extremely negative. Frederick Douglass later wrote, "A discussion of the rights of animals would be regarded with far more complacency by...the wise and the good of our land, than would be a discussion of the rights of woman." But Stanton claimed to be thrilled anyway, taking the tack that "all press is good press." "Imagine the publicity given to our ideas," she said, "by thus appearing in a widely circulated sheet like the [New York] Herald. It will start women thinking, and men too; and when men and women think about a new question, the first step in progress is taken."

"MY HEART IS WITH ALL WOMEN WHO VOTE"

As it turned out, the dreams of most who attended the convention would not come to fruition in their lifetime. Though slavery was abolished in 1865, it wasn't until 1920 that the U.S. Congress passed the 19th Amendment to the U.S. Constitution, giving women the right to vote. Only one of the conference's attendees lived long enough to see it happen: Charlotte Woodward Pierce had been 19 years old at the convention. Even though she never did manage to vote in an election (she was sick on election day in 1920, and died the next year), she always remained committed to the cause, saying, "My heart is with all women who vote."

As for the village of Seneca Falls, the National Women's Hall of Fame was established there in 1969, and today several of the buildings used for the planning and convention are National Historic Sites. It wasn't until 2004, though, that residents of the hamlet elected their first female mayor, Diana M. Smith. And she would be their last. In 2010, citizens voted to dissolve their tiny village and join the larger, similarly named city of Seneca Falls in 2012.

* * *

NYU BY THE NUMBERS

3.63: Average high school grade point average of the incoming 2011 undergraduate class.

10: Percentage of NYU students who come from one of New York City's five boroughs.

33: Ranking on the 2011 *U.S. News* "Best Colleges" list (out of 1,400 schools).

70 percent: Number of freshman applications that the school rejects each year.

$40,000: Annual tuition for a freshman who enrolls in 2011. (That doesn't include $13,500 for room and board, and about $700 per semester for books.)

40,000+: Undergraduate and graduate students.

$100,000: Amount of private money it took to start the school in 1831.

$2.43 billion: Amount it takes to run the school today.

THERE GOES THE NEIGHBORHOOD: QUEENS

If you've ever wondered why that neighborhood is called that, here's why.

• The Dutch settled **Queens** in the early 1600s, but it didn't get its modern name until after the British moved in. It was originally part of an area called Yorkshire, but in 1683, the borough (and its county) were renamed Queens for Queen Catherine, the wife of England's King Charles II.

• **Blissville** was named for Neziah Bliss, a shipbuilder and entrepreneur. In the 1830s and '40s, Bliss owned the land where the neighborhood now sits.

• **Flushing** began in 1645 as a Dutch settlement. The area was originally named Vlissingen after a port in the Netherlands, but the British thought the word sounded like "flushing," so when they took over, they renamed the town. In 1657, Quakers living in Flushing rebelled against Governor Peter Stuyvesant's decree that Dutch Reformism was the only religion colonists could practice. The Quakers drafted the "Flushing Remonstrance," arguing for religious freedom. Stuyvesant retaliated against the Quakers, arresting and fining those who refused to give up their religion. But some historians believe that the document was an inspiration for the creation of the First Amendment to the U.S. Constitution, written more than 100 years later.

• A "neck" is an elongated piece of land, so **Little Neck** is part of a small piece of land—which also includes Douglaston—that protrudes into Little Neck Bay of Long Island Sound.

• **Jamaica** comes from the English name for the Native American tribe that lived there: the Jameco. (Jamaica Avenue is an old Indian road and was, at one time, the only way to get from Queens to Brooklyn.)

Ellis Island's busiest day: April 17, 1907: 11,797 immigrants were admitted in 12 hours.

MORE NYC THEN AND NOW

Our comparison of New York City in 1964 and New York City now continues. (Part 1 on page 89.)

THEN: The passenger car toll across the George Washington Bridge into New York was 50¢ at all hours. (And you paid another 50¢ when you went back to New Jersey.)
NOW: At peak hours, with or without an E-ZPass, the eastbound toll into New York City is $8. No charge for the westbound return to Jersey.

THEN: One of New York's best bakeries was William Greenberg, Jr., Desserts, Inc. on Madison Avenue between 86th and 87th Streets. It was famous for luscious brownies, fresh coconut layer cake, crisp popovers, and especially their melt-in-your-mouth butter cookies at $2.80 a pound.
NOW: Greenberg's has moved to Madison between 82nd and 83rd, but it's still a favorite and still sells the same delicious butter cookies...for $27.00 a pound.

THEN: The Yorkville area in the east 80s of Manhattan was a flourishing German community. Schaller & Weber, a German grocery, specialized in 50 different kinds of sausage and a variety of smoked meats. *Lachsschinken* (thinly sliced smoked pork reminiscent of prosciutto) cost $2.60 per pound.
NOW: Not much is left of the old Yorkville, but Schaller & Weber is still going strong. You can still indulge in *lachsschinken*, for $18.99 per pound.

THEN: The Brooklyn Botanic Garden was open every day from 8 a.m. to sunset, free to all. The Brooklyn Museum, right next door, was open every day except Christmas, and admission was free there too.
NOW: The Botanic Garden is closed on Thanksgiving, Christmas, New Year's Day, Labor Day, and most Mondays—adult admission

---

"New York had all the iridescence of the beginning of the world." —F. Scott Fitzgerald

costs $8. The Brooklyn Museum is open Wednesdays through Sundays, closed on Thanksgiving, Christmas, and New Year's Day, and has a suggested admission price of $10 for adults.

THEN: The Staten Island Ferry ran day and night, every day of the year. The fare: 5¢ for a passenger, 60¢ for a car, 20¢ for a motorcycle (30¢ with sidecar), 10¢ for a bicycle, 15¢ for a tricycle, and 20¢ for a baby carriage.

NOW: The Staten Island Ferry still runs every day, all day and night, but cars are no longer allowed and everyone rides for free. (You can bring your bike or scooter along, as long as you walk it onto the boat.)

* * *

THE BOSS SPEAKS

When Yankees owner George "the Boss" Steinbrenner died in 2010 at the age of 80, he left behind a legacy that includes one of America's most successful baseball teams ever and many colorful quotes...like these.

• "I am tough. Sometimes I'm unreasonable. I have to catch myself every once in a while."

• "New Yorkers are strong people. They've got to fight in the morning to get a cab. They go to a lunch place at noon, they gotta fight to get a table or a stool off the counter. You have to give the city a team that's filled with battlers."

• "Second place is really the first loser."

• "I wouldn't sell the Yankees for anything. Owning the Yankees is like owning the *Mona Lisa*. You don't sell it."

• "I'm really 95 percent Mr. Rogers and only 5 percent Oscar the Grouch."

• "Winning is the most important thing in my life, after breathing. Breathing first, winning second."

The Statue of Liberty's torch stood on display in Madison Square Park for five...

RADIO CITY

Every great city needs a great public radio station, and WNYC is New York City's. Here's a timeline of the station's history.

1922–24: Regularly scheduled commercial radio broadcasting started in America around 1920. But New York City had no public-owned station even in the works until 1922, when Grover A. Whalen—Commissioner for Plants and Structures—convinced the city to approve $50,000 for a "Municipal Wireless Broadcasting Station." It took two more years for Whalen to wrangle a transmitter: He finally located one in Brazil and had it shipped to New York. Nonprofit, noncommercial, municipally funded WNYC-AM hit the airwaves on July 8, 1924, and New York became one of the first city governments in the country to be directly involved in radio broadcasting.

1926–29: WNYC, run by Commissioner Whalen, made radio history in 1926, when it aired radio's first quiz program, *The Current Events Bee*, and covered Admiral Richard E. Byrd's return from his legendary flight to the North Pole. In 1927, the station reported Charles Lindbergh's landing in New York after his solo flight to Paris, and two years later, it introduced *The Masterwork Hour*, the longest-lasting program of recorded classical music on radio.

1938–43: In 1938, Mayor La Guardia created a special city agency (the Municipal Broadcasting System) to run the station, and on December 7, 1941, WNYC was the first U.S. station to report the bombing of Pearl Harbor by the Japanese. WNYC was still just a tinny-sounding daytime-only AM station, though; it wasn't until it added FM in 1943 that it was able to broadcast higher quality sound around the clock. WNYC-FM was the only FM station in the country to create programs specifically for FM, like *Nights at the Ballet* from the orchestras of the Metropolitan Opera and New York City Center, and live opera broadcasts from City Center Opera Company.

1945: In one of the station's most iconic moments, during a newspaper strike, Mayor La Guardia started reading the newspaper cartoons "Dick Tracy" and "Little Orphan Annie" to the city's children. He read only three times, but the concept became a regularly featured program called *The Comic Parade*, with comedians doing the readings.

1970–79: Hard times came with the city's fiscal problems of the 1970s. Mayor John Lindsay cut WNYC's funding, and 55 staffers had to be laid off. The relationship between the city and its broadcast media was an uneasy one: The stations (WNYC-AM and FM, and WNYC-TV) depended on the city for money, and that made them vulnerable both to cutbacks and to political pressure. The stations' head, Mary Perot Nichols, was worried, and in 1979 she started raising money from private sources so that the stations could survive the city's cutbacks.

It was also becoming difficult to shield the stations from political pressure. In the same year that Nichols established the foundation, Mayor Ed Koch introduced the "John Hour"—he wanted WNYC to broadcast the names of men ("johns") who were arrested for soliciting prostitutes. Station management was furious, announcers threatened to walk out, and the idea was ditched after just one broadcast. But this was not the last time a mayor tried to influence the radio station.

1994–96: Newly elected Mayor Rudy Giuliani thought the city shouldn't be in the broadcasting business at all, and his transition team recommended selling the valuable WNYC radio and TV licenses to a private company. Giuliani offered two options to the station: sell all or part of the WNYC "assets" (AM, FM, and the TV station), or find a way to make the entire group self-sufficient. In the end, the mayor compromised: The city turned over the licenses for WNYC-AM and WNYC-FM to a nonprofit group called the WNYC Foundation—for a price of $20 million. The foundation had six years to raise the money and could stay rent-free in its studios in the Municipal Building on Centre Street. WNYC-TV was sold to a partnership of Dow Jones & Company and ITT Corporation for $207 million.

2001–02: The last payment from the WNYC Foundation to the city for the radio stations was due in January 2002, but just as management was planning the final fund drives, September 11, 2001, stopped everything in its tracks.

On 9/11, WNYC's FM and backup transmitters went down with the twin towers. The staffers had to evacuate their offices (which were close to Ground Zero) and couldn't return for three weeks. They camped out at NPR's offices in Midtown, and continued broadcasting via an AM signal and by a live Internet stream. In the wake of the disaster, the station was averaging more than a million listeners per week—the first time any public radio station had seen such high numbers. But as a result of the disaster, WNYC had to raise more than $4 million to replace the destroyed transmitters and get itself back on the air full-time—at the same moment that it was trying to raise the last payment to the city. An emergency on-air fundraiser in October pulled in the money for the new transmitters, but the January 2002 fund drive for the final payment to the city came up short. It took until spring 2002 to finish paying off the city and achieve complete autonomy.

But with independence came trouble: staff shake-ups and resignations, abrupt changes in programming, and constant pressure to raise enough money to keep the stations going. Many loyal listeners were confused—even outraged—by the changes, especially when the station eliminated five hours of daytime classical music in favor of news and cultural shows.

2006–08: But even bigger plans were in the works: In 2006 CEO Laura Walker announced that the station would leave its dilapidated old home in the Municipal Building and move to a brand-new space across town at 160 Varick Street.

The old Municipal Building studios were inconvenient and scattered over eight floors, the front-door security lines were frustrating for guests coming for interviews, and there were endless maintenance problems. The Varick Street space would give the station 2½ floors of new offices, twice as many recording studios and recording booths, and a lot more square footage. And there would be a 140-seat street-level studio for live broadcasts and other special events. It was expensive (about $61.3 million for rent, renovation, and new programming), but the 189 staffers were eager for the improvements. At 10 a.m. on June 17, 2008, roughly two years after the move was announced, Brian Lehrer, host of the popular *Brian Lehrer Show* for more than 20 years, flipped the "On Air" switch in the new building and the move was complete.

Number of streetlights in NYC: 330,000.

2009–10: In October 2009, WNYC acquired WQXR, a well-known classical music station. With WQXR in the fold, WNYC-FM dropped the remainder of its classical music programming and switched to round-the-clock news and information.

Today, New York's public radio station has podcasting, live streaming, and a handful of prestigious Peabody Awards for broadcast excellence. It's one of National Public Radio's most important customers—WNYC has more than 100,000 paying members, with many nonprofit foundations and other entities adding to its funding. It reaches more than 1.1 million listeners each week—the largest public radio audience in the country—and it's the most listened-to station (commercial or non) in Manhattan. Its stated mission is "to make the mind more curious, the heart more tolerant, and the spirit more joyful through excellent radio programming."

* * *

WHO ARE YOU CALLING A SLACKER?

In the early 17th century, when European explorers arrived in what is now New York, they encountered the Lenape tribe of Native Americans, who had a very different division of labor than the Europeans were used to. Among the Lenape, women did the farming and harvesting, while the men hunted and fished. This caused some confusion for the Europeans, who viewed hunting and fishing as leisurely activities to be enjoyed by the wealthy—"real" men were supposed to do backbreaking farm work. As a result, the Europeans considered the Lenape men to be lazy.

However, the Europeans overlooked the fact that the Lenape men were the ones to prepare the soil at the start of the farming season, a task that required a great deal of backbreaking work. And far from being leisurely activities, hunting and fishing for game were tough jobs that involved as many as a hundred men on foot chasing deer and other animals into the water, where they could be killed more easily.

THE NAKED COWBOY

*When it comes to tourist attractions, New York City has some of
the most spectacular: the Empire State Building, the Statue
of Liberty, the Brooklyn Bridge…and this guy.*

DUDE IN THE NUDE

Street performers in New York City are a dime a dozen.
No matter the corner, the time of day, or the weather,
buskers are always out—singing, doing flips and other gymnastics,
break-dancing, even miming to earn a buck. But since the early
2000s, visitors to Times Square have been entertained by a unique
performer whom the New York State Tourism Department has
called "more recognizable than the Statue of Liberty." Who is he?
The Naked Cowboy, of course.

It all began in southern California in 1997, when a recent college
graduate named Robert John Burck dressed up like a cowboy, took
his guitar to the boardwalk in Venice Beach, and started playing for
tips. He made only a dollar, but a friend suggested that he try
again—wearing just his underwear—and see if that made a difference. It did. Says Burck, "I made $100 and a TV crew came out and
filmed me."

"KING OF PLANET EARTH"

Pretty soon, Burck had taken his show on the road. He landed in
New York City and set up a "performance space" in the middle of
Times Square. His schtick was simple: Rain or shine, sleet or snow,
he wore only a cowboy hat, cowboy boots, and tighty-whiteys with
the words "Naked Cowboy" stenciled on the back in red, white,
and blue. He also carried a guitar, which he placed "strategically"
in photos to make it look like he was wearing nothing at all.
He posed for pictures, played music (including his original songs
"Naked Cowboy" and "Balls of Steel"), and became a popular stop
on New York City bus tours. Visitors lined up to see him, hot dog
vendors loved the business he brought in, and NYPD cops came by
to say hello.

By 2005 Burck was making up to $1,000 a day, and he had the
ego to match. When one reporter asked what kind of performer he

considered himself to be (singer, actor, busker, etc.), Burck replied simply, "I'm the king of planet Earth."

MORE THAN JUST A PRETTY FACE

Burck was a savvy businessman who trademarked his stage name and its female variant (the Naked Cowboy *and* Naked Cowgirl) and had a keen eye for branding. While building his business, he sent out thousands of postcards each month to friends and acquaintances to remind them of who he was and what he did. (The picture showed him in the middle of Times Square, surrounded by his adoring public.)

He also had his eye on bigger and better things. In 2009 Burck announced that he planned to challenge Michael Bloomberg in the mayoral race. He had to drop out because he hadn't filled out the proper paperwork, but politics remained in his sights. The next year, a freshly shaven Burck (fully dressed in a suit and tie) announced that he would be a 2012 Republican primary presidential candidate, running for the Tea Party. Why? According to Burck, "Politicians are selling out America and its most cherished institution, that being capitalism." Reporters didn't take Burck's announcement seriously, peppering him with questions like "Where's your underwear?" and "Aren't you just another dishonest politician since you're not *technically* naked while performing in Times Square?" But Burck waved them off, announcing that he had "no time for games." Soon after, he was back on the street in his tighty-whiteys, guitar in hand.

* * *

NEW YORK NUMBERS

• There are more than 18,000 restaurants in New York City.

• About 46 million tourists visit the city every year.

• The Federal Reserve Bank of New York at 33 Liberty Street in Manhattan holds 25 percent of the world's gold bullion.

Percentage of NYC residents it would take to occupy every inch of pavement in Midtown: 6.

SAVE THAT SITE!

*Sometimes it seems as if New York City is all about
knocking down the old and replacing it with the new.
Not so—at least, not while the Landmarks
Preservation Commission is on the job.*

WAKE-UP CALL
On October 28, 1963, to the horror of many New
Yorkers, the demolition of Pennsylvania Station began.
Built in 1910, the iconic railroad station was the largest indoor
space in the city—more than seven acres, taking up two whole
blocks—and a landmark that anchored the west side of Manhattan. Penn Station had its heyday during World War II, but by the
1950s, fewer people were traveling by train because of the influx of
cars and planes.

The Pennsylvania Railroad decided that Penn Station was
underused, and that the cost of operating it was too high. In
1955 a real-estate firm bought the station, with an agreement to
build a new underground railroad station on the site. But the
plans weren't made public until 1961, when shocked New Yorkers
learned that the old Penn Station would be demolished and
replaced with the 29-story Madison Square Garden complex and
a new station. Suddenly the public realized that without official
protection of certain buildings and areas, New York could easily
lose even more of its irreplaceable architectural, cultural, and historical heritage. It was too late to save Penn Station, but in 1965
Mayor Robert Wagner signed the Landmarks Law and appointed
the first Landmarks Preservation Commission (LPC) to protect
important districts, buildings, and other sites in all five boroughs.

ROUGH ROAD

The LPC's mission hasn't always gone smoothly: Choosing a site is
a long, complicated process that's often fraught with controversy.
Developers, for example, may want to knock down historically
significant buildings in order to build new ones. Or residents of
a neighborhood may want the city to get rid of something they
perceive as an eyesore but the LPC deems valuable. Nonetheless,
the serious work of the commission (the largest local preservation

New York was the first state to require automobile occupants to wear seat belts.

agency in the United States) has resulted in the rescue and recovery of hundreds of unique locations.

HOW TO BE A LANDMARK

Currently, the LPC is responsible for 24,000 properties that have been deemed landmark. Here's how a site becomes eligible: It must be at least 30 years old, and can be an office building, church, house, tavern, store, bridge, pier, cemetery, fence, clock, or even a tree. It also has to stand in one of the five boroughs and go through an eight-step designation procedure, which includes an evaluation request, a public hearing, a commission vote, and a lot of waiting. But finally, if the city council approves, the site can become a landmark.

Official landmarks fall into four categories:

• Individual (exterior): properties or objects, such as the Edgar Allan Poe Cottage in the Bronx or the old-fashioned lampposts on Patchin Place in Greenwich Village.

• Interior: inside spaces, accessible to the public, like the ground floor of the Empire State Building or the Woolworth Building.

• Scenic: a landscape feature or group of features on city-owned property, such as Prospect Park in Brooklyn or the colonial-era Remsen Cemetery in Queens.

• Historic district: a whole neighborhood or area that represents an architectural style or historical period, and has what the LPC calls a "sense of place," such as the Soho-Cast Iron Historic District (HD), the African Burial Ground HD, or the Brooklyn Heights HD.

CONGRATULATIONS—YOU'VE MADE IT!

Some interesting and unusual historic sites around the city:

• **Bowne House in Queens,** designated in 1966. The earliest parts of this house were built in 1661—the kitchen wing is the oldest surviving structure in Queens, and one of the oldest in New York City. In 1662 John Bowne allowed Quaker meetings in his home, defying Governor Stuyvesant's ban on Quaker worship. Bowne was arrested, tried, and acquitted, a crucial step in establishing the right of religious freedom in America.

The Big Apple nickname was born when sportswriter John Fitzgerald overheard...

- **William and Catherine Cass House in Staten Island,** designated in 1990. It's New York City's only residence designed by famous architect Frank Lloyd Wright.

- **Weeping Beech Tree in Queens,** designated in 1966. American landscape architect Samuel Parsons planted the Weeping Beech in 1847, and the tree—which sadly died in 1998—was one of only two tree designations (the other is the Magnolia Grandiflora in Bed-Stuy, Brooklyn).

- **Sidewalk Clock,** Fifth Avenue at West 44th Street in Manhattan, designated 1981. The American Trust Company installed the clock in 1907, and it's a piece of what the LPC calls "street furniture." Nineteen feet tall, it cost (at the time) about $600.

- **Voorlezer's House,** in Richmond Town, Staten Island, built around 1695 and designated 1968. It's the oldest surviving elementary school in America—in Dutch, a *voorlezer* was a teacher or assistant minister.

* * *

GOOD NEWS

Artist Melinda Hackett is one of New York's lucky few: She owns a townhouse in Greenwich Village that includes a small backyard, a little bit of nature in the otherwise crowded city, and in 2005 she built a round treehouse, complete with a circular staircase, in the yard for her three young daughters. The small playhouse seemed harmless enough, but a neighbor complained to the city that the structure was "nailed to a tree," looked "unsafe," and lacked a proper building permit. The city sent the police and firefighters, and when Hackett returned home one afternoon a few weeks after the structure went up, they were all waiting at her front door.

The next thing Hackett knew, she was defending her treehouse to judges at the Department of Buildings. It took five years, but finally, in 2010, the city approved the structure—the Landmarks Preservation Commission granted it a landmark permit because it (and the house whose yard it's in) are in a landmark district. And according to Hackett, the kids still "use it as a clubhouse. They plot. They scheme. They gossip."

...stable hands in New Orleans refer to an NYC racetrack as "The Big Apple."

NEW YORK'S #1! PART II

Our list of New York firsts continues.
(Part I appears on page 196.)

FIRST CHILD PROTECTIVE SERVICES. Animals had their own protective agency (the ASPCA, established in 1866) before children did. So in 1874, when missionary Etta Wheeler couldn't get help for an abused 10-year-old girl named Mary Ellen, who lived in a Manhattan tenement, she sought out the ASPCA's president, Henry Bergh. Bergh succeeded in removing Mary Ellen from her abusive home, and Wheeler's family later adopted the little girl. But the case underscored the need for a Society for the Prevention of Cruelty to Children (SPCC), which was founded the next year, with Bergh as its president. At first, the group targeted children of indigent immigrants, and it removed many kids from their homes primarily because their families were poor. But by the early 1900s, the SPCC aimed to preserve families when possible, and it formed the foundation for the modern child-welfare system.

FIRST SLIDING SEAT AND ROWING MACHINE. In 1870 New Yorker John Babcock invented every serious rower's dream: a wooden sliding seat covered with leather and lubricated with lard. It was the world's first rowing machine, and crew teams at Yale and Oxford quickly snatched it up for practice and competitions.

FIRST MARSHMALLOW FACTORY. People have been eating marshmallows as candy since ancient Egypt, but for most of their history, the treats were handmade and expensive. In 1895 confectioner Joseph Demerath improved the sweets by mass producing them *and* making them fun. He started the Rochester Marshmallow Works, which used a machine he invented to mold marshmallows into shapes such as fish, rabbits, cones, and bananas. The plant also mass-produced the sticky sweets, which allowed candymakers nationwide to add marshmallows to recipes, creating chocolate-dipped marshmallow squares with nuts, mallow walnut cups, S'mores, and others candies still available.

The Statue of Liberty weighs 450,000 pounds.

FIRST NIGHT COURT. In the 1870s, the Jefferson Market Courthouse opened a night court to deal with prostitutes caught after dark in Greenwich Village. The court's association with prostitutes became well-known, and "proper" women were mortified to be tried there. So sometimes, the police used the court's reputation to embarrass women they arrested. For example, the night court tried female workers striking for humane conditions at the Triangle Shirtwaist factory in 1909. Many of the women received jail time and harsh fines, and two years later, 125 workers died in a notorious fire at the same factory. (*More about that on page 324.*)

FIRST PRO-GAY RIGHTS MISS AMERICA CONTESTANT. In 2010, Claire Buffie won the Miss New York title with a platform that had never been tried in the entire 90-year history of Miss America pageants. (As part of the competition, each Miss America contestant must devote herself to a cause.) Called "Straight for Equality: Let's Talk," Buffie's campaign aimed to support members of the lesbian, gay, bisexual, and transgender community by fighting discrimination of LGBT students in schools and encouraging political reform. (She placed 12th in the 2011 Miss America Pageant.)

* * *

BLACKOUT STATS

On page 68, we told you the story of New York City's 1977 blackout. Here are some statistics about the event:

- Actual fires during the blackout: 1,037

- False alarms: 1,700

- Firefighters injured: between 45 and 55

- Cops on night duty on July 13: 2,500

- Cops on night duty on July 14: 12,000

- Sanitation Department staff mobilized on July 14: 3,800

- Number of 911 calls: 3,000 per hour (70,680 total)

- Amount given to NYC by the federal government to pay for damages: $11 million

"PUBLISHERS OF CHEAP AND POPULAR PICTURES"

Currier & Ives began as a small printing shop on Broadway, but eventually produced some of the most famous pictures in American history.

EARLY IMPRESSIONS

Eight-year-old Nathaniel Currier went to work to help his family in 1821, after his father died. His mother had four young children to support, so Nathaniel and his older brother did odd jobs in their hometown of Boston, Massachusetts, to make enough money to keep them all going. When he was 15, Nathaniel got an apprenticeship at a lithography shop near the family's home. Lithography, a type of printing in which an image is created with a grease pencil on a smooth stone or metal plate and then pressed onto paper, was a relatively inexpensive way to print.

At 20, Currier set out on his own, first moving to Philadelphia to work with a printer and engraver there, and then heading to New York City and a job at a print shop owned by John Pendleton, the lithographer he'd apprenticed with as a teenager. Pendleton's shop at 137 Broadway gave Currier the opportunity to hone his skills, and in 1834, when Pendleton decided to move back to Boston, he left the shop in the care of Currier.

DISASTERS ARE WORTH A FORTUNE

During the next decade, Currier moved his shop to Wall Street and continued making lithographs. He started experimenting with his own scenes, particularly images of contemporary disasters. In the days before TV news and photojournalism, images of the disasters people read about in newspapers—shipwrecks, fires, and explosions—were hot sellers because the papers didn't include any images at all. Various printers would produce single scenes and sell them individually, and the first lithograph print Currier created himself was of the collapsed Planter's Hotel in New Orleans. Customers to his print shop snatched them up. In 1840 he got a big break when one of his lithographs—of the sinking of a ship in New York Harbor—ran as a supplement in an issue of the *New York Sun*.

Both Nathanial Currier and James Merritt Ives...

Currier's shop had to work nonstop for several months to print enough copies.

In 1852 Currier met a young man named James Merritt Ives, a New York bookkeeper who was friends with his youngest brother. Ives became Currier's go-to guy: He kept the books, managed the shop's finances, helped with the creative process, and made the production process more efficient. Within five years, Currier had made him a full partner. The printing company was renamed Currier & Ives.

PICTURES FOR THE PEOPLE

Around that time, the company also changed from a job press (one that took on jobs from outside clients) to a full-time print publisher of its own line of prints. Currier & Ives moved its operation one more time—to Spruce Street—and focused solely on producing artistic lithographs. The company had dozens of in-house artists who created images and were paid anywhere from a penny per print for a 3 ½ x 5-inch image to eight or ten cents for a larger one. Each image was pressed by hand, and there were no limits on print runs. So no one knows for sure how many prints Currier & Ives produced, but estimates run as high as one million...of about 7,500 different scenes.

The prints were marketed to average customers ("colored engravings for the people," Currier & Ives called them), so that everyone had the opportunity to see the things they read about in newspapers and so they could have art to enjoy. Nathaniel Currier and James Ives even called themselves "Publishers of Cheap and Popular Pictures." The prints detailed everything from Civil War battles and presidential portraits to everyday life—fishing on the Harlem River, families at home, horse races, and landscapes, in color and in black and white. Small prints were affordable, selling for 20¢ each (or about $5 today). Large prints, though, could run as high as $5 (about $125 today), and these were often considered works of art.

Nathaniel Currier retired in 1880 and sold his shares to his son Edward. James Ives worked every day until he died in 1895; then his son Chauncey took over. Edward and Chauncey co-managed the company until 1902, when Edward Currier had to retire after contracting tuberculosis. Chauncey stayed on until 1907, when

---

...served as volunteer firemen in New York City.

Currier & Ives officially closed. But the prints it made became collector's items—today, creations made by those "Publishers of Cheap and Popular Pictures" sell for hundreds, sometimes thousands, of dollars.

FAMOUS FINDS

During the more than 70 years it was in business, Currier & Ives employed some of the 19th century's most famous artists. People like...

• Thomas Nast, who became a famous caricaturist and editorial cartoonist. Often called "the father of the American cartoon," Nast created the symbols of the Democratic and Republican parties (the donkey and elephant, respectively) and is usually given credit for drawing the first modern image of Santa Claus.

• Eastman Johnson, known for his portraits of both everyday people (including some of the most famous images of slaves in the American South) and prominent Americans. He was also a co-founder of the Metropolitan Museum of Art.

• George Inness, well known for his panoramic American landscapes.

• Frances (Fanny) Flora Palmer, who worked for Currier & Ives for 20 years and was known for creating panoramas of American landscapes. She's generally called the most famous female American lithographer of her day.

• Napoleon Sarony, who became a famous photographer, shooting pictures of everyone from Mark Twain to General William Tecumseh Sherman. One of Sarony's photographs of Sherman was used on an 1893 postage stamp.

* * *

THE OLDEST

• The first nursing home and hospital for retired seamen is on Staten Island—Sailors' Snug Harbor opened in 1883.

• New York's City Hall is the oldest city hall in the country still being used as a government center.

Most populous bird species in Central Park: the common grackle.

DUMB CROOKS

*Attention, all criminals! Need proof that crime
doesn't pay? Read these…and weep.*

BIG THANKS TO THE BIG SCREEN

In October 2010, Brooklyn resident Earle Barranco allegedly shot and killed a man in Chelsea after an argument but disappeared after the murder. There were no leads… until Barranco went to a basketball game in North Carolina and showed up on the arena's jumbotron. Someone at the game recognized him and later reported him to police. When he went to another game at the same arena, police picked him up and sent him back to New York. And how did that witness (and police) identify him? Barranco was wearing the same diamond-encrusted pendant he'd had on during the murder.

WATCH OUT ABOVE!

In August 2010, Sherin Brown was walking down a sidewalk in Brooklyn when a tractor-trailer jumped the curb and careened into a light pole, knocking it over. When paramedics arrived, they found Brown pinned beneath the pole and screaming in pain. They pulled her out and took her to the hospital, where she was treated and released. And then she started preparing a lawsuit. But what Brown didn't know was that a nearby surveillance camera caught the entire accident on tape…including Brown walking up to the light pole *after* the accident and pinning herself underneath it. Brown's lawsuit was thrown out, and police arrested her for falsely reporting an emergency.

GIMME ALL YOUR DOUGH

One evening in November 2010, Salvatore LaRosa and an accomplice followed two men out of the Brothers Pizzeria in Staten Island. The men carried a large bag that LaRosa believed held all the day's earnings, so he and his buddy pulled on ski masks, pointed guns at the men, and demanded they hand over the bag. They did, and the criminals ran off with their haul…which they soon realized held pizza dough, not money. In the end, LaRosa gave himself up.

First U.S. hockey franchise to win a Stanley Cup: the New York Rangers, 1928.

MADISON SQUARE GARDEN DID IT FIRST

"The World's Most Famous Arena" has hosted countless star-studded events since opening its doors in 1874. Come along as we celebrate some of the fabulous firsts that have happened at the Garden over the past 130+ years.

NORTH AMERICA'S FIRST ARTIFICIAL ICE RINK Madison Square Garden was transformed into a winter wonderland on February 12, 1879, with the installation of a 6,000-square-foot indoor ice rink, the first in North America. The opening coincided with a gala ice carnival that attracted thousands of revelers to the arena.

FIRST INDOOR FOOTBALL GAME

Football came in out of the cold on December 28, 1902, when Syracuse defeated "New York" (a team made up of several professional football players from around the state) in the inaugural game of the World Series of Pro Football. Organized by the Garden's operations manager, Tom O'Rourke, the innovative event was an attempt to attract patrons to the building during its slowest time of the year. Unfortunately, New Yorkers continued to stay away in droves, and the short-lived, six-day series was discontinued in 1904.

FIRST TELEVISED BASKETBALL GAME

Basketball made its small-screen debut on February 28, 1940, when the local NBC affiliate W2XBS broadcast a regular-season game between Fordham University and the University of Pittsburgh live from Madison Square Garden. Only one camera was used in the no-frills telecast as the Fordham Rams defeated Pitt's Panthers, 57–37.

THE JACKSON 5'S FIRST TELEVISION APPEARANCE

The pop group was still relatively unknown on August 22, 1969, when they made their television debut at the Miss Black America Pageant at Madison Square Garden. The event gave the group some much-needed exposure and paved the way for a series of sold-out Michael Jackson shows at the Garden over the next four decades.

FIRST SPECIAL BENEFIT CONCERT
The Garden made headlines around the world on August 1, 1971, when it played host to the Concert for Bangladesh, the first humanitarian benefit concert. Organized by former Beatle George Harrison and featuring artists like Eric Clapton, Bob Dylan, Billy Preston, and Ringo Starr, the one-day event raised money for Bangladeshi refugees victimized by the 1970 Bhola cyclone and the bloody fallout from the Bangladesh Liberation War. The initiative generated more than $243,000 in ticket sales and led to the creation of future benefit concerts such as Live Aid and Farm Aid.

FIRST WRESTLEMANIA
Big-time wrestling overtook the Garden on March 31, 1985, when the World Wrestling Federation presented its first WrestleMania. Billed as "The greatest wrestling event of all time," the show featured nine wrestling matches, including a heavily hyped tag-team bout with Hulk Hogan and Mr. T battling another team. (Hogan's side won.) WrestleMania has since become an annual tradition that attracts millions of viewers each year.

FIRST HDTV SCOREBOARD
In October 2000, the Garden changed the way fans watch live sporting events when it installed the world's first high-definition scoreboard system. Unveiled at the New York Rangers' regular-season opener, the system included four huge screens on the Garden's main hanging structure and 150 smaller screens scattered throughout the building. Other arenas around the world have since followed the Garden's lead in an attempt to give fans crisper images and higher resolution replays.

* * *

HOME SWEET HOME
It's a fact: In the 1998 movie *Godzilla*, the enormous, menacing lizard made a nest for its 200 eggs inside Madison Square Garden.

NEW YORK ON $0 A DAY

New York is one of the most expensive cities in the world.
But there are lots of things to do and see for free.

• You'll have to get them in advance—and sometimes get on a waiting list—but TV shows with studio audiences that tape in New York offer free tickets. Some of them include *The View, Saturday Night Live, Late Night With Jimmy Fallon,* and *The Daily Show.*

• Can't get tickets? Get up early, make a homemade sign, and stand outside the glass windows behind the hosts on *Today.*

• Central Park—all 843 acres (1.3 square miles) of it—is free and available to walk around, explore, take a nap, or throw a frisbee. The Central Park Conservancy also offers free walking tours, offering information on the park's history and plant life.

• Lots of New York City museums offer free admission on Friday evenings. The list includes the Museum of Modern Art, the Museum of the Moving Image, the New York Historical Society, the Whitney Museum of American Art, the Bronx Museum of the Arts, and the American Folk Art Museum.

• From June to August, there are nighttime outdoor classic movie screenings in Bryant Park. The grounds open at 5 p.m. (thousands bring blankets and picnics), and the show starts at sunset.

• The summer months also bring Shakespeare in the Park. Presented by the Public Theater (*more about that on page 297*), these are full productions of Shakespeare plays staged in Central Park by world-class actors.

• You don't *have* to buy anything at the city's fancy world-famous department stores, such as Saks Fifth Avenue, Bergdorf Goodman, or FAO Schwartz—you can gawk or live vicariously.

• Almost every weekday afternoon during the school year, students from the Juilliard School put on free classical concerts at Lincoln Center.

- The city operates a program called Big Apple Greeters, which matches up volunteer tour guides with visitors based on common interests. Visitors then get a guided tour of New York City tailor-made to what they're most interested in.

- Flushing Meadows Corona Park in Queens is bigger than Central Park. For free, you can see the Unisphere, take a walk around Meadow Lake, and walk by two of the country's most famous sports complexes: Citi Field (home of the Mets) and the U.S. National Tennis Center (home of the U.S. Open).

- The Strand bookstore at the corner of 12th and Broadway houses 18 miles of books. It's also a hot-spot for celebrity sightings: Patti Smith, Robert Pattinson, Orlando Bloom, and others have all been caught shopping there. But browsing and people-watching are free.

- The Downtown Boathouse offers free kayaking lessons and tours of New York Harbor on the weekends and weekday evenings between May and October. Classes meet at Pier 40, Pier 96, and 72nd Street and are all first come, first served.

- Admission to the New York Stock Exchange is free. (Investing is another story.)

* * *

DUNKIN' DOUGHNUTS

There's no way to know for sure who was the first person to dunk a doughnut into a cup of coffee, but we do know who made it popular. In the 1920s, silent film star Mae Murray—best-known for her full, pouty lips—accidentally dropped a piece of her doughnut into a cup of coffee while eating a New York deli. Her friends were aghast, waiting to see what she'd do, but Murray just fished out the doughnut, popped it into her mouth, and declared it "delicious." Word of Murray's unusual eating habit spread to Hollywood, and suddenly doughnut-dunking appeared in movies like *Duck Soup* (with Groucho Marx) and *It Happened One Night* (with Clark Gable and Claudette Colbert). Thanks, Mae!

I ARRRRGH NEW YORK

*In New York's early days, some people thought pirates were dastardly criminals,
while others considered them to be good business partners. It all depended
on who got a share of the treasure…and who had to walk the plank.*

THE PIRATE'S LIFE FOR ME

In the late 1600s, pirates were a common sight in New York's saloons, where they could spend their stolen doubloons and pieces of eight. They also did business with local merchants, who traded with or sold them ships and provisions. One colonial governor of New York, the Earl of Bellomont, said that the eastern area of Long Island was a "great receptacle for pirates…The people there have many of them been pirates themselves, and naturally are not averse to the trade."

Gradually, New York began to take a dimmer view of piracy, and by the 1700s, the Jolly Roger welcome mat was pulled. Still, pirates continued to plunder the bustling shores of New York.

THOMAS TEW

One of the reasons so many pirates flocked to New York was that they could pass as legal "privateers," sailors hired by the government (British, at the time) to attack and rob ships belonging to enemy governments. Privateers were perfectly respectable and often very wealthy. So impersonating a privateer was the perfect cover for a pirate. So goes the story of pirate Thomas Tew and Governor Benjamin Fletcher, who helped Tew perpetuate his charade.

Not much is known about Thomas Tew before he showed up in Bermuda in 1692 with enough money to buy a share in the eight-gun sloop *Amity* and sail as a privateer for the British. His commission was to take only enemy French ships, but out at sea, Tew convinced his crewmates that there was more money to be made in pure piracy. Sailing to the Red Sea, Tew captured an Indian ship filled with jewels, silks, gold, and silver. By 1694, when Tew arrived in Rhode Island to reunite with his wife and daughters, he was an extremely rich man.

Tew visited New York, enjoyed its high society, and met with

Governor Benjamin Fletcher. Though nearly every governor of the colony of New York made quiet deals with pirates, Fletcher was open about it, accepting "gifts" in return for protecting them from legal problems. Fletcher made no secret of his friendship with the pirate Tew, whom he described as "a pleasant fellow" and "a man of courage and activity." Fletcher even gave Tew a gold watch to encourage him to dock his ship in New York instead of Rhode Island. Fletcher also gave Tew an "official" privateering assignment...and paid him 300 pounds to do it.

Tew rounded up another crew and sailed back to the Red Sea, where he tried to take another ship. This didn't go so well, and Tew was shot and killed. But by then, the jig was up anyway: Before the English government learned of Tew's death, it put out a warrant for his arrest, calling him a "wicked and ill-disposed person." England also removed Governor Fletcher from his post.

CAPTAIN WILLIAM KIDD

New York's most famous pirate was Captain William Kidd, though for most of his career, Kidd actually was a privateer. He made a fine living taking French ships for the English government, and he had a sloop called *Antigua* and money in his pockets when he showed up in New York in 1690. In 1691 Kidd married the rich widow Sarah Oort and soon became one of New York's most prominent citizens. He owned land and homes, and even a pew in Wall Street's Trinity Church.

Then, in 1696, the King of England gave Kidd a commission to catch pirates (including Thomas Tew). Kidd sailed out of New York on the *Adventure Galley*, a 284-ton ship with 34 cannons. The voyage was difficult; pirates were elusive, and Kidd's crew grew mutinous. Finally, either because the crew forced him to, or because he wanted to return home with something to show for his time at sea, Kidd turned pirate himself. He plundered ships off the Indian coast, including one called the *Quedagh Merchant*, which gave him a fortune in gold and jewels.

When Kidd returned to New York around 1699, he found that times had changed. The Earl of Bellomont was now governor, and he arrested Kidd for piracy. In 1701 Kidd was tried and hanged in London; his corpse was covered with tar and hung out over the River Thames as a lesson to pirates. But his story still wasn't over.

Kidd had collected a treasure that included gold, diamonds, and rubies and had buried some of the loot on East Hampton's Gardiners Island, where authorities found it. But legends persist that more of his enormous wealth was buried elsewhere. Over the centuries, treasure hunters have scoured New York, digging holes everywhere from Montauk to the Hudson River Valley. They'll have to keep looking—so far, Kidd's treasure remains as elusive as the pirates he hunted.

CHARLES GIBBS

In the 1760s, an island off New York became known as Gibbet Island (now Ellis Island). Condemned pirates were hanged there for their crimes, and their dead bodies were placed in a metal device called a "gibbet" to hold the corpse erect. Hung from iron chains, gibbeted pirate corpses dangled in the view of passing ships. Government officials hoped that these corpses would be a deterrent to any sailor who might get buccaneering ideas.

In 1831 Charles Gibbs (aka James Jeffers) became the last pirate executed on Gibbet Island. Born in Rhode Island, Gibbs soon decided he wanted no part of his family's farm, and would go to sea. He joined the Navy during the War of 1812 and, after the war, sailed the Caribbean as a privateer on the schooner *Maria*. Eventually he led a mutiny and became the captain of the *Maria*, which he turned into a pirate ship and used to attack merchants in the Caribbean and along the Atlantic Coast. According to his later confessions to New York police, Gibbs made a fortune and killed almost 400 people during his career as a pirate.

Gibbs eventually lost the *Maria* when it ran aground, and according to some accounts, he hid out in England, where he might have stayed except that he spent all his money on liquor and gambling. When he returned to sea, Gibbs worked on merchant ships. In 1830 Gibbs and his pals signed on to the *Vineyard*, which left New Orleans carrying a load of Mexican silver coins. Leading another mutiny, Gibbs killed the ship's captain and stole the *Vineyard*—and the silver. New York authorities caught the pirates and took them to jail, but the silver was gone. Some say that it was lost in rough seas, but legends place the treasure on Barren's Island, under beaches in Canarsie on Coney Island, or off of Long Island Sound. It's never been found.

Q: What do Herman Melville's *Moby Dick* and the Ramones album...

SADIE THE GOAT

Most piracy took place on the high seas, but New Yorkers faced pirates on rivers too. In 1850 more than 400 pirates terrorized the East River. Unlike their oceangoing counterparts, river pirate gangs lived on land and did their robbing from small rowboats. The pay for a river pirate wasn't usually great—instead of making hauls of doubloons, they often attacked ships to steal coils of rope worth a few dollars. But even if they weren't as glamorous as ocean pirates, river pirates were just as feared as seafaring ones. They often murdered sailors who got in their way and kidnapped passengers for ransom. And sometimes they made great hauls.

One of the most unusual river swashbucklers was Sadie "the Goat" Farrell. Like most river pirates, Farrell was trying to escape poverty-stricken life. She lived in the slums of the 4th Ward, along the riverfront in lower Manhattan, where she first became a mugger. Farrell earned the nickname "Goat" because she butted her mugging victims with her head, knocking them out so her gang could rob them. (She was also famous for having only one ear. The other was bitten off by Gallus Mag, a six-foot-tall female bouncer who ran a Water Street bar called Hole-in-the-Wall. The ear went into a pickling jar behind Mag's bar.)

In the late 1860s, Farrell decided to try her hand at piracy. Successful river pirates could make decent money, and Farrell was tough. Unlike most river pirates who lived on land, Farrell and her crew (the Charlton Street Gang) hijacked a sloop to live on. Hoisting the Jolly Roger, she sailed away from the East River waterfront and traveled up the Hudson River toward Albany, and extended her pirating territory.

For a few months in early 1869, Farrell's ship terrorized the Hudson River Valley, robbing large estates and small farms. She and her gang kidnapped wealthy victims and were not afraid to kill, and newspapers of the day told horror stories of Farrell forcing victims to walk the plank. Finally, a group of citizen vigilantes banded together to fight her, and Farrell and the Charlton Street Gang were forced back into the streets of the 4th Ward. It wasn't a great loss, however. Farrell made up with Mag and got her ear back from Mag's jar—according to legend, Farrell put it into a locket and wore it around her neck.

HEY, TAXI!

Some facts and trivia about those ubiquitous New York cabs.

• The first metered taxis showed up on New York City streets in 1907, the brainchild of Harry N. Allen, a New Yorker who was angry that a hansom cab driver charged a friend $5 (about $113 today) for a .75-mile trip.

• Allen's first taxis were red and French-made; he introduced 65 of them to Manhattan on October 1. A year later, he had a fleet of 700.

• The first taxi strike took place in October 1908, when 500 drivers at Allen's New York Taxicab Company walked out because they wanted to be considered full-time employees and they wanted Allen to supply free gas. (Rising gas prices were making them lose money, they said.) But Allen wanted to keep in place the system he'd set up: Cabbies rented their uniforms, cabs, etc. from him and used the money from their fares to pay for it all. After a violent month of protests, the strikers gave in. A similar system still exists today.

• Businessman John Hertz founded the Yellow Cab Company in 1915. He was the first to paint taxis yellow. Why? He thought it was the easiest color for the eye to see. (Hertz went on to also found Hertz Rent-a-Car.) In 1967, New York City mandated that all of its taxis had to be yellow.

• New York City's most famous taxi model was the Checker cab, which first appeared in 1922 and had its heyday in the 1930s and '40s. Checker cabs became iconic to the city, but most of them were actually manufactured in Michigan.

• The first woman to drive a New York City taxi appeared in 1925, and in the 1960s, about 10 percent of all cab drivers were women. By 2008, that number had dropped to 1 percent.

• There are more than 12,000 licensed cabs in New York City... 50,000 if you also include limousines and other types of hired cars.

Football coach Knute Rockne's "win one for the Gipper speech" took place at Yankee Stadium.

FROM HAARLEM
TO HARLEM

Harlem is as much a state of mind as a geographically defined part of Manhattan. Here's the story of Harlem from its beginning, with an update on its new face.

HARLEM ON MY MIND

In 1969, the Metropolitan Museum of Art mounted an exhibit called "Harlem on My Mind." It explored the history and life of a part of the city that had frightened white New Yorkers for decades. At the time, it was the most controversial exhibit ever presented in an American art museum. But curator Allon Schoener—who had overseen a groundbreaking exhibit about Jewish immigration three years earlier at the Jewish Museum—felt that if New Yorkers had been fascinated by the story of poor Jewish immigrants, the story of the city's most famous black neighborhood would be no less interesting.

Still, the exhibit caused a firestorm of protest, disagreement, press hysteria, and charges from all sides. Prominent black leaders complained that the exhibit featured photographs of blacks but did not include art by Harlem artists, and they didn't like that organizers hadn't consulted Harlem residents in their planning. Black and white demonstrators disrupted the press preview and the opening. Perhaps the most shocking aspect of the controversy, though, was one of the simplest: whether an exhibition about Harlem belonged in the Metropolitan Museum of Art. According to Schoener, it did. He said, "it brought African-American history and culture to one of the world's preeminent art museums and placed it on a par with the established icons of the Western tradition." Harlem was, after all, a deeply important part of New York and America.

HARLEM HISTORY

In the 1630s, in the far northern part of the Dutch colony of New Amsterdam, settlers founded a small rural village. In 1658, Governor Peter Stuyvesant formally established it as *Nieuw Haarlem*

First NYC district to be designated a national historic landmark: Brooklyn Heights (1966).

(New Harlem), named after the city of Haarlem in Holland. In 1664, the English conquered New Amsterdam and renamed it New York, and Nieuw Haarlem became just Harlem. Dutch and English settlers lived together peacefully there, and over the next century, Harlem became an area of country estates and grand houses built by gentleman farmers and wealthy merchants.

The population of Harlem stayed small, mainly because the area wasn't easily accessible. Transportation finally changed that: in the 1870s and 1880s, the elevated railroads on Second, Third, and Eighth Avenues reached into Harlem, and real-estate development began with a vengeance. Builders put up low-rent tenement housing, and Jewish, Irish, Italian, and German immigrants flocked from the Lower East Side to the new apartments, especially in East Harlem—even though the new housing wasn't a whole lot better than the tenements downtown. At least it was far away from the worst of the slums.

BOOM AND BUST

The west side of Harlem had a different fate. There were already single-family brownstones with upper- and middle-class white tenants there. Anticipating that the subway would open a Lenox Avenue Line along Harlem's west side in 1902, real-estate speculators rushed to build more luxury apartment buildings and townhouses to accommodate what they assumed would be an instant influx of rich new (white) renters. Unfortunately, the builders were hit with two pieces of bad luck: First, the subway didn't open until 1904, so they were stuck paying mortgages and taxes on half-empty buildings. And second, they overestimated the market and built way too much. Residential demand wasn't as large as expected—and suddenly there was a housing glut and a drop in real-estate prices.

Meanwhile, black communities in midtown Manhattan were being displaced by the Pennsylvania Railroad and by new department stores that razed black-occupied tenement buildings. Since so many landlords (citywide) refused to rent to black citizens, where could they go?

THE REAL-ESTATE MAN

The answer came from a black real-estate developer named Philip A. Payton. Born in Massachusetts in 1876—his father was a barber, and his mother a hairdresser—Payton became a barber too, but couldn't settle to it and decided to move to New York. In 1900, he got a job as a janitor in a real-estate office, which paid more than barbering and opened his eyes to a new career. Payton started his own firm and eventually began to get contracts to manage apartment houses. Saving his money, he invested it by buying the small apartment house he lived in, then bought two more houses, sold them for a profit, bought another house—and he was on his way.

But his real inspiration came after he and several other black businessmen formed the Afro-American Realty Company. When the Harlem real-estate boom went bust in 1904, Payton convinced financially strapped white owners of under-rented buildings to rent out their empty apartments to black tenants at higher rates. Then he brought in the black tenants (who couldn't actually afford the high rents) and convinced them to sublet some of their rooms to other black tenants in order to make the rent payments. The white landlords, who normally wouldn't have rented to blacks, reluctantly allowed Payton's plan to proceed—and their buildings filled up. Suddenly Harlem was a housing mecca for black people. By 1911 blacks were renting tenements, row houses, and luxurious apartments, according to their means. In less than a decade, Philip Payton changed the face of Harlem. Some white landlords in the traditionally white neighborhoods of West Harlem tried to stop the incursion of blacks, but it was too late. Not only were blacks renting, they were buying: It was the beginning of an era of black-owned real estate, and by 1925, when some states didn't even allow blacks to own real estate, African Americans owned $60 million worth of Harlem's property.

THE GREAT MIGRATION

According to the 1910 census, Harlem had a population of 500,000: 50,000 of them blacks. Ten years later, the black population had doubled, and two thirds of New York's African Americans lived in Harlem. This was partly due to the Great Migration of 1910–30, when blacks from the American South moved north to escape the racist climate there and to find work in big cities. Thousands of black Americans headed for Harlem, crowding into the now-deteriorating inner-city housing and turning more and more buildings into tenements. As more people moved in, signs of ghetto life began to show: high infant mortality, epidemics of tuberculosis and other diseases, street crime, scarcity of jobs, and inadequate political leadership. In the 1920s, the population density of Harlem was more than 215,000 per square mile, compared to about 104,000 per square mile in Manhattan as a whole.

Most Harlemites were working class and many were poor, but at the same time, Harlem was also home to many middle class and rich African Americans: doctors, lawyers, ministers, and businessmen who lived in fancy apartment houses on Sugar Hill or in the beautiful townhouses of Strivers' Row. There were 60 churches, two renowned newspapers (the *New York Age* and the *Amsterdam News*), a YMCA and a YWCA, Harlem Hospital, a branch of the NAACP, a branch of the New York Public Library, and many black-owned small businesses such as barber and beauty shops, funeral homes, banks, and insurance companies. Harlem was a city within a city.

THE RENAISSANCE

Through the 1920s and into the mid-1930s, Harlem experienced what author and civil rights activist James Weldon Johnson called a "flowering of Negro literature." The era came to be known as the Harlem Renaissance for the astonishing proliferation of theater, poetry, fiction, art, dance, and jazz music that took place during those years. This flowering of black culture was a source of great pride for Harlem residents.

Harlem had become a refuge for African Americans, yet racism remained a powerful institution even there. In central Harlem, there were more than 125 theaters, supper clubs, lounges, and other entertainment spots that were run and patronized by black people, but some of the most famous nightclubs and dancehalls were not. The Cotton Club, for instance, was owned by white gangster Owney Madden, and although it featured some of the greatest black talents in history (Duke Ellington, Lena Horne, Cab Calloway), its patrons were almost exclusively white. The dancers in the chorus line were black—but according to the club's policy, they had to be light-skinned.

On the other hand, the Savoy Ballroom—the birthplace of dozens of dance fads from the Lindy Hop to the Jitterbug Jive—was the opposite: It was owned by Moe Gale, a white man, and managed by Charles Buchanan, a black man. Called the "World's Finest Ballroom," the Savoy was one of the first racially integrated public places in the country. Live bands played all night, and black and white patrons danced together under colorful spotlights.

HARLEM TODAY

The atmosphere in Harlem from the 1940s to the 1990s is all too familiar to most Americans: unemployment, poverty, decaying housing and schools, and violent crime. Even the 1989 election of David Dinkins, New York City's first black mayor, didn't have much impact on those problems. But in 1994, Harlem was designated as the Upper Manhattan Empowerment Zone, one of nine areas created by the Clinton Administration to revive failing communities by using city, state, and federal funding and tax incentives to encourage private investment. More than $250 million poured into Harlem for new construction, rehabbing of older buildings, loans to small businesses, and grants to nonprofit organizations.

By the late 1990s and 2000s, Harlem was seeing a second real estate boom, with people (black and white) moving into the area in large numbers again. Restaurants, movie theaters, and stores began to flourish—125th Street has two Starbucks, a Staples, and an Old Navy. Jazz clubs reopened, and the Apollo Theater currently draws more than a million visitors each year.

But Harlem hasn't completely overcome its history yet. Some of the major avenues still don't have enough retail stores to make their surrounding neighborhoods attractive to renters or buyers. Many of the public schools lag far behind schools in other parts of the city, a deficit that hasn't been corrected by the neighborhood's few charter schools; in fact, only one in five Harlem kids is enrolled in a charter school. Asthma, obesity, and other health problems haven't gone away, and pockets of deep poverty persist.

And not everyone is happy about the new gentrification. In 2008 the average price of a new Harlem condo was $900,000, even though the average household income was less than $25,000. The *New York Times* wrote, "No one…is wishing for a return of row upon row of boarded-up buildings…but residents say they do miss having a neighborhood with familiar faces to greet, familiar foods to eat, and no fear of being forced out of their homes."

CITY HODGEPODGE

Quick! Some facts about the city of New York.

• New York County (Manhattan) is the most densely populated county in the United States. Kings County (Brooklyn) is #2.

• Some of Rikers Island's inmate dormitories are located inside former Staten Island Ferry boats docked at the prison.

• Manhattan lies along the same latitude as the temperate Mediterranean region of Europe, so when the early Dutch settlers arrived in New York, they were shocked that the winters were so cold and snowy.

• Average hotel room rate in New York City: about $200 a night.

• Central Park is larger than the kingdom of Monaco.

• There is no Main Street in Manhattan, but each of the other boroughs has one.

• Trees required to print the Sunday *New York Times*: 75,000.

• Only school in the world to offer a college degree in Cosmetics and Fragrance Marketing: the Fashion Institute of Technology in Manhattan.

• About 47 percent of New York City residents older than five speak a language other than English at home.

• Alexander Hamilton founded the *New York Post* in Manhattan in 1801. It's the longest continuously running daily paper in the United States.

• More than 3 million people have been buried in Calvary Cemetery in Queens, making it the "most populous" cemetery in the United States.

• About 40,000 location shoots for movies, TV shows, and commercials take place in New York City every year.

• The Brooklyn Children's Museum, which opened in 1899, was the first museum in the world created specifically for kids.

DOINK, DOINK!

The Law & Order *franchise has been investigating crime and prosecuting offenders in New York City for more than two decades.*

• The original *Law & Order* ran for 20 seasons on NBC (from September 1990 to May 2010) and holds the distinction of being TV's longest-running crime show. (It's tied with *Gunsmoke* for longest-running drama.)

• The show was originally supposed to be set in Los Angeles, but creator Dick Wolf thought his hometown of New York City offered more dramatic possibilities so he convinced the network to let him set the show there instead.

• The franchise now has three major shows: *Law & Order* (the original series), *Law & Order: Special Victims Unit* (or *SVU*), and *Law & Order: Criminal Intent*. Most recently, in 2010, NBC began airing *Law & Order: Los Angeles*.

• *Law & Order* is filmed almost exclusively in New York City, though parts of northern New Jersey occasionally stand in for New York locations. For instance, exterior shots of the Queens home of *SVU*'s Detective Elliot Stabler (Christopher Meloni) are actually filmed in Fort Lee, New Jersey.

• Chris Noth (*Sex and the City*'s Mr. Big) played Detective Mike Logan in the first five seasons of the original *Law & Order*. At the end of season 5, Wolf decided not to renew Noth's contract because he didn't think there was enough dramatic tension between Logan and the other lead cop, Lennie Briscoe (Jerry Orbach). Fans were shocked because Logan was a popular character, but there weren't any hard feelings for Noth: He went on to star for three years on *Criminal Intent*.

• Actor Dann Florek (Captain Donald Cragen) was let go in the third season of the original series—Wolf wanted to add female characters and needed to reduce the number of cast members. Again, no hard feelings: Florek (as Cragen) was the first one cast on *SVU* in 1999 and is still on that show.

Full name of toy magnate FAO Schwarz: Frederick August Otto.

• The narrator of the famous intro ("In the criminal justice system...") is voice-over actor Steven Zirnkilton. He does the intros for all three shows and is the only credited cast member to appear in every episode of the franchise. (His narration didn't appear in the original series pilot, but he had an on-camera cameo.)

• The first regular on any *Law & Order* series to receive an Emmy: *SVU*'s Mariska Hargitay (Detective Olivia Benson), who won for Outstanding Lead Actress in a Drama in 2006.

• From 1999 to 2001, the opening credits for *SVU* contained shots of the World Trade Center. After 9/11, producers removed the images.

• Two actors—Richard Brooks and Carey Lowell—began their *Law & Order* careers playing prosecutors. Both left the show and then returned to play the same characters...who had become defense attorneys.

• Richard Belzer has played the character of Detective John Munch on *SVU* since the show began and on the original *Law & Order* before that. But the character debuted on another show entirely: the 1993–99 series *Homicide: Life on the Street*. The shows were all on NBC, and they did crossovers several times.

• Jill Hennessey played District Attorney Claire Kincaid on the original series from 1993–96. In 1997, she also appeared on *Homicide: Life on the Street*, which presented a logistical problem...she couldn't film both shows at once. Fortunately, Hennessey has a twin sister, also an actress, who appeared as Kincaid in at least one *Law & Order* episode.

• Actor Fred Thompson, who played District Attorney Arthur Branch on the original series, spent eight years as a real-life senator from Tennessee. In 2008 he ran for president, but lost the Republican nomination to John McCain.

• The fate of villain Nicole Wallace (Olivia d'Abo) on *Criminal Intent* was supposed to be decided by a fan poll: In 2004 viewers voted online and by phone for her to keep escaping, but in a 2008 episode, she was killed by another character—the murder wasn't shown onscreen, though, so fans remain skeptical.

New York State's highest waterfall: Taughannock Falls (215 feet) in Ulysses.

LOST LANDMARKS

New York is famous for its big showy landmarks like the Brooklyn Bridge and the Empire State Building. Here are a few that aren't so easy to find—because they've nearly disappeared.

ST. AUGUSTINIAN ACADEMY, STATEN ISLAND

Elegant and vine-covered on the outside but graffiti-covered and neglected on the inside, St. Augustinian Academy once stood dignified on Campus Road in Grymes Hill. Built in the 1920s, St. Augustinian was originally a private Catholic high school for boys, but it closed about 40 years later, due to lack of enrollment. The following year, the building was used as a retreat, but that didn't last long, either—the grounds were soon abandoned and fell into disrepair. Despite the "no trespassing" signs, amateur explorers have been traipsing around the site for decades. Reportedly, there are three floors above ground in the main building and 10 stories below ground. The crumbling old bell tower still stands, and rumors of ghosts, eerie hallways, and creepy rooms abound.

Today, nearby Wagner College owns the property—they bought it from developers. But in 2009, the old site got a little respect: The Staten Island City Council renamed the stretch of Campus Road that passes by the site "St. Augustinian Academy Way."

THE KINGDOM OF ZOG, LONG ISLAND

Knollwood Estate, a mansion built in the early 20th century by steel magnate Charles Hudson, had the look of a palace. Built between 1906 and 1920, it sported columns, stone balconies, 60 rooms, spiral staircases, and stone walkways. It was surrounded by a working farm, several gardens, and many outbuildings. But Hudson didn't live in his palace for long—he died in 1921.

Thirty years later, Zog I—the self-proclaimed King of Albania who was then living in exile in Egypt—bought Knollwood. The mansion and 150 acres of grounds fetched a price of $102,000, and rumor had it that Zog paid the bill with a bucket of diamonds. Like most new homeowners, Zog could see possibilities—he dreamed of setting up a new kingdom, even bringing over some of his Albanian countrymen to populate it.

First American–born and trained director of the N.Y. Philharmonic: Leonard Bernstein.

But Zog overextended his credit and never lived in the mansion. Knollwood stood vacant for many years and was ransacked by looters, who'd heard rumors that Zog's fortune was hidden somewhere in its walls. (They never found it.) Finally, in 1959, the building was mostly demolished. Now part of the Muttontown Preserve, its crumbling stone walls are covered with moss, vines, and trees.

NEXT STOP: NOWHERE

With almost 700 miles of subway track beneath New York City, it's not surprising that there are a few forgotten places:

• The 91st Street Station, part of the original New York subway system, opened in October 1904 and closed in February 1959 because the platform wasn't long enough to accommodate modern trains. Today, if you take the number 1, 2, or 3 trains, you can briefly see the old station as the train whizzes from 86th to 96th Street in Manhattan.

• If you take the number 6 train to the Brooklyn Bridge and stay onboard as it turns around, you should be able to see the old City Hall station. With colorfully tiled walls and ceilings, sweeping mezzanines, arches, and a grand entranceway, this forgotten bit of New York was closed in 1945 because its short platforms (which had huge gaps between the platform and trains) were considered safety hazards.

• Hidden in Grand Central Terminal is the unlisted Track 61, which has a secret entrance—a freight elevator went directly into the Waldorf-Astoria Hotel on the street above. Legend says that President Franklin Delano Roosevelt used it to leave New York without being hassled by reporters and gawkers. If you take a Metro Train North from Grand Central, look out the right side of the train as you're leaving the station and you might catch a glimpse of the old Track 61.

*   *   *

"Traffic signals in New York are just rough guidelines."

—**David Letterman**

Average time it takes to swim around the island of Manhattan: 7 hours, 15 minutes.

THE BIGGEST FAIR ON EARTH

Putting on a fair is a great community builder for counties and small towns. But putting on a World's Fair is a little riskier.

WHAT EVER HAPPENED TO THE FAIRS? We don't hear much about World's Fairs anymore—probably because the United States is no longer a member of the Bureau of International Expositions, the group that oversees the fairs' production. But the rest of the world still participates in them—Expo 2010 was held in Shanghai, China, and attracted more than 70 million visitors. During the 19th and early 20th centuries, World's Fairs were internationally celebrated events that exhibited new ideas and technology; today, they're a way for participating countries to showcase their culture and achievements on the international stage. Over the years, New York City hosted three World's Fairs, all ambitious events...that turned out to be financial busts.

1853 WORLD'S FAIR

Theme: The Exhibition of the Industry of All Nations

Where: Midtown Manhattan

The Plan: Following the first World's Fair in London in 1851, a group of New York civic leaders drew up plans to host their own World's Fair in 1853. Publicly, the fair's purpose was to display the fruits of the industrial revolution, but organizers were also driven by the tourism dollars and prestige that the fair could bring.

What You Could See: The fair itself was housed in the Crystal Palace, a lavish iron-and-glass building shaped like a Greek cross. The New York fair's commission wanted a replica of the London fair's Crystal Palace, but they eventually settled on a unique design. New York's structure was topped with a dome 100 feet in diameter, and reached 123 feet high. The building housed more than 4,800 exhibits from 23 countries.

The NYFD officially began in 1865, when the city replaced volunteers with paid firefighters.

- A mineralogical section showcased thousands of ore samples from across the globe, including gold from California, where the gold rush was in full swing.

- The next year, after the fair closed, Elisha Otis demonstrated his safety elevator in a dramatic stunt at the Crystal Palace. Otis proved that his invention was safe, thus freeing up architects to design ever taller buildings.

Aftermath: The fair lost more than $300,000 due to delays in opening some exhibits, as well as low attendance by foreign visitors. The Crystal Palace burned down in 1858. Bryant Park, which is adjoined by the New York Public Library, sits on the site today.

1939–40 WORLD'S FAIR

Theme: The World of Tomorrow
Where: Flushing Meadows–Corona Park, Queens
The Plan: As the worldwide Depression dragged on, people were weary but hopeful of what the future held. The stated goals of this fair were to provide a peek at the "World of Tomorrow." But at its core, the fair was a business enterprise. So the organizers encouraged corporations to use the event as a platform for new products.

Notable Exhibits: The fair's centerpiece was the 700-foot Trylon, a slim, three-sided tower that stood beside the Perisphere, a 200-foot orb containing a model city of the future.

- In General Motors' Futurama, visitors sat in moving chairs that toured a scale representation of a futuristic (1960s) city.

- New inventions that made an appearance: the color camera, air conditioner, automatic dishwasher, and television, which was demonstrated to the public for the first time.

- Most popular attraction: the Amusements Area—which offered a roller coaster, parachute jump, carnival acts, and "girlie shows."

Aftermath: The onset of World War II caused many of the international exhibitors to return to Europe, and high ticket prices were another obstacle for visitors. The fair lost nearly $21 million, and declared bankruptcy. Flushing Meadows–Corona Park, created specifically for the fair, was left unfinished.

1964–65 WORLD'S FAIR

Theme: Peace Through Understanding

Where: Flushing Meadows–Corona Park, Queens

The Plan: A new generation of New Yorkers wanted to re-create their memories of the 1939–40 fair for their children. So Robert Moses, the Big Apple's "master builder," was hired to lead the charge. Moses saw the fair as a way to raise enough money to complete Flushing Meadows–Corona Park, so the 1964–65 World's Fair, held there again, was under even more pressure to make money than the previous fair had been.

Notable Exhibits: With the space race heating up, NASA sought public support for its efforts by sponsoring the two-acre Space Park, which included full-scale models of rockets and satellites.

• Futurama made a return, and was updated with models of a city under the ocean, a port on the Antarctic ice shelf, an automated farm in the desert, and a lunar colony.

• New technologies on display: a picture phone, computer modem, and the first model of the now-classic Ford Mustang.

• The Unisphere, a 140-foot steel globe, was the fair's most recognizable structure. It still stands in Flushing Meadows–Corona Park today.

Aftermath: The fair again fell far short of its attendance goals, and was forced to declare bankruptcy. But when all was said and done, New York did make enough money to finish Flushing Meadows–Corona Park. Today, the park is home to both the U.S. National Tennis Center, which hosts the U.S. Open, and Citi Field, stomping grounds of the New York Mets.

* * *

FLUSHED

In 1983 New Yorkers were so riveted by the final episode of the TV show M*A*S*H that, when it ended (2½ hours after it began), so many people rushed to the bathroom—and flushed their toilets—that water pressure throughout the city dropped. According to many reports, it was the largest use of water at one time ever in the United States.

NEW YORK FOOD FROM "Q" TO "Z"

Our smorgasbord of New York's favorite edibles and grazing grounds continues. (A through P appears on page 32.)

QUEENS: The city's most culturally diverse borough, famous for its diverse restaurants. Among the cuisine you'll find: Greek, Moroccan, Middle Eastern, Egyptian, Afghan, Czech, Spanish, French, Italian, Romanian, Indian, Pakistani, Filipino, Cuban, Mexican, Brazilian, Peruvian, Chilean, Colombian, Argentine, Ecuadoran, Salvadoran, Uruguayan, Thai, Japanese, Chinese, and Korean.

REUBEN SANDWICH: This grilled sandwich of corned beef, Swiss cheese, sauerkraut, and Russian dressing on rye has murky origins. New York deli owner Arnold Reuben either invented it or let it be named for him, but food historians continue to argue the point. (A few claim it was invented in Nebraska, but no New Yorker believes that for a minute.)

SNAPPLE: Born in Greenwich Village in 1972, when Hyman Golden, Leonard Marsh, and Arnold Greenburg (owner of a health food store on St. Mark's Place) started making and selling fruit drinks. Their small company, Unadulterated Food Products, had grown to 26 plants bottling more than 50 all-natural beverages.

THOUSAND ISLAND DRESSING: Invented in the Thousand Islands-Seaway resort region of upstate New York, probably around 1910, by the wife of a popular fishing guide. She gave her recipe to actress May Irwin, who coined the dressing's name. May passed the recipe to George Boldt, proprietor of the Waldorf-Astoria, and George gave it to his maitre d'—who promptly put it on the hotel's menu.

UKRAINIAN FOOD IN BRIGHTON BEACH: Brighton Beach is where the great Russian food is, and serious foodies are happy to make the pilgrimage out there to eat dumplings, kebabs,

---

Truman Capote's first choice for Holly Golightly in *Breakfast at Tiffany's:* Marilyn Monroe.

kasha, pickled vegetables, and a *lot* more (quantity is part of the experience). BYOB (vodka, of course), but the custom is to keep the bottle out of sight under the table.

VIETNAMESE BÁNH MÌ: These sandwiches have taken New York by storm, especially in Queens, Brooklyn, and Manhattan. Think French/Vietnamese fusion: a Vietnamese baguette (made with wheat and rice flours) stuffed with ham, pork, pâtè, pickled vegetables, and sometimes basil, cilantro, mayo, cucumbers, or bean sprouts.

WHITEFISH, SMOKED: Like chopped liver, smoked fish isn't a New York invention, but it's been raised to a high art at Zabar's, Barney Greengrass, and Murray's Sturgeon on the Upper West Side, Russ & Daughters on the Lower East Side, and other "appetizing shops." (An "appetizing shop" is a store that specializes in things you can eat on bagels.)

XO SAUCE: Chinese sauce made with dried shrimp, dried fish, and dried scallops cooked with red chile peppers, onion, garlic, and oil; typically served with Cantonese meals and dim sum in restaurants. Invented in Hong Kong in the 1980s, but it's a New York City staple now.

YONAH SCHIMMEL'S KNISHES: In 1910, Yonah Schimmel, a rabbi from Romania, opened his bakery on East Houston Street, when he made only kasha, potato, and fruit-and-cheese knishes (filled dumplings). The shop is still there, and it hasn't changed much—except now you can get a veggie egg roll, potato kugel, or even a chocolate knish.

ZITO'S BREAD: This one got away, and New Yorkers still miss it. Zito's coal-oven-baked white, semolina, and whole wheat were the best breads you could get until well into the 1960s. A family-run fixture on Bleecker Street since 1924, it closed in 2004.

* * *

New York is the only American city in which less than 50 percent of households do not own a car.

Bushwick (Brooklyn) is an English corruption *boswijck*, meaning "little town in the woods."

MONUMENTS
TO HERSTORY

*The New York City Department of Parks and Recreation has
named dozens of monuments, parks, and playgrounds
after notable women. Here are just a few.*

LADY MOODY TRIANGLE

Where: Brooklyn

Named for... Lady Deborah Moody (1583–1659), who founded Gravesend, the only English town in what is now Brooklyn, when New York City was still the Dutch colony of New Netherlands. Moody was the first woman in the New World to buy a plot of land—an incredible accomplishment, given that women had few rights at the time. She reportedly paid "one blanket, one gun, and one kettle" for the land that became Gravesend. The Lady Moody Triangle is formed by Village Road North, Lake Street, and Avenue U, but it might have been more appropriate to honor Moody with a "square" instead—Gravesend's street design was one of the earliest in the colonies to employ a block grid system.

MARGARET CORBIN CIRCLE

Where: Manhattan

Named for...the first woman to fight to receive a U.S. military pension, Margaret Corbin (1751–1800). On November 16, 1776, during the American Revolution's Battle of Fort Washington, Corbin took control of her fallen husband's cannon and fired on invading troops. She was injured in the fighting and captured. Eventually the British released her, but Corbin suffered injuries that left her disabled for the rest of her life, making her eligible for a military pension. Margaret Corbin Circle is at the entrance to Fort Tryon Park in Washington Heights, where that long-ago battle was fought.

HATTIE CARTHAN GARDEN

Where: Brooklyn

Named for... Bedford-Stuyvesant resident Hattie Carthan

(1900–84). In the early 1970s, bothered by the decline of green space and the overall deterioration of her neighborhood, Carthan began replanting trees and helped found the Bedford-Stuyvesant Neighborhood Tree Corps and the Green Guerrillas, which nurtured urban community green spaces. (The "Guerrillas" were known for their inventive tactics—among other things, they often threw water balloons filled with seeds into abandoned lots.) Carthan and her groups ultimately added more than 1,500 trees to the neighborhood of Bed-Stuy, earning her the nickname "First Lady of the Environment."

Carthan was in her 70s when she began her environmental crusade, and she often joked about her age, saying "I've got one foot in the grave and the other on a banana peel." She was responsible for saving the Bed-Stuy magnolia on Lafayette Avenue—it had been slated for demolition. That tree became a symbol of the neighborhood and was eventually declared an official city landmark. The Hattie Carthan Garden is bound by Lafayette and Marcy Avenues and Clifton Place. There is also a Hattie Carthan Playground a few blocks south, between Monroe and Madison streets.

JENNIE JEROME PARK
Where: The Bronx
Named for... Jeanette "Jennie" Jerome (1854–1921), who, in 1874, gave birth to Winston Churchill, who became Prime Minister of England and helped lead the Allied Forces to victory in World War II. Born and raised in New York City, Jeanette Jerome was the daughter of Leonard Jerome, a successful New York financier (nicknamed "The King of Wall Street") and patron of the arts. In 1873, Jennie traveled to Europe with her family, where she met Lord Randolph Churchill, a handsome young English nobleman. They married in 1874 and the rest, as they say, is history. The Jennie Jerome Playground sits next to Jerome Avenue, which is named for her father.

ILKA TANYA PAYÁN PARK
Where: Manhattan
Named for... Dominican-born and New York City–raised Ilka Tanya Payán (1943–96)—an immigration lawyer, a newspaper columnist, member of the Dominican Women's Caucus, and a

dedicated AIDS activist. Before all of this, though, Payán made a name for herself as an actress, portraying the villainous Carmen Delia in the Spanish-language soap opera *Angelica, Mi Vida* (*Angelica, My Life*). She was also very involved in promoting and developing New York's Latino theater community. Payán contracted AIDS in 1981 and died of complications from the illness in 1996. Her park is located at 157th and Broadway.

* * *

FIRST LADY

Eleanor Roosevelt was New York born and bred: She began her life in 1884 in a mansion on Manhattan's Upper West Side, lived with her grandmother in Dutchess County after her parents died, had her debut at the Waldorf-Astoria, married future president Franklin Delano Roosevelt in New York City, and died in Manhattan in 1962. Throughout her life, Roosevelt was an author, speaker, and ardent advocate for civil rights. Today a statue in Riverside Park—the first statue of a woman ever commissioned by the city—honors her life's work.

Roosevelt was well-known for speaking her mind—here are five of her most famous quotes.

• "A little simplification would be the first step toward rational living."

• "A woman is like a tea bag—you can't tell how strong she is until you put her in hot water."

• "Do what you feel in your heart to be right, for you'll be criticized anyway."

• "Great minds discuss ideas; average minds discuss events; small minds discuss people."

• "No one can make you feel inferior without your consent."

MURDER'S BIG BUSINESS

In the 1920s and '30s, mob bosses ruled the mean streets of New York City.

L A COSA NOSTRA
Throughout the 1920s, New York was terrorized by criminals. Gangs threatened business owners, extorted money, corrupted labor unions, and formed gambling, prostitution, and drug rings. Some of the most successful criminal organizations were controlled by Italian American immigrants who, in 1931, stopped battling each other, joined forces, and created a criminal syndicate known as La Cosa Nostra, or the American Mafia.

La Cosa Nostra ran its illegal activities like a corporation: The newly allied gang lords served on an executive board called the Commission, which gave orders to the rest of the mob. Charles "Lucky" Luciano, the architect of Cosa Nostra, was the first head of the Commission. Like all good businessmen, Luciano ran his corporation to create big profits. And like all good criminals, he used violence to intimidate people and keep his enemies in check.

MOBILIZING THE TROOPS

To help provide the kind of "muscle" La Cosa Nostra needed, Luciano enlisted two gangster pals—Meyer Lansky and Benjamin "Bugsy" Siegel. Lansky was known for his business brains and organizational skills, and Siegel was an accomplished hit man. Even though they were not Italians (they were from Jewish crime networks), Luciano brought Lansky and Siegel into La Cosa Nostra because they had done "enforcement" for other gang lords—dealing out beatings and killing people who ran afoul of organized crime. Together, Luciano, Lansky, and Siegel formed a Brooklyn-based gang of contract killers whose job was to commit murders for La Cosa Nostra.

Luciano also brought in Louis Buchalter, a gangster who had taken control of New York's garment industry unions and then used that influence to extort factory owners by threatening strikes and walk-outs. On Luciano's watch, Buchalter became the boss of the contract killers. Albert Anastasia, who controlled the city's waterfront, was put in charge of day-to-day operations. Buchalter was said to be so cold that his eyes "were like blocks of ice," and Anastasia was a brutal bully known as the "Lord High Executioner." Under this grim pair, the Brooklyn hit squad became so efficient at killing victims for the mafia that the public began calling it "Murder Inc."

BUSINESS AT MIDNIGHT

The headquarters for Murder Inc. was in the Brownsville section of Brooklyn, in a 24-hour candy store called Midnight Rose, on Lovinia Avenue at Saratoga. The location was convenient for the hit men, who came mainly from the Jewish, Irish, and Italian gangs in the neighborhoods of Brownsville, Ocean Hill, and East New York. They gathered at the store for meetings and used pay phones out back to get their assignments from the Commission. Orders to kill usually came directly from Buchalter himself.

The victims, whom the assassins called "bums," were usually other gang members. Many were suspected police informants or had committed some act of disloyalty, such as pocketing gang profits that were supposed to be paid to the bosses. Police officers and other lawmen were rarely targets because La Cosa Nostra wanted to avoid retribution from the authorities.

MURDER'S HEYDAY

Like traveling salesmen, the members of Murder Inc. often took their deadly services on the road. In 1939, when the New York bosses worried that union mobster Harry "Big Greenie" Greenberg was no longer loyal and might turn informant, a Murder Inc. assassin was called in to kill him. The hit man chased Greenberg from Montreal to Los Angeles. There, the hired killer stalked and assassinated Greenberg, the first organized-crime murder in L.A.

Buchalter paid his hit men about $12,000 a year (nearly $200,000 in today's dollars), plus bonuses. The mob expected professionalism, and Murder Inc. operatives prided themselves on their skill and efficiency. They could kill with a knife, an ice pick, a garrote, a machine gun, or their bare hands, depending on what would get the job done quickly and not get them caught.

HARD TO CATCH

The U.S. government estimated that Murder Inc. killed about 1,000 people across the country, and the hit men were hard to

---

The oldest state park in the U.S.: Niagara Falls (est. 1885).

catch. When the law did track one down, La Cosa Nostra guaranteed him the best defense possible. The mob also tended to kill witnesses and tamper with juries, so hit men often walked.

One other problem was that police and lawyers didn't even know how far La Cosa Nostra's reach was. In 1940, when Burton Turkus became Brooklyn's assistant district attorney, he inherited a collection of unsolved murders. At the time, no one knew they were all connected to Murder Inc. As Turkus later wrote: "If anyone had suggested that the 200 or so unsolved murders plaguing us…could be laid to the same group of killers, we would have laughed at them."

BRINGING DOWN MURDER INC.

In the end, a simple case of loyalty finally unraveled Murder Inc.'s reign of terror. In 1940 small-time hoodlum Harry Rudolph saw a 19-year-old friend get shot in the back by members of Murder Inc., so he wrote to the district attorney's office, volunteering information. When detectives followed up on Rudolph's tip, they were able to arrest three members of Murder Inc., including Abe "Kid Twist" Reles—a man so high in the gang hierarchy that he knew all the inside details.

To save himself from the electric chair, Reles spilled all his secrets. After he'd outlined the workings of Murder Inc., 85 unsolved murders in New York were solved and six members of the gang were convicted of homicide and executed. Even the powerful Louis Buchalter went to his death in Sing Sing's electric chair. As Murder Inc. weakened, more of its members scrambled to avoid the death penalty by turning informant. And within a few years, the deadliest gang in America was disbanded. And as for the leaders:

• Lucky Luciano ran La Cosa Nostra until 1935, when he was finally sent to jail for running a prostitution ring. (Many of his associates insisted that Luciano was framed, arguing that he was too high up in the organization to deal directly with prostitutes.) During World War II, his mob contacts spied for the U.S. government, and to reward him, he was freed and deported to Italy in 1946. He died there of a heart attack in 1962.

• Bugsy Siegel moved to California in 1935, where he continued working for the mob. In 1946 he built the Flamingo, a luxury hotel and casino in Las Vegas. After construction problems delayed the opening of the casino, his investors thought Siegel was skimming profits. They had him gunned down in 1947.

• Meyer Lansky became Luciano's financial advisor and ran things when Luciano went to prison. The government prosecuted Lansky for tax evasion in the early 1970s, but the mobster fled to Israel. He tried to become a citizen there, but was returned to the United States. He was acquitted at trial and lived quietly, dying of lung cancer in 1983. Because Lansky had been expert at hiding money in Swiss banks, some said he went to his death leaving $400 million in secret accounts...even though his family said he was broke.

* * *

FORGIVE AND FORGET

In the 1970s, Elvis Costello was hugely famous as a British punk and new wave rocker, so of course *Saturday Night Live* wanted him to be a musical guest. On December 17, 1977, Costello got the gig...by accident. The Sex Pistols, who were supposed to perform that night, couldn't get their passports in order so they couldn't travel. *SNL* producer Lorne Michaels called on Costello, who agreed to do the show.

Michaels had some conditions, though. Mainly he insisted that Costello not perform the song "Radio Radio," which criticized the media's power to decide what the public would and would not hear, a form of censorship...just what Michaels was trying to do. Surprisingly, Costello agreed and showed up to perform as scheduled.

When Costello and his band, the Attractions, stepped onstage, they launched into another hit, "Less Than Zero," but suddenly, Costello signaled for the band to stop, said there was no reason to play that song, and then proceeded to play "Radio Radio."

Lorne Michaels was furious. Not only had Costello violated his directive, but the stop and start made the entire show run long. Michaels banned Costello from future appearances on *SNL*.

It took 12 years for Michaels to get over the incident, but on September 26, 1999, Costello made his second *Saturday Night Live* appearance...and played "Radio Radio."

Montana, Nevada, Illinois, and Kansas each contain a town called Manhattan.

A LONG SHORTZ LIST

From New York Times *crossword puzzle editor Will Shortz's own list of famous people who are* New York Times *crossword fans.*

- Bill Clinton
- Bill Gates
- Stephen King
- Jon Stewart
- Stephen Sondheim
- Ed Asner
- Lee Iacocca
- John Lithgow
- Jane Curtin
- Paul Sorvino
- Teri Garr
- Anne Meara
- Dana Delany
- Matthew Modine
- Ellen Burstyn
- Eli Wallach
- Joan Rivers
- Martha Stewart
- Keith Hernandez
- Tom Seaver
- Yo-Yo Ma
- Dick Cavett
- Ken Burns
- Jack Kevorkian
- Brett Favre

- Lou Piniella
- Sting
- Noah Wyle
- Rachel Dratch
- Philip Seymour Hoffman
- Carol Burnett
- Keith Olbermann
- Claire Danes
- Elijah Wood
- Morgan Freeman
- Catherine Zeta-Jones
- Michael Douglas
- Natalie Portman
- Dustin Hoffman
- Jake Gyllenhaal
- Christina Applegate
- Diane Lane
- Ed Begley Jr.
- Nora Ephron
- Kate Hudson
- Zachary Quinto
- Kristen Bell
- David Bowie
- Olivia Wilde
- Dick Gautier

NYC was home to the world's first system of urban highways.

GOING GREENMARKET

New Yorkers love to buy food on the street. And in the 1970s, a couple of local guys tapped into that passion when they came up with the idea of bringing together the farmers of New York State and the citizens of New York City.

PUSHING OUT THE PUSHCARTS

Long before supermarkets, Korean groceries, and gourmet food palaces, many New Yorkers, especially in immigrant neighborhoods, bought their fresh vegetables and fruits from peddlers who set up pushcarts on city streets. The peddlers were mostly European immigrants who had arrived in America in the mid- to late 19th and early 20th centuries. In Europe, it was common to see open-air markets with proprietors running small stalls, so pushcarts—small open stalls on wheels—were a logical leap for immigrants, and a familiar way of earning a living. Customers looked over the goods, haggled over the prices, and went home with their daily bread, fish, meat, and produce.

As late as the 1960s, there were still a few Italian vendors operating vegetable pushcarts on Bleecker Street in the West Village, but they were anomalies. In 1938, Mayor La Guardia had pretty much done away with pushcarts (which he considered messy, unsanitary, and degrading to the city), moving them off the streets and into new indoor market buildings. So when Bob Lewis and Barry Benepe hit on the idea for Greenmarket in the 1970s, it was a concept that felt new to a lot of New Yorkers.

THE BOB AND BARRY SHOW

Native New Yorker Barry Benepe had been trained as an architect and city planner, committed to making cities more livable for ordinary people. While he was working upstate, he began to think about the connection between struggling rural farmers and the poor quality of produce in New York City supermarkets. His friend Bob Lewis, another city native, had gone into regional and town planning in the Catskill Mountains. And both men were interested in the relationship between cities and agriculture.

Benepe and Lewis were concerned by the fact that family farms

---

The Brooklyn Dodgers were originally called the Trolley Dodgers...

were becoming an endangered species in the Hudson Valley; thousands of acres of local farmland had already been lost, and thousands more were going to be lost because farmers couldn't make a living when they sold their crops to wholesalers at low prices. Benepe and Lewis figured that if farmers could sell directly to consumers—without the middlemen—they could get full retail price, make a decent living, and be far less likely to lose their land to developers. So in the early 1970s, they came up with the concept of Greenmarket, an umbrella organization that would oversee open-air sites where New York State farmers could set up stands and sell their fresh produce directly to New York City residents. New York City already had a lot of food stores that called themselves "farmers' markets," but they weren't actually getting their produce from local farmers. Benepe and Lewis's Greenmarket would guarantee that consumers got locally grown farm food.

In 1975, the two men pitched their idea to the nonprofit Council on the Environment of New York City, and the council agreed to sponsor the program. The next year, Benepe and Lewis opened the first Greenmarket site on a city-owned parking lot at 59th Street and Second Avenue in Manhattan, with just 12 farmers. By noon, the stands were completely sold out. Two more markets (one at Union Square and another near the Brooklyn Academy of Music) opened that summer, and Greenmarket was off and running.

MAKING IT WORK

Not everyone liked the idea of Greenmarket. Neighborhood merchants and supermarkets were afraid the farmers would steal business from them and complained that the farmers didn't have to pay rent and city taxes. Customers had to be convinced that the farmers' fresh produce (unpackaged and with actual *dirt* clinging to the lettuce leaves) was safe to eat. And farmers had to be persuaded that the Big Apple wasn't full of dangerous criminals and rude New Yorkers. In the end, it was the high-quality locally grown food that sold residents on the Greenmarkets—and the eager customers who sold the farmers on the wisdom and profitability of bringing their goods to the city.

Growing the Greenmarket project was a step-by-step process. Benepe and Lewis got many calls from people all over the city who wanted both the fresh food and a boost to their neighborhoods. The men learned to choose their new sites carefully, looking for high visibility and serious customers. The Union Square Greenmarket, for example, wasn't a rousing success at first. The area was neglected, crime-ridden, discouraging to visitors, and rife with dilapidated buildings—not a great candidate for attracting food buyers. But eventually, the market started to prove what Benepe and Lewis had anticipated: Greenmarket helped to improve and sustain New York City neighborhoods. The small collection of stands at Union Square started to bring in customers, who then also shopped the local businesses. More businesses opened around the square, real estate values went up, and the neighborhood improved. Today Union Square is a magnet for local visitors, foreign tourists, and neighbors alike—full of stores, restaurants, office buildings, and residences, and a lot of the credit goes to Greenmarket.

THE SWEET TASTE OF SUCCESS

Since that first summer, Greenmarket has grown to include more than 50 locations in all five boroughs, with 18 markets running year-round and more than 250,000 customers per week at peak season. Around 200 family farmers and fishermen take part in the program, and they come from New York, New Jersey, Pennsylvania, Connecticut, and other parts of New England. Depending on which market you attend, you can find everything from vegetables, fruits, and flowers to honey, jam, pies, houseplants, herbs, breads, fish, meat, poultry, eggs, cheese, cider, wine, and wool yarn.

These are products grown, raised, or made only in New York State and the surrounding regions. (In fact, one of the market managers' jobs is to check that farmers are selling only what they grow, raise, or make themselves.) What you won't find are oranges from Florida or strawberries from California at Greenmarket; neither will you find out-of-season produce—no asparagus in October or corn in November. The whole point is *local, in season,* and *direct to the consumer.* In addition, Greenmarket has turned out to be good for the environment: All Greenmarket farmers are committed to the quality of the soil, air, and water on their farms. Their food is safe and healthy to eat—and if you have a question about that, you can march right up to the farmer and ask about it face-to-face.

For many New Yorkers, Greenmarket has become part of a weekly routine, as much a social experience as a nutritional one. They bump into old friends there or make new ones, chatting over the crisp green beans or the juicy tomatoes. They buy flowers for their parties and houseplants for their windowsills, pumpkins at Halloween and fragrant wreaths at Christmas. Local restaurants pride themselves on planning seasonal menus based on what's available at Greenmarket; chefs cart off the prizes of the day, and shoppers trail them to find out what's cooking. For the hours that each Greenmarket is open, that space in the big city becomes a small town.

* * *

"EMPIRE STATE OF MIND"

Before 2009 no song about New York City came close to touching the iconic "New York, New York." But when rapper Jay-Z and R&B artist Alicia Keys teamed up to record the 2009 Billboard hit "Empire State of Mind," a new anthem for important New York events was born. The song talks about New York's places, people, and character and was written by Angela Hunte, who, like Jay-Z, grew up in Brooklyn, and her writing partner, Jane't Sewell-Ulepic. While on a trip to London, the pair had gotten homesick for New York and penned the tune.

Jay-Z first performed "Empire State of Mind" solo on September 11, 2009, at Madison Square Garden during the "Answer the Call" benefit for the New York Police and Fire Widows' and Children's Fund. Two days later, at Radio City Music Hall, he performed it again, this time with Alicia Keys (who grew up in Manhattan), when they closed the 2009 MTV Video Music Awards. The duo also performed the hit during Game 2 of baseball's 2009 World Series at Yankee Stadium.

Keeping true to the spirit of the lyrics, the music video for "Empire State of Mind" was filmed at locations around the city, including Ground Zero, Times Square, and in Tribeca. In the video, Keys plays a piano that features an image of the New York City skyline around the case and an image of the Statue of Liberty on the closed lid.

DISASTER!

A timeline of some of the biggest disasters in New York's history.
(For the history of big New York fires, go to pages 324 and 353.)

1668: A yellow fever epidemic hit New York City, one of the first recorded outbreaks of the mosquito-borne disease in Colonial America. (The disease isn't endemic to the Americas; it was brought by the Europeans.) The number of fatalities is unknown, but Governor Francis Lovelace noted that "many people" died every day. Yellow fever epidemics occurred several more times in New York City; the last recorded outbreak came in 1870.

1836: The *Mexico*, a ship that had departed from Liverpool, England, ran aground off of Long Island on New Year's Eve. A rescue boat didn't arrive until the next afternoon, and 115 passengers and crew froze to death while waiting.

1896: Temperatures in New York City rose above 90°F for 10 days—day *and* night. In the stifling heat, nearly 1,500 died, mostly as a result of crowded tenements and a citywide ban on sleeping outdoors.

1915: A dynamite blast set off by subway workers under Seventh Avenue and 25th Street in Manhattan caused an entire block of the crowded street above to collapse. Seven people were killed; nearly 100 more were seriously injured.

1918: A subway train derailed beneath Flatbush Avenue, Ocean Avenue, and Malbone Street. The "Malbone Street Wreck" killed 97 people, most of whom were heading home from work. It remains the worst subway wreck in history.

1920: A bomb hidden in a horse-drawn carriage went off on Wall Street at noon. More than 300 were injured and 38 killed. The perpetrators were never found.

1928: A defective switch caused a subway to derail underneath Times Square. The car smashed through a tunnel wall and was cut in half. The crash killed 16 and injured 100.

1957–65: During this eight-year span, six passenger jets crashed in and around New York City, caused by a variety of electrical problems and pilot errors. The crashes killed 399 people, including passengers, crew, and six people on the ground.

1975: On December 29, a bomb exploded in the crowded baggage-claim area of LaGuardia Airport's TWA terminal. More than 70 holiday travelers were injured and 11 were killed. The bombing remains unsolved.

1990: Avianca Flight 52 crashed at Cove Neck, Long Island, killing 73 of 158 passengers and crew.

1993: A truck bomb exploded in the World Trade Center's underground garage, killing six and injuring more than a thousand.

1996: TWA Flight 800 exploded 12 minutes after takeoff from JFK and crashed into the Atlantic Ocean south of Long Island. All 230 people onboard were killed. The explosion was at first thought to be a bomb, but was later determined to be an explosion of fuel vapors caused by an electrical short circuit.

2001: The 9/11 terrorist attacks by Al-Qaeda brought down the two 110-story World Trade Center towers and several surrounding buildings. A total of 2,996 people were killed, including the 19 attackers. It was the worst terrorist attack in U.S. history.

2001: On November 21, American Airlines Flight 587 crashed into the Belle Harbor neighborhood of Queens shortly after takeoff from JFK Airport, killing all 260 on board and five people on the ground. The cause was later determined to be the result of turbulence from another plane and overuse of the rudder by the pilot.

2003: The Staten Island Ferry crashed into a pier at the St. George Ferry Terminal of Staten Island, killing 11 and injuring 70.

2009: On January 15, U.S. Airways Flight 1549 flew into a flock of Canada geese, causing both engines to fail. Captain Chesley "Sully" Sullenberger carefully ditched the plane in the Hudson River—and all of the 155 people on board survived. One member of the National Transportation Safety Board said, "It has to go down [as] the most successful ditching in aviation history."

Total manpower used to cut the 20 miles of tunnels for the NYC subway: **7,700 men.**

COMIC RELIEF

Looking for wisdom? Consider the words of these Borscht Belt comedians. (More about them on page 93.)

"I once wanted to become an atheist, but I gave up—they have no holidays."

—**Henny Youngman**

"I could tell my parents hated me. My bath toys were a toaster and a radio."

—**Rodney Dangerfield**

"Anytime three New Yorkers get into a cab without an argument, a bank has just been robbed."

—**Phyllis Diller**

"My doctor is wonderful. Once, in 1955, when I couldn't afford an operation, he touched up the X-rays."

—**Joey Bishop**

"The guy who invented the first wheel was an idiot. The guy who invented the other three, he was a genius."

—**Sid Caesar**

"As the poet said, 'Only God can make a tree.' Probably because it's so hard to figure out how to get the bark on."

—**Woody Allen**

"Marriage is an attempt to solve problems together which you didn't even have when you were on your own."

—**Eddie Cantor**

"An undertaker calls a son-in-law: 'About your mother-in-law, should we embalm her, cremate her, or bury her?' He says, 'Do all three. Don't take chances.'"

—**Myron Cohen**

"Age does not bring you wisdom. Age brings you wrinkles."

—**Estelle Getty**

"I wasn't born a fool. It took work to get this way."

—**Danny Kaye**

"Anytime a person goes into a delicatessen and orders a pastrami on white bread, somewhere a Jew dies."

—**Milton Berle**

"I don't exercise. If God had wanted me to bend over, he would have put diamonds on the floor."

—**Joan Rivers**

The Rockefeller Center's Christmas tree is almost always a Norway spruce.

PAPP AND THE PUBLIC

*At 8:00 p.m. on November 1, 1991, Broadway theaters
dimmed their lights to honor the death of Joseph Papp, a man
whom critic Frank Rich said left "the New York theater an
almost completely different place than he found it."*

MEET THE PUBLIC
Theater in New York City is divided into Broadway and
everything else. "Everything else" includes off-off-Broadway theaters, off-Broadway theaters, nonprofit organizations, and a
few major institutions like Lincoln Center's Vivian Beaumont
Theater, the Brooklyn Academy of Music, and the Public Theater.

The Public is a complex of six theaters on Lafayette Street in
Manhattan. Since its founding in 1966, the Public has produced
hundreds of avant garde, experimental, culturally diverse, ambitious, and crowd-pleasing works. It's had a handful of failures, but
an abundance of triumphs. The Public has championed many new
playwrights (like David Rabe, David Mamet, Ntozake Shange, and
John Guare) and advanced the careers of many actors (like Kevin
Kline, Meryl Streep, and James Earl Jones). It's sent shows to Broadway (*Hair* and *A Chorus Line*) and won dozens of awards. But the
Public Theater would never have been created if not for the genius
of a man named Joseph Papp.

REBEL WITH A CAUSE

Papp was born Yosl Papirofsky in 1921, the son of Yiddish-speaking
Eastern European immigrants. Growing up poor and Jewish in
Brooklyn, he was the target of a lot of anti-Semitism, which, he
said, made him want to "fight for things, for any aspect of minority
rights—black, Hispanic, and so on. To me, intolerance [was] a
greater threat than poverty." By the time he left high school, Papp
was involved in the liberal political activism that would influence
the rest of his life—including his life in the theater. Papp was convinced that "culture, by itself, was not significant. It had to be always doing something for the masses, for ordinary people, not just
servicing an elite."

After a stint in the navy during World War II, where he put

Technically, Coney Island is a peninsula.

together shows for the troops, Papp went to California and joined a theater group called the Actors' Lab, where he rose to the position of director, his first real job in theater. He missed New York, though, and moved back to the city in the early 1950s, initially working as a stage manager at CBS. But his real goal was to start a Shakespeare repertory company. He'd fallen in love with Shakespeare during his time at the Actor's Lab and believed that ordinary theatergoers could love it too…if they could just see it for free in an unintimidating venue. In 1954, Papp founded the New York Shakespeare Festival, and soon, he was producing free Shakespeare in a Lower East Side church. Then, in the summer of 1956, he put on free Shakespeare plays at the 2,000-seat East River Park Amphitheater (also on the Lower East Side), with support from the New York City Parks Department. Just as he'd anticipated, crowds were eager to see plays like *Julius Caesar* and *Taming of the Shrew*.

The following year, Papp's company began performing—still for free—in a makeshift theater in Central Park in the summer. "When I got into doing Shakespeare," Papp said, "the whole idea was to give it to people in the parks so that there would be large numbers there who might be influenced." It worked. New Yorkers went crazy for "Shakespeare in the park." On performance days, people lined up hours before showtime to make sure they'd get their free tickets. In 1962 the New York Shakespeare Festival opened its permanent summer home in Central Park: the outdoor Delacorte Theater.

A LIBRARY BECOMES A THEATER

With Shakespeare solidly established in the park, Papp began to think about producing contemporary works—and for that, he'd need an all-weather theater. In the 1960s, the beautiful old Astor Library, on Lafayette Street just south of Astor Place, was scheduled for demolition, but Papp was sure it would make a great home for a complex of performance spaces. He convinced the city to halt the demolition and, in 1966, acquired the property and turned it into the New York Shakespeare Festival Public Theater.

The first production at the Public was the rock musical *Hair*. To the surprise of everyone (except Joe Papp), it was a huge success and, in 1968, became one of the first shows to make the leap from off-Broadway to Broadway. In fact, Papp pioneered the transfer of

To for his role in *Gangs of New York*, actor Daniel Day-Lewis listened to the music of Eminem.

off-Broadway shows to Broadway—before him, Broadway shows were always big-budget affairs produced specifically for a huge stage; no one imagined that a quirky show that originally played in a small theater would appeal to the big audiences. But *Hair* ran for four years on Broadway, proving that it could. That first Public season also included *No Place to Be Somebody* by Charles Gordone (in 1970, it became the first Pulitzer Prize–winning play by an African-American writer), a play by Václav Havel (who was later elected president of the Czech Republic), *Down the Morning Line* by Ramon G. Estevez (better known as actor Martin Sheen), *The Figures at Chartres* by Edgar White (a West Indian playwright), and a modern version of *Hamlet* directed by Papp and starring Martin Sheen. And just to round out the ambitious program, there was a concert series that season, too.

STANDING FIRM

Throughout the late 1970s and '80s, Papp continued to produce Shakespeare, as well as productions by new playwrights and plays that dealt with social issues. He gave theater space and time to writers of all ethnicities, races, genders, sexual orientations, and political views. And he was ruthless where artistic freedom was concerned. In 1973, he learned that CBS had postponed its promised telecast of *Sticks & Bones*—David Rabe's play about the aftermath of the Vietnam War—because the network considered the play too controversial. Furious, Papp canceled his $7 million contract with the network and refused to produce the additional 11 plays he'd agreed to do for CBS. In 1990 he turned down a badly needed $50,000 grant from the National Endowment for the Arts (and deferred applying for $323,000 more funding) because, if he accepted the money, he would have had to agree to obscenity restrictions in the plays he produced. He wrote to the chair of the NEA that he "could not in good conscience accept any money...as long as the...amendment on obscenity is part of our agreement."

As Papp continued to fight the theater's battles, he was losing his own. He died of prostate cancer in 1991. After his death, the Public was officially renamed the Joseph Papp Public Theater.

GLORY DAYS

Joe Papp's theaters have produced hundreds of plays, and his

New York State is home to 58 species of wild orchids.

productions have collected an impressive number of prestigious theater awards, including 42 Tonys, 40 Drama Desk Awards, and 4 Pulitzers. So far, the Public has sent 54 shows to Broadway. Here are a few highlights:

1972: *That Championship Season*, by Jason Miller, which won a Tony Award for Best Play and Best Director, and a Pulitzer Prize in 1973.

1973: *The Cherry Orchard*, by Russian playwright Anton Checkov, was staged with an all-black cast in what was then called "color-blind casting." It was typical Papp, politically radical and provocative.

1975: *A Chorus Line*, written by James Kirkwood Jr. and Nicholas Dante, directed by Michael Bennett, was a smash hit that transferred to Broadway and ran until 1990, the longest-running musical up to that time. It won nine Tonys and a Pulitzer. Best of all, Papp had the foresight to make sure that the Public Theater benefited from the play's success: Almost $40 million in royalties went into the Public's coffers over the years, and *A Chorus Line* continues to bring in money, since the show is produced worldwide and often.

1982: *Hamlet*, starring Diane Venora in the title role, was one of Papp's first cross-gender casting experiments. She was the first woman to play Hamlet in the history of the New York Shakespeare Festival.

1985: *The Normal Heart*, Larry Kramer's play about AIDS, premiered at the Public and became the longest-running play there.

1987: *Talk Radio*, actor and writer Eric Bogosian's first play.

1996: *Bring in 'da Noise, Bring in 'da Funk*, starred a then-unknown tap dancer named Savion Glover.

1999: *Caroline, or Change*, by Tony Kushner, told the story of racism during the 1960s. Actress Anika Noni Rose (best known for her roles in the movies *Dreamgirls* and *The Princess and the Frog*) won a Tony for Best Featured Actress in a Musical.

MORE NEW YORK INVENTORS

*Our list of important New York inventors
continues. (Part I appears on page 231.)*

HERMAN HOLLERITH

In 1889, Buffalo-born statistician Herman Hollerith invented an electric tabulating system that could be used to read and collect data from punched cards. The machine soon became an indispensable tool at the U.S. Census Bureau, and Hollerith used the money generated from his invention to form the Tabulating Machine Company in 1896. That company merged with three other high-tech businesses in 1911 to form the International Business Machines Corporation...better known as IBM.

ELMER SPERRY

Cincinnatus-born and Cortland-schooled inventor Elmer Sperry achieved a breakthrough in 1908 when he created the spinning gyroscopic compass. The device is far more reliable on a moving platform than a traditional magnetic compass, and the U.S. military uses Sperry's compass to steer ships, guide torpedoes, and stabilize airplanes during both world wars.

PETER COOPER

In 1845 New York City–born industrialist, philanthropist, and 1876 U.S. presidential candidate Peter Cooper patented a formula for powdered gelatin. He later sold his colorless, odorless, and flavorless creation to Pearl B. Wait, a cough-syrup manufacturer from Le Roy, New York. Wait then infused it with a variety of artificial flavors and renamed it Jell-O.

GEORGE PULLMAN

Overnight railroad travel became a lot more bearable in 1857 when Brocton-born cabinetmaker George Pullman invented the Pullman Sleeping Car. Modeled after the most luxurious hotel rooms of the day, the "Palace Car" was longer, higher, and wider than traditional coaches and featured folding upper berths, polished brass fixtures, deep pile carpeting, and a spacious washroom. Sales of the lavish cars picked up steam in 1865 when one was attached to President Abraham Lincoln's funeral train, and by 1893 Pullman's company was worth $62 million.

GERTRUDE ELION

The daughter of Lithuanian and Polish immigrants, New York City scientist Gertrude Elion made headlines around the world in 1954 when she patented the leukemia-fighting drug 6-mercaptopurine. Later in her career, Elion did research that was also critical in the creation of azathioprine, a drug that reduces the rejection of kidney transplants, and acyclovir, a medication used to fight herpes. The chemotherapy medicine and other drugs she invented earned her the 1988 Nobel Prize in Medicine and a place in the National Inventors Hall of Fame.

*　　*　　*

THERE'S MORE TO BUFFALO THAN WINGS

The beef on weck is a local favorite around Buffalo, New York, but it's hardly known outside the region. What is it? A sandwich that consists of thinly sliced rare roast beef dipped in its own juices and piled high on a salty, crusty, hard kummelweck roll. The roll (whose name is shortened to "weck") is key to the sandwich—it's a Kaiser roll covered with pretzel salt and caraway or cumin seeds. The sandwich is usually served in a bar, and diners typically apply horseradish liberally. Traditional accompaniments include French fries and a dill pickle.

The sandwich first appeared in Buffalo's German American community around the turn of the 20th century. According to most historians, a baker named William Wahr, who emigrated from Germany's Black Forest region, created the kummelweck roll. Wahr worked for a saloon-owner named Joe Gohn, who liked the roll's unique taste, added thinly sliced beef, and began serving the sandwich to tourists visiting Buffalo for the 1901 Pan American Expo.

Albany began as a Dutch fur-trading post called *Beverwijck*—"beaver district."

DIRTY ROTTEN SCOUNDRELS

*Wall Street is notorious for swindling honest taxpayers
out of their money, but the crimes aren't new. In fact,
in the early days of American business, fraud
and profiteering were the name of the game.*

WILLIAM DUER

The Crime: Insider trading

The Scoundrel: A lawyer and wealthy landowner from England, Duer came to America in 1773 and settled in New York, eventually buying a home on Broadway near Trinity Church. He was elected to the Continental Congress and the New York Assembly. Then, in 1789, when the U.S. Treasury was established, Duer was made Assistant Secretary of the Treasury, under Alexander Hamilton.

The Scandal: Duer is regarded as one of the first insider traders in U.S. history. (Insider trading occurs when someone uses confidential information that the average investor doesn't know about to make money in the stock market.) Duer decided to use information he learned while working at the Treasury—about the country's finances and the health of its banks—to make himself rich. He planned to buy up bank stocks, beginning with the Bank of New York (now called Bank of New York Mellon), which had been founded by Alexander Hamilton in 1784. Duer's Treasury job afforded him the information that the Bank of New York (BNY) was planning to merge with another, larger bank (the Bank of the U.S.). When that happened, BNY's stock prices were sure to soar.

In 1790, Duer quit his job at the Treasury and, the next year, teamed up with Alexander Macomb, a prominent New Yorker, who had the money to back Duer's plans. Duer also brought in other creditors to buy up stock in other American banks in preparation for the day when their stock would soar, too. Macomb and the other creditors were eager to lend Duer money, since they knew he had insider information.

But then in 1792, the Livingstons—an extremely wealthy and prominent New York family—decided they didn't want the merger to go through. What they wanted was for interest rates to rise...so they could make more on money they loaned out. So they began withdrawing substantial amounts of silver and gold from the banks, creating a cash-flow problem as the banks had less and less money to lend, driving up interest rates.

The Aftermath: The Livingstons won out. Interest rates began rising as much as one percent a day, and bank stocks tanked. The event became known as the Panic of 1792, and it took a government bailout of the American banking system to keep the country's economy afloat. Hundreds of investors who had followed Duer's lead in buying up bank stocks lost hundreds of thousands of dollars. And Duer himself, who had made most of his stock purchases with borrowed money he now couldn't pay back, ended up in debtor's prison.

Despite the scandal, strict insider trading laws didn't appear on U.S. books until the 20th century. Still, one good thing did come of it all...depending on your perspective. America's stock dealers and auctioneers who had, until then, been a disorganized group with no central trading place, met beneath a tree at the spot that is now 68 Wall Street and formally established the New York Stock Exchange. The first stock to trade on the new NYSE: the Bank of New York.

THOMAS CLARK DURANT

The Crime: Fraud, profiteering

The Scoundrel: Thomas Clark Durant's parents sent him to Albany Medical College, and he graduated (and called himself "the Doctor"), but he never went into practice. There was much bigger money to be made in disreputable business dealings. Durant founded his first railroad—the Missouri & Mississippi (M & M)—in 1854, but he made his first real fortune during the Civil War, smuggling Confederate contraband cotton into the North. With those ill-gotten gains, he bought up more railroad companies. He wasn't particularly good at constructing or managing railroad lines, but he was a genius at manipulating the price of their stock and then cashing in. For example, as vice president and general manager of the Union Pacific Railroad—which gained fame as one of two companies the federal government had contracted with to build the Transcontinental Railroad—he announced that the Union Pacific would meet up with his own M & M line, driving up the price of M & M stock. Then Durant bought stock in competing lines and reneged on the deal, which drove up the competitors' stock value, making him millions, and devalued M & M's, which he bought back at bargain prices. According to one of his acquaintances, "It [was] the smartest operation ever done in stocks and could never be done again."

The Scandal: But that wasn't Durant's biggest swindle. In 1864, the Doctor launched the Crédit Mobilier of America construction company, which he secretly owned. Crédit Mobilier charged Union Pacific exorbitant prices for every mile of railroad track it laid—including on the Transcontinental Railroad—and Durant used his position at Union Pacific to force the railroad to approve the high charges. Durant also chose to build long, winding train routes that required more track than direct lines. The cost overruns nearly bankrupted Union Pacific, and the railroad's shareholders and American taxpayers lost millions of dollars.

To make matters worse, Durant wanted to ensure that Crédit Mobilier got as many railroad construction contracts as possible and that his dirty dealings weren't exposed. So he gave Crédit Mobilier stock to influential members of its board of directors. Then board member—and U.S. congressman—Oakes Ames bribed members of the Senate and the House of Representatives to "overlook" Durant's scheme by offering them Crédit Mobilier shares.

The Aftermath: Union Pacific finished the Transcontinental Railroad in 1869, even though the Crédit Mobilier scandal nearly derailed its construction. But it wasn't until 1872 that a newspaper—the *New York Sun*—finally figured out what had gone on and exposed the truth. In the end, Union Pacific, via Crédit Mobilier, had built a railroad that was worth about $50 million. The cost: more than $70 million. The $20 million difference had gone right into the pocket of Crédit Mobilier—and Thomas Clark Durant.

The public was furious, and there was an investigation, but it went nowhere. Railroad fraud and scandals like Crédit Mobilier happened all the time during the late 1800s. And although many politicians were exposed for taking bribes (including the future

NYC power runs through 83,043 miles of underground cables.

president James Garfield), the Republican-controlled Congress censured only Ames and one other bribe-taking congressman—a Democrat. As for Durant, by then, he'd already resigned from Union Pacific and went free.

WILLIAM FRANKLIN MILLER

The Crime: Fraud

The Scoundrel: William Miller was a young bookkeeper from the Ridgewood neighborhood of Brooklyn. With a pregnant wife and a small salary, he badly needed extra cash. First he borrowed money to invest in the stock market, but crooked brokers sold him worthless stock. With loan sharks coming after him, Miller decided that the only solution was to figure out how to pull his own swindle.

The Scandal: In 1899 Miller set up a phony investment company called the Franklin Syndicate and began collecting money from his neighbors. He talked a good game, claiming he'd worked on Wall Street and had insider information on stocks. According to Miller, everyone who invested with him would receive profits of 10 percent a week, no matter the amount of the initial investment. That attracted a lot of working-class people with just a little money to spare. He opened an office at 144 Floyd Street in Brooklyn and began collecting cash and sending out advertisements. As word spread of the enormous interest that could be made, Miller even hired employees to help handle all the new investors.

Miller himself never invested a dime. He pocketed some of the money, but was careful to pay out the promised 10 percent per week...at first. It worked for a while because he could afford to pay his first investors as new investors kept bringing him money.

The Aftermath: Ultimately Miller's Franklin Syndicate lasted a year and swindled "investors" out of $1 million (about $25 million today) before it imploded. Miller was exposed and indicted, and spent three years in jail. He wasn't the last grifter to "rob Peter to pay Paul," though. Two decades later, a Boston businessman named Charles Ponzi pulled the same con, swindling thousands of people out of millions of dollars...and giving the scheme its official name.

THE MIRACLE METS

Only 25 percent of New Yorkers admit to being Mets fans. But over the years, the Amazins have managed some amazing comebacks.

• The Mets played their inaugural season in 1962 and didn't get a win until the 10th game. They ultimately lost 120, the most losses in one year in modern MLB history. But by 1969 the team was playing its best season yet, winning 100 games, sweeping the Atlanta Braves to win the National League pennant, and finally beating the Baltimore Orioles in five games to win the World Series, the first expansion team ever to take the title. The season earned them the nickname "the Miracle Mets."

• During a May 1973 game at Shea Stadium, Atlanta Brave Marty Perez cracked a line drive right into the forehead of Mets pitcher Jon Matlack. The ball hit Matlack so hard that it fractured his skull and then bounced off one of the dugouts. Many Mets players and fans thought Matlack's career was over, but he returned to the mound just 11 days later to pitch a win in Pittsburgh.

• By the late 1970s, the Mets had fallen into the "losers" category once again, and in 1979, they posted their worst record ever: just 63 wins...and 99 losses. Shea Stadium sat nearly empty throughout the season, earning it the nickname "Grant's Tomb." But the team rallied during the 1980s, signing stars like Darryl Strawberry and Gary Carter. By 1986 they'd rebounded once again to appear opposite the Boston Red Sox in the World Series. By game six, all appeared to be lost—the Red Sox were up 3–2, and one of the scoreboards even flashed a congratulatory message to the Boston team. But the Mets went on to stage one of the most impressive comebacks in baseball history. Thanks to a lot of impressive hitting—and an infamous error from Boston first baseman Bill Buckner, who let a slow ball roll through his legs—the Mets went on to win game six, and then game seven, to take their second World Series title.

• On April 17, 2010, the Mets beat the St. Louis Cardinals 2–1 in a 20-inning game that lasted for seven hours. It was the first time in MLB history that neither team scored for the first 18 consecutive innings.

EMILY'S BRIDGE

*How one exceptional New Yorker saved
the day…and the Brooklyn Bridge.*

LOVE STORY

Emily Warren came of age in the mid-19th century, at a time when women were denied the right to vote and were taught that they were best suited to a life of homemaking. Growing up in Cold Spring, New York, Emily was the eleventh of 12 children. She was particularly close to her older brother Gouverneur, and when their father died in 1859, Gouverneur became responsible for the 16-year-old Emily. A Civil War hero and an engineer who advocated education, Gouverneur made sure Emily studied math and science—subjects usually reserved for men.

In 1864 Gouverneur invited his little sister to a military ball, where she met Washington Roebling, one of Gouverneur's aides. Emily and Washington hit it off immediately, and within a year, they'd married. From the start, the couple broke the social rules of the day by declaring themselves partners and equals. Washington encouraged Emily's enthusiasm for learning and helped her study civil engineering so that she could understand his work, building suspension bridges.

FOLLOWING IN FATHER'S FOOTSTEPS

Washington's father, John Roebling, manufactured wire cables. These cables, strung from high towers, were used to support the roadways of suspension bridges. After the Civil War, Washington helped his father build the Cincinnati Bridge, which still spans the Ohio River. Then, in 1868, Washington and Emily traveled to Europe, studying suspension bridges there that were built on *caissons*.

Constructed deep underwater, caissons were airtight chambers that formed solid foundations to build on. When built on caissons, a suspension bridge tower—even a heavy one—could rise high out of the water. The towers were central to John Roebling's newest and most ambitious project: He wanted to build a bridge with two stone towers more than 300 feet high supporting a 1,595-foot span. He planned to use the structure to connect Manhattan and Brooklyn across the East River.

BRIDGE TO DISASTERS

Washington Roebling started out as his father's assistant, but one day, while the elder Roebling was out surveying the location for one of the towers, he suffered a freak accident that crushed his foot. Tetanus set in, and before construction on the bridge could even begin, John died. His grieving son took over as chief engineer. Construction finally began on January 3, 1870.

As the great stone towers of the bridge began to take shape, Washington often worked underwater inside the caissons that supported them. The caissons were an engineering marvel, but working inside them was a dangerous job. Many of the men who toiled inside the chambers contracted an illness called "caisson disease," which brought on joint pain, itchy skin, vision problems, headaches, paralysis, and other debilitating symptoms. Today the ailment is known as "decompression sickness" or "the bends." It occurs when a body is exposed to a severe change in barometric pressure—like flying at high altitudes in an unpressurized plane, scuba diving, or working inside a caisson many feet underwater. The changes in air pressure cause dissolved nitrogen in the blood to turn into bubbles, which then circulate and damage a variety of organs.

Decompression sickness can now be treated with time in an oxygen chamber, but in the mid-1800s, there was no effective treatment. So by 1872, Washington Roebling, stricken with caisson disease, was paralyzed and bedridden. His business partners and workers assumed he'd bow out of the project or let another bridge-builder finish the job. Instead, he maintained his position and appointed his 29-year-old wife, Emily, to be his eyes and ears at the worksite.

STEPPING IN

The Brooklyn Bridge was the longest suspension bridge ever built, and it came with enormous engineering challenges. The caisson on the Brooklyn side, for example, rested firmly on bedrock 45 feet below the water's surface, but on the Manhattan side, workers dug down more than 70 feet below the surface and still couldn't find solid rock to support the caisson. Digging finally stopped at 78 feet, both because it was so dangerous for the workers (the deeper they went, the more likely a cave-in or other disaster was) and because

Most career minutes played by a member of the Knicks: 37,586 (Patrick Ewing).

Washington Roebling decided that the immense weight of the Manhattan stone tower would hold the caisson in place even if the caisson didn't rest on solid rock. More problems arose during the project, but Washington believed Emily could handle the herculean task.

And handle it she did. Besides caring for her bedridden husband and the couple's young son, she kept business and financial records on the project. She also studied civil engineering, including how to test materials to gauge their strength and safety, and how to make suspension cables that could safely support a bridge deck and the traffic moving across it. Thanks to her studies, when Emily showed up at the bridge site each day, she could direct construction and take accurate notes on any technological or practical problems. Then she went home and relayed the information to her husband, who remained bedridden.

TROUBLED WATERS
Building the bridge took 11 more years, and as the work progressed, Emily's knowledge and confidence grew. She dealt with contractors, assistant engineers, city officials, and politicians, some of whom worried that the bridge was taking too long to build and costing too much money—$15 million, or about $320 million today. Some of the city officials and politicians wanted to replace the sickly Washington, complaining that all the back-and-forth between the man and his wife was slowing down construction even further. So, in 1882, it fell to Emily to convince them that her husband should keep his job.

That was how Emily Roebling became the first woman to give a speech before the American Society of Civil Engineers, founded in New York in 1852. She argued that Washington should remain chief engineer, reminding the engineers of the enormous problems he'd solved and that his work was essential to the project's completion. Emily so impressed the group that Washington kept his position...although by then, many people believed that it was really Emily Roebling running the show.

HAIL TO THE CHIEF
May 24, 1883, was the Brooklyn Bridge's official opening day, and Emily Roebling—in an open carriage—was the first person to cross

---

The interlocking "NY" logo used on Yankees caps first appeared in 1877 on a...

it. Abram Hewitt (who became mayor of New York in 1886) delivered a famous speech, pointing out that the new bridge was "an everlasting monument to the self-sacrificing devotion of a woman and of her capacity for that higher education from which she has been too long disbarred." Emily's bridge had not only connected Manhattan and Brooklyn, but it also had helped change opinions about what women could achieve. Today Emily Roebling is recognized as America's first female civil engineer.

* * *

GUERRILLAS IN THE MIST

Street art has come a long way since the 1980s, when gangs began tagging their territories in New York City's subways, storefronts, and just about anything they could put their spray cans to. But what was once a symbol of tough turf and unsavory characters has evolved into a legitimate art scene.

New York has become a favorite canvas for guerrilla artists because it provides a venue where their work can be seen by many people, especially those who might not typically venture into a gallery. It's also a way for them to make political statements or even brighten up city blocks that are otherwise considered "dumps."

These days, graffiti artists like Banksy, Shepard Fairey, and Nick Walker have become so popular that people from all around the world come to New York and other cities to see their work. In February 2011, fans of Nick Walker stood in line overnight to buy limited edition prints of his mural *The Morning After: New York*, painted on the side of a building at 35 Cooper Square in the East Village. The mural depicts a silhouetted man in a rowboat in New York Harbor looking at the city's skyline, which is dripping with graffiti paint. The building where the mural is painted is scheduled to be torn down...taking the mural with it and showing fans just how fleeting graffiti art can be.

Unlike Walker, some muralists prefer to keep their identities a secret. Technically, street art is still graffiti and illegal. The mysterious British artist Banksy even stayed away from the 2011 Academy Awards (where a movie he directed, *Exit through the Gift Shop*, was nominated) to make sure he wouldn't be arrested for previous acts of vandalism.

KEEP OFF THE GRASS!

A look at Gramercy Park, Manhattan's only surviving private park.

LOOK, BUT DON'T TOUCH

If you were strolling down Park Avenue South from 23rd Street, you probably wouldn't even notice that just east of the walls of tall office buildings there's a small, secluded, formal park that looks as if it were plucked out of 19th-century London. That two-acre green space is the 175-year-old Gramercy Park, and it's bordered by its very own streets: Gramercy Park West, East, North (actually East 21st Street), and South (actually East 20th Street). In fact, the park is so special that even the surrounding neighborhood has taken the name Gramercy Park.

The park is enclosed by a wrought-iron fence made of eight-foot-high bars. Inside the fence are huge trees, carefully tended shrubs and flower beds, clipped lawns, raked gravel paths, and old-fashioned wooden benches. No litter, no Frisbees, no pets, no parties. It's beautiful, but it's also off-limits: On each side of the park are gates with heavy-duty locks. Only the people whose apartment buildings or townhouses face directly onto the park get the privilege of receiving a key to the gates—and they have to pay for it.

Gramercy Park has rarely been open to the public. In 1863 it was briefly turned into an encampment for Union soldiers sent to control riots that broke out in protest of Civil War conscription. And the gates used to be open for one day each year (Gramercy Day, usually the first Saturday in May), but that tradition was abandoned in 2007. It's still open for a few hours for caroling on Christmas Eve. And on 9/11, even Gramercy Park's rules were suspended, and the south and north gates were unlocked to allow hundreds of New Yorkers to hurry through the park as they escaped from downtown Manhattan.

NICE SWAMP

Early Dutch settlers called the Gramercy area *Krom Moerasje* ("little crooked swamp") or *Krom Mesje* ("little crooked knife," because of the shape of the swamp and brook on the site). Those names gradually transformed to *Crommessie*, which over time became Gramercy.

In the early 1800s, Manhattan was growing and moving northward. Samuel B. Ruggles, a clever real-estate developer, bought the "little crooked swamp" in 1831 with the intention of turning it into a level, dry, open square surrounded by lots that would be sold for the construction of townhouses. The central square would be privately maintained as a park and cooperatively used by the owners of the lots, with no government support or interference. Ruggles spent $180,000 to drain the swamp and level the terrain. Then he laid out the park, divided the surrounding land into 66 parcels, and began to sell the lots. He decreed that no owner could "erect within forty feet of the front of any of the…lots any other buildings saving brick or stone dwelling houses of at least three stories in height." According to this rule, the park would be ringed *only* by gracious homes—no stores or businesses. To complete his plan, in 1833 Ruggles deeded the park to a group of trustees who would act on behalf of the owners to maintain the character of the park and the surrounding area.

A GOOD MANSE IS HARD TO FIND

By the 1860s, Gramercy Park—exclusive, quiet, beautiful—had become a fashionable enclave of the wealthy, the accomplished, and the politically powerful. Here are some of the important addresses in the neighborhood:

• **#3 and #4 Gramercy Park West.** Two of the most unusual townhouses on the park, these two were built in the 1840s and have iron lacework porches that look a lot like the French Quarter of New Orleans. James Harper, founder of Harper & Brothers publishing company and mayor of New York in the mid-1840s, lived in #4 from 1847 until his death in 1869. When he moved in, "Mayor's Lamps" were installed at the entrance, an old Dutch custom for making it easier to find the mayor's house at night. But for Harper they were purely ceremonial, since he wasn't actually the mayor anymore.

• **#15 Gramercy Park South.** Politician Samuel J. Tilden bought this house in the 1860s and hired Calvert Vaux (co-designer of Central Park) to give it an overhaul. Vaux added bay windows and Gothic ornamentation, and the renovation was completed in

1874, the year Tilden was elected governor of New York. Two years later, after he ran for president and lost, Tilden decided he'd better do a few more renovations—politics, he'd found, could get a little rough—so he installed rolling steel doors behind the bay windows and built an underground tunnel to 19th Street…just in case he needed to get out fast.

• **#16 Gramercy Park South.** In 1888, Edwin Booth, America's most celebrated actor (and brother of John Wilkes Booth, assassin of President Abraham Lincoln), bought the mansion at #16. That same year, Booth joined with Mark Twain, General William T. Sherman, and 13 others to found the Players—a gentlemen's club for actors, artists, writers, lawyers, and other professionals interested in the arts. Booth deeded #16 to the Players, on the condition that he be allowed to keep his apartment on the third floor; he died there in 1893. The Players still own #16, which now functions as a social club, a repository of theater memorabilia, and a performance space.

• **#36 Gramercy Park East.** Designed in 1909, with elaborate pointed arches, protruding stone gargoyles, and a pair of knights in armor guarding the exterior, this 12-story building has been home to several more historical figures: actor John Barrymore, circus founder Alfred Ringling, sculptor Daniel Chester French (who created the seated figure of Abraham Lincoln at Washington, D.C.'s Lincoln Memorial), and playwright Eugene O'Neill.

* * *

DID YOU KNOW?

George Washington had no navy during the Revolutionary War, so he used privateers. One of New York's best known was Stewart Dean, who captained a six-gun sloop called *Beaver* which sailed from New York in 1776, 1779, and 1781. Dean took *Beaver* throughout the Caribbean and the Atlantic—attacking British ships and confiscating their cargoes to help feed and clothe the American army and help fill the depleted American war treasury.

The first "subway series" took place in 1921 between the Giants and the Yankees.

MURDER, HE WROTE

How did New York City, a famous cigar girl, and Edgar Allan Poe combine to create one of the world's first murder mystery stories? Read on.

PROLOGUE
Anyone who enjoys murder mysteries owes a debt of gratitude to Edgar Allan Poe. Before there was a Sherlock Holmes or a Nancy Drew, before the word "detective" was even in common usage, Poe created the character of C. Auguste Dupin, an eccentric Parisian genius who solved murder cases that baffled the city's police force. Dupin first appeared in April 1841 in a short story called "The Murders in the Rue Morgue" and reappeared in two more stories after that. To create his detective stories, Poe did plenty of research on real crimes, including one of his century's most notorious murder mysteries.

CHAPTER ONE: THE BODY

On July 28, 1841, the body of 21-year-old Mary Cecilia Rogers was found floating in the Hudson River near Hoboken, New Jersey. The discovery was shocking, not just because the body was battered beyond recognition (she could be identified only by her clothing and a birthmark on her arm), but because Rogers was famous in New York City. One of America's first celebrities, she was nicknamed the "beautiful cigar girl."

Until shortly before her death, Rogers had worked at a huge tobacco and cigar shop on Broadway. She had an unusual job: enticing men into the shop. According to legend, she was so beautiful that men would come inside just to see her, and wouldn't leave without buying tobacco. Some of those admirers even published poems in local papers, singing of her charms. One besotted "poet" wrote, "She's picked for her beauty from many a belle / And placed near the window Havanas to sell." Other patrons were more talented, including New York City newspaper reporters and a writer named Edgar Allan Poe.

CHAPTER TWO: THE DISAPPEARANCE

By July 1841, Rogers had quit her job at the tobacco shop to help

---

Longest underwater car tunnel in North America: the Brooklyn–Battery Tunnel at 9,117 feet.

her mother run a boarding house on Nassau Street. She had plenty of admirers there, too, including a sailor named William Kiekuck, clerk Alfred Crommelin, and the dashingly handsome (but hard-drinking) Daniel Payne. To her mother's dismay, Rogers chose Payne and accepted his marriage proposal, though there were rumors later that the young woman was planning to leave him.

On Sunday, July 25, Rogers told her fiancé that she was going to visit her aunt, who lived uptown. She never made it. When she hadn't returned home the next morning, Payne took out a missing-persons ad in the *New York Sun*. Reporters jumped on the story—search teams formed and started combing the city. But Rogers was nowhere to be found...until Wednesday, when her body was pulled from the river.

The coroner found strangulation marks on Rogers's neck, and part of her dress had been torn off and tied around her mouth and neck with a sailor's slipknot. Another piece of her dress was missing, and the coroner speculated that it had been used to drag the body to the river. He also noted that Rogers was not pregnant, she had been severely beaten and sexually assaulted, and her body still showed signs of rigor mortis (when a corpse's limbs go stiff). He concluded that she'd been murdered on Sunday night, just after she left home, and that she may have been killed by more than one assailant, perhaps one of the gangs that plagued New York City's streets at the time.

CHAPTER THREE: THE INVESTIGATION

The discovery of the beautiful cigar girl's body launched an intensive inquiry to find out who had killed her. Some people thought she'd drowned accidentally, but that didn't explain her injuries. One witness claimed to have spotted her on Sunday on the Hoboken Ferry with a "dark-complected man." Daniel Payne and the other men she knew from the boarding house came under suspicion immediately; newspapers even published libelous stories accusing them of her murder. Payne had to bring witness affidavits to several city newspaper offices to get them to stop calling for his arrest.

About three weeks after Rogers disappeared, a woman named Frederica Loss, who ran a tavern in Hoboken near the spot where Rogers's body was found, came forward and produced some stained, mildewed pieces of clothing that she said her sons had found nearby. The items looked like things Rogers had owned—one handkerchief was even monogrammed with the initials "MR." But no one could say for sure that the items had belonged to Mary Rogers, and there were rumors that the belongings had been planted to lure gawkers. Loss's tavern had been doing a brisk business serving tourists who came to visit the site of Rogers's demise.

CHAPTER FOUR: THE REVELATION

Despite having several leads, police couldn't find Rogers's killer. Every suspect they questioned (including her fiancé, Daniel Payne) had an alibi. But events began to take a strange turn. In October 1841, a few months after Rogers's death, Payne walked to the thicket near Hoboken where Rogers's clothes had been found. There, he penned a vague note about his "misspent life" and drank a fatal overdose of laudanum, a liquid form of opium.

Then, in the fall of 1842, one of Frederica Loss' sons accidentally shot her. On her deathbed, a delirious Loss confessed that on that fateful Sunday, Mary Rogers and a doctor had rented a room in the tavern. Rogers was pregnant, Loss said, and she died in the rented room from complications after the doctor performed an abortion.

That story appeared in all of New York City's major newspapers and churned up reader interest again. Police found nothing to corroborate the confession, but the case was back in the spotlight. Questions abounded: A botched abortion contradicted the coroner's report that Rogers had died of strangulation. Had the coroner been lying? Or had the mysterious doctor tried to cover the whole thing up by beating Rogers's body, simulating a strangulation, and dumping her in the river? Could the wounds from the abortion have looked to the coroner like sexual assault? Maybe Mary Rogers was planning to leave Daniel Payne after all, and when he found out about that and the abortion, he killed her in a fit of rage. Or was Frederica Loss simply a delusional dying woman still trying to drum up business for her tavern? No one knew, and no one ever figured it out. To this day, Mary Rogers's murder remains unsolved.

CHAPTER FIVE: THE DETECTIVE STORY

In 1841, Edgar Allan Poe wasn't yet the legend he is today, but he was an up-and-coming writer. He'd held jobs at various literary magazines and had published several short stories, including "The Murders in the Rue Morgue," starring that early fictional detective C. Auguste Dupin. Poe had always been attracted to stories of supernatural melancholy and horror, and Mary Rogers's murder caught his attention. He decided to try to solve the case in fictional form, and to write a compelling story in the process. The result was "The Mystery of Marie Rogêt," a three-part serial that appeared in a magazine called *Snowden's Ladies' Companion* in late 1842 and early 1843. Poe wrote later, "Under the pretense of showing how Dupin...unraveled the mystery of Marie's assassination, I, in fact, enter into a very rigorous analysis of the real tragedy in New York."

Poe's story went like this: The body of a young woman named Marie Rogêt was pulled out of the Seine River in Paris. The young perfume-shop worker had been brutally beaten and died as the result of some kind of "accident." Part of her dress had been removed and tied in a sailor's knot, which was used to drag the body to the river. In the story, Dupin essentially "solved" the crime by implying that Rogêt had been killed by a "naval officer with [a] dark complexion." But Poe never named names.

"The Mystery of Marie Rogêt" was a hit for Poe, and so was the final Dupin story, "The Purloined Letter," published in 1845. It also spawned an entirely new fictional genre: the detective novel, which turned crimesolving into literature.

* * *

STALL OF FAME

On Earth Day 2007, the Bronx Zoo introduced the most expensive bathroom ever installed in New York City: the $1.6 million Eco Restroom, which is situated at the zoo's busy Bronx River entrance. The restroom includes frosted glass windows to let in sunlight and reduce energy consumption and 14 composting toilets. The restroom also uses a *greywater system*, meaning it's not connected to New York's sewer system. All the waste that goes into the toilet gets composted, and the water from the sinks is recycled to irrigate plants. As a result, the Eco Restroom uses 99 percent less water than a regular one.

CHEERS FOR BEERS

Move over, Milwaukee. Step aside, St. Louis. We're paying tribute to another American brewing capital: Brooklyn.

BROOKLYN BORN AND BREWED
Between the 1840s and Prohibition in 1920, there were at least 35—some say as many as 50—breweries in Brooklyn. In Williamsburg and Bushwick alone, a dozen of them dotted a 12-block section that became known as Brewer's Row (Scholes and Meserole streets from Bushwick Avenue to Lorimer Street). Heavy, British-style ales came first. Later, German immigrants introduced their own style of Bavarian lager. But for all the popularity of Brooklyn beers, even big brand names like Rheingold and Schaefer, they never could compete with national brands, so they remained regional favorites.

MY BEER IS RHEINGOLD

Of all the beers brewed in Brooklyn, Rheingold was the one people knew best, thanks to a ubiquitous ad slogan, "My beer is Rheingold, the dry beer." By the 1950s, the phrase had been turned into a jingle that played all over New York City's TV and radio stations. The brand was introduced by the Leibmann family—father Samuel and sons Joseph, Charles, and Henry—who came to Brooklyn from Bavaria around 1850. Soon after, they opened their first brewery on Meserole Street, and then moved to expanded facilities at Forrest and Bremen streets in Bushwick 1855.

Expert marketers, Rheingold hired a list of celebrity endorsers that would make today's promoters foam with envy: Groucho Marx, John Wayne, Marlene Dietrich, Gene Kelly, Dean Martin, Ella Fitzgerald, Cab Calloway, Carmen Miranda, and many more. In 1956, when *The Nat King Cole Show*—the first successful TV variety program to feature a black host—had trouble finding sponsors, Rheingold signed on. When the New York Mets set out to fill the baseball gap created after the turncoat Dodgers and Giants fled to California, Rheingold was among the team's charter sponsors. The Miss Rheingold competition, held annually from 1941 to 1964, generated millions of votes from the public, occasionally

---

...pianos in the neighborhood being played at once.

outpacing national elections. The beauty contest also attracted a number of young women who became Hollywood stars, including Hope Lange and Tippi Hedren. (Neither won the title.) Competition was tough: In the 1948 Miss Rheingold contest, Grace Kelly didn't even make the final cut.

"WHEN YOU'RE HAVING MORE THAN ONE"

The Bavarian-style lager beer introduced by the F. & M. Schaefer brewing company in the 1840s was a revelation to New York beer drinkers. "Its merits were many," wrote the *New York Times* in 1885, "including vivacity, brilliancy, and coolness, without the 'gummy,' soporific, and changeable characteristics of ale."

Light, thirst-quenching Schaefer quickly became, as its slogan said, "the one beer to have when you're having more than one." And beer drinkers did indeed have more than one. In 1885 Schaefer was brewing 150,000 barrels a year, in 1938 the company passed the million-barrel mark, and in 1944 it produced two million barrels a year. Not bad for a business started by two kids from Germany.

Frederick and Maximilian Schaefer immigrated to New York in the 1830s. After working at a brewery in Manhattan for a couple of years, they bought it in 1842. Frederick was 25 years old; Maximilian was 23. They built new facilities on Seventh Avenue and 17th Street, and then moved uptown to Fourth Avenue (now Park Avenue) and 51st Street, where the company headquarters remained for 67 years before it relocated to Kent Avenue in Brooklyn. (St. Bartholomew's Church and the Waldorf-Astoria were built on Park Avenue sites once owned by Schaefer.)

As Schaefer expanded, its production branched out to Pennsylvania and Maryland. But by the 1970s, sales had dropped and the big Brooklyn plant was no longer a jewel in the company crown. Schaefer announced it would close the plant in 1976, just a week after Rheingold revealed it was closing its own Brooklyn facility. Thus, the reign of the big-time Brooklyn breweries came to an end.

HONORABLE MENTION: McSORLEY'S

This one's not in Brooklyn, but old-time New York drinking establishments don't get more old-timey than McSorley's Old Ale House at 15 East 7th Street in Manhattan. The place has been going strong since John McSorley opened the doors in 1854.

Abraham Lincoln drank there. Woody Guthrie sang there. E.E. Cummings wrote a poem about it. But for the bar's first 116 years, if you wanted that old-time experience and you happened to be a woman, you were out of luck. McSorley's didn't have a lot of rules, but "no ladies" was one of them. Even when the bar was owned by a woman, which it was from 1939 to 1974, women didn't drink there. The owner, Dorothy O'Connell Kirwan, who inherited the place from her father, only came in on Sundays after the bar was closed. Finally, in 1970, a judge's ruling forced McSorley's to let women in. (It took another 16 years for a women's restroom to be installed.)

The other rule at McSorley's—one that remains essentially un-broken—is that the bar serves only ale. No wine, no cosmopolitans or appletinis, no light beer or lager. Just McSorley's ale—in light and dark varieties, served two at a time in half-pint glasses. Fidelio Brewery on First Avenue and 29th Street brewed the first ales for McSorley's, but today they're brewed by Pabst. And while you can buy McSorley's in bottles now, nothing compares to hoisting a cold one at the ale house itself.

* * *

"START SPREADIN' THE NEWS"
Frank Sinatra's 1980 version of "New York, New York" may be the best-known song about the Big Apple, but Sinatra wasn't the first to sing it. Liza Minnelli sang "New York, New York" in Martin Scorsese's 1977 film of the same title. The song was written for the film by Fred Ebb and composed by John Candor, and in the years since, it's been covered by countless other artists in various genres, including Queen, Sammy Davis Jr., Phish, Michael Bublé, and Devin Townsend, who did a heavy-metal version for a compilation album called *SIN-atra*.

The song, which captures the pride and spirit of the "city that never sleeps," is played regularly during the Macy's Thanksgiving Day Parade, in Times Square on New Year's Day just after the ball drops, and at the end of every home game in Yankee Stadium— Sinatra's version when they win; Minnelli's version when they lose.

Before Zane Grey wrote bestselling Westerns, he was a dentist in Manhattan.

ON BROADWAY

You can't have a Broadway play without a Broadway theater. Here are some behind-the-scenes facts about the big-money theaters that make it all happen.

- A "Broadway play" does not necessarily mean that a show is being produced at a theater on Broadway itself. Instead, it indicates the size of the theater. Broadway venues are the ones with the most seats: 500 or more. (Off-Broadway theaters have 100 to 499 seats; off-off-Broadway have fewer than 100.)

- All of the Broadway theaters happen to be in New York's main theater district in Times Square, through which Broadway Avenue runs. One exception: the Vivian Beaumont Theater, which is at Lincoln Center.

- Only five theaters have a Broadway address. The rest are in the West 40s and 50s.

- Currently, there are 40 Broadway theaters. Most are large—30 of them seat more than 1,000.

- Largest Broadway theater: the Gershwin, with 1,935 seats. Smallest: the Helen Hayes Theater, with 597 seats.

- Of the 40 theaters, 17 are owned by the Shubert Organization, which owns more than 50 theaters in New York City...including the Shubert Theater.

- Total number of seats in all the Broadway theaters put together: 49,670. (Total number of seats in the new Yankee Stadium: 52,325.)

- Oldest operating Broadway theaters: the Lyceum and the New Amsterdam, both built in 1903. In 1974 the Lyceum became the first Broadway theater to be named a historical landmark. The New Amsterdam is the earliest example of the Art Nouveau architectural style in New York City

- Latest Broadway theater to close: the Stephen Sondheim, in

In a year, one pair of sewer rats can produce 15,000 descendants.

2004, although a new theater was built on the site, and the name carried over.

• Newest Broadway theater: In 2010, the Henry Miller Theatre was built directly behind the famous Studio 54 disco, which had been converted into its own theater in 1998. The first production on Studio 54's stage: *Cabaret*.

• Like sports stadiums, many Broadway theaters have changed their names to reflect corporate sponsorship. Two current examples: the American Airlines Theater and the Cadillac Winter Garden Theatre.

• Other theaters are named after theatrical icons, such as musical composer Richard Rodgers, playwright Eugene O'Neill, actress Ethel Barrymore, and longtime *New York Times* theater critic Brooks Atkinson.

• The New Amsterdam is corporate-owned by Disney, for its stage-musical adaptations, but the company opted not to rename it because of the building's historical importance.

* * *

QUOTE ME

"Being on Broadway is the modern equivalent of being a monk. I sleep a lot, eat a lot, and rest a lot."

—**Hugh Jackman**

"Broadway has been very good to me. But then, I've been very good to Broadway."

—**Ethel Merman**

"People wear shorts to the Broadway theater. There should be a law against that."

—**Stanley Tucci**

"The only stuff I don't like are Broadway musicals. I hate them. I don't even like to talk about it. I can't bear musicals."

—**Laurie Anderson**

The U.N. Peace Garden contains more than 1,000 rosebushes.

CHANGE BY FIRE

*One of the greatest tragedies in New York's history led to some of today's
most important safety regulations. If you've ever wondered
why your office is always holding fire drills, read on.*

UNLUCKY #9
On March 25, 1911, the Saturday shift was just ending
at the Triangle Shirtwaist Factory, which occupied the
eighth, ninth, and tenth floors of the Asch Building near Washington Square. Shirtwaists—light cotton women's blouses—were all
the rage at the time, and the factory floor was lined with bins full
of cotton waste scraps. Fabric was draped over sewing tables, and
tissue-paper patterns hung from clotheslines. Workers—mostly
young Jewish women who'd recently immigrated—were collecting
their pay and getting ready to go home. but what they didn't know
was that a small fire had started in one of the waste bins on the
eighth floor. The fire quickly spread to fabric and paper nearby, and
within minutes, the whole eighth floor was engulfed in flames.

Most of the workers on the eighth floor escaped. A bookkeeper
called up to the offices on the tenth floor and warned the owners.
They immediately fled, along with almost everyone on the tenth
floor. But no one was able to get through to the workers on the
ninth floor. As the fire spread below them, the ninth-floor workers
were trapped. One survivor said, "All of a sudden, the fire was all
around."

NO WAY OUT
At the time, garment factories like the Triangle Shirtwaist one dotted Manhattan, and safety regulations were well-established. But
many factories ignored them, and Triangle, owned by Max Blanck
and Isaac Harris, was among the worst violators. When the Asch
Building was built in 1901, an automatic sprinkler system would
have cost $5,000, so the owners decided to leave it out. The building's fire hose wasn't maintained—a manager tried to use it to put
out the flames, but found that the hose had rotted and the valve
rusted shut. Some workers knew there was a fire escape, but those
who climbed out onto it found that the drop ladder, which was

supposed to extend down to the alley, had never been installed. The weight of so many workers on the narrow fire escape tore it from the building, plunging two dozen people to their deaths.

Worst of all, only one of the doors to the two stairwells could be opened—the other was kept locked to prevent employee theft. The stairwell that was open was quickly blocked by fire when a barrel of machine oil (that had been stored in the stairwell) exploded. The fire spread so fast that many workers never even had time to leave their sewing machines. And those who tried to escape were faced with an impossible choice: Helpless onlookers watched in horror as dozens of people jumped to their deaths to avoid the flames.

NYU TO THE RESCUE!

From a neighboring building, law students at New York University could see hundreds of people, mostly from the tenth floor, on the roof of the Asch Building. The students sprang into action, laying ladders across the gap between roofs and rescuing about 150 people. Firemen arrived at the scene within minutes and quenched the blaze a half an hour after it started, but it was too late—146 people were dead.

The Asch Building, which had been certified fireproof, had lived up to its billing—it didn't burn, but *everything* inside did.

CHANGES

After the Triangle fire, the city sent inspectors out to other factories. Most were found to be violating city safety codes. Within a few years, New York passed comprehensive building codes and fire safety laws—at the time, the strictest in the nation, all as a direct result of the Triangle fire. The tragedy was a turning point for the safety of American workers in other industries, too. It served as a catalyst to the growing union movement, which gave workers more leverage to force factory owners to improve working conditions, and New York State reorganized its Department of Labor so it could more effectively regulate factories. Other states adopted the changes too, and eventually, the reaction to this fire—which killed so many low-income workers—even laid the groundwork for the creation of a federal minimum wage.

The owners of the Triangle Shirtwaist Factory, meanwhile, were charged with manslaughter for locking the stairwell...but were acquitted. The insurance claims they filed for the fire made them a tidy profit of $400 for every victim. ($75 of that was eventually awarded to each victim's family, after a civil suit.) Two years after the Triangle fire, one of the owners was arrested for locking an exit door in another factory he owned. This time he was found guilty...and fined $20.

The Asch Building still stands. Renovated and renamed the Brown Building, it's now part of the NYU science department.

For more New York City fires, turn to page 353.

* * *

WHY'S IT CALLED THAT?

Buffalo, New York, was named for a small waterway called Buffalo Creek, but where the creek got its name seems to be a mystery. There are several theories:

The French: Some historians say that when French explorer Louis Hennepin first saw the Niagara River, he exclaimed, "Belle fleuve!" (Beautiful river!) The area then took on that name. When the English moved in, they anglicized the term and began calling the creek (and then the trading post and city that grew up around it) Buffalo.

The French, again: According to other historians, when French explorers first crossed the Niagara River from what's now Canada, they saw a lot of buffalo, so they named the small waterway Buffalo Creek.

The Native Americans: Supposedly, a Seneca Indian lived along Buffalo Creek. Some historians theorize that his name meant "buffalo" (though the actual name has been lost to history), so the first Europeans who settled the area named the creek after him.

The English: A final theory says that the English may have confused the French words for "buffalo" and "beaver." There were a lot of beaver in the area when the Europeans arrived, and some of the French terms may have just been poorly translated. But since the French word for buffalo is *buffalo*, and beaver is *castor*, that seems unlikely.

America's first known abolitionist group was founded in Rochester in 1838.

ART IMITATES LIFE

*New York is filled with characters, and some of them
have inspired famous fictional counterparts.
(Remember, we said "some" of them.)*

JAY GATSBY

The Great Gatsby, F. Scott Fitzgerald's melancholy chronicle of
Jazz Age hedonism in Manhattan and on Long Island, is recognized as an era-defining novel, a kind of snapshot of the roaring
twenties in New York. So who served as the real-life models for the
book's characters?

From 1922 to 1924, Fitzgerald lived in the Long Island village
of Great Neck, the inspiration for the novel's nouveau-riche
enclave, West Egg. Other notable Great Neck residents at the
time were Groucho Marx, author P. G. Wodehouse, and sportswriter Ring Lardner, whose parties helped to shape the depictions
of hectic decadence in Gatsby. No one knows for sure who
inspired the main character, Jay Gatsby, but it might have been
Max von Gerlach, a mysterious bootlegger, or wealthy New York
stockbroker Robert Kerr, both of whom Fitzgerald met at the Long
Island soirees.

OSCAR THE GROUCH

This crabby, trash-can-dwelling misanthrope with the matted green
fur has been a fixture on *Sesame Street* for all of the 40-plus years the
popular kids' show has been on the air. Master of muppets Jim Hen-
son and former show director Jon Stone came up with the idea for
the prickly character during a lunch meeting at a Manhattan restaurant. Their waiter was particularly rude and surly—so much so that
his behavior went beyond offensive and became entertaining. The
name of the restaurant? Oscar's Salt of the Sea.

As for the voice of Oscar the Grouch, muppeteer Caroll Spinney (who also does the voice for Oscar's personality opposite, Big
Bird) drew inspiration from a different source. When Spinney
caught a New York City taxi to the TV studio on the day of his
debut performance as Oscar, he hadn't yet decided on a voice for
the muppet. But then his cabbie, a crusty character from the Bronx

---

Novelist Jack London spent several weeks in his early 20s living homeless in City Hall Park.

with a cigar clenched between his teeth, asked a simple question: "Where to, Mac?" During the ride, the cabby aired his gripes about then-mayor John Lindsay and how he was ruining New York City. "As he was talking, I was taking it in," Spinney remembers. "When I got out, I kept repeating, 'Where to Mac?' just as he said it. It was like nothing I had in my repertoire of voices." The cabbie's voice became Oscar the Grouch's.

THE SOUP NAZI

In Season 7 of *Seinfeld*, viewers were introduced to one of TV's most memorable sitcom villains: "The Soup Nazi," a dictatorial purveyor of high-quality soup who barked "No soup for you! NEXT!" at customers he deemed unworthy of his delicious creations. Scriptwriter Spike Feresten was encouraged by show creators Jerry Seinfeld and Larry David to write the episode after he told them about a restaurant called Soup Kitchen International in Manhattan. The restaurant's chef and proprietor, Al Yeganeh, had a reputation for barking orders, and long before the episode aired in 1995, customers had nicknamed him "The Terrorist." The Midtown eatery closed in 2004, but Yeganeh pursued a new cross-country soup-serving enterprise: He launched the Original SoupMan franchise, now with 500 locations across the U.S., and a line of "heat-and-serve" soups. Despite the fame and free publicity brought to him by *Seinfeld*, Yeganeh was apparently offended by the characterization—employees of the franchise are forbidden from making "Soup Nazi" references.

The original restaurant at 55th Street and 8th Avenue reopened in 2010 as part of the Original SoupMan franchise. And although Yeganeh no longer operates that location, his authoritarian manner still abides in a sign posted there: "The line must keep moving! Pick the soup you want! Have your money ready! Move to the extreme left after ordering!"

PRIVATE JAMES RYAN

Steven Spielberg's 1998 World War II epic *Saving Private Ryan* follows a company of Army infantrymen assigned the task of bringing Private James Ryan, the last surviving brother of three servicemen killed in action, home safely. In the film, the mother of the Ryan boys grieves at home on a farm in Iowa, but the real-life inspira-

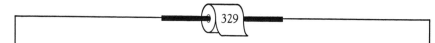

tions behind the story—the Niland brothers—were from the town of Tonawanda, New York, north of Buffalo.

All four Niland sons—Robert, Preston, Edward, and Frederick—served in World War II. When the Army discovered in 1944 that all but one, Frederick, had been reported killed in action, the last remaining brother was sent stateside to safety where he served as an MP in New York for the rest of the war. However, in a twist not shown in the movie, it was discovered in 1945 that Edward was alive, too. British troops liberated him from a Japanese prison camp in Burma. Frederick died in San Francisco in 1983 at age 63, but Edward lived in Tonawanda until his death in 1984 at age 72.

TONY MANERO

Like *The Great Gatsby*, the film *Saturday Night Fever* (1977) defines an era in New York's social history. *Saturday Night Fever* is about a group of young Italian Americans from Brooklyn in the 1970s who used the ecstatic abandon of disco dancing to overcome economic, ethnic, and class boundaries…and just to have a good time. John Travolta played the role of iconic disco stud Tony Manero.

The idea for Manero came from a 1976 *New York* magazine article called "Tribal Rites of the New Saturday Night," written by Nik Cohn, a British pop-culture journalist living in New York. The article told the story of a young Italian American man named Vincent, who was described as "the very best dancer in Bay Ridge—the Ultimate Face." But 18 years after the article was published, Cohn admitted that the story he'd written was pure fiction. "My story was a fraud," confessed Cohn. "I'd only recently arrived in New York. Far from being steeped in Brooklyn street life, I hardly knew the place. As for Vincent, he was largely inspired by a [Londoner] whom I'd known in the '60s."

*   *   *

"Campaign behavior for wives: Always be on time. Do as little talking as humanly possible. Lean back in the parade car so everybody can see the president."

—Eleanor Roosevelt

INSIDE THE BLUE BOX

Tiffany & Co. has been creating incredible collectibles since Charles L. Tiffany opened the first store in 1837. Here are some of the most beautiful creations ever to come wrapped in Tiffany's trademark Blue Box.

• In 1848, one of Tiffany's partners (John F. Young) went to Paris as a buyer....just after the French monarchy was overthrown. Young made a few extraordinary purchases there, including the French Crown Jewels and a jeweled corset that reportedly belonged to Marie Antoinette. Some of these were taken apart and their gems reset in other Tiffany items; others were sold at stores in New York and Paris.

• In 1863, Tiffany teamed up with circus showman P. T. Barnum to create a one-of-a-kind wedding gift for Charles Sherwood Stratton (a.k.a. General Tom Thumb), a dwarf who performed in Barnum's circus, and his bride, Lavinia Warren. The gift: a jewel-studded miniature horse and carriage.

• During the late 19th century, tycoon "Diamond" Jim Brady commissioned Tiffany to design a gold chamber pot for his girlfriend, actress Lillian Russell.

• In 1878 Tiffany acquired the world's largest flawless diamond from a mine in South Africa. The 128.5-carat stone was designated the "Tiffany Yellow Diamond" and today is valued at $22 million. It's usually on display at the flagship store on Fifth Avenue.

• In 1886 Tiffany introduced an engagement ring with what the company called a "Tiffany setting"—the diamond is lifted above the band with six platinum prongs. It's still one of the most popular engagement ring styles today.

• Magician and escape artist Harry Houdini bought an appropriate item in 1891: a diamond-studded Tiffany pocket watch, complete with a chain made of tiny gold handcuffs.

• Since the first Super Bowl in 1967, Tiffany's has created the Vince Lombardi Trophy that's given to the game's winning team.

WHAT IN THE DICKENS? PART II

Here we continue with Charles Dickens's observations about Manhattan during an 1842 tour of New York City. The excerpts appear in the book American Notes. *(Part I is on page 119.)*

THE TOMBS PRISON

"A long, narrow, lofty building, stove-heated as usual, with four galleries, one above the other, going round it, and communicating by stairs. Between the two sides of each gallery, and in its center, a bridge, for the greater convenience of crossing. On each of these bridges sits a man: dozing or reading or talking to an idle companion. On each tier are two opposite rows of small iron doors. They look like furnace-doors, but are cold and black, as though the fires within had all gone out. Some two or three are open, and [visitors], with drooping heads bent down, are talking to the inmates. The whole is lighted by a skylight, but it is fast closed; and from the roof there dangle, limp and drooping, two useless windsails [hatches]…

The fastenings jar and rattle, and one of the doors turns slowly on its hinges. Let us look in. A small bare cell, into which the light enters through a high chink in the wall. There is a rude means of washing, a table, and a bedstead. Upon the latter, sits a man of sixty; reading. He looks up for a moment; gives an impatient dogged shake; and fixes his eyes upon his book again. As we withdraw our heads, the door closes on him, and is fastened as before. This man has murdered his wife, and will probably be hanged…

Each cell door on this side has a square aperture in it. Some of the women peep anxiously through it at the sound of footsteps; others shrink away in shame. [Dickens asks the jailer] 'For what offence can that lonely child, of ten or twelve years old, be shut up here?'

'Oh! That boy? He is the son of the prisoner we saw just now; is a witness against his father; and is detained here for safe keeping, until the trial; that's all.'"

THE FIVE POINTS

"We have seen no beggars in the streets by night or day; but of other kinds of strollers, plenty. Poverty, wretchedness, and vice, are rife enough where we are going now.

This is the place: these narrow ways, diverging to the right and left, and reeking everywhere with dirt and filth. Such lives as are led here, bear the same fruits here as elsewhere. The coarse and bloated faces at the doors have counterparts at home, and all the wide world over. Debauchery has made the very houses prematurely old. See how the rotten beams are tumbling down, and how the patched and broken windows seem to scowl dimly, like eyes that have been hurt in drunken frays...

So far, nearly every house is a low tavern; and on the bar-room walls are coloured prints of [George] Washington and Queen Victoria of England and the American Eagle. Among the pigeon-holes that hold the bottles, are pieces of plate-glass and coloured paper, for there is, in some sort, a taste for decoration, even here. And as seamen frequent these haunts, there are maritime pictures by the dozen: of partings between sailors and their lady-loves."

LOWER MANHATTAN TENEMENTS

"What place is this, to which the squalid street conducts us? A kind of square of leprous houses, some of which are attainable only by crazy wooden stairs without. What lies beyond this tottering flight of steps that creak beneath our tread? A miserable room lighted by one dim candle and destitute of all comfort, save that which may be hidden in a wretched bed. Beside it, sits a man: his elbows on his knees: his forehead hidden in his hands. 'What ails that man?' asks the foremost officer. 'Fever,' he sullenly replies, without looking up. Conceive the fancies of a feverish brain, in such a place as this!

Ascend these pitch-dark stairs, heedful of a false footing on the trembling boards, and grope your way with me into this wolfish den, where neither ray of light nor breath of air, appears to come. A negro lad, startled from his sleep by the officer's voice—he knows it well—but comforted by his assurance that he has not come on business, officiously bestirs himself to light a candle. The match flickers for a moment, and shows great mounds of dusty rags upon the ground; then dies away and leaves a denser darkness than before, if there can be degrees in such extremes. He stumbles down the stairs and presently comes back, shading a flaring taper with his hand.

While living in NYC in 1790, George Washington ran up a...

Then the mounds of rags are seen to be astir, and rise slowly up, and the floor is covered with heaps of negro women, waking from their sleep: their white teeth chattering, and their bright eyes glistening and winking on all sides with surprise and fear, like the countless repetition of one astonished African face in some strange mirror.

Mount up these other stairs with no less caution (there are traps and pitfalls here, for those who are not so well escorted as ourselves) into the housetop; where the bare beams and rafters meet overhead, and calm night looks down through the crevices in the roof. Open the door of one of these cramped hutches full of sleeping negroes. Pah! They have a charcoal fire within; there is a smell of singeing clothes, or flesh, so close they gather round the brazier; and vapours issue forth that blind and suffocate. From every corner, as you glance about you in these dark retreats, some figure crawls half-awakened, as if the judgment-hour were near at hand, and every obscene grave were giving up its dead. Where dogs would howl to lie, women, and men, and boys slink off to sleep, forcing the dislodged rats to move away in quest of better lodgings."

* * *

IS THAT A MERMAN?

What's the most crowded day of the year to visit Coney Island? The annual Mermaid Parade, held in mid-to-late June on the first Saturday after the summer solstice. It began in 1983 and celebrates "artistic self-expression" with participants who dress in handmade costumes as mermaids, mermen, Neptune, and other sea creatures. The parade begins promptly at 2:00 pm, starting on West 21st Street and Surf Avenue and ends some three hours later on Stillwell Avenue. Every year, a different celebrity king and queen are chosen to ride in the parade. In 2010 Lou Reed and Laurie Anderson had the honors. Others have included David Byrne, Queen Latifah, Ron Kuby, Moby, Adam Savage, and Harvey Keitel.

The parade is also a celebration of start of summer, so the king and queen always walk up 10th Street to the beach and "open" the ocean for the summer swimming season by throwing offerings of fruit into the ocean to appease the sea gods.

FOR SALE: A BRIDGE IN BROOKLYN

"If you believe that, I have a bridge to sell you" has insulted gullible people since the 1800s. It comes from the days when con artists actually "sold" the Brooklyn Bridge to tourists and immigrants, most of whom expected to make a fortune on tolls from travelers between Brooklyn and Manhattan. (They didn't.)

SWINDLER: Reed C. Waddell
SALE DATE: 1880s through mid-1890s
PRICE: Unknown
DETAILS: Born in Springfield, Illinois, Waddell moved to New York in 1880 and started conning people right away. He offered the Brooklyn Bridge to gullible folks and pioneered a "gold-brick scandal" in which he passed off lead bricks plated with gold as solid-gold ones. Over several years, he made about $250,000.
CLOSING COSTS: In 1895, Waddell was shot and killed by fellow criminal Tom O'Brien, with whom he'd been arguing over shares of a heist.

SWINDLERS: Brothers Charles and Fred Gondorf
SALE DATE: Early 1900s
PRICE: $200 to $1,000 (Once, the Gondorfs sold *half* the bridge for $250 to someone who couldn't afford the whole thing.)
DETAILS: The brothers were professional conmen who had a surefire way to avoid detection: As soon as police officers crossed the bridge one way on their beat, the Gondorfs whipped out "Bridge for Sale" signs, chose their marks, and collected cash. They knew roughly the length of a beat path (though it varied, depending on how much crime was going on at a given time) and always broke down the enterprise before the cops returned.
CLOSING COSTS: The men also ran a horseracing scam. In 1915, Charlie was caught and imprisoned for that. Fred soon joined his brother after he was arrested for wire fraud. Neither was

---

ever arrested for the Brooklyn Bridge con. In 1973, long after they'd died, the brothers gained fame on the big screen: They were the inspiration for the grifters Johnny Hooker (Robert Redford) and Henry Gondorf (Paul Newman) in the 1973 movie *The Sting*.

SWINDLER: George C. Parker
SALE DATE: Twice a week for several years during the 1920s
PRICE: From $50 to $50,000, with payment plans available
DETAILS: Parker convinced his marks that he was a legitimate businessman by presenting them with "official" ownership documents that listed him as the property holder for the Brooklyn Bridge. The documents were forged, of course, but they fooled many people. Sometimes it took months for the duped buyers to realize the bridge wasn't theirs—and often they figured out they'd been conned only after they tried to set up toll booths and were stopped by police. Parker went on to "sell" Madison Square Garden, General Ulysses S. Grant's Tomb, and even the Statue of Liberty.
CLOSING COSTS: Parker was caught when he scammed three Texans who had him arrested. Facing his third fraud conviction, he got a life sentence. He died in Sing Sing in 1936.

HONORABLE MENTION
SWINDLER: Bugs Bunny
SALE DATE: 1949
PRICE: Unknown
DETAILS: In the cartoon short *Bowery Bugs*, the rascally rabbit met up with an elderly man and spun a tale of his encounter with a character named Steve Brody… based on the real-life Steve Brody, who claimed to have survived a jump from the Brooklyn Bridge in 1886. Some people claimed that the real Brody's jump was all a hoax (they said he used a dummy), but the fictional Steve Brody, fed up with a string of bad luck, also jumped into the East River. The old man, mesmerized by the story and as gullible as any tourist, announced that he'd "buy it!" and handed over a fistful of cash to purchase the bridge from Bugs.
CLOSING COSTS: Bugs hopped off scot-free.

LOCATION, LOCATION, LOCATION

*New York City has been the backdrop of so many Hollywood films
that it's hard to keep all the filming locations straight. Can you
match the movie with the New York landmark it featured?
(Answers are on page 364.)*

1. *Wall Street* (1987)

2. *Trading Places* (1983)

3. *The Wiz* (1978)

4. *The Warriors* (1979)

5. *The Squid and the Whale* (2005)

6. *Saturday Night Fever* (1977)

7. *Rosemary's Baby* (1968)

8. *North by Northwest* (1959)

9. *Miracle on 34th Street* (1947)

10. *Marathon Man* (1976)

11. *Manhattan* (1979)

12. *Goodfellas* (1990)

13. *The Godfather Part II* (1974)

14. *The French Connection* (1971)

15. *Big* (1988)

a. Dakota apartment building

b. Ellis Island

c. Jacqueline Kennedy Onassis Reservoir, Central Park

d. Kennedy Airport (formerly Idlewild)

e. Macy's Department Store

f. Museum of Natural History

g. Queensboro Bridge

h. Shea Stadium

i. Tavern on the Green

j. The U.N. Headquarters

k. The Wonder Wheel, Coney Island

l. Triborough Bridge

m. Verrazano-Narrows Bridge

n. World Trade Center

o. Yankee Stadium

The word graffiti is from the Italian *graffiato,* meaning "scratched."

THE ERIE CANAL

The story of the most famous and important manmade waterways in American history.

DILEMMA
As the United States expanded westward in the 1700s, the new nation ran up against a problem: Settlers were pushing their way into the new "Northwest Territories"—modern-day Ohio, Indiana, and Michigan—and found extremely fertile plains there, perfect for growing grain...and lots of it. But unfortunately, the area was separated from the Eastern Seaboard by the Appalachian Mountains. If anybody wanted to bring anything back from the plains to sell in Eastern cities, they had to carry it over the mountains. The roads were crude: hard and baked in the summer, and overrun with water and mud in the winter. That made it more costly to transport the grain than it was worth.

A MAN, A PLAN, A CANAL

For years, politicians and engineers kicked around ideas for solving the problem. The key seemed to be finding a way to connect Lake Erie with the Atlantic Ocean. Even Robert Fulton, best known for inventing the first commercially successful steam engine, stepped forward with a canal plan. In 1797 he asked President George Washington for federal funding to complete the project. Nothing came of it.

The man who finally got the job done was named Jesse Hawley. In 1805 he began farming grain in Geneva, in western New York, with plans to sell it in New York City. But within two years, he'd lost so much money transporting the grain that he wound up in debtors' prison. With nothing to do but think about how to improve his business, Hawley began writing letters to New York newspapers and officials arguing for a canal from Lake Erie to the Mohawk River, a tributary of the Hudson, which would then run to the Atlantic Ocean by way of New York City. A canal in this area would make the transport of freight—and settlers—extremely cheap and fast.

CLINTON'S FOLLY

Cawley's essays got through to at least one person: DeWitt Clinton, a New York senator, New York City mayor, and later governor of the state. Clinton saw the value in Cawley's proposed canal, and he took it on as a personal project. Arguing before the legislature in 1817, he called for a canal from Buffalo, on the eastern shore of Lake Erie, to Albany, on the upper part of the Hudson River. Clinton argued that the channel would make New York City "the granary of the world, the emporium of commerce, the seat of manufacturers, the focus of great moneyed operations."

But such an endeavor wouldn't be cheap. The legislature reluctantly earmarked $7 million (about $93 million today) for construction of the canal. Its size: 40 feet wide, 4 feet deep, and a staggering 363 miles long, and it would require an unprecedented 77 locks to make up for the rise (650 feet at its highest point) from the Hudson to Lake Erie. And because this was the 19th century, before modern machinery, it would all have to be constructed by man and horsepower. The media wasn't convinced the canal would ever be built, and the project was nicknamed "Clinton's Folly."

IF YOU BUILD IT

Construction began on July 4, 1817, in Rome, New York. The first 15 miles were finished…more than a year later. That took far longer than planners had hoped, but there was a steep learning curve. The two planners, James Geddes and Benjamin Wright, weren't engineers or builders. They were former judges whose only useful experience was surveying to settle boundary disputes. And they weren't the only novices—everyone on the project was. With no engineers and little supervision, builders had to think up on the fly how to do even basic things, like blast through rock. (Solution: gunpowder.)

As construction continued and the people involved gained experience, the process sped up. Ninety-six miles were completed by 1819, and a 250-mile portion, from Brockport to Albany, took just three more years to finish.

CURRENT AFFAIRS

A shallow, unnatural waterway doesn't generate much movement—no waves or current to push boats along. That meant the Erie Canal also needed a towpath alongside it, where horses and mules could walk while pulling the boats along. Even the paths were a project—they had to be cut out of the soil and then lined with stone and clay just like the bottom of the canal itself.

The labor required for the canal led to a massive immigration boom. Stone masons to make the canal's stone linings were especially in demand, so thousands of workers moved to the Hudson River Valley from Germany to work on the project. Many of them also went on to help build Manhattan's first skyscrapers and iconic buildings in the mid-19th century.

GRAND OPENING

The Erie Canal opened officially on October 26, 1825. The event was commemorated by Governor Clinton, who led a flotilla in a boat called the *Seneca Chief* the length of the 363-mile canal from Buffalo to Albany, and then down the Hudson River all the way to New York City. There, he emptied two casks of Lake Erie water into the Atlantic, a ceremonial "marriage of the waters," and then repeated the ceremony in reverse, sailing back to Lake Erie with casks of ocean water.

The impact of the Erie Canal was immediate and dramatic. The newly created freight route from Buffalo allowed grain to be transported for a rate of about $10 per ton (beating, by far, the over-mountain cost of $100 per ton). By 1837, 500,000 bushels of wheat came to New York City via the canal every year. Four years later, the figure was up to a million. The economic boom in western New York created a population boom, too, of immigrants and farmers looking to cash in on the new grain economy in the region. (How'd they get there? Via passenger ships on the canal, of course.)

Within nine years of the Erie Canal's opening, toll fees recouped the entire $7 million construction cost. Clinton's "folly" had paid off—by 1841, New York City was the busiest port in the country, moving more freight than Boston, Baltimore, and New Orleans combined.

Waverly Place in Greenwich Village was named for Sir Walter Scott's novel *Waverly*.

LADIES' ROOMS

In the 20th century, as single women from all economic classes came to New York to earn a living, women-only residence hotels became part of the city scene.

THE MARTHA WASHINGTON
One block east of Fifth Avenue, at 29 East 29th Street, the Martha Washington was the first New York hotel "exclusively for women." It opened on March 2, 1903 with 416 rooms and was initially managed as a cheap flophouse, or transient hotel, for women. But by 1907 the building's stockholders (who included many businesswomen) got fed up and decided to lease the building to an experienced hotel owner. The Martha Washington continued to be a women-only hotel, but, reported the *New York Times* on January 29, it would be "brought up to hotel par and run at as reasonable rates as possible…it will be run for no particular class of women, but women will find there a certain seclusion and protection that they do not have in an ordinary hotel."

In 1907 a single room cost $1.50 to $5.00 per day, depending on whether it had just a sink or a full private bath; there were free shared baths on every floor. In 1915 the rates were the same, but ads boasted a telephone in every room, convenience to surface and subway transportation, and exceptionally good cuisine in the restaurant. In 1934 the rates for a single without private bath started at $2. Jump ahead to 1988: the block-wide Martha Washington now had the address of 30 East 30th and advertised rooms at $119 to $175 per week for a single studio.

As the years went on, the Martha Washington became what New Yorkers call an SRO: a "single-room-occupancy" hotel, which usually means a decrepit, decaying, dangerous old building full of tenants with no place else to go. (In the 1960s, the once-famous 1940s-era blonde bombshell Veronica Lake, destitute and struggling with alcoholism and mental illness, worked in the hotel's bar.) By the 1990s, developers wanted to revamp the place into a trendy new hotel, but when they tried to get the old tenants out, charges of harassment flew. Later the building's crime rate soared, especially when a dance club called Danceteria rented space in the lobby and drug dealing became a problem. Danceteria morphed into another club called the Melting Pot, and in 1994 eight patrons were injured there when gunshots caused a stampede. Finally, in 2003, the poor old Martha Washington was emptied, completely renovated, and renamed the Hotel Thirty/Thirty, with 243 smallish, inexpensive rooms…for women and men.

THE PARKSIDE EVANGELINE

Recently, an online brochure for a new luxury condo on Gramercy Park South—at the corner of Irving Place—rhapsodized over the elegance of the building and the neighborhood: "In each great city of the world, the most privileged residents claim an area of refuge…a cloistered realm of domestic tranquility…a place where genteel living is its own reward." What the brochure didn't mention was that before the luxury conversion, the residents claiming refuge, cloister, and genteel living in this building were all women of modest means. From 1963 to 2008, the handsome 17-story Georgian-style structure was the Parkside Evangeline, an SRO women's residence run by the Salvation Army.

Right up until it closed, Parkside Evangeline was occupied by about 300 students, models, actresses, former secretaries and teachers, and other women willing to follow strict rules in exchange for relatively low rent (about $1,000 per month in 2005) that included breakfast, dinner, and maid services. Most rooms in the building, which started out as a hotel in 1927, were only 100 square feet, with private baths and simple wood furniture. Some of the rules: no men allowed above the first floor; no visitors after 11 p.m. during the week; no microwaves, hot plates, or candles; no smoking; and no alcohol. One of the upsides: a key to the locked gate of Gramercy Park (*see page 312*)—but only for an hour at a time.

THE BARBIZON

This was the women's hotel that had the reputation for glamour and class—partly because of its fancy address at Lexington and 63rd, but more because during its heyday, from its beginning in 1927 through the 1950s, only the elite could stay there. The Barbizon admitted residents based on references, looks, clothes, and ladylike behavior. Over the years, it was home to stars like

---

NYC's first subway car sat 22 passengers and traveled at 10 mph.

Joan Crawford, Candice Bergen, Cybill Shepard, and Liza Minnelli. Inside, though, the 23-story neo-Gothic building was far from glamorous: It had 700 tiny rooms—each barely big enough to hold a bed, desk, and dresser—with one window and no private bath.

Rules were strict for dress (stylish but demure) and conduct (no men were allowed above the ground floor), and rule-breakers were chastised—sometimes the management even called their parents. In the 1960s (when a single room cost $6.25 to $13 a day), there were social activities (teas, bridge, amateur dramas) and amenities like piano practice rooms, studios for artists, even a swimming pool and a sun deck. Several floors served as dormitories for girls attending a nearby secretarial school. And Eileen Ford, owner of the Ford Modeling Agency, often rented rooms for her models so that they wouldn't get into trouble, or into the tabloids. (Ford once said of the Barbizon, "It was safe, it was a good location, and they couldn't get out.")

But the days of this deluxe sorority house didn't last: On February 14, 1981, the hotel hung a big Valentine heart from its window and began renting rooms to men as well. In 2002 it was completely renovated and became the Melrose Hotel. Four years later, the owners converted it to luxurious condos, and all but 14 long-term residents left. The holdouts, protected by New York City's rent-control laws, were permitted to stay, paying their old monthly rents...which ranged from $113 to $424.

* * *

SHE DID WHAT...WHERE?

One of the Barbizon's most famous residents was actress Grace Kelly, who starred in 1950s hits like To Catch a Thief, High Noon, and Rear Window. In the late 1940s, though, she was just another hotel resident, attending an acting school nearby. According to legend (and a handful of witnesses), to the amusement of her hotel-mates—and the delight of any men who had managed to sneak upstairs—Kelly used to dance in the hotel's hallways in her underwear.

GET YOUR (EVERYTHING) HERE!

Street vendors are as ubiquitous in New York City as World Series rings in the Yankees dugout. But where did all those food carts come from?

OPPORTUNITY KNOCKS

Food carts have been part of New York's street scene since the 17th century, but after the Civil War, when the city's population quintupled (from 400,000 to about two million by 1880), farmers living close by couldn't grow enough produce to feed everyone. Fruits and vegetables started coming into New York by rail and ship, and were delivered to wholesale markets, which also sold fish, olives, nuts, cheese, and other foodstuffs. At the end of the day, whatever the wholesale marketers couldn't sell to stores could be purchased for very little, so a new group of entrepreneurs emerged: peddlers who bought up the excess food and sold it from wooden pushcarts in the street. Pushcart vendors mostly sold surplus produce, but they also sold fresh and pickled fish, hot corn, hot sweet potatoes, hot chestnuts, pickles, pretzels, eggs, and even soda water.

LIFE ON THE STREET

Pushcart peddlers were legally forbidden from selling in one spot for more than 30 minutes, but to make it harder for the police to single out violators, the peddlers congregated in groups on streets like Hester, Orchard, and Grand on the Lower East Side. These open-air markets attracted crowds of local customers. Business was brisk, noisy, and nonstop, often lasting into the night. Most pushcart peddlers were immigrants—without speaking much English or raising much capital (renting a cart cost between 10¢ and 25¢ per day), they could work in familiar neighborhoods close to home. But it wasn't easy. Peddling was backbreaking work for long hours in every kind of weather, and on a good day, a pushcart owner could make just enough to feed his family.

In 1900 there were about 25,000 pushcart peddlers all over the city. And by 1925 there were nearly 31,000 of them. Plus,

53 stationary open-air markets had sprung up around the city. During the Great Depression, with jobs so scarce, there were even more. In one of the most famous photographs of the Great Depression, a well-dressed former businessman sold apples for 5 cents each from a box on a city street corner. He was one of thousands.

NO PEDDLING HERE

Local shopkeepers didn't like the pushcarts, though—they competed with stores, and aggressive peddlers sometimes drove customers away. The storeowners had support from very high places—including Mayor Fiorello La Guardia, who was known to hate pushcart peddlers, even the Good Humor ice cream men. In 1938 he confronted one at a public hearing, saying, "I'm going to abolish all itinerant peddling from the streets...I have to protect the city...This whole thing of pushcarts has been abused."

In 1936 La Guardia used federal money (which was pouring into the Depression-strapped city to create jobs) to build indoor markets that would get the pushcarts off the streets—a process that he called "professionalizing" the peddlers. The first opened on Park Avenue, between 111th and 116th Streets in East Harlem, and eventually, at least four others started up. But there was one major problem: The new market buildings didn't have enough room for all the peddlers. Plus, many of them were unable to afford the $4-per-week fee charged for renting a stall. Thanks to La Guardia, the poorest peddlers were simply put out of work, and others weren't able to get a spot in the markets. By 1939 La Guardia had reduced the number of licensed peddlers from 6,000 to 2,700.

NICE TRY, NO CIGAR

The indoor market experiment was a huge failure. The stallholders hated all the rules and regulations: They had to wear neat white coats, keep their merchandise stacked in an orderly arrangement, and stay behind their counters while they did business. There was to be "no shouting or hawking by vendors nor abusive and lewd language." And, according to the new rules, they had to be American citizens.

Many of the vendors missed their previous lives on the street.

And surprisingly, the shopkeepers missed them, too. As it turned out, the street peddlers had brought foot traffic to neighborhoods—shops all over New York City started to lose money for lack of customers. New Yorkers also missed the convenience, noise, low prices, and color of the street vendors. La Guardia's indoor markets didn't provide the same experience: They were scattered throughout the city (and there weren't many to begin with). So customers chose to shop at supermarkets and local groceries instead, and over the years, many peddlers chose to go back to selling on the sidewalks.

LICENSE FOR SALE?

But the local government still didn't want all those vendors on city streets. They were hard to keep track of, and the city didn't have enough resources to make sure they all adhered to sanitation regulations. In 1979, despite the fact that there was a huge demand for food-vending licenses, Mayor Ed Koch's administration capped the number at a very low 3,000. Before long, the waiting list for licenses was up to 10,000. As a result, from the 1980s on, many peddlers took to the streets illegally and without regulation. But vendors *wanted* licenses to avoid being fined or harassed by the police. And what's a street peddler to do if the city won't let him peddle legally?

He turns to a thriving black market in licenses. Today, there are only 3,100 legal licenses issued at one time, and a new one is issued only when someone gives up one of the 3,100. Licenses are good for two years and renewable as many times as the *original* license holder likes...for a fee of $200 per renewal. But a lot of the people who own those licenses don't actually vend. Instead, they make big money by illegally renting their licenses...for as much as $15,000 for two years. The black market is an open secret, and no city agency has cracked down on it. In 2006, the City Council introduced legislation that would have raised the number of available licenses to 25,000. But at the end of 2009, after three years of discussion and debate, nothing had changed, and the number of licenses held at 3,100.

That doesn't mean the city just ignores unlicensed vendors, though. More than 60,000 vending-related tickets are written each year—sometimes for minor violations, like being more than 18 inches from the curb or neglecting to offer a receipt to a customer. The biggest ticket comes for failing to display a license in an easy-to-see place—that $1,000 fine can put a cart out of business.

FOOD FIGHTS
Vendors also get into turf wars with each other over who gets what space on what street, who's horning in on whose business, and how many vendors should occupy a given stretch of sidewalk. One vendor who sells baked goods from her truck had her tires slashed in 2007. She told the *New York Times*, "The street is like a playground when you're a kid, and you have to learn your way around." Another owner of a cupcake truck thought that cupcakes wouldn't be a problem for hot dog vendors. Wrong. He says, "When a hot dog guy sees a line in front of my truck, he thinks: 'That [should be] my line.'" Competition can even get violent: One vendor vying for a street corner in the Bronx followed his rival after work one night, pulled a knife on him, stole his money, slashed a tire on his food cart, and threatened to kill him.

ROLLING STOCK
Most of today's street-food vendors sell their wares from four basic kinds of vehicles: processing carts and trucks and nonprocessing carts and trucks. Processing carts and trucks handle "the sale or distribution of any foods that require cooking or any other treatment, e.g., slicing, mixing, packaging, or any other alteration that exposes the food to possible contamination," says the Department of Health and Mental Hygiene (DOHMH), the city agency that regulates the carts and trucks. Examples: freshly made sandwiches or falafel, grilled meat or vegetables, roasted nuts, barbecue, or freshly squeezed fruit juice.

Nonprocessing carts and trucks handle only prepackaged foods or foods that don't need cooking. That includes whole fruits and vegetables, packaged snacks and ice cream, and—oddly enough—coffee and boiled hot dogs. (Hot dogs contain sodium nitrate, which acts as a preservative and protects against bacteria.) Each kind of vehicle has to meet a slew of requirements about size, shape, structure, surfaces, equipment, and so on.

The DOHMH inspects every food cart and truck at least once a year and also spot-checks randomly, to be sure that food is being cooked and stored at the right temperatures, if there's a clean water supply for hand-washing, if the surfaces are sanitary, etc. But the DOHMH inspection system isn't foolproof. Because street-food vending can have such a low profit margin, owners often cut corners to save a few dollars. For example, all licensed carts are *supposed* to go into a garage each night, where they're *supposed* to be thoroughly "showered." Vendors don't always do this—some leave their carts on the street all night.

BEST IN CHOW

Today, the street vendors even have their own Academy Awards... sort of. One day in 2003, some members of the Street Vendor Project—a legal-aid society for the city's vendors—were sitting around, discussing ways to raise money for the organization. They hit upon an idea: Why not hold a public awards ceremony for street vendors, complete with judging and prizes for the best street food? The annual Vendy Awards were born, and the first competition and ceremony were held in 2005. Chef Mario Batali of *Iron Chef America* calls the Vendy Cup (the Vendy's grand prize) the "Oscar of food for the real New York."

The process works like this: Over a six-month period, customers send testimonials to the Street Vendor Project, nominating their favorite food vendors. The nominees are winnowed down to the 18 most popular, and those semifinalists gather in one place (Flushing Meadows–Corona Park in Queens in 2009, Governor's Island in 2010) for a cook-off. The competition has four major awards: Best Street Food Vendor (the Vendy Cup), the People's Taste Award, Rookie Vendor of the Year, and the Dessert Category. Anyone can buy a ticket and attend the cook-off. In 2010 Fares "Freddy" Zeidaies, the King of Falafel & Shawarma, won both the first prize Vendy Cup *and* the People's Choice Award. Freddy, a West Bank Palestinian, started his cart in Astoria in 2002 and made it to the Vendy semifinals twice before winning. Like Freddy, many vendors today are immigrants—Dominican, Bangladeshi, Vietnamese—working long hours for minimal income, a lot like those early peddlers more than a century ago, who stood on street corners selling peaches and pickles and roasted potatoes to busy, hungry New Yorkers.

BANNED IN NEW YORK!

Saturday Night Live has been offending network censors since it first hit the airwaves in 1975. But some performers go too far even for SNL. Here are four who've been banned from the show.

LOUISE LASSER. The first performer ever banned from *Saturday Night Live*, Lasser hosted an episode in July 1976. According to some on the *SNL* set, she was high throughout the broadcast, refused to do scenes with any other cast members except Chevy Chase, and insulted the cast and crew. The reason? She later cited "personal problems."

MILTON BERLE. In 1979 *SNL* hired Mr. Television himself, Milton Berle, to host its April 14 episode. Berle was America's first TV superstar, a comedian who had his own show during the 1950s. But he didn't seem to like being part of *SNL's* ensemble: Berle reportedly upstaged the other performers and even inserted his own, unapproved, racist jokes. For many years, producer Lorne Michaels wouldn't even let Berle's episode be shown in reruns because he thought the performance "brought the show down."

ANDY KAUFMAN. In 1982, Kaufman and producer Dick Ebersol got into a shouting match at *SNL's* Rockefeller Plaza studios. Then, on the November 20 show, Ebersol came onstage and told audiences that it was up to them whether or not the show should "dump Andy." Nearly 400,000 people called in, and Kaufman lost by about 26,000 votes. But the whole thing turned out to be a hoax, staged by Kaufman himself (who was well-known for his pranks). He'd actually suggested the "dump Andy" stunt to Ebersol. The ban stood, though, and Kaufman never returned.

SINEAD O'CONNOR. On October 3, 1992, O'Connor sang Bob Marley's "War," a song about racism, but changed some of the lyrics to be about child abuse. When the song was over, she pulled out a picture of Pope John Paul II, tore it in half, and shouted, "Fight the real enemy!" The stunt was a reference to the Catholic Church's child-abuse scandals, but it was too much for Michaels and got her banned from future appearances on the show.

Q: What's the claim to fame of the town of Palenville, at the foot of the Catskills?...

HOLLYWOOD ON
THE HUDSON

*Since 2000, hundreds of feature films and TV episodes have been filmed in
New York. The city has a dozen film schools, three major production
studios, and about 40 film festivals per year. Here's a timeline of
how the film and television industry evolved in New York.*

1896: The public was invited to attend an "exhibition of
[Thomas] Edison's latest marvel, THE VITASCOPE," one of several new systems that projected moving images onto a screen. At a
popular music hall on West 34th Street in Manhattan, an audience of astonished New Yorkers watched hand-tinted, black-and-white images actually move on a 20-foot screen. Pink- and
blue-togged girls danced, wild surf broke on a shore, two comedians (one tall, one short) boxed with each other. From the balcony
of the theater, Edison accepted the excited cheers. The commercial movie business had arrived in New York City.

1900–20: New York had skilled workers, money, theaters, and
audiences, so in 1901 Edison moved his movie company from
New Jersey to West 28th Street. His main rival, the American
Mutoscope and Biograph Company, opened offices in a loft on
13th Street and Broadway, and the American Vitagraph Company (another Edison rival) rented offices on Nassau Street. To
take advantage of as much light as they could, these companies
built rotating open-air stages on the roofs of their buildings so
they could track the sun as it moved during a shoot. Up there,
they filmed circus performers, magic acts, dancers, and other
entertainments. But camera operators also began to set up their
equipment around the city, filming what came to be called "actualities"—short movies that documented day-to-day events all
over New York: tenements, businesses, rich people, police and
firefighters at work, subway scenes, and construction projects.
The actualities, which had no story lines, were the precursors to
modern documentaries.

...A: It's the fictional home of Rip Van Winkle.

Soon the new film companies also began to make short fictional movies with simple plots. For that they needed bigger spaces to accommodate sets, costumes, editing equipment, booking offices— and they needed stable shooting stages. Vitagraph moved to Brooklyn and Edison to the Bronx in 1906; Biograph went to the Bronx in 1913. A host of smaller companies crossed the river and found space in Fort Lee, New Jersey, working there between 1910 and 1919.

1920–30: In 1920 Adolph Zukor, head of Famous Players-Lasky Corporation (which was renamed Paramount Pictures in 1935) chose Astoria, Queens, as the site for his new production facilities. The area was easily accessible to Manhattan (via the new Queensboro Bridge), plenty of available workers lived nearby, and there was plenty of room for expansion. During the 1920s, more than 100 silent films were made there with stars like Rudolph Valentino, Gloria Swanson, and Lillian Gish. When "talkies" came in, the Marx Brothers made The Cocoanuts (1929) and Animal Crackers (1930) in the Astoria Studios. But by 1927, most sound film production had moved to Hollywood. To make movies with outdoor scenes, you need constant, reliable light—and that's what ultimately sent most feature film production to the open spaces and sunshine of Los Angeles. Besides the light issue, there was just too much loud city noise in New York.

Still, much of the financial and administrative end of the movie business remained in New York, and the big new motion-picture companies (Warner Bros., Paramount, MGM, Fox) showcased their films in the fabulous movie palaces on Broadway. Many film studios found their new talent in New York, too, among the vaudeville acts that still entertained on stage. The Marx Brothers, Al Jolson, Mae West, W. C. Fields, Fred Astaire, James Cagney, and many others all made the transition from New York's vaudeville stages to the movies.

1942–45: During World War II, the federal government took over the Astoria Studios and turned it into the Signal Corps Photographic Center, or SCPC (later the Army Pictorial Center, or APC). Production units made training films on everything from personal hygiene to camouflage to field conditions, as well as

---

The Jackie Chan movie *Rumble in the Bronx* was actually filmed in Vancouver, Canada.

propaganda films such as director Frank Capra's famous series of films called *Why We Fight*, which helped galvanize support for the war effort. In 1945 the U.S. War Department used the APC to make an inspirational film called *Diary of a Sergeant*, starring Harold Russell, a soldier who had lost both hands in a training accident and been rehabilitated at Walter Reed Army Medical Center. Russell was so good in the movie that director William Wyler cast him in the 1946 film *The Best Years of Our Lives*...and Russell, who was not a professional actor, won two Academy Awards for his role, Best Supporting Actor and an honorary Oscar.

The SCPC/APC was used by the government all the way until the Vietnam War. It closed in 1970.

1966: When John V. Lindsay began his tenure as mayor in 1966, he immediately created the Mayor's Film Office, the first agency of its kind in the world, to encourage location filmmaking in New York City. The agency (now called the Mayor's Office of Film, Theatre and Broadcasting) set up a simple one-stop permit process for movie production companies, created a special police unit to help filmmakers, and ordered all other city agencies to cooperate with producers and directors.

A year later, 42 feature films—or parts of them—were produced in New York, including *Barefoot in the Park* (with the young Jane Fonda and Robert Redford) and *Wait Until Dark* (a thriller starring Audrey Hepburn). That year the *Wall Street Journal* declared "New York, New York, a wonderful town for making movies."

1977: The old Astoria Studios—now the Army Pictorial Center—had fallen into disrepair, but it came back into play when the nonprofit Astoria Motion Picture and Television Center Foundation acquired the lease from the government and restored the run-down facilities. The first major film made in the newly refurbished studios: *The Wiz* (1978), starring Diana Ross and Michael Jackson, directed by Sidney Lumet.

1980: The new Astoria Studios made a good start, but it wasn't until real-estate developer George Kaufman took on the project in 1980 that serious studio-based movie-making returned to New York City. Kaufman found investors from the entertainment world—

Johnny Carson, Neil Simon, Jimmy Nederlander (owner of Broadway theaters), comedian Alan King, actor Gregory Peck—and raised $50 million to renovate and expand the Astoria Studio. He renamed it Kaufman Astoria Studios, and today, with seven soundstages, it's the nation's biggest moviemaking studio outside of Hollywood. Interiors for *Moonstruck*, *The Cotton Club*, *Presumed Innocent*, *The Bourne Ultimatum*, the 2009 version of *The Taking of Pelham 1 2 3*, *Eat, Pray, Love*, and many other films have been shot there. *Sesame Street* began taping at Kaufman Astoria Studios in 1993, and TV shows like *The Cosby Show*, *Sex and the City*, and *Law & Order* have been taped there, too.

1996 to the present: Kaufman Astoria Studios isn't the only active studio in New York. The Silvercup Studios in Queens has filmed parts of *Gangs of New York*, *Big Daddy*, *When Harry Met Sally*, TV's *30 Rock* and *The Sopranos*, and more than 400 commercials per year. The Steiner Studios in Brooklyn had *Inside Man*, *Sex and the City 2*, *Revolutionary Road*, and *Spider-Man 3*, as well as HBO's *In Treatment* and *Boardwalk Empire*. New York's film industry now generates more than $5 billion per year and employs more than 100,000 New Yorkers.

* * *

SOME BIG APPLE MOVIE-MAKING FACTS

• In 2006 the city scored 34,718 on-location shooting days, up from 21,286 in 1996.

• In 2007, 88 percent of New Yorkers said they had seen filming taking place in the city—and 95 percent of Manhattan residents had.

• Los Angeles's share of total production dropped from 54 to 48 percent in 2008, but New York's climbed from 12 to 15 percent.

• New York City offers a free "production assistant training program" for low-income or unemployed residents as part of its Made in NY campaign to bring movie-making to the city.

In 1861 NYC mayor Fernando Wood proposed the creation of a new country, Tri-Insula...

BRIGHT LIGHTS, BLAZING CITY

On page 324, we told you about the Triangle Shirtwaist Fire, one of the worst blazes in the history of New York City. Here are four more.

THE POTTER BUILDING FIRE

At 10:00 in the evening of January 31, 1882, a messenger on the street noticed smoke coming from the old Potter Building (also called the World Building) at 38 Park Row. Until a few months before, the structure had been the home of the *New York World* newspaper. When firefighters showed up—just three minutes after the alarm sounded—the building was already engulfed in flames. The old building was a lair of narrow passages and offices, with a stairwell that went straight up the center—making it the perfect conduit for flames. Within an hour, the Potter Building's wood interior was completely gutted, leaving only its four stone outer walls standing. The heat was so intense that it broke all the windows in a neighboring building. Firefighters tried to fight the blaze, but a fierce winter storm got in their way, as did the tangle of electrical and telegraph wires around the building. And to make matters worse, as they tried to rescue people from the upper floors, their ladders proved to be too short.

Despite the fire's speed and heat, most of the 150 occupants of the building managed to escape, including three who climbed down a telegraph wire. But 12 people lost their lives. The Potter Building became notorious for going up like a box of matches, so when the new Potter Building was constructed in its place in 1886, builders used brick and terra cotta to cover the iron frame, making the new structure "virtually fireproof." (So far, so good.)

THE GENERAL SLOCUM FIRE

On June 15, 1904, the Sunday school of St. Mark's German Lutheran Church, on the Lower East Side, gathered to head out for its annual summer picnic. About 1,500 people, mostly women and children, left the neighborhood known as *Kleindeutschland*, or Little Germany. For many of the people from the working-class neighborhood, this excursion was their one indulgence of the year.

To take them to the picnic location on Long Island Sound, the church had chartered a paddle steamer ship called the *General Slocum*. As they paddled up the East River, a cabin boy noticed smoke coming from under the door of a compartment on the bow that held several boxes of drinking glasses, packed in hay. No one ever determined how the fire started, but within moments, it was out of control.

Word of the fire reached the ship's captain, who should have immediately put the *General Slocum* ashore so the passengers could escape, but he couldn't—flammable oil tankers and lumber yards lined the shore. So he kept going full-steam down the middle of the East River…as flames spread. The passengers rushed to the back of the boat. They tried the lifeboats, only to find them rusted to the deck. The life jackets were 13 years old, and many disintegrated as passengers pulled them on.

As the fire picked up speed, people leapt overboard—but most of them couldn't swim and drowned. Finally, the captain grounded the boat on North Brother Island, between the Bronx and Riker's Island, but by then the *General Slocum* was completely engulfed and caving in on itself. An estimated 1,021 people died in the fire or drowned in the river, making it the worst disaster in New York history until the September 11, 2001, attacks.

In the Kleindeutschland neighborhood, almost every tenement had lost someone. Within a few years, the community had disappeared—survivors moved away. The boat's owners were tried and acquitted, but the captain was convicted of negligence and sentenced to 10 years in Sing Sing. He served three and then was released on probation. President William Howard Taft pardoned him in 1912.

THE DREAMLAND FIRE

During Coney Island's heyday in the early 20th century, it was home to three legendary amusement parks: Luna Park, Dreamland, and Steeplechase. In 1911 Dreamland, which featured animal acts and sideshows, in addition to rides, was undergoing renovations to try to compete with neighboring Luna Park. At 1:30 a.m. on May 27, a roofing company was doing last-minute repairs on a ride called Hell Gate, a boat ride through creepy caverns, when *some-*

thing—maybe an electrical short, but no one is sure—caused the light bulbs to explode. In the dark, a worker knocked over a bucket of hot pitch (a resin used for caulking), and soon the whole park—whose buildings were made mostly of wood—was ablaze. During the ensuing chaos, as the park's lion tamer tried to save his lions, one of the animals escaped and charged a crowd of gawkers. It was shot by police.

By the time the fire was put out, 60 animals had died, and one employee was listed as "missing." Another casualty of the fire was Dreamland itself, which was never rebuilt. But that didn't stop the park from making money. Shortly after the fire was subdued, Dreamland's owners had wooden walkways built throughout the wreckage so crowds could get a closer look at the damage…for a fee.

THE HOLLAND TUNNEL FIRE

On May 13, 1949, a truck carrying eighty 55-gallon drums of carbon disulfide, a volatile chemical used to make solvents and insecticides, drove into the Holland Tunnel, which connects New York City and New Jersey…in clear violation of a law that said you *could not* drive carbon disulfide through the tunnel. At the height of rush-hour traffic, one of the drums came loose and ignited when it hit the road. Ten trucks near the burning barrel caught fire. As toxic fumes billowed into the tunnel, drivers in about 125 other cars abandoned their vehicles and ran for the exits.

The fire burned hotter than 1,000° F, disabling several of the tunnel's exhaust fans.…which caused the ceiling to cave in. Boats on the Hudson River above sat waiting, watching for signs that the tunnel had breached. (It never happened.) In the end, the fire destroyed 600 feet of the tunnel. Telephone and telegraph lines inside it were severed, and more than 650 tons of debris eventually had to be hauled away. But despite all that, no one was killed, and the tunnel reopened to traffic less than three days later.

* * *

New York's subway system runs 24-hours a day, one of only three public transportation systems in the world that does. (Chicago's El trains and some of the PATH trains to New Jersey are the others.)

THE DOCTOR WILL SEE YOU

*For modern immigrants, getting into America can be tough—there
are health exams to pass and civics tests to take. But all that pales
in comparison to what immigrants who came through Ellis Island
between 1907 and 1954 faced. Watch out for the button-hook!*

WELCOME TO AMERICA—NOW GO HOME

Eighteen-year-old Anna Segla from Hungary arrived at
Ellis Island in 1910, and as they did with all new immigrants, doctors from the Public Health Service (PHS) examined
her. Even though Segla explained that she was a hard-working
housekeeper whose hunchback "never interfered with my ability to
earn my living," the doctors noted her "curvature of the spine, de-
formity of the chest," and dwarfism as reasons for sending her
home. But how did those doctors get the power to decide who
could enter the United States, and who went back across the
ocean?

THE GOOD OLD DAYS

Until 1855 anyone who could buy a ticket for a steamship could
immigrate to the United States. Passengers simply disembarked
on the wharf in New York, San Francisco, New Orleans, or other
ports, and began life as an American. The only person from the
government that they had to deal with was a customs official, who
checked to see if the new arrivals had any valuables to declare and
pay taxes on. But between 1845 and 1851, Ireland suffered a terrible famine—a fungus spread throughout Irish potato plants, the
staple of the working-class diet, and killed thousands of acres of
crops. The poor, who made up most of Ireland's population, had
nothing to eat. About 1 million people died as a result, and another 1.5 million fled…most of them to the United States. Suddenly thousands of destitute people were landing each year in New
York City.

Theory Irish were joined by Italians, Greeks, Germans, and Eastern
European Jews escaping their own economic and political hard-

ships, and pretty soon, the overwhelmed U.S. government realized it had to get organized. So in 1855, the United States established an immigration depot in Castle Garden, at the southwest tip of Manhattan. But even that wasn't enough—the immigrants just kept coming... some four million people between 1841 and 1860 alone. So in 1892, the Federal Government opened a larger, more secure immigration complex on Ellis Island. In the facility's first year, 450,000 immigrants were processed there.

GIVE US YOUR TIRED, YOUR POOR, YOUR DISEASED

Still, pretty much anyone could enter the country. The steamship companies performed cursory disease screenings of passengers, but there were few restrictions. The United States was, after all, a nation of immigrants. But then, in January 1892, the steamship *Massilia* arrived from France with 700 Eastern European passengers who hadn't been screened for typhus. Before long, 70 of them—mostly Italians and Russian Jews who'd sailed on that ship and then moved into New York's densely populated Lower East Side—came down with the disease.

Typhus is a painful and deadly bacterial illness usually spread by lice or fleas, and 19th-century New Yorkers were all too familiar with it. There had been periodic epidemics, including one in 1863 that had killed 400 people. Hoping to prevent an outbreak, frantic Public Health Service officials rounded up all of the *Massilia*'s third-class (or steerage) passengers that they could find, whether the people were sick or not, and quarantined them, first in two tenement buildings and then on North Brother Island in the East River. Fifty people died, but it looked like the drastic approach had worked...until a few months later, when another ship arrived with passengers dying from cholera. Two more cholera-infected ships arrived just days after that.

The new immigration complex at Ellis Island wasn't equipped to handle cholera patients, so the ships had to sit offshore for three weeks while officials figured out where to put the sick passengers. Meanwhile, New Yorkers—many of them immigrants themselves—had grown wary of the newcomers constantly arriving on their shores. As the *New York Times* put it, "We have enough dirt, crime, misery, sickness, and death of our own without permitting any more to be thrust upon us."

LOOKING FOR THE "RIGHT KIND"

Even as the protests against immigration grew, America's expanding industries were badly in need of cheap labor. So in 1907, in an effort to calm the critics and appease the factory owners, Theodore Roosevelt announced that immigrants were welcome in the United States as long as they were the "right kind." People who were sick or of unsound mind, or who were guilty of "moral turpitude" (adultery or illegitimate pregnancy) wouldn't be allowed on American soil. Also, no anarchists and no children traveling alone would be let in. Examinations began at Ellis Island to weed out the "wrong kind" of immigrants from the "right" ones.

TESTING, TESTING...

When it came to immigrating to America, money mattered. People who could afford first- or second-class passage (as opposed to steerage, the below-decks accommodations) were nearly always allowed to land. The assumption was that if you had enough money to buy a good ticket, you probably weren't sick and weren't a criminal, prostitute, unwed mother, or anarchist. But most of the people who came to America came in steerage. And for those poorer applicants—who passed through Ellis Island at a rate of more than 2,000 a day—the Public Health Service (PHS) came up with a system of complicated, humiliating, and sometimes painful tests to prove their eligibility.

The medical exam began as immigrants arrived, while climbing the stairs into the depot's Great Hall. Doctors stood on the landing, watching to see if anyone limped, shuffled, coughed, wheezed, or exhibited symptoms of "spastic paralysis." Once in the Great Hall, each immigrant entered a long line that led to a PHS doctor who performed a physical exam, looking at an immigrant's scalp, face, neck, and hands as he assessed the person's general mental and physical health. Immigrants were asked to unbutton high collars to check for goiters (enlarged thyroid glands). Shawls and coats were removed to see if patients looked thin or sickly, and their hands were examined for skin disease, possible deformities, and nail fungus. Children older than two had to walk and speak to prove they weren't physically or mentally disabled.

Then came the psychological exam. At a time when the newcomers were emotionally and physically exhausted after spending more than a week on a steamship in cramped, unsanitary conditions, the PHS doctors studied their reactions, speech patterns, and overall behavior, looking for mental problems. As one PHS doctor said, people were questioned to gauge their intelligence and mental health, especially if they were "inattentive and stupid-looking."

Next, the new arrivals proceeded to a meeting with the dreaded "button-hook man"—an official who conducted the vision exam. He probed each person's eyes, searching for diseases from conjunctivitis to "bulgy eyes." Then he turned the patient's eyelids inside out with his own unwashed fingers, an unsterilized hairpin, or a button hook—a long, steel instrument with a tight hook at one end—and searched for (and probably spread) contagious diseases like trachoma, which could result in blindness or death.

ELLIS ISLAND CODE

After all that, about 80 percent of immigrants passed their exams and were directed to the railroad depot, where they could buy tickets to travel to the rest of the country. The ones who didn't pass the initial inspection had their right shoulders marked with chalk and then were pulled out of line and sent to another, more thorough examination

The chalk marks were a type of code. If an officer suspected a health problem, he might write C for conjunctivitis; CT for trachoma; G for goiter; H for heart; K for hernia; L for lameness; Pg for pregnancy; S for senility; and so on. An X meant that doctors suspected the immigrant had "subnormal" intelligence; a circled X meant that he or she might be mentally ill.

The chalk-marked people then underwent the next examination process, in which doctors took their temperatures, examined them with stethoscopes, and asked them to read from eye charts. People who failed the psychological tests had to solve puzzles, manipulate cubes, or interpret events from a photograph. Sometimes just a simple chat was enough for officials to decide that someone wouldn't make it in America. One wrong answer, and you could be banned from the country.

At the end of the exams, PHS officials either gave the immigrant the OK to leave the island or detained the person for an appearance before a Board of Special Inquiry, where the immigrant would have one last chance to prove that he or she was "clearly and beyond a doubt entitled to land." By that point, though, the decision rarely changed, and people were usually deported back to where they came from, at the expense of the shipping company that had brought them.

News of the strict examination process at Ellis Island spread to other countries, angering foreign governments that resented the United States for taking their best workers and leaving the sick and infirm behind. But despite the rigid rules and lengthy examination process, the PHS actually deported very few people. Only about 2 percent of the 12 million who passed through Ellis Island between 1892 and 1954, when the facility closed, were denied admission. And today, about 40 percent of Americans can trace their ancestry back to at least one person who arrived at the immigration complex on Ellis Island.

*　　*　　*

MORE BARBIZON SHENANIGANS

Officially, no men were allowed above the first floor in the Barbizon Hotel at 63rd Street and Lexington, and many of the women who lived there respected that rule. Actress Cybil Shepherd, who called the hotel home during the 1960s, said, "That's my speciality—sneaking 'em in, sneaking 'em out. But I wouldn't have dared to do that there. It was an institution."

Not everyone was so reverent, however. Malachy McCourt—writer, actor, and brother to Frank McCourt, author of *Angela's Ashes*—opened an Irish pub at 63rd Street and Third Avenue. The year was 1958, and most bars didn't allow women, but McCourt made an exception. Among his primary clientele were residents at the Barbizon, just around the corner. McCourt called the Barbizon "a large building throbbing with post-pubescent sexuality," and later told stories of being sneaked inside (more than once) by the young women who lived there. Supposedly, the women would distract the hotel's matron while McCourt raced upstairs, only to leave several hours later more brave than he'd arrived—when he left, McCourt usually just walked right out the front door.

An estimated 200 languages are spoken in NYC.

THE LAST LIST

*The world is full of firsts, but from the city that
has everything, we bring you a list of lasts.*

LAST TIME THE MACY'S THANKSGIVING DAY PA-
RADE WENT DOWN BROADWAY: November 27,
2008. In 2009, the city changed the route to accommodate
more viewers, eliminating the run down Broadway.

**LAST TIME THERE WAS A SHUTOUT AT EBBETS
FIELD:** September 24, 1957, when lefty Danny McDevitt and the
Brooklyn Dodgers beat the Pittsburgh Pirates 2–0. That game also
happened to be the last played at Ebbets Field.

LAST TIME TO SHOP AT GIMBEL'S: September 26, 1986.
The department store, much loved and co-featured in the movie
Miracle on 34th Street, closed September 27.

LAST TIME STREETCARS RAN IN BROOKLYN: October
31, 1956. (But there's talk of bringing them back on a limited
basis.)

**LAST TIME EDDIE CANTOR FLOATED DOWN BROAD-
WAY:** November 21, 1940, when his likeness was made into a
balloon for the Macy's Thanksgiving Day Parade. Technically, this
was also the only time the Eddie Cantor balloon was featured in
the parade. Kids found his image "scary." (The Three Stooges also
once enjoyed their own balloon images.)

**LAST TIME NEW YORK WAS NOT AMERICA'S
LARGEST CITY:** 1809. The following year, New York City
surpassed Philadelphia in population to reach #1, a title it hasn't
relinquished since.

**LAST TIME YOU COULD DANCE AT THE ORIGINAL
STUDIO 54:** Early in the morning of February 4, 1980. The club

closed later that day when managers Steve Rubell and Ian Schrager were fined and sent to prison for 3½ years on charges of conspiracy and tax evasion. The club reopened briefly several times over the years, but never achieved the original's notoriety or fame.

LAST TIME TO SEE JUDY GARLAND ONSTAGE IN THE BIG APPLE: August 26, 1967, when she performed at the Palace Theatre with her two youngest children, Lorna and Joey Luft.

LAST TIME YOU COULD SMOKE IN NEW YORK CITY'S BARS AND RESTAURANTS: 2003, when the City Council passed a resolution banning smoking inside public places. In 2011, the City Council passed another law banning smoking at the city's parks and beaches. The punishment for defying the ban: a "quality of life" summons that'll cost you $50.

LAST TIME YOU COULD BE PART OF THE STUDIO AUDIENCE FOR THE *ED SULLIVAN SHOW*: February 7, 1971. The program was canceled shortly afterward.

LAST TIME YOU COULD RIDE IN A CHECKER CAB IN THE CITY: July 26, 1999. The last vehicle was about 17 years old at its retirement.

LAST TIME YOU COULD CHECK INTO ST. VINCENT'S HOSPITAL IN MANHATTAN: 2010. In April, the board voted to close the hospital due to Chapter 11 bankruptcy.

LAST TIME YOU COULD DUMP YOUR TRASH AT FRESH KILLS LANDFILL ON STATEN ISLAND: March 22, 2001, although the dump was temporarily reopened for burial of 9/11 attack debris. The 2,200-acre area is now being developed into a park.

LAST TIME TO SEE A LIVE MASTODON IN THE CITY: Around 11,000 years ago, according to scientists who studied a mastodon jawbone found by construction workers near Broadway and Dyckman Streets back in 1925.

Last time a New Yorker was nominated on a national ticket by a major party...

ANSWERS

GIVE OUR REGARDS TO BROADWAY
(page 35)
1. b. *Carousel* ran for 890 performances...*Oklahoma!* ran for 2,212.

2. d. Although *West Side Story* was nominated for Best Musical in 1957 (the year it opened on Broadway), *The Music Man* beat it out for the award.

3. d. John Guare is the American playwright of *The House of Blue Leaves* and *Six Degrees of Separation*.

4. b. *Chicago* opened on Broadway in 1975, and then again in 1996; the film came out in 2002.

5. a. *The Sound of Music*; b. *My Fair Lady*; c. *Cabaret*; d. *Hello, Dolly!*

6. d. So far, the longest-running one-word-title play on Broadway is *Cats*, with 7,485 performances.

7. c. All of these plays were also made into movies.

8. c. As of January 2011, *The Phantom of the Opera* had more than 9,500 performances and had been running on Broadway since 1988.

NEW YORK I.Q. QUIZ
(page 136)
1. c; **2.** b; **3.** d; **4.** b; **5.** d; **6.** b; **7.** d; **8.** c; **9.** a

KNOW YOUR POLITICIANS
(page 205)
1. William M. "Boss" Tweed. The courthouse at 52 Chambers Street in Manhattan is better known as the Tweed Courthouse because "Boss" used his corrupt influence to embezzle millions via its construction. Ironically, Tweed's 1873 fraud trial was held in one of the building's courtrooms—he was convicted and sentenced to 13 years in prison.

2. Al Smith ran for president in 1928, giving up his job as New York's governor, but Smith supported the man who ran for governor

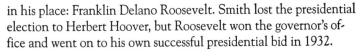

in his place: Franklin Delano Roosevelt. Smith lost the presidential election to Herbert Hoover, but Roosevelt won the governor's office and went on to his own successful presidential bid in 1932.

3. Rudy Giuliani. On the eve of 9/11, Giuliani's approval rating had dropped nearly 32 percent since the start of his first term in 1994, the result of several public scandals—including alleged police brutality and the discovery that he had a mistress. But in the days after 9/11, he became a hero to many, inspiring a terrified public with comforting words like "Tomorrow, New York is going to be here. And we're going to rebuild, and we're going to be stronger than we were before."

4. Fiorello La Guardia. Until 1939, there was no major airport serving New York City. Flights landed in New Jersey, and travelers had to cross the Hudson River to get to New York. La Guardia insisted that the city needed an airport of its own to make it more accessible to tourists and business travelers. But he couldn't get much support for the project, so on his way home from a business trip, when his TWA flight from Chicago landed in Newark, the mayor refused to get off the plane. He insisted that he be flown to a small airstrip in Brooklyn...and on the way, he gave a press conference explaining that if New York had its own airport, the extra trip wouldn't be necessary. The grandstanding worked: City officials and the public started talking about a New York airport, the federal government approved use of New Deal money for the project, and New York Municipal Airport (now LaGuardia Airport) opened in Queens in 1939.

5. Ed Koch was one of only four three-term New York City mayors (La Guardia, Robert F. Wagner, and Michael Bloomberg are the others), and his larger-than-life personality was well known to New Yorkers. According to former *Daily News* editor Michael Goodwin, "Mayor Koch was so in your face for so long that a whole generation of children grew up thinking 'Mayor' was his first name."

LOCATION, LOCATION, LOCATION
(page 336)

1. i; **2.** n; **3.** h; **4.** k; **5.** f; **6.** m; **7.** a; **8.** j; **9.** e; **10.** c; **11.** g; **12.** d; **13.** b; **14.** l; **15.** o

More Bathroom Reader Titles!

Find these and other great *Uncle John's Bathroom Reader* titles online at ***www.bathroomreader.com.*** Or contact us:

Bathroom Readers' Institute

P.O. Box 1117

Ashland, OR 97520

THE LAST PAGE

FELLOW BATHROOM READERS:
The fight for good bathroom reading should never be taken loosely—we must do our duty and sit firmly for what we believe in, even while the rest of the world is taking potshots at us.

We'll be brief. Now that we've proven we're not simply a flush-in-the-pan, we invite you to take the plunge: Sit Down and Be Counted! Log on to *www.bathroomreader.com* and earn a permanent spot on the BRI honor roll!

If you like reading our books...
VISIT THE BRI'S WEB SITE!
www.bathroomreader.com

- Visit "The Throne Room"—a great place to read!
- Receive our irregular newsletters via e-mail.
- Order additional *Bathroom Readers.*
- Read our blog.

Go with the Flow...

Well, we're out of space, and when you've gotta go, you've gotta go. Tanks for all your support. Hope to hear from you soon. Meanwhile remember...

Keep on flushin'!